# NO FREE MAN

McGILL-QUEEN'S STUDIES IN ETHNIC HISTORY
SERIES ONE    DONALD HARMAN AKENSON, EDITOR

## McGILL-QUEEN'S STUDIES IN ETHNIC HISTORY
## SERIES TWO   JOHN ZUCCHI, EDITOR

Internees under guard, Kapuskasing, Ontario. Ron Morel Memorial Museum

# NO FREE MAN

## Canada, the Great War, and the Enemy Alien Experience

### BOHDAN S. KORDAN

McGill-Queen's University Press
Montreal & Kingston • London • Chicago

ISBN 978-0-7735-4778-0 (cloth)
ISBN 978-0-7735-9963-5 (ePDF)
ISBN 978-0-7735-9964-2 (ePUB)

Legal deposit third quarter 2016
Bibliothèque nationale du Québec

Printed in Canada on acid-free paper that is 100% ancient forest free
(100% post-consumer recycled), processed chlorine free

This book has been published with the help of a grant from the Canadian Federation
for the Humanities and Social Sciences, through the Awards to Scholarly Publications
Program, using funds provided by the Social Sciences and Humanities Research
Council of Canada. This project has been made possible by a grant from the
Endowment Council of the Canadian First World War Internment Recognition Fund.
Funding has also been received from the Canadian Foundation for Ukrainian Studies,
the University of Saskatchewan Publications Fund, and St Thomas More College
Publications Fund.

McGill-Queen's University Press acknowledges the support of the Canada Council
for the Arts for our publishing program. We also acknowledge the financial
support of the Government of Canada through the Canada Book Fund for
our publishing activities.

---

**Library and Archives Canada Cataloguing in Publication** ·

Kordan, Bohdan S., author
No free man: Canada, the Great War, and the enemy alien experience/
Bohdan S. Kordan.
(McGill-Queen's studies in ethnic history. Series two; 39)

Includes bibliographical references and index.
Issued in print and electronic formats.
ISBN 978-0-7735-4778-0 (hardback). – ISBN 978-0-7735-9963-5 (EPDF). –
ISBN 978-0-7735-9964-2 (EPUB)

1. World War, 1914–1918 – Evacuation of civilians – Canada. 2. World War,
1914–1918 – Concentration camps – Canada. 3. Immigrants – Government policy –
Canada – History – 20th century. 4. Aliens – Government policy – Canada –
History – 20th century. 5. Canada – Emigration and immigration – Government
policy – History – 20th century. 6. Immigrants – Canada – History – 20th century.
7. Aliens – Canada – History – 20th century. I. Title. II. Series: McGill-Queen's
studies in ethnic history. Series two ; 39

D627 C2 K665 2016          940.3'1771          C2016-902413-X

---

This book was typeset by Interscript in 10.5/13 Sabon.

*For Christian*

*My joy, my love, my life, my son*

# CONTENTS

# ILLUSTRATIONS

# ACKNOWLEDGMENTS

Human rights are a passion of mine. It stems from the twin belief that freedom is indispensable to human dignity and that communities, to be whole, must be mindful of the rights they hold in common. This belief is central to the story of those who arrived in Canada at the start of the twentieth century, facing as they did the enormous challenge of acceptance during a period of extreme crisis and conflict. It is not an uncommon story in Canadian history, but in the case of the Great War it is a narrative that is neither widely known nor fully understood. Many years ago, speaking publicly on the topic of internment, I was approached by a historian whose roots were in the Ukrainian community of pre–Second World War rural Alberta. He conveyed to me his skepticism about those long-ago events and their significance. He had never heard of internment and told me that there was no talk of it while he was growing up. I was utterly dumbfounded to learn that events so widely experienced and felt, and which had impinged on our constitutional make-up as a rights-bearing people, could be so lost to time and memory. I resolved then and there to devote some effort to making the history and politics of the experience more accessible. This book is a product of that resolution made so many years ago.

Along this journey I benefited from the good counsel, sage advice, as well as knowledge and talents of a number of individuals. Peter Melnycky, Lubomyr Luciuk, Craig Mahovsky, and James Farney were fellow travellers on this knowledge quest and I have gained mightily from their insights and work in the area. The convivial Margaret Sanche kindly agreed to read the original manuscript in its entirety and made a great number of editorial suggestions that unquestionably improved the text. I was ably assisted by several graduate and undergraduate research assistants over the years who generously helped secure and/or organize archival materials: James Farney, Eric Woods, Kyle Christensen, Joel Seaman, and Vanessa Leon. St Thomas More College at the University of Saskatchewan funded the research and awarded me a sabbatical to undertake the work. I am truly grateful to have received this support. The Canadian First World War Internment Recognition Fund (CFWWIRF) liberally funded a research leave that afforded me an extraordinary opportunity to write without interruption for an entire year; I deeply appreciate the vote of confidence by the board of directors, which led to the grant. I would especially like to thank Andrea Malysh who assisted me throughout the granting process. Over the years, I have worked on a number of projects with McGill-Queen's University Press. I am impressed with MQUP and its people, particularly James MacNevin and Ryan Van Huijstee with whom I worked closely on this book. At the Press, copyediting was entrusted to the ever-capable James Leahy, who gently reminded me of the importance of keeping it simple and direct. Subventions received from the Social Sciences and Humanities Research Council of Canada, St Thomas More College, the University of Saskatchewan, and the Canadian Foundation for Ukrainian Studies made the publication of this book possible, for which I am much obliged.

My home in the mountains served as a base for writing. It is a splendorous venue. There is nothing quite like the quiet of the autumn and the stirrings of spring in the Rockies to heighten one's senses and instill an appreciation for this remarkable setting. But it is my neighbours at Folding Mountain – Paul, Jocelyn, Bob, Glenda, Morgan, Debbie, Erika, and Wilmut – who, inquiring about the topic as well as my progress, made writing all the more agreeable and easy. Good neighbours and friends are to be treasured.

Finally, I wish to acknowledge my family, Danya and Christian, whose steadfast support and boundless love sustain me. I am, if only because of them. No words can begin to express my deep respect for them both and the endless joy and comfort that I gain from their cheerful and selfless company each and every day.

# NO FREE MAN

# INTRODUCTION

On 11 November 1918, the guns of war fell silent. After four and a half years of fighting, an armistice was signed, compelling all the warring powers to put an end, if not to their grievances, then at least to the hostilities. After so many years of destruction and death, there was a collective sigh of relief. Instinctively, as though responding to the deep sense of loss and insecurity, people began to ask questions. What went wrong? Who was responsible? What about justice? Perhaps it was too early, but the pain and sorrow demanded soul-searching if not answers. It was a time for reflection and assessment.

In a faraway corner of the British Empire, in Vernon, a small outpost on the Canadian frontier, where a collection of civilian prisoners were interned, a band of these individuals took pen to paper, three months after the armistice, to write a petition to the king's representative in Canada, the governor general. They, like so many others at the time, felt obliged to give their interpretation, at least with respect to their misfortune as to what had gone wrong and who was responsible. Having been interned, they were also motivated by a desire to make their claim against Canada. But most importantly, they wanted their grievances to go on record, persuaded as they were by their profound sense of betrayal with the country they had once claimed as their own.

Their long and involved statement, informed as much by political philosophy as by an understanding of the law, was articulate and cogent. Central to their argument was the notion that Canada had invited them to leave their land of birth and settle within its borders. This placed Canada under a moral obligation that was not shared by other countries. More especially, the obligation was binding in that

[Canada] was also under a legal contract with us, insofar as in consideration for our coming and settling in the country she had, among others, guaranteed us two things:

1) The FULL PROTECTION OF CANADIAN LAWS and

2) That no immigrant should be deported from this country on any ground after three years continued residents here [*sic*] …

The "FULL PROTECTION OF CANADIAN LAWS," promised to us (in the official Immigration literature), was explained to mean that we should enjoy ALL THE RIGHTS and privileges of a CANADIAN CITIZEN, except franchise rights. No time limit was set for these guarantees, nor was there any reservation made for a possible cessation or suspension of them in case of war. It was a contract as binding as that which the Canada Government made with the Mennonites, who by its virtue are exempted from military service.

Of particular note, the authors of the petition argued that, on the issue of rights, liberty was a foundational right, to which all were entitled as long as they did not contravene the law. However, according to them, they were deprived of this right as a result of a discriminatory and ill-considered policy that exposed them to a host of injustices:

By Order in Council, dated August 16th 1914 [*sic*], this recognition of our equal rights, which up to this time had been extended to us without dispute, was suddenly withdrawn from us and we as "enemy aliens" – a term especially coined for this purpose – were placed under an exceptional law, inasmuch as this order decreed that under certain circumstances we might be interned, a procedure not applying to Canadian "citizens." They were liable to prosecution and punishment for certain measures under the War Measures Act, but not to internment until the end of the war as we were. This proves legal discrimination against us contrary to the agreement.

At a superficial reading, the order mentioned seems to decree internment for us only in exceptional cases, but it contains an enlarging clause to the effect that we might be interned anyhow. Consequently, in the case of nearly all of us, WE WERE DEPRIVED OF OUR LIBERTY for no other reason than JUST BECAUSE WE WERE GERMANS and since no proof of guilt was required against us and suspicion, however unfounded, sufficed it was a welcome opportunity for many, who owed us money, wanted our farms, or thought they had a grievance against us to denounce us as pro-German in order to escape the necessity of paying their debts or getting a cheap, but powerfully effective revenge for their supposed grievances.[1]

The authors were quick to point out that the government was obligated to protect them from such abuses or, alternatively, give those who wished to leave time to quit the country. That the government chose not to make this allowance, prohibiting their departure while simultaneously making them outlaws, indicated that Canada "[was] dictated by her political interests." Political interests were felt to be at work here because "*force majeure* cannot be pleaded in defence of this action." In addition, "a *force majeure* is distinguished by not making an intelligent selection of its victims." Speaking on behalf of the internees at the Vernon camp, most of whom were professionals and therefore entitled under international law to be considered prisoners of an officer class, the petitioners further protested that they were being treated as mere common criminals – "appalling in its details." So as not to be misunderstood, the authors made it clear that the petition was not intended to solicit sympathy in order to prevent their deportation, but rather "the majority will be heartily glad to leave this land of broken promises and persistent and purposely incited hatred against us." They had had enough of Canada and all that it stood for.

The document was a powerful indictment. It was also insightful. The authors highlighted the issue of rights but also signalled the special obligation (moral and political) that Canada owed to those it had invited to its shores. That obligation, they declared, pertained especially in the context of war, placing an even greater responsibility on Canada to protect. Abandoning that responsibility by both failing to extend the full protection of Canadian laws and designating individuals of German and Austro-Hungarian birth as "enemies," Canada, so they claimed, had created the conditions for their internment. Internment deprived them of their personal liberty – the basis for a free and just society. In this regard, the petitioners hearkened back to the ancient principle contained in the Magna Carta which stated: "No free man shall be seized or imprisoned, or stripped of his rights or possessions, or outlawed or exiled, or deprived of his standing in any other way, nor will we proceed with force against him, or send others to do so, except by the lawful judgment of his equals or by the law of the land." For the petitioners, arrest and internment had represented a broken promise. It was also, however, seen as a failure of duty and responsibility to safeguard the rights and liberties of every man.

The petitioners argued that arrest and internment were instigated in many cases by the cruel and vicious subterfuge of those who sought to use the laws either to enrich themselves or to pursue a grievance against individuals who were now made vulnerable.[2] In being deprived of their rights under the 15 August Proclamation and being designated "enemy aliens" so that they might be brought under this exceptional law ("a term especially coined for this purpose"), the authors noted that the conditions were in place for further injustices to occur. Internment, originally meant to address the issue of security, had now been so enlarged as to make it possible for any alien of enemy birth to be interned – not because of what they did but because of who they were. As to any military or political considerations that necessitated the introduction of emergency security measures, the authors pointed out, the war in Europe was far away. There was nothing that prevented Canada from fulfilling its obligations and responsibility to those who came to the country in good faith.

From the perspective of the petitioners, Canada had failed them. But how did it come to this? What possibly could have motivated authorities to act in so rash a manner? War brings with it many challenges. Certainly one of those challenges in a democratic polity is to balance security considerations with the rule of law. The language of the 15 August Proclamation was carefully crafted to ensure that security concerns were addressed and to show sensitivity to the predicament of innocents who might be caught up in the vagaries of war. But the Proclamation and the War Measures Act that followed also made "enemies" of those who were born in lands now at war with Canada by designating them "enemy aliens." What precisely did this mean and what effect did the designation have on the public imagination? Moreover, what responsibility did the government have in allaying the fears and anxieties of a public that had come to accept the idea of an alien subject as enemy? To the degree that alien subjects of German or Austro-Hungarian birth (and subsequently others) were identified as potential enemies, social and political acceptance was limited and the question of their rights moot. Yet, labelling was one thing, actions an entirely different matter. What then did government measures adopted at the outset of the war say about the nature of the relationship between the government and the enemy alien and how are we to interpret this relationship, especially in the context of the nation-building project?[3] Equally, what obligations did the government have toward those it cast in the role of enemy?

The designation "enemy alien" was profoundly important in the context of war. It established the limits of social and political acceptance of the alien of enemy origin. For a society positioning itself in the struggle that lay ahead, the term served conceptually to frame an understanding of what if any obligation was owed these people and what approaches should be taken. War did not define who was friend or foe – that was already done by way of the official designation. What the war did, however, was impress upon the public at large as well as officials the urgency of dealing with the enemy alien as a "problem." This occurred despite the struggle of enemy aliens to demonstrate their loyalty, raising important questions about whether it was even possible that they would ever be accepted.[4] Existing on the periphery of society without social or political standing, except as a prospective enemy, aliens of German or Austro-Hungarian origin were considered a liability. This fact would be understood differently in both official and non-official settings. But no matter what was meant, the fundamental premise was that enemy aliens represented a "problem" that required attention.

In dealing with the perceived problem, the government prioritized the issue of security over individual rights. The state, of course, has a right to defend itself, as is understood in international custom and law. Yet the war in Europe was distant. Characteristically, therefore, the threat posed by the enemy alien was more hypothetical than real. What then are we to make of the emergency war measures? What was their intent? To answer these questions requires a close reading of the orders-in-council, especially order-in-council PC 2721, which would prove pivotal in both scope and purpose. How do we understand this order and what did it convey about the problem that was to be managed? Finally, what do the decisions taken say about the political choices being made and the prerogatives of state in the context of rule of law?

In Canada, some 8,579 enemy aliens were interned during the Great War. That statistic looms large in the narrative of the enemy alien experience. Internment was central to the enemy alien story because of the enormity of its consequences. It deprived certain individuals of their basic human right – freedom. It also placed them in a position where they would be treated as prisoners of war. But how did it come to pass that civilian internees could be interned and then treated as prisoners of war?

The story of internment, its general outline and details, has been fairly well documented.[5] Less understood are the implications that the prisoner-of-war designation had on the mindset of those in authority and what this meant, practically speaking, for the internees. The authors of the petition, for instance, noted that as professionals they had not been accorded treatment that corresponded to their social standing. They claimed to have been handled as common criminals. It stood to reason then that with respect to those internees whose social class status was still lower, they would be given even less consideration. Forced to work on public works projects, they were exposed to treatment that went beyond the customary military regulations applying to prisoners of war. Why did this occur and how was it justified? What did the designation mean for those behind barbed wire? And did it have bearing on the conditions and the specifics of their treatment?

Internment, an extraordinary measure, was used to manage the enemy alien problem. How the problem was approached depended on the context. The context, however, invariably changed because of the effect of war. This meant that government would have to adapt. Internment would continue to play a role in dealing with the enemy alien problem, but as the problem changed so too would the policy of internment. In particular, the rise of radicalism, thought to be linked to foreigner activity, resulted in a realignment in internment. But what did this entail? Did it mean there was a fundamental shift in the purpose and function of internment? Radicalism was seen as a political threat. That internment could be used to address this problem underscored the unique vulnerability of the enemy alien engaged in politics.[6] It highlighted the government's disposition to privilege security over rights. But it also suggested the utilitarian nature of internment. Internment could and would be used to deal cleanly and clearly with a host of problems considered menacing, something that was characteristically demonstrated by the role deportation would play – as an ancillary aspect of internment that would rid the country of those deemed undesirable.[7]

Internment was a defining feature of the enemy alien experience. But the experience included more than internment. Registration and monitoring affected an additional 85,000 enemy aliens across the country. It constituted a mass surveillance system that sought to control and manage this segment of the population. But what did control and management mean and what was the impact on the target population? What role did public opinion play in driving government policy? Was nativism a factor?[8] How did the government respond? The enemy alien population was clearly under pressure at this time. Returning veterans and other members of society were mobilizing around issues seen as vital to the war effort. To the degree that enemy aliens were the object of many of these campaigns, how did they understand what was occurring and what are we to make of their reaction? Finally, how are we to understand and make sense of their dilemma – being inside and outside the community – and what were the implications for the country's future?

This book is about the enemy alien experience in Canada during the Great War. It does not pretend to be a definitive statement. It does, however, aim to add to an understanding of that experience. It includes a critical reading of government policy and decision making, examining the role that internment played in the government's strategic engagement with the enemy alien "problem." The manner in which the problem was understood is also described and explored with a view to revealing the nature of the relationship between government and enemy aliens while placing the issue within the wider context of community and belonging. Because internment is so central to the enemy alien experience, this book focuses on the many contradictory and problematic aspects of its character and conduct. Of interest as well is the effect of war, with all of its attendant concerns and consequences, in shaping public attitudes and sentiment toward the alien subject of enemy birth, and in assessing its meaning and implications for the wider national project.

Chapter 1 deals with the effect of war in shaping public attitudes and the government's response to the challenges posed by the presence of enemy aliens, highlighting the limits of their social and political acceptance. Chapter 2 examines and assesses the rationale, character, and effect of the political choices made by officials regarding the enemy alien, drawing attention to the unique part that internment played. Chapter 3 explores the policy and practice of internment, highlighting its role while bringing attention to the precarious existence of the enemy alien. Chapter 4 describes the nature of government policy and public attitudes toward the alien as enemy during the final years of the war, sketching out the difficulties associated with their social and political acceptance within the context of the wider issue of belonging. Finally, chapter 5 offers an analysis and assessment of the enemy alien experience, focusing on the factors, issues, and dynamics that gave shape to the experience.

This book seeks to contextualize the enemy alien experience in Canada during the Great War. That experience was shaped by the decisions and policies adopted at the start of the war. The narrative, as a consequence, is skewed toward a discussion of the early stages of the conflict when government action and its impact were greatest and most widely felt. Yet the enemy alien experience needs to be understood in its totality. Internment did not end in mid-1916 when the bulk of the internees were released. It continued well after hostilities had ceased in 1918, pointing to the deep issues at work. The enemy alien experience

must be read as a continuum from war's start to end, with all of its per-
mutations and inconsistencies, in order to give us a better appreciation
of what was at stake.

Being a general survey of the enemy alien experience, the following
narrative does not treat all of the many specific issues and questions.
There is still much to do in terms of research and investigation. For
example, the topic of diplomacy and the interned enemy alien remains a
fertile area of inquiry, as does the study of the Canadian experience as
part of the global phenomenon of internment. A description and analysis
of the various orders-in-council and legislation affecting enemy aliens
during the war is much needed. An assessment of the nexus between
provincial interests and federal decision making would offer some
understanding of policy developments at this time. Another important
issue is the impact of public and private interventions on decision
making. There are, of course, other avenues of inquiry that will shed
even more light on the larger question of state–minority relations during
moments of war and crisis. In the meantime, this book offers insight into
the reasoning behind the choices that would affect the lives of thousands
who at one time called Canada home.

## CHAPTER ONE

# The Uncertainty of War
# and the Limits of Acceptance:
# Aliens of Enemy Nationality

## FEAR AND SECURITY

In the early morning of 28 August 1914, Private Gordon J. Betts of the 5th Royal Highlanders was placed on sentry duty guarding the shipping canal at Soulanges, Quebec, on the north shore of the St Lawrence River. While standing guard, Private Betts was shot through the eye, reportedly ambushed by an unseen assailant. He was killed instantly. His father, Thomas Betts, on being informed of his son's death, told the coroner that his son, all of fifteen years of age, was "a good boy." In an instant, Private Betts had become one of Canada's first casualties of the Great War.[1]

For the young Betts, perhaps it was a case of being at the wrong place at the wrong time. But the job was not without risk. From the start of the war and prior to the Betts shooting, guards placed at the canal were reported to have been fired upon. Elsewhere in the country, similar incidents were said to have taken place at various security points. Private William Buck of the 103rd Rifles in East Calgary, while standing guard, was allegedly shot at by persons unknown, as was Private Harry Tebbutt of the 79th Cameron Highlanders, who, patrolling the armoury in Winnipeg at night, returned fire in the direction of what was taken to be the flash from a revolver.[2] Guarding a grain elevator in Portage la Prairie, Private M. Hooper of the 96th Manitoba Rangers was allegedly set upon by an unknown assailant.[3] The assailant, brandishing a sharp instrument, cut a gash in the sentry's thick overcoat and managed to escape at the last moment. Also reported was an incident on the new railway bridge at St Louis, Saskatchewan, where guards were nearly overpowered by a gang of six attackers who, before they made their getaway, declared that it was their intention to blow up the bridge.[4] The report was neither confirmed nor denied by the local RNWMP inspector in charge of the district. Meanwhile, the back of the observation car on the No. 2 Express en route from Vancouver and carrying British officers to the European theatre was purportedly struck by a bullet as it was leaving the station in Sudbury, shattering the glass window.[5]

Overwhelmingly, these attacks were attributed to enemy spies and saboteurs. Reporting the incident on the No. 2 Express, the press made the point that Sudbury contained a large number of aliens, in particular Austro-Hungarians, whose birth country was now at war with Canada. The death of Betts was thought to have been the work of a spy, as was the fatal shooting of Trooper P. Moran, who had been tasked with guarding the CPR track in the north end of Smith Falls, Ontario.[6] The frequency of reported events suggested the active presence of agents, necessitating increased vigilance.

With so many reports of saboteurs, it was both right and natural for guards to be alert. But this also resulted in rifles regularly and indiscriminately discharging, with disastrous results. When fishermen in a rowboat on the Kaministiquia River near Port Arthur, Ontario, were commanded to halt and failed to do so, they were fired upon by soldiers guarding the nearby grain terminal.[7] The bullets missed their mark, but one hit a watchman standing on the opposite bank, fatally wounding him. In Montreal, Antoine Notter, a recently arrived French immigrant, was about to have his photograph taken near the Craig Armoury when he was approached by Sergeant George Hooton. A disturbance ensued, in part brought on by Notter's inability to speak English, which led Sergeant Hooton to level his rifle and shoot the unfortunate man dead. A coroner's inquest found Hooton criminally liable, to which the minister of the militia, the Hon. Sam Hughes, responded that if Notter had been a German leader of a force bent on seizing ammunition in the armoury, the situation would have turned out even worse.[8] Hughes commended the soldier for his resolve, an opinion seconded by an editorial published in the *Calgary Daily Herald,* which stated it was a justifiable killing: "The difficult thing for the individual to understand is that Canada is today in a state of war, with all that such a state implies."[9]

Being in a state of war, Canada was also in a state of high anxiety. The various incidents described above demonstrated that accidents brought on by either excitement, nervousness, or bad judgment proved to be the source of much of the misfortune – not saboteurs or agents. It was determined, for instance, after a brief inquiry, that the rifle used by the young Betts exploded in his face after being discharged while reloading. Trooper

1.1 Sentry on duty, Toronto, Ontario, 1914

Moran was shot after stumbling upon a botched robbery. Meanwhile, it was discovered during court proceedings that Sergeant Hooton and other guards had been drinking alcohol prior to the Notter killing, significantly impairing his judgment. As for the Port Arthur incident, it caused the Toronto *Globe* to question sentry protocol and the competence of officers and men alike. Challenged by a sentry whose language the men in the boat more than likely could not understand, the *Globe* asked what the soldiers expected to accomplish by shooting at the boat, especially since they could have no more information about the Canadian forces than might have been obtained in any newspaper. The editors believed that the actions of the guards demonstrated "a lack of comprehension of the sacredness of human life" and concluded, "A man walking up and down at a distance and shouting something generally unintelligible will not do, and the people innocently disregarding such a challenge must not be exposed to danger." They urged, "Let no officer name a man for sentry duty who is not sufficiently discerning to be safely trusted with arms."[10]

There was, of course, every good reason to exercise caution. After all, Canada was at war. But rumours were rife, contributing to the heightened level of public insecurity. Spies, poised to do maximum damage to Canada's war effort and harm the population, were thought to be everywhere.[11] The *Calgary Daily Herald* reported the Canadian government had discovered that information regarding British war preparations was being sent by secret agents in Canada to Germany, part of an alleged spy network operating in Canada for five years. The authorities, according to the paper, had the situation in hand, although the agents apparently succeeded in recruiting among the German-speaking population in Canada – a few of whom, it was alleged, were in the active pay of the kaiser's war party. According to the paper, German Canadians could only blame the kaiser for the pall of suspicion that was cast over the entire community. As for the loyal citizens of Canada, "it is a time when public safety demands that [they] should take no chances," the *Herald* insisted, "even though to act may seem to be doing an injustice."[12]

Rumours of organized espionage appeared to be supported by evidence of a range of suspect activities across the country. In Halifax, two Germans were arrested after various papers and plans were found in their possession, suggesting they were acting as spies in preparation for an invasion of the south shore of Nova Scotia.[13] Foreigners were seen prowling around the Sault Ste Marie wireless station, fleeing only after shots were fired in their direction.[14] While in Port Burwell, a small fishing hamlet located on the north shore of Lake Erie, a suspicious character loitering around the government wireless was arrested.[15] He managed to escape but not before a photograph of the village harbour was found in his possession, leading authorities to believe that he was a German spy. In Saint John, New Brunswick, an elevator fire that destroyed 350,000 barrels of grain – suspiciously started before guards could be posted – was believed to be deliberate.[16] Fire at the Thompson elevator in Spring Coulee, Alberta, was similarly determined to be the work of German sympathizers.[17] In Ontario, the city of London was abuzz after someone had attempted to enter the yard of the Wolseley Barracks. The intruder was prevented from doing so only by the quick action of a sentry, who fired a bullet that pierced the wall of a distant residence, narrowly missing a sleeping mother and child. It was presumed that the attempted breach was to gain access to the gunpowder in the barracks magazine so as to blow up the London powerhouse. After the incident, and despite the near tragedy, the local militia were given explicit orders: "Shoot to kill."[18]

Railways were thought to be especially vulnerable to attack. On 7 August, dynamite was found on the CNR track outside of Parry Sound, prompting the CNR to request arms and ammunition from military authorities for use by men in the company's employ.[19] Near the town of Revelstoke in British Columbia reports circulated that gunfire was exchanged with a gang of marauders who attempted to blow up the Mountain Creek Bridge in advance of a troop train carrying 150 sailors bound for the Atlantic coast.[20] A CNR train also transporting troops from Montreal to the military camp at Valcartier hit a rail that had been left on the track, evidently placed there, according to newspaper accounts, with the intention of derailing and wrecking the military transport.[21] Meanwhile, a number of Austrian homesteaders were arrested near Wadena, Saskatchewan, when spikes between rails were discovered on the track.[22] Released for lack of evidence, the trying magistrate remarked that had a similar incident occurred in Austria-Hungary and British subjects were arrested on suspicion, they would have been executed, but that living in Canada, any man, regardless of nationality, enjoyed the protection of British justice.

The question of British justice no doubt weighed heavily on Herman Wiermeir of Lethbridge, Alberta. The arresting officers who had seized Wiermeir in a bid to capture a suspect responsible for the theft of a number of kegs of blasting powder publicly crowed that there was enough evidence against the man "to warrant taking him out to be shot."[23] Although friends rushed to his defence, attesting to his peaceful disposition, it was his Canadian citizenship that would eventually garner his release. As for Henry Gercke, his Canadian-born wife pleaded with authorities for special consideration after sticks of dynamite had been discovered in their Scarborough, Ontario, home when police, acting on rumours that Gercke had explosives, raided his house.[24] Speaking in court on behalf of her husband, who had a poor command of English, she claimed that a box of dynamite had been found on the road a year earlier, presumably having fallen off a wagon, and was kept by her husband for safekeeping after several attempts to dispose of the explosives at local hardware stores failed. Further investigation corroborated the story, but Gercke was nevertheless fined and jailed for possession of explosives. The nervous panic caused by the Gercke episode as well as another find of lost dynamite near Weston, Ontario, forced the Toronto *Globe* to call for closer supervision of explosives.[25] Dynamite found on the side of the road, the *Globe* argued, was not particularly reassuring, from the perspective of either the danger it posed to those ignorant of its nature or those bent on sabotage.

The concern expressed by the *Globe* foreshadowed an event that sparked widespread panic in Montreal. A devastating explosion took place on 21 October, reportedly killing two men while critically injuring many more and razing the tenement block that served as home for a large number of immigrants.[26] The explosion was attributed to a bomb, the alleged handiwork of the two dead men. The intended device was presumed for a more nefarious purpose, but "that being an illustration of the occasional strangely accurate workings of the hand of fate," it was believed the bombers had received their comeuppance. It was not clear, however, whether they acted alone. Indeed, in the aftermath of the explosion, the mayor received a letter claiming that there was an organized gang of German and Austro-Hungarian nationals, possessing explosives, firearms, and wireless machines, prepared to wreak even more havoc on the city.[27] When blasting by public works employees took place shortly thereafter on a construction project to deepen the channel at the south end of Montreal's St Helen's Island, panic understandably gripped the city.[28] It did not appear to make any difference that the initial investigation, later confirmed, pointed to a faulty gas line as the source of the tenement explosion, and the victims were not bombers as was originally reported, but rather a mother and child and an elderly woman. The story of the alleged bombing in Montreal had a predictable effect elsewhere. The Ottawa police immediately began carrying out a search of the homes of suspect foreigners in the city.[29] In Hull, Quebec, the municipal council instructed the city engineer that contractors working on public work projects discharge foreigners in their employ, presumably because of their access to dynamite.

Public talk of bullets, bombs, sabotage, and foreigners was rampant, but government authorities, for the most part, were circumspect in their assessment of a possible threat. It was appropriate, of course, for the Ontario attorney general to be concerned about reports claiming that foreigners were buying up all of the ammunition in Cobalt, Ontario.[30] And when Prime Minister Sir Robert Borden authorized the employ of an additional five hundred RNWMP officers before it was even discussed in parliament, this was seen as a necessary precaution.[31] But by and large federal officials were guarded in their evaluation of the threat on the basis of the information being received.

Part of the information addressed to government authorities for their attention consisted of private communication from ordinary citizens. Some of it was harmless enough, if nonsensical.[32] Much of it, however, was made up of denunciations borne of envy, malice, and hatred.[33] To check the veracity of the allegations, all of the correspondence, regardless of its content, was sent to the dominion police and the RNWMP for follow-up. Still other letters, especially those received from persons of stature and who had access to officials, were set aside for special treatment and comment. George Bury, vice-president of the Canadian Pacific Railway, urged the deployment of a fighting ship to protect Vancouver's harbour from seizure by German naval vessels that were reportedly plying BC's coastal waters. The minister of militia praised the proposal, declaring it to be an "an excellent idea."[34] On the other hand, nervous communication from M. Donaldson, vice-president and general manager of the Grand Trunk Pacific Railway to the RNWMP commissioner, Colonel A. Perry, regarding reports of foreigner unrest and the need for an additional 2,500 members to protect the railway lines, was skeptically received. The RNWMP comptroller, Laurence Fortescue, in particular, noted the impracticality of the suggestion, not only because of the expanse of the track but also because, of the 1,907 miles of CPR track alone, only 736 miles lay within the territorial jurisdiction of the RNWMP. This, however, did not dissuade Donaldson, who organized a large public meeting in Winnipeg to bring pressure on the government for an increase of three thousand additional RNWMP officers. The action appeared to have influenced the government's decision to increase the force by 1,200 men, with an additional 300 if required. As Prime Minister Borden instructed, although the men would not be used to guard the railways, they could be called upon for assistance if needed.[35]

For the most part, the government looked to its own counsel in making decisions and, as such, depended heavily on information from its own sources. In this regard the government looked to reports from the militia, dominion police (operating in eastern Canada), and the RNWMP (western Canada). In addition, immigration officers were called upon to provide information on border activity, passenger traffic, and activity at railway terminals. The government also contracted with detective agencies and relied on information provided by the dominion office in London as well as the British embassy in the United States regarding activity that could have bearing on the security situation at home. All of the reports were to shed light as much as possible on the threat, especially in light of the rumours and speculation.

The militia regularly provided intelligence reports to government officials on the activity and attitudes among the foreign-born element in the early months of the war. They were particularly on the lookout for Austro-Hungarian and German reservists who wished to return to their native land. Closely monitoring the railways, they collected information and sent it directly to military district headquarters, all of which was then compiled and forwarded to Ottawa. The reports detailed both the movement among foreigners and the security steps taken. Apprised, for example, of the release of some four hundred alien construction workers from Algoma Central Railways, detachments from the 51st Regiment Soo Rifles had intercepted the group before their arrival in Sault Ste Marie with a view to investigating their status as reservists.[36] Several were arrested. In the Clyde district of Alberta, where large numbers of foreigners had settled, the officer commanding in Edmonton, hearing of possible unrest, recommended that a mounted squadron be dispatched to the area.[37] Although there were no outward signs of trouble, there was a sense that, here as elsewhere, a show of force would have a sobering effect on the foreign element while reassuring British settlers in the district.

The reports received from militia provided general background intelligence on developments in various parts of the country. But this was also true of the dominion police, which supplied the prime minister with regular confidential reports in the form of weekly synopses.[38] The reports, concerned with gauging the temperament of the foreign-born population not only in Canada but also in the US (where it was thought that events might trigger a response in Canada), all underscored the finding that the population was largely docile and, contrary to the rumours and allegations made, there appeared to be no organization or planning involved. Nothing was discovered by the RNWMP, either its uniformed or undercover officers, that was concerning, let alone alarming, a conclusion shared not only with the prime minister but with other senior government officials as well. Threatening attitudes among the German settler population near Irma and Wainright, Alberta, for example, were found to be non-existent, according to one investigation. The report that German homesteaders in the Happyland district of Saskatchewan had purchased large quantities of arms and ammunition was determined to be false. Nor, according to police intelligence officers in Winnipeg, was there any evidence to rumours that Austro-Hungarian or German nationals were preparing to attack public or private property in the city. For that matter, the chief commissioner of the dominion police, Colonel A.P. Sherwood, noted from a general read of police reports there was no evidence anywhere in the country that any planned attack was being organized or prepared.[39]

The police view that nothing untoward was occurring was confirmed by sources from other parts of the country. The dominion immigration agent for New Brunswick reported to the superintendent of immigration, W.D. Scott, that "the [Austro-Hungarians] have gone to work in the lumber woods and appear to take no interest whatever in the European

War ... [and that] none of them show the slightest inclination to cause trouble or do other than proceed in the usual way to earn a living."[40] An immigration report from northern Ontario was equally sanguine with respect to the disposition of the foreign-born element there: "It seems that as long as the majority of these foreigners are kept in work there will be no cause for anxiety"; further, they were "quiet and inclined to mind their own business."[41]

The persistence of the rumours, nevertheless, was troubling. Anxious to stay on top of the situation, the police sought independently to ascertain the extent of the possible threat. Inquiries and investigations, as a consequence, were made all around. A police request, for instance, was made of the registrar at the University of Toronto to provide names and addresses of students of German descent who had entered the university.[42] There was also some concern that the American consul in Montreal harboured pro-German sympathizers. Wishing to determine the extent of the consul's support for Germany, an undercover police officer, posing as an American citizen, was sent to his office to secretly gauge his views.[43] Desiring to know the scope of the challenge facing the federal police, the dominion police commissioner, Colonel Sherwood, also requested information from the immigration branch on the numbers of aliens of enemy nationality resident in the country. He was informed that as of 1 June 1911 there were 393,320 Germans living in Canada and a further 15,868 had arrived since then. Austro-Hungarians, on the other hand, numbered 129,103 in 1911 with an additional 66,911 having arrived during the intervening period. In total, there were approximately 600,000 individuals living in Canada who had close ties to Germany and Austria-Hungary, lands now at war with Britain and the empire.[44]

The numbers were indeed large, pointing to the scale of the possible threat. But in the end what mattered most was the attitude of the population and, more particularly, whether there was political motivation behind any activity. It was for this reason that the actions of the Ukrainian Ruthenian League and the Association of an Independent Ukraine were felt to be somewhat worrisome. Both organizations, agitating for Ukrainian independence, were decidedly anti-Russian in their views. Although unopposed to British participation in the war, the group's amity toward Austria-Hungary, as a more benevolent power offering greater autonomy to Ukrainians, was considered disconcerting. Their leadership warranted greater scrutiny and surveillance, prompting RNWMP comptroller Laurence Fortescue to recommend to the prime minister that the activities of the two, but especially the more vociferous League, be put under closer watch.[45]

Although information on the League and the Association hinted at conspiracy, RNWMP commissioner A.B. Perry thought that in general the views of the Austro-Hungarian population were not particularly problematic, especially since, as he concluded, "Most of the people from the dual kingdom are from Galicia and their sympathy is not very warm towards their homeland." He did venture to say, however, in his communication to the RNWMP comptroller that "the German is the one who is antagonistic, and it is the German-Canadian whom we have to fear." Perry concluded, "I am not desiring of alarming you, but I think that the situation must be carefully watched and preparation made to meet all eventualities."[46]

Perry's remarks may have been coloured by rumours and reports regarding the possibility of an attack by raiders from the United States, in particular German settlers along the Canada-US border. Memories of the Fenian raids in the mid-nineteenth century – when the Irish republican element in the US organized and conducted military forays against British Canada – added to the general urgency of obtaining a better understanding of what was transpiring there. The situation became even more urgent when the press began covering statements made by the German ambassador to the US, Count Von Bernstorff, who claimed that Germany reserved the right to attack Canada given that it had violated the Monroe Doctrine by engaging in European affairs.[47] These statements gave credence to information, widely reported, that contingents of armed German Americans were ready to invade Canada from Buffalo and other US centres.[48] To the degree that such attacks might encourage local extremists in Canada, the government was praised for its decision not to allow members of the RNWMP to enlist for fighting service abroad. As the *Calgary Daily Herald* editorialized, "it is impossible to know at what moment the spirit of unrest may occur."[49] Concluding that the mounted police were best equipped to handle the situation, the *Herald* further stated that the fight at home could prove to be as significant as the fight overseas. "It may yet develop that in remaining at their posts here in the West they will be serving the cause of the Allies better than they ever could hope to do in the firing line over in Europe."

Reports of an invasion had been received from the war's outset, notably through British channels in the United States. On 8 August, the British embassy in Washington alerted the governor general in Ottawa of imminent raids on the dominion through the woods of New England

and that steps had been taken to inform the US authorities with a view to preventing a border crossing.[50] When learning of the report, the special counsellor to the US secretary of state, Robert Lansing, communicated with British representatives that Maine had but few German inhabitants and none lived near the Canadian border, leading him to conclude that the rumour of a raid was unfounded.[51] More to the point, Maine's governor described the rumour as "absurd." As for Vermont, the governor there promised to investigate, but deplored the lack of specific information.

The scarcity of detailed, reliable information prompted the Canadian government to engage in a full-scale effort to collect particulars in the US.[52] On the diplomatic front, Sir Joseph Pope, Canada's undersecretary of state for external affairs, conveyed the need for regular, full reports from the British embassy. The embassy replied that consular officers across the United States would be instructed to "exercise great care in watching for raids into Canadian territory, and to report any movement of the kind."[53] In terms of strategic intelligence, arrangements were also made through the dominion police to station secret service agents in both large and small US cities, where Austro-Hungarians and Germans were concentrated, for the purpose of providing regular, detailed reports and following up on leads obtained by the government.

In the end very little was discovered except for strong anti-British sentiment in various parts of the German-American community, which was being incited by certain German-language newspapers. As for planning, there was no evidence of a conspiracy, including the widely reported story of an organized effort to stage a raid from Buffalo on behalf of thirty-nine enemy aliens held near Niagara Falls, which had caused Canadian military authorities to overreact and move those arrested further inland for safekeeping. Indeed, it was determined that the rumours, whose principal source was the press, were "altogether exaggerated and wholly founded on individual utterances, behind which there is no effective organization."[54]

This was not to say that there were no threats. But if there was danger, it was by way of lawless individuals who might undertake single acts of sabotage and destruction. This knowledge, however, did little to temper the ongoing anxiety and belief that large numbers of German and Austro-Hungarian reservists, as part of the growing unemployed in the US, and being destitute and desperate, might yet be instigated to attack Canada.

With this risk in mind, and given the widespread unease in the country about an imminent invasion, Prime Minister Borden sought assurance from the dominion police commissioner Colonel Sherwood that there was sufficient ammunition to repel an attack on the city of Toronto.[55] When asked by a member of parliament what measures would be taken to help address the "perilous situation" in which the country had been "denuded of its rifles and cannons," Borden, having been reassured by the commissioner, replied that adequate defences were in place. He was quick to point out that seventy-one thousand rifles were in the hands of the local militia, with an additional ten thousand Lee-Enfield rifles and eight thousand Ross rifles. Eighty twelve-pound cannons were at the ready, and carriages were being constructed at the Ottawa Car Works for twenty-eight fifteen-pound cannons. Repeating the commissioner's observation that there was "no evidence that anything of importance is being attempted except possibly through certain thugs and gun-men who are being carefully watched and shadowed," Borden's response revealed that, in terms of preparation, the government was nevertheless ready for any eventuality.[56]

## A QUESTION OF LOYALTY

The promise of a citizens' group in Kingston, Ontario, to purchase four heavy machine guns for use by the local militia underlined the general sense of unease in the country.[57] It also pointed to a larger concern: namely, that the alien population could not be trusted. As a number of writers noted in their correspondence with the government, if the Allies were to suffer military reversals in Europe it could be expected that German and Austro-Hungarian elements in the country would take advantage of the situation and engage in possible insurrection or other activity that would be equally harmful to the national interest. Indeed, the fall of the fortress city of Namur in Belgium, believed to be impregnable but taken after only three days of fighting, was attributed to the activities of spies and saboteurs and served as a useful reminder about the importance of increased vigilance and surveillance.

Distrust of the alien immigrant was clear and unmistakable. The source of that distrust was their questionable loyalty, of which there was some evidence. Weeks before the start of hostilities in Europe, countless hundreds of Austro-Hungarian and German subjects resident in Canada had presented themselves for duty to consular representatives in Canada, responding to patriotic declarations in the foreign-language press calling to arms reservists and others willing to serve.[58] And although they were not alone – Swedes, Greeks, Swiss, Belgians, and others were heading home as well, heeding the call to arms by their respective mother countries – the departure of Germans and Austro-Hungarians was an altogether different matter. Prepared to take up arms against Britain and the empire, these individuals made no pretence about their allegiance.[59]

Also adding to the climate of mistrust was the pastoral letter written on 27 July 1914 by the Ruthenian Greco-Catholic hierarch in Canada, Bishop Nykyta Budka, and read in Ukrainian Catholic parishes across the country.[60] The letter, reflecting the bishop's conservative and hierarchical views, spoke of the looming war between the Austro-Hungarian and Russian empires and encouraged Ukrainians in Canada, former nationals of the dual kingdom, to come to its defence against a rapacious Russia, which was threatening Ukrainian autonomy under the Hapsburgs. Although the letter was written before British involvement in the war, the liberal-oriented *Manitoba Free Press*, seizing an opportunity to discredit the conservative Roblin government that had recently claimed electoral victory by courting the Ukrainian vote with its support for bilingual education in the province, published a translation of the pastoral letter on 4 August – the day Britain declared war on Germany. It created an extraordinary public furor, exacerbated by the persistent baiting of the *Free Press*.[61]

It did not matter that in the aftermath of Britain's declaration of war, Bishop Budka released a subsequent letter asking that under the changed geopolitical circumstances his former missive be ignored and the faithful perform the duties expected of them as Canadians. Nor did it matter that Prime Minister Borden, having received correspondence explaining the bishop's position, acknowledged in a widely quoted communication that the patriotism of the bishop "commend[ed] itself to the approval and sympathy of the Government and people of Canada."[62] What mattered was that the bishop was cast in the role of an "Austrian mobilizer," accused of using his ecclesiastical authority "to shepherd his flock into the Austrian army to fight against the British Empire."[63] His actions served as sufficient evidence of the perfidy of those Canada had invited to its shores but who were now taking advantage of the country's freedoms.

Much of the outrage directed against Bishop Budka's alleged betrayal and those who were returning to their respective homelands to fight was played out against a backdrop of patriotic fervour. News of the declaration of war was met throughout the country with unbounded enthusiasm and joy. In Regina, throngs of people listened to news bulletins read from specially erected platforms near the newspaper offices, cheering wildly with every announcement and singing patriotic songs to the

accompaniment of a local boy scout band. In Fort William, thousands
lined the streets singing "God Save the King" and "Rule Britannia." All-
night bands paraded the streets of Toronto to scenes of celebration and
outbursts of "patriotism and whole-souled loyalty to the empire," neither seen nor heard since the Boer War. In Quebec City, English, French,
and Irish inhabitants gathered together as never before in a common
display of loyalty. Similar scenes of jubilation were replicated across the
country in various other centres with calls being made for the native-
born to enlist.

The sentiments accompanying the revelry spoke to the importance of
honour, pride, and, above all, duty. War would be successful only if every
man was prepared to make a contribution and, if need be, sacrifice.
Individuals were being called upon to give of themselves and to sacrifice
everything, injecting into the political atmosphere and discourse a dose
of high moral conviction, delineating between those for and against the
cause.[64] It was not surprising, therefore, that interspersed among the
celebratory statements were declarations denouncing both Germany and
those who favoured that country.

The powerful and genuine emotions stemmed from a profound respect
for king and country. But, arguably, it also sprang from a deeper understanding that the conflict ahead was about principles. As was repeated in
a number of editorials in the major dailies, although there was no denying the importance of devotion to country, behind patriotism were principles that would also guide and inspire.[65] In the war against autocracy,
so it was argued, freedom, justice, and the independence of peoples were
ideals that informed the British temperament. These also necessarily
made the cause both just and right and roused in Canadians the spirit to
fight.[66] Patriotism was about king and country. Canadians, however,
were being called upon to balance simple love of country with ideals that
would hold promise for the future.

The manner in which patriotism was being expressed and articulated,
not only as a natural demonstration of devotion to country but also as a
political project, posed some important questions with respect to the
foreigner.[67] If it were natural for the native-born to show signs of attachment and regard for their homeland, then would a similar condition also
apply in the case of those recently arrived? Was it not expected that they
too would exhibit the same concern about their kindred back home?
The question, therefore, was what should be the proper attitude toward
foreigners, who were faced simultaneously with concern for their birth
country and adopted country? Further, if the fight was about freedom,

then what role might this principle play in shaping the attitude of foreigners so that they might understand and appreciate the opportunity presented by their country of choice?

For Private J.W. Wendt of Alberta's 101st Regiment training at Valcartier, the predicament was real. In a letter to the militia council in Ottawa, Colonel J.P. Landry, commander of the 5th Military District (Quebec), indicated that Trooper Wendt requested a discharge after learning that two of his siblings were fighting for Germany and that "he threatened to blow his brains out if he was obliged to fight against his brothers."[68] Wendt further asked that the reason for his discharge not be divulged, "as the men might think of him as a spy." Wendt, who had six years of military service with the US army and two years with the Alberta Dragoons, was considered an efficient and able soldier. However, on the date of the declaration of war and before the case for his discharge could be considered, Wendt attempted suicide by ingesting arsenic. Deemed to be of sound mind, Wendt was arrested on suspicion of being a reservist. Wendt, however, was a naturalized Canadian citizen, and after an investigation he was released and discharged. Colonel Cruickshank, the commanding officer of Military District No. 13 (Alberta), noted that Wendt should not have been allowed to enlist in the first instance. His personal predicament made for difficult choices.[69]

Private Wendt was not alone in his emotional turmoil. A number of requests were received for discharge on the grounds that they were not prepared to fight against their ethnic kindred. The problem of divided loyalties was widespread and endemic. In the Hope Valley district of central Alberta, where large numbers of Galician and other Slav homesteaders had settled, it was reported that their sympathy was with their kindred back home.[70] This did not imply that they wished to return, let alone fight for their former homelands. It did suggest, however, that there was much anxiety and misgiving about the days ahead.[71]

For Sir Wilfrid Laurier, former prime minister and leader of the opposition in parliament, what was required was a sympathetic hearing of the plight of those with divided loyalties. Laurier acknowledged that just as they were proud of their country of adoption, Canadians of German descent were equally proud of their country of birth and that "there [was] nothing perhaps so painful as the situation in which mind and heart are driven in opposite directions."[72] He wished to assure Canadians of German origin that Britain and Canada had no quarrel with the German people, but also reminded them that, in the struggle for constitutional freedom, if Germany had had the institutions of democracy then

the cruelty of war could have been avoided. Prime Minister Borden similarly noted that there was no problem regarding the Canadian attitude
toward the German people. Rather, the fight was with the reactionary
autocracy in Germany that had dominated them. Moreover, with hundreds of thousands of "the very best citizens of Canada" being of German
origin, he was sure "that no one in this country ... would for one moment
desire to utter any word or use any expression in our debates, in regard
to this matter, which would wound the self-respect or hurt the feelings of
any man or woman in the country of German descent."[73]

Both Laurier and Borden sought to make clear that a distinction
had to be made between attachment to place of birth and support for
militarism. They also wished to make plain that it was important for
native-born Canadians to distinguish between atavistic German militarism and the German people. In this way Canadians would not only
show magnanimity, intelligence, and courage but also highlight the
value of freedom and help to inculcate democratic principles among the
immigrant element. "When he becomes inoculated with the principles
of democracy which find expression in all Anglo-Saxon governments,
the German takes his place among the foremost advocates of democracy."[74] As for those who would leave Canada if permitted, "they would
receive no help from their German Canadian compatriots. The Canadian
German knows that this is a war of autocracy against democracy – and
he is with democracy."

Expressions of loyalty were a comforting reminder that foreigners recognized the principles behind the fight and its significance. It was further
evidence that they were prepared to sacrifice for the cause of liberty.
Louis Gurofsky, an ex-sergeant of the 10th Royal Grenadiers, offered to
raise at his own expense a regiment of "Hebrew Volunteers" who would
show "their Loyalty and appreciation of the many courtesies and freedoms extended to our people under the British Flag in all parts of
the world."[75] The Russian, Serbian, and Montenegrin Committee of
Vancouver, anxious to demonstrate their loyalty to Britain and Canada,
telegraphed the governor general in Ottawa asking for approval and
authorization to mobilize a foreign legion of a thousand men for active
service at the front.[76] Italian residents of Toronto promised an entire regiment in support of the effort in Europe.[77] Ukrainians in Winnipeg made
a similar promise at a meeting of some three thousand individuals.[78]

Monetary contributions to local patriotic funds or the Red Cross
Society exceeded targets as various groups began donating more than was
expected. The small town of Rosthern, Saskatchewan, whose population

was estimated to be two-thirds of German descent, succeeded in raising $2,000 in two days. The residents of Berlin, Ontario, a city preponderantly of German origin, raised in excess of $95,000 for the Patriotic Fund. The large sum merited a cablegram to Lord Kitchener, the British war secretary, who was informed of "the success of the campaign in this German center."[79] Collections no matter how small were also seen as evidence of patriotism and widely acknowledged as such while those who were not in a position to make a financial contribution but felt compelled to demonstrate their loyalty did so in other ways that were considered equally meaningful.[80]

Political statements of loyalty accompanied these simple acts of patriotism. A few days after the declaration of war, the three thousand Ukrainians who gathered together at the convention hall of the Industrial Bureau in Winnipeg passed a resolution not only reaffirming their allegiance to the British flag as citizens of Canada but also asserting that the British cause was their cause, a point reiterated by W. Arsenych, a keynote speaker, who declared: "Our homes and our fortunes are now at stake. Great Britain is at war and the welfare of the British Empire is at stake. Whatever friction might have existed among foreigners in this country in the past should be forgotten at this time and all should stand together in one common purpose."[81] When a general meeting of several thousand, representing a variety of nationalities, was held a month later in the same venue, the message was made even clearer. The assembled lot were resolute in their support for Britain and Canada because of the justice of the cause to which they were witness as free men:

Resolved by this meeting of British citizens by adoption, representing practically all of the civilized nations of the earth, that this meeting of citizens, who have been born in other lands, but who have exercised the right of free choice, which should belong to every man, of deciding what country he shall live and to whom he shall give his allegiance, and holding that the ballots of the people alone should decide how they shall be governed, have become citizens of this country, and without disparagement of the lands of our births, believing that in the present cruel and unjust war which has been thrust upon us, that Great Britain and her allies represent the cause of democracy and rule by the people as against military despotism;

That we hereby pledge our moral and material support to Great Britain and to the cause of human freedom, and we hereby declare

that we are ready to contribute of our financial means and our
personal services to the destruction of autocracy and triumph
of liberty as represented by the British Empire and her allies in
this crisis.[82]

Freedom and liberty became the watchwords that defined the nature
of the struggle for the many who had left their homelands. These words
were not seen as empty gestures but represented a goal to be applied
back home. For Poles in Canada, the war as a struggle for freedom meant
that Polish independence might once more be restored. After Poland had
lost territory to Prussia, Austria-Hungary, and Russia in the late eight-
eenth century, the restoration of Polish sovereignty was very much on
the minds of Polish patriots, including those who had left their occupied
home for opportunity and freedom elsewhere, including Canada. The
war was a means to achieve freedom for Poland, but this could only be
fulfilled if Russia, an ally in the conflict, would abide by the principles
governing the struggle. In Winnipeg, Polish inhabitants organized a mass
meeting of eight hundred, expressing thanks to Britain, France, and the
other nations for their defence of liberty, but also voicing their belief that
greater autonomy and freedom for Poland would be endorsed and guaranteed by Britain and France "not as a gift or favour of the Czar, but as
a deposit on account of the rights the world owes us."[83]

Although the Polish position elicited some sympathy, it was also met
with perplexity regarding the timing and seeming conditionality of the
loyalty of Canadians of Polish descent. Was it appropriate at this crucial
hour to make declarations that complicated the alliance and which
framed allegiance in terms that placed loyalty to Canada in a secondary
role? It was an argument that also applied in the case of Ukrainians. Like
the Poles, they seized the opportunity to make a claim on behalf of
Ukrainian independence, which historically had been denied by Russia.
It was an argument, however, that, when combined with the Bishop
Budka affair, raised doubts about Slav loyalty generally.[84]

The *Manitoba Free Press* was particularly harsh in its criticism of
advocates of both Polish and Ukrainian independence, arguing that
Canada did not ask newcomers to forget their birthplace but did have
the right to insist they become Canadians, noting their primary obligation was to the country they now called home. The newspaper declared
that this was of national importance and those who did not feel their
first duty was to Canada and the empire "had better be got out of
Canada and kept out," especially those agitators who have "imported

the lingo and catch phrases of the nationalist crusade in Galicia [Western Ukraine]" and clerics "who fear the Anglicization of their people."[85] The *Free Press* further noted "the mischievous anti-Canadian propaganda carried on amongst the Poles and Ruthenians [Ukrainians] in Manitoba … [was] potentially strong enough to prejudice the future of Manitoba for more than a generation."[86] Insisting that it was neither against the foreigner nor fanatical in its position, the newspaper, nonetheless, evoked the spectre of chaos unless the threat was averted:

> With the terrible example of Europe before their eyes, the people of Canada will see to it that this vast western plain is not divided up among races, nourishing age-long animosities and cherishing divergent racial ideals. Our gates are open to the oppressed of Europe; but when they come here they must forget their feuds, forswear the racial aspirations and become Canadians, not only in name but also in fact. Otherwise Western Canada will see in fifty years a repetition of the conditions which have turned Central Europe into a shambles.[87]

In Alberta, reports of clubs being created for the purpose of supporting the cause of Ukrainian independence, notably the Society for an Independent Ukraine, were met with outrage and indignation. Ukrainian independence should be of no concern to Canada, declared the *Edmonton Bulletin*: "Canada is Canada and those who become Canadian citizens are expected to limit their activities to Canada and to Canada's place and duty in the British Empire. Whether the Ukraine is to be a republic, or a province of Russia or of Austria is none of Canada's business, and whoever tries to carry on in Canada a propaganda for settling the political status of the Ukraine is making trouble for Canada and therefore for himself." As for the agitators whose avowed aim was starting an insurgency against Russia, a country in alliance with Britain, their work made them no less than agents acting on behalf of Austria-Hungary. On this point, the *Edmonton Bulletin* was clear: "The business should be put a stop to."[88]

A number of individuals and organizations, concerned about the public perception of Slav and German loyalty, especially as the press was shaping it, sought to explain and clarify the statements of community representatives. They claimed that these were being either misconstrued or misinterpreted.[89] Others urged the public not to overreact. If the public were able to openly understand the predicament of these people, their criticism would be much tempered. If a more charitable and sympathetic view of the challenges facing the newcomer were adopted, it would do much to alleviate their concerns and help integrate them into the mainstream. Furthermore, the fact that they had proven themselves as settlers surely meant they deserved the respect and assurance of not being subjected to "any act, however trivial, which would make their sojourn amongst us any harder or more trying than the developments from day to day are sure to make it."[90] There were a number of calls for the public to be "self-respecting" and to refrain from wanton denunciations and mob rule. Menacing opinions and vicious accusations served no other purpose except to incite public disorder, which had to be avoided and resisted at all costs.

Justice Rupert Kingsford, for instance, appealed for calm and sanity in his remarks at the opening of the police court in Toronto. He stated that the immigrants who came from countries at war with Canada and had been living among Canadians for years were "respectable citizens." He declared that they deserved the full protection of the law so long as they reciprocated by not contravening the laws of the land. Moreover, they were entitled to fairness and justice and to be shielded from accusations and judgments that prejudiced their place and role in society. Judge Kingsford concluded by encouraging members of the bar "to use all your influence in the direction of impressing on our own people the necessity for the preservation of law and order, and the protection of foreigners remaining within our borders."[91]

The appeal of Justice Kingsford and the singular calls for moderation and tolerance were in response to the growing number of attacks on persons and property animated by anti-foreigner sentiment. Shortly after war's outbreak, an unruly and vicious mob cornered a number of immigrants on the streets of Toronto, forcing them to kneel and kiss the Union Jack.[92] In Vancouver, the windows of the German consulate as well as shops believed to be foreign-owned were smashed by youth, whose misplaced patriotism, according to the local police, was fuelled by alcohol.[93] In Fort William, eighteen Austrians were forcibly ejected from a train by a troop of naval reservists after two highland pipers were allegedly insulted.[94] When street orators whipped up the emotions of a group of Winnipeggers during the local parading of troops, the mob proceeded to march on the German and Austro-Hungarian consulates and the local German club, where they stoned the buildings, doing considerable damage before the police finally arrived and dispersed the crowd.[95] Meanwhile, in Calgary, vigilantism was openly encouraged to deal with purported pro-German sympathizers, who were voicing their views, albeit clandestinely.[96]

1.2 Effigies and anti-foreign sentiment, Calgary, Alberta

In the face of allegations of treachery and spying, a number of individuals felt compelled to defend themselves. F.O. Willhofft, a Queen's University engineering professor, accused of being a German spy, was forced to publicly declare his innocence, adding in his defence that "since my word would not be respected by persons who believe me capable of such treachery, all I can say is, that if I were offered a fortune for each word, with all my knowledge of Canada and Canadian conditions, I could not think of any information that would be of any earthly use to the German Government."[97] F.M. Shunck of Toronto, a third-generation Canadian of German descent, offered $100 for information that would enable him to prosecute individuals unknown who were injuring his name and business by engaging in slander and insinuating that he was a German spy.[98] When Reverend John Oberhiemer was accused by a local magistrate of preaching sedition to his congregation in Irvine, Alberta, the Lutheran pastor thought it necessary to swear an affidavit and assert his innocence in a letter to the prime minister.[99] As a pastor of the Lutheran Church of Canada, he objected against statements "imputing to our teachings doctrines opposed to the principles of our Church as a whole." As a naturalized citizen, he also protested being described as a so-called "enemy." He claimed that such provocations only served to jeopardize both peace and harmony.

Prime Minister Borden expressed satisfaction on learning Reverend Oberhiemer had instructed his congregation that "they must be obedient to the authority and perform their duty as good citizens of this country." Borden assured the reverend that he was mindful of the fact Canadian citizens of German and Austro-Hungarian nationality were conscious of their civic duty and that he personally took great pleasure in testifying to this on many occasions.[100] Privately, however, the prime minister asked the RNWMP to investigate. In its report to Borden, the RNWMP stated that it was unclear whether the allegations against Reverend Oberhiemer were true or false, but if there was a concern, it was the considerable agitation in the district "caused to a great extent by the action of the home population."[101]

For the German-Canadian Provincial Alliance of Saskatchewan, the attacks and other challenges facing Germans and Austro-Hungarians warranted a response. In a petition to Prime Minister Borden they drew attention to the harmful effect of newspaper articles that incited "race hatred and ill-feeling" against the foreign population.[102] These not only undermined the efforts at nation building, according to the organization, but also prevented recent immigrants from becoming true and loyal citizens. The issue was whether the government would continue to tolerate a press that wantonly "hurt the feelings of a considerable percentage of the total population of Canada," endangering the work of building the country. The prime minister responded carefully, stating that the country would never contemplate controlling a free press, if only because it was a cherished right that was highly prized in Canada. And although he preferred that such newspapers abstain from any criticism directed against Canadian citizens of German or Austro-Hungarian origin, there was little he could do, save exercise his personal influence for this purpose.[103]

When news of the petition was made public, several papers felt obliged to comment. Describing the petition an impertinence, the *Manitoba Free Press* roundly condemned the Alliance for its hypocrisy: for opposing the mainstream press that reported on German cruelty and treachery, yet remaining silent on pro-German newspapers that it was in a position to control. Pro-German sympathy such as this, the *Free Press* argued, was the source of much of the misfortune of German Canadians. It was the wish of the *Free Press* editors that "those Western Canadians of German descent who today are sympathizing with a ruthless military autocracy will live to see their mistake and be ashamed of it."[104] In the surge of untrammelled patriotism brought on by war, with few defenders and even fewer supplicants, immigrants of "enemy nationality" would find themselves increasingly isolated and even more apprehensive for the future.

## THE PREDICAMENT OF BELONGING

Unchecked news and opinions expressed by the foreign-language press were considered harmful to the British cause. The newspapers commented freely on the victories of enemy states, giving rise to the criticism that "[foreigners] imagined Canada was some sort of indefinite frontier country or some exalted mining camp where each nationality was a law unto itself." It was a disturbing development that prompted the questions: How was it that Canada found itself in this situation and what might be done to best address the failure? The response was: more effective citizenship. Only by teaching the principles of citizenship would "a new and virile nation" emerge, one that would be neither Scotch, Irish, German, Polish, French, nor anything else but Canadian.[105]

The importance of citizenship was a lesson that needed to be learned, if only because the rights of citizenship imposed certain obligations, the first of which was loyalty. By understanding and valuing that rights and freedoms followed from citizenship, newcomers would see the significance and importance of fidelity and their commitment to their country of choice. Only through the knowledge and experience of citizenship would the newcomer be drawn into the political community and encouraged to stand in its defence.[106] In placing emphasis on civic education, however, the debate presumed that there was public acceptance of the idea that recent arrivals could or should become citizens. War brought with it many lessons, not the least of which was the importance of distinguishing between friend and foe. War, regrettably, insisted on the following questions: Who constituted the community and who did not belong? Citizenship was a category of belonging that helped make that distinction and, therefore, was something not to be easily negotiated or casually surrendered.

However, there remained a perceptible gap between those hoping to engage the foreigner through the lessons of citizenship and those who were skeptical of the process. No better example of this can be found than in the discussion of naturalization – the granting and acquisition of citizenship by immigrants. Could, for example, applications for naturalization by Austro-Hungarians and Germans be accepted under the conditions of war? For Justice H. Gervais of the court of appeal in Montreal, the answer was "No!" War had politicized the issue of allegiance, making it nearly impossible to accurately assess the motivations of those applying. Accordingly, he informed the naturalization commissioner in Montreal that naturalization of a subject of an enemy country could not be obtained during wartime and instructed him not to process any more applications.[107]

There remained some uncertainty, however, as to whether this could legally be done, and a ruling from the Justice Department was sought, especially as there did not appear to be any authority upon the subject and no statute relating to the matter. On the bench, the issue was being dealt with as a matter of expediency. Policy, however, was what was needed. After some deliberation, the Justice Department advised that, as long as there was compliance with the Naturalization Act, the prevailing state of war did not affect the duty of the court to grant naturalization certificates to Germans and Austro-Hungarian subjects.[108] This position stood in contrast to the attitude in the United Kingdom, where certificates of naturalization were not granted to subjects of enemy states except to persons performing public service or for other special reasons.[109] Given the importance and tradition of following the British lead, the divergence between Canadian and British policies pointed to an altogether different understanding of the role that naturalization could play in the context of the war.

An important consideration in the naturalization of subjects of enemy states was the principle behind the grant. Thomas Mulvey, the undersecretary of state, held that "one of the most elementary and far-reaching principles which can be invoked for the purpose of deciding questions raised between belligerents is this: that either of the belligerents may take any action which is not prohibited by international law which will weaken the other."[110] From this perspective, Mulvey argued, the best way to take the enemy's men out of the fight was by naturalizing them. To be sure, there were some obvious difficulties with this approach. Naturalization could serve as a means by which spies might be introduced into the country. It would also give the necessary protection and opportunity for reservists and others to cross the border unmolested, making their way back to their respective homelands to take up arms against Britain and the empire. Consequently, Mulvey advised that it was the responsibility of judges to exercise discretion, establishing the bona fides of the applicants and refusing naturalization to those who would abuse the privilege.

A striking characteristic of the debate was the fact that the loyalty of the foreigner was in question either way. Whether naturalization was used by the applicant as a means to cloak his real intentions or by authorities to draw them out of the fight, the presumption was that his allegiance lay elsewhere. It was a widespread sentiment, prevalent even in the highest courts of the land. In Montreal, the chief justice of the circuit court, Justice M. Lebeuf, for instance, stated that "in numerous instances, the petitions were based on ulterior motives" and expressed personal dismay because the law was being "made a mockery of by persons desirous of taking up arms against us."[111] Lebeuf was not alone in his suspicions. The *Calgary Daily Herald* also expressed uneasiness with extending citizenship to subjects of enemy birth during wartime.[112] The duties of citizenship were being taken lightly, placing doubt not only on its value but on the question of who rightfully belonged to the community.

No such ambiguity, however, rested with another political category that operated concurrently alongside that of citizenship. All those born in Canada under the flag of the British sovereign enjoyed subject status. In Canada, it was a defining political characteristic that established, within the context of imperial rule, a political and legal relationship between the individual and the crown. Individuals received protection and benefits from the crown as a result of their subject status, while those who were not subjects merited only limited rights and security.[113] This condition reciprocally followed from the allegiance naturally owed the sovereign in a hierarchical political and social order. Most importantly, however, by defining a legal and political relationship with the crown, one that could neither be easily forsaken nor abandoned, subjectship established in a clear and unambiguous way a framework for answering the question of who belonged.[114]

In the context of war, in which the relationship between individuals and the crown was militarized, the idea of subjectship had serious implications. Subjects of the British crown were exhorted to stand in its defence. Those who owed their allegiance as subjects to another sovereign would be recognized as "enemy subjects." Immigrants of enemy nationality, accordingly, were saddled with the ignominious label "enemy alien."[115] Most importantly, however, from the perspective of modern war, where entire nations were mobilized for the conflict and mass mobilization made every able-bodied man a potential combatant, the enemy alien became a possible enemy combatant against whom sanctions could be employed and the laws of war applied. When the editors

of the *Edmonton Daily Bulletin* noted that Canadians in Germany and
Austria-Hungary were being treated as enemies because they were British
subjects, they maintained that a similar principle also applied with
respect to German and Austro-Hungarian subjects in Canada: "We are
at war with Germany and Austria today. As a consequence, our residents
of German and Austrian citizenship are technically enemies – whatever
their personal sympathies or actions."[116]

By imposing the tag "enemy alien" on an individual because of the person's subject status, that individual was immediately cast in the role of an
enemy. "Enemy alien," however, was not simply a normative declaration;
it had real legal and juridical import. As Justice J.B. Archambault, sitting
in the circuit court, noted in his remarks during naturalization proceedings of some 153 "enemy alien" applicants, whether they were naturalized
or not such individuals were entitled to the protection of the courts. But
he also went on to say: "The fact that an Austrian or German subject may
be, and is at present, in a state of war against His Majesty King George,
no matter in what part of his Dominions the Austrian or German is
located, does not bar him from ceasing to be in a state of war by assuming
British citizenship."[117] Subject status thus became an important determin-
ant in the conflict about one's standing in the political community.

Archambault's views on extending legal protection to enemy aliens
(despite the contradiction) followed from the government's attitude that
subjects of enemy nationality were not to be interfered with as long as
they obeyed the laws of the land. It was a position clearly articulated in
the Proclamation published 15 August 1914. The Proclamation was
explicit, claiming that persons of German or Austro-Hungarian nationality would be accorded the respect and consideration due to law-abiding
citizens. Moreover, they would not be arrested, detained, or interfered
with in any way unless there were reasonable grounds to suggest that they
were engaged in hostile activity or were in contravention of any law or
order-in-council. But also implied in the Proclamation was the idea that
these individuals were in fact enemy subjects. This was apparent from the
state's discretionary power to grant rights; enemy aliens would enjoy
rights but these were provisionally given and could be limited or taken
away at any time. It was also evident in the provision contained in the
Proclamation that allowed enemy aliens to sign an "Undertaking" which
committed those individuals to forswear behaviour seen as either inimical
or prejudicial to the country's national interests. The Undertaking, a preventative measure, presumed the possibility of enemy activity, underscoring their enemy status.

According to international understanding and convention, every sovereign state has both the right and duty to protect itself and to provide security to its citizens. The Proclamation therefore was a legitimate act of state. In taking preventative measures against enemy aliens, the government operated in self-defence. But immigration, which included the migration of subjects of enemy nationality to Canada, posed something of a conundrum. Having invited them to the country as settlers, did the government have any obligation to these people? In point of fact, it did, and it acknowledged as much. The government, therefore, was careful in the sense that it wished to make clear, through the Proclamation, that enemy subjects, if they followed their avocations peacefully, would be neither molested nor interfered with in any way. Yet they were also subjects of enemy states that were at war with Britain and the empire – a point that was not lost on Justice Archambault. It was also not lost on other officials, who, as fair warning, gave instructions to provide "due publicity" to the Proclamation, notably in those areas and communities where suspicious activity was reportedly taking place and the potential for disturbances was possible.[118]

The Proclamation of 15 August represented an important first step in providing security. The dominion police, for instance, collected the signed Undertakings in order to have "a complete record" from which intelligence reports could be made.[119] The Undertakings as outlined in the Proclamation further imposed a duty on those who were arrested and on parole to report regularly to officials as a condition of their exemption from detention. From the point of view of government, these measures were necessary but fair to the alien of enemy nationality whose country was at war with Canada. Not everyone, however, shared this perspective.

Wild rumours and public speculation about the threat that enemy aliens posed created the conditions whereby individuals and agencies called upon Canadian officials to do more. T.J. Parkes, regional manager for Sun Life Canada in Quebec's Eastern Townships, for instance, complained that "any German or Austrian spy will go about his business in a quiet and orderly manner, without awakening any suspicion until his plans are ripe for execution, and therefore the opportunity is presented for them to do incalculable damage before the authorities can interfere."[120] Describing the government's policy as "locking the stable door after the steed is stolen," he declared that there was "only one way" to treat enemy aliens, which was to dictate that the entire enemy alien population register with the local police within a forty-eight-hour period

and declare in a formal affidavit that they would not aid or abet the
enemy. Failure to do so, Parkes continued, should result in a penalty of
either jail or some other confinement under suitable guard.

When contacted by the crown prosecutor in Brockville as to what
steps should be taken against "mysterious strangers" in town who were
believed to be spies, the deputy minister in Ontario's Department of the
Solicitor General advised the prosecutor that he should use "drastic"
measures, "even if you had to remand them from week to week and let
them apply for a habeas corpus." This would have been both awkward
and difficult, the deputy minister acknowledged, but he was hopeful of
some positive developments on this score. He confided to the Brockville
crown attorney that he raised with the federal Justice Department the
matter of habeas corpus being an impediment to maintaining order, suggesting to them "the advisability of the Government taking power to
suspend the Habeas Corpus Act."[121] In the opinion of the senior law
officer, legal protection of enemy aliens was a detriment to the wider
public interest and had to be disposed of.

Others were equally prepared to dispense with the formalities in handling the enemy alien problem. Writing to the general superintendent of
the Grand Trunk Pacific Railway in Winnipeg, N.B. Walton observed
that in the village of Coblenz, Manitoba, he had heard of reports of anti-
British sentiment and purported talk among the local German-speaking
settlers about doing damage to railway property. Walton suggested that
it was a waste of time patrolling the tracks or conducting investigations.
Rather, he recommended that two or three company men might be sent
down from Winnipeg to "make an example" of those who were talking
treason. He also recommended the dismissal of the local railway agent,
W.H. Bergman, a German speaker, who supposedly was in sympathy
with the locals, having failed to report threats against the company's
property.[122]

Dismissal from work became a common trial facing enemy aliens in
the prevailing climate of fear, panic, resentment, and spite. It prompted
the German-Canadian Alliance of Saskatchewan to raise with the government their concern that the assurance granted in the initial Proclamation, allowing law-abiding subjects of enemy nationality to go
about their business without fear, was not being heeded.[123] Hundreds
had been discharged from their place of employ since the first week of
August. It was a matter, the Alliance insisted, that required the government's attention.

Government officials were under tremendous pressure to do something. They were also, however, mindful of the threat of possible raids from the US, reports of alleged espionage, and rumours of organized enemy activity on Canadian soil. Officials were compelled to act. A bill was introduced in parliament 19 August 1914 granting the federal cabinet extraordinary executive powers. Based on Britain's Defence of the Realm Act, the War Measures Act (wma), as it was called, permitted the governor-in-council to introduce whatever rules and regulations were deemed necessary to maintain security, defence, peace, order, and welfare as long as the conditions of war pertained, whether real or perceived. Enacted 22 August and in force retroactively from 4 August, the act granted the governor-in-council unparalleled authority to exercise sovereign powers and to severely curtail traditional rights. These included arrest without charge, deportation without trial, censorship, and the expropriation, control, and disposal of property. Local agents were also given wide powers of arrest and detention.

The act and its executive decrees caused a considerable stir both inside and outside the country. In the United States, several newspapers reported that the entire German and Austro-Hungarian population in Canada would be arrested.[124] US officials wished to receive assurance from British authorities that Canada would respect the rights of Arnold von Eitlinger, a naturalized American citizen who had been serving as the German honorary consul in Vancouver.[125] Along with other diplomatic representatives of enemy states, von Eitlinger was instructed to leave the country but remained in Canada, having applied for an exemption. From the American perspective, it was not clear that he would be protected without diplomatic intervention.

The question of rightful arrest also figured prominently in the dispatch to Ottawa from the US secretary of state, William Jennings Bryan, who raised the issue of American consular intervention in cases of the possible arrest of Austro-Hungarians for whom the US was now responsible as a neutral state. The undersecretary of state for external affairs, Joseph Pope, noting that it could prove "embarrassing to us," suggested to the prime minister that Canada should agree to the more routine aspects of American representation but "ignore" the portion of the dispatch referring to intervention in cases of arrest.[126] The recommended approach – to avoid discussion of the matter until necessary – highlighted the uncertainty and anxiety around the propriety of making arrests. That these could prove awkward and problematic suggested an awareness,

1.3  Police arrest, Toronto, Ontario

given their wide implications, that the powers granted under the act could be unduly used.

The issue of arrests was also a concern for the Saskatchewan-based German-Canadian Alliance, which claimed that a number of Germans and Austro-Hungarians had been arrested, some of whom were Canadian citizens. They requested that the government conduct an investigation into the situation; if it could be proven that arrests were being made without proper cause, then it was the responsibility of the government "to bring the full measure of their influence to make further outrages of this kind impossible." Fully aware of the importance of citizenship in the trying days ahead, they also encouraged the government to facilitate the acquisition of British imperial citizenship so that German Canadians "might avail themselves of the protection of the authorities of the British Empire in foreign countries."[127] The underlying belief was that British subject status not only would serve as protection in Canada but also, on balance, offered greater personal protection than simple naturalized Canadian citizenship, which could be revoked at any time.

The extensive powers under the War Measures Act proved to be unsettling for Canada's German and Austro-Hungarian population. Concerned about its effects, Sir Thomas Shaughnessy of Montreal, president of the CNR and a close confidant of Sir Robert Borden, wrote the prime minister recommending the government reassure subjects of enemy nationality that their person and property would be respected and safe-guarded. "We find that there is a good deal of nervousness because of the fear that their property will be confiscated and there have been some cases where they have abandoned their lands and left for the States," noted Shaughnessy.[128] On 2 September, acknowledging the fear, the government issued a public notice, widely disseminated, reaffirming its commitment to not interfere with those subjects of German and Austro-Hungarian nationality who peaceably carried on with their lives.

The original intent of the War Measures Act was to provide the government with the necessary powers to ensure security. The 31 August order-in-council, PC 2283, issued under the act, for example, introduced an immediate ban on the possession and use of firearms, ammunition, and explosives by enemy aliens – a response to the RNWMP concern that stricter controls be placed on firearms and on the handling and disposition of dynamite, gunpowder, and other explosives. In this case, security was obtained by imposing restrictions and sanctions against a class of individuals designated enemies. In the process, however, the act became much more than ensuring security. Security, in effect, was being achieved at the expense of the rights of individuals. But by limiting individual rights in the name of security, the government was also testing the boundaries of its own commitment to democracy and the principles of natural justice. Government officials understood this political conundrum and sought to alleviate hardship where possible.

Writing to the government in German, Fritz Broo of Maisonville, Quebec, appealed for a personal exemption regarding the possession of firearms by enemy aliens. He reported that a local official who was hostile to him as a person of German origin had seized his hunting weapons.[129] These were working guns, he claimed, which were indispensible for preserving his safety and quality of life in the countryside. A number of local citizens vouchsafed for Broo's character, claiming that he had left Germany so that his son might avoid military service. On the basis of these and other creditable reports, Thomas Mulvey, undersecretary of state, informed Broo that his guns would be returned to him.[130] Similar appeals were entertained from others, who insisted that their rifles were needed to hunt for wild game to sustain their families.

When Joseph Wall, a barrister in Antigonish, Nova Scotia, wrote to the undersecretary of state, he described the difficult circumstances that Anton Wadzka and his family faced. Having bought a small farm, the Polish immigrant, who was also an Austro-Hungarian subject, found it necessary to secure a mortgage. The Mortgage Corporation of Nova

Scotia, predisposed to accept the application, was reluctant to do so without permission in light of the executive prohibition under the WMA on entering into contracts with enemy aliens. Upon consulting with the Justice Department, the undersecretary of state, Thomas Mulvey, communicated that as long as the company was satisfied that the funds would be used for legitimate purposes, and not assist the enemy, then there was no objection to making the advance.[131]

Then there was the case of Fred Erhard, an Austro-Hungarian subject. Working as a die and toolmaker with the Canadian General Electric Co. in Peterborough, Ontario, the young Erhard had been permanently laid off from work because of the deepening recession. Unemployed and with a wife and child in tow and rent due, Erhard had become desperate. He applied for an exeat to the United States, which prompted a number of individuals, including the city solicitor, to speak on his behalf. Stressing the urgency of the matter, they pressed the government to grant him permission to leave Canada for the US, where friends were prepared to offer the family shelter and support. The deputy minister of justice, Edmund Newcombe, to whom the case was referred, declared it to be a discretionary matter and that he was personally disposed to think that there was nothing preventing Erhard and his family from going to the United States. Satisfied that the circumstances as represented were legitimate and that he was not a reservist, the dominion police commissioner, A.P. Sherwood, sent the necessary permission for the Erhard family to leave the country.[132]

Other requests for special consideration were similarly entertained. An appeal from Baer Brothers Manufacturing of New York was favourably received for the release of one Mr S. Henle, an oil businessman, described as completely trustworthy but who had been seized from a passenger ship by the British navy on the high seas and interned at Halifax.[133] Also approved was a request from Isaac Cohen for the release of Saul Fanger and Judah Einhorn, who were interned at Fort Henry in Kingston as German reservists. Described as a "responsible merchant," Cohen interested himself in the welfare of both men who shared his faith. With Cohen guaranteeing work for them, they were both given parole.[134]

The goodwill extended by government officials complemented the judgment of others who were prepared to temper a number of the more unrestrained calls for government intervention. When officials in Prince Rupert, British Columbia, recommended that authority be given to the local police chief to have the entire population of four hundred and more foreigners (aliens and enemy aliens alike) register so that their movements might be closely monitored, the request was denied.[135] Also rebuffed was the petition of the inhabitants of Canning Parish in the vicinity of Minto, New Brunswick, for federal authorities to send troops to control the local enemy alien population. Militia headquarters in Ottawa indicated that "no grave condition" existed as to warrant such action and that "there cannot be nearly so many of German and Austro-Hungarian nationality in that vicinity as in many other places in Canada where the Provisions of the Order-in-Council [firearms] have been carried out without any difficulty."[136] Officials would demonstrate charity and liberality when they saw fit. They would not be stampeded into making rash decisions or forced into taking unnecessary action.

And yet Canada was at war and the emergency powers extended to the government under the War Measures Act provided it with the means to protect the country and punish those who would threaten it. Moreover, the enemy alien designation and the War Measures Act provided the political and legal framework by which such actions could be taken. The criminal code, for example, had abolished forfeiture in the case of those convicted of treason. But for the Hon. Charles Doherty, minister of justice, the notion that there could be enemy aliens who would leave the country to take up arms against it without penalty was unconscionable. They would not only be prevented from returning but, as he recommended, the property of such persons would be confiscated under the forfeiture powers of the War Measures Act.[137] As to whether enemy subjects had the right to sue in the courts during war, Edmund Newcombe, the deputy minister of justice, was of the view that they did not have that right, although they themselves could be sued.[138]

When more stringent measures were required to discipline those who did not abide by the general regulations set out in the act, these were introduced and applied as needed. Although section 6 of the War Measures Act provided the general means for a conviction against what were considered to be "decidedly anti-British" German-language newspapers in the Canadian west, it was not until a 12 September order-in-council was issued under the act, which explicitly addressed various aspects of censorship, that the government felt it was on firmer ground in dealing with offending newspapers in Regina and Winnipeg.[139] The editors in particular were to be held personally liable and made to account for their actions. As for those individuals who had signed an Undertaking but violated their parole by ignoring the restrictions regulating their behaviour, Laurence Fortescue, the RNWMP comptroller, noted that the

15 August Proclamation contained no penalty for breaking parole. Rather than simply interning these individuals, he recommended imprisonment with hard labour, a view shared by the chief commissioner of dominion police, Colonel Sherwood.[140] For those who would abuse the leniency, generosity, and goodwill of the government, they would be forced to pay for their actions with not only their loss of freedom but also the penalty of hard labour as a reminder of their duplicity.

### INITIAL DAYS: MUDDLING THROUGH

In keeping with international understanding, reservists were considered enemy combatants. Representing a security threat, they were subject to possible internment as prisoners of war. On 13 August, the SS *Ruthenia*, a passenger ship from Antwerp, arrived at the port of Montreal. A squad of local police boarded the ship, apprehending thirteen of its crew – stokers, firemen, and stewards – who were identified as German reservists. They were to be taken to the police station, but because they could not be separated from common criminals and the itinerant, the crew were marched off to the detention quarters of the immigration authorities located on rue St Antoine. According to the Montreal police chief, Oliver Campeau, they were prisoners of war and had to be treated as such. The group joined twenty-two others, German and Austro-Hungarian reservists who had been apprehended after attempting to make their way to the United States. On being escorted under police guard to the detention facility, one of the detained crew declared, "It cannot be helped. It is one of the things we must put up with in times of war."[141]

A retired captain of the Royal Artillery and a resident of the village of Balfour in British Columbia's Kootenay Mountains, R.H. Manley was on the lookout for suspicious activity.[142] In particular, he was concerned about the activity of one A.H. Catrin, a resident of the nearby village of Riondel. Manley had learned that Catrin, a former German cavalry officer and aviator, had left the province for Washington state, from where he intended to go on to Germany in order to join the colours. While he was in Seattle the German consular official advised Catrin to return to Canada and take no part in the trouble. He did so.

Originally, Manley had attempted to block the route of Catrin, but to no avail. Now that Catrin had returned, Manley thought it necessary to alert government officials because he felt the local police were "quite ignorant as to what steps should be taken under the conditions, at present existing, to effectively deal with such potential enemies as Herr Catrin, so as to make them ineffective for war." Manley, writing to the governor general, specifically noted that Catrin, as an enemy reservist, had been arrested upon his return yet released. He was neither interned as a prisoner of war nor, at a minimum, placed on parole. This was unacceptable, according to Manley, since there were a large number of foreigners of enemy origin in the vicinity who would shortly be set adrift because of the imminent closure of the mines. To prevent a similar occurrence, he suggested that, as a matter of policy, all enemy aliens should be required to carry a passport identifying a place of residence from which they could not leave. He further recommended they report regularly to local authorities. Moreover, for reservists like Catrin he suggested that they be granted limited freedom only after being given their parole and that the parole be framed "so comprehensively" as to curtail their activity for the duration of the war.

The governor general asked for a confidential report on Catrin and his activities, especially with regard to his departure from Canada. The ensuing police report indicated that Catrin had, indeed, left for the United States the day after war's declaration but had returned shortly after, whereupon he was arrested and released after being cautioned. The reporting officer opined that Catrin posed no threat and there was "no cause for alarm," but if there was fault regarding dereliction of duty it did not rest with the police. The accusing finger pointed to immigration authorities who allowed his re-entry into Canada. The problem, therefore, was not that he was allowed to leave but that he was allowed to return. The governor general, His Royal Highness the Duke of Connaught, was surprised by the cavalier and peculiar attitude of those entrusted with Canada's security, which no doubt impressed upon him the importance of Manley's recommendations that more be done in terms of securing the borders and monitoring those whose loyalties were in doubt. The governor general, noting his concern, passed these recommendations on to the government for its consideration.[143]

Both the SS *Ruthenia* episode and the Catrin incident underlined for Canadian authorities certain realities they faced with the advent of war. Although the security threat posed by enemy aliens was thought to be exaggerated, the potential harm posed by reservists – individuals with prior military training who could be called upon to render service to the enemy – was nevertheless real. Whether it was the reservist who had settled in Canada or the merchant seaman sailing in Canadian waters, the question of what to do with this class of individual was uppermost in the mind of the government.

What both cases also revealed was that at the start of the war, Canada was ill-prepared to deal with reservists in its midst. Not only was there an absence of effective policy guiding government action, but there was no real organization in place for the possible long-term internment of such individuals. Both the policy and practice of detention required that decisions be made in line with calculations about the appropriateness and sufficiency of the response. In times of war, the country needed to defend itself. But exactly against whom and how the policy and practice of internment would be executed was not entirely clear at the war's start.

International law governing land wars made provision for the detention of potential enemy combatants as prisoners of war – individuals with military standing in the reserves as well as those civilians who actively aided and abetted the enemy. In this sense, this was a good beginning. But the issue could not be entirely separated from the larger imperial war policy that governed aspects of Canadian participation and conduct in the war. How should Canada respond in the light of its imperial ties? Were there specific Canadian conditions that demanded a more subtle response? For instance, did Canadian conditions warrant the detention of all reservists? After all, the war was far away and the historical understanding regarding non-combatants of military reserve status was that internment should be used only against those who actively sought to take up arms against the country in which they resided.

Canada had entered the war as part of the British Empire. Self-rule had provided Canada with a considerable degree of autonomy on domestic matters in the late nineteenth and early twentieth centuries but, as to its external sovereignty, Canada continued to be bound by its imperial connection. It is from this perspective that the political relationship between Canada and Britain must be understood. It also meant, however, that in August of 1914 external relations would be handled through the colonial office and imperial defence through the war office in London. Moreover, as the king's representative in Canada, the governor general would become an important conduit for British information, advice, and directives concerning the war. Within this imperial framework, the expectation was that Canada would follow Britain's lead on all matters governing war policy, including taking direction on policy toward potential enemy combatants – those reservists who might make their way back home and take up arms against Britain and its allies.

The initial position of Britain was communicated to the governor general on 3 August when it was advised that the most advantageous course of action by Canada was to permit the departure of German army reservists (excepting those suspected of espionage) and, wishing to maintain naval superiority, detaining only naval reservists if hostilities commenced.[144] War between Germany and Britain had not yet been declared and there was much ambiguity among the parties as to what constituted an appropriate response. Canada answered by stating that it was very difficult to distinguish between army and naval reservists, while detention was logistically impossible "unless we resort to actual imprisonment."[145] Following Britain's declaration of war on 4 August, the instructions from London were repeated, but this time calling for the arrest and detention of all German officers and reservists in Canada. Austro-Hungarian personnel were also to be watched and similar action taken given the possibility of war between the Hapsburg and British empires.

On 7 August, the Canadian government reiterated the special circumstances that made it neither feasible nor desirable to arrest and detain German reservists "in the comprehensive manner set forth in the imperial directive."[146] As was pointed out, the expanse of the land made any such plan difficult to execute, and the sheer numbers that would need to be arrested and detained made it an impractical idea. In a carefully crafted response, one that showed a strain of independence yet responsibility, Canadian officials recommended that, unless there were reasonable grounds to suspect that reservists were engaged in espionage or other acts of a hostile nature, the approach most suited was not to interfere with such individuals as long as they quietly went about their business. But the Canadian government was also aware of the potential harm that could result from the return of German officers or reservists to the European theatre, and therefore officials indicated that measures would be introduced to prevent their departure from Canadian ports, including interning them as prisoners of war. Despite Canada's limited ability to guard the border, Canadian authorities further communicated to London that precautions would be adopted at important centres to prevent officers or reservists from leaving Canada for the purpose of entering the United States by land.

The proposed policy, framed within order-in-council PC 2085, was one of qualified compromise, trending toward the maxim "live and let live." Not everyone, however, was satisfied with the plan. The governor general, for one, expressed "shock" that "stricter steps" were not taken.[147] But as the prime minister noted in his correspondence with the

Canadian high commissioner to Britain, the proposed course of action was "perfectly sound" and he had no intention of departing from it.[148] The governor general would eventually approve of the approach but remained critical of its implementation.[149] Imperial authorities accepted the proposal not only because it was reasonable under the circumstances, but also because there was no alternative.

In preparation for the measures adopted under the new order-in-council, the government instructed the dominion police and the RNWMP to cooperate with immigration and customs officials as well as municipal police detachments in securing the names and addresses of German military personnel resident in Canada.[150] It was important that information be available regarding those whose activities needed to be monitored. Necessary steps, in effect, were being taken, suggesting the semblance of organization and procedure. It became apparent in short order, however, that lines of authority and responsibility between the agencies were neither fully established nor clearly defined. There was also the question of whether what was being proposed was legal.

As members of the militia began conducting arrests, inter-agency tensions became apparent. Powers of arrest were extended to both police and immigration authorities, the latter being best placed to intercept the movement of individuals seeking to cross the international border. But immigration inspectors in the field protested that customs officials and the militia were hampering them, operating as they were in a casual manner, given the climate of uncertainty and confusion.[151] They insisted on more authority as it related to cross-border activity. Ultimate command and authority, however, would rest with the militia because the detention of reservists and other potential combatants was considered to be a military matter with the provision for their internment being sanctioned under international law governing war.[152]

Adding to inter-agency conflict was the shortage of facilities to keep individuals in custody. Lacking military prisons or lock-ups, those arrested by the militia were being immediately turned over to police authorities. But as police officials observed, these were military prisoners who rightfully fell under the authority of the militia; unless the military took control, the conditions "might easily become serious, as we have neither the guards nor accommodation for a considerable number of prisoners of any sort, [let alone] the indiscriminate arrest of persons who, under momentary stimulation, might talk carelessly and reach large proportions."[153] When the militia turned to immigration for the use of their facilities, immigration officials complained that the business of immigration was being hindered at a number of locations by the presence of military sentries who, guarding enemy alien prisoners, frightened away immigrants seeking assistance. They insisted that the arrangement on the use of their facilities be made temporary.[154]

Finding a place to hold those arrested became a difficult question, as was the issue of police authority in the matter of powers of arrest. There was much uncertainty among the police, who, being instructed to assist, questioned whether the arrest and receipt of reservists could take place by civil authorities without a legal warrant. The belief was that "martial law did not provide for this." The doubt, initially articulated by the assistant commissioner of the RNWMP, stemmed from the fact that since the civil courts were still sitting, persons arrested by the RNWMP and not by the military would automatically be released by way of habeas corpus.[155] On this point, the assistant commissioner felt that direction from the Justice Department was required, suggesting that more comprehensive security legislation was needed, a development that would lead in part to the War Measures Act.

The order-in-council PC 2085, which prohibited the departure of reservists, had an immediate effect. Individuals were apprehended both at the border and on US-bound trains. Railway stations, serving as points of embarkation, also soon became focal points of arrest by the militia and immigration agents. It was evident however from the arrests that a disproportionate number were subjects of Austria-Hungary, many of whom did not appear to be motivated by military or patriotic concerns. German reservists, better acquainted with the political situation in Europe, reportedly had departed before the outbreak of war.[156] But among Austro-Hungarians, it appeared that more mundane reasons were at work.

The growing unemployment situation in Canada and the unlikely prospect of finding work in the growing anti-alien climate prompted some to look to the United States for relief.[157] For others, given the seemingly arbitrary nature of arrests and the rumours of what might yet come, the neutrality of the US offered the promise of personal well-being and safety.[158] And then there were those who simply wished to return home, anxious about the prospect of being cut off from their families during the uncertainty of the war.[159] They, however, were to be disappointed. With the war on, American authorities, committed to preserving their neutral status in the conflict, placed a prohibition on nationals at war seeking a return to their homelands. The embargo meant that no Germans or Austro-Hungarians were accepted as passengers for Europe on ships bound from US ports. Counselling against travelling to the United States to secure a transatlantic crossing, the Austro-Hungarian consul in Canada advised many to remain in the country and obey the law.[160] Ever hopeful, and though small in number, people continued to seek a passage home through the US.[161]

At train stations and Canadian ports, reservists were automatically arrested and processed for internment. Yet, every enemy alien as a potential combatant was suspect and it remained for officials to ascertain their military status and the purpose of their travel. This was no easy task. Language and literacy proved to be a problem. A serious obstacle to assessing the status of a suspect was the inability of the person in question to communicate adequately in English. Requests for interpreters became commonplace among military authorities, immigration agents, customs inspectors, and police.[162] The absence of interpreters, not surprisingly, resulted in individuals being detained and initially processed for internment on the basis of insufficient or unreliable information. It was one of the many problems that finally convinced the government that the most propitious course of action was to advise and instruct those in the field to exercise reasonable judgment in determining the intentions of the enemy alien held in custody.

An important measure by which to establish the intentions of those arrested and interrogated was whether they would sign the Undertaking that was part of the 15 August Proclamation obliging them not to take up arms and to follow government rules concerning their conduct.[163] A further consideration was whether they also agreed to report to designated agents of the crown under terms that were prescribed after their release. The signing of such an Undertaking as well as reporting to officials imposed a significant burden on the individual. On one level, for those who failed to sign the Undertaking, it provided clear and undeniable evidence of hostile intent and the necessary grounds to intern such individuals as prisoners of war.[164] On another level, the proviso to routinely report also introduced a program of monitoring that could only be established by maintaining lists that were closely scrutinized.[165] A monitoring system, as a result, was slowly being put into place, but, most importantly, the failure to report regularly as a condition of their parole – a signal of hostile intent – also meant they could be subject to internment as prisoners of war.

On the face of it, the provision allowing parole in exchange for signing an Undertaking appeared to be in keeping with the government's assurance that enemy aliens would not be interfered with as long as they complied with the laws of the land. In actual fact, however, it stemmed from necessity. Thousands of suspected enemy aliens were arrested and interrogated on suspicion of being a reservist or engaging in a hostile act. The difficulty of holding these individuals, however, soon became apparent. It would lead to what could be best described as a situation of "catch and release."[166] Faced with a choice between parole and internment, the majority of those arrested signed the Undertakings, and the question of what to do with them was effectively resolved since the military had but few installations to hold the numbers, even temporarily. There were, of course, permanent military installations that could suffice – Fort Henry in Kingston and the Citadel in Halifax – but these were constructed in the nineteenth century and were never meant to detain more than a hundred or more prisoners at a time. The Undertakings, therefore, at least initially, became an important means by which officials could offset the logistical difficulty of interning large numbers of reservists and others. Colonel E. Cruickshank, commanding officer of Military District No. 13 (Alberta), for one, thought that the acquisition of large buildings for internment purposes was unnecessary since "it is anticipated that a very small number, if any, will be committed for internment as up to the present, without exception, every person arrested has signed the 'Undertaking.'"[167]

Cruickshank, however, was speaking from a limited perspective and limited experience. At Sarnia, Fort Frances, Niagara Falls, Windsor, Winnipeg, Vancouver, and Lethbridge, enemy aliens were attempting to cross the border, including some who were reservists. Once they were caught and their status determined, the question was not whether they would be interned but where. Immigration facilities with holding areas equipped to deal with groups of individuals, as was the case in Montreal, became, early on, important detention centres. Elsewhere public or government buildings that could be converted into secure spaces were pressed into service. These included the Winter Fair building in Brandon and the poultry building at the Lethbridge fairgrounds (both offered up by municipal authorities), the Gouin Street arena in Sault Ste Marie (again offered up by city officials), the provincial jails in Regina and Nanaimo, the Stanley Barracks in Toronto, and the Fort Osborne Barracks in Winnipeg.[168] At the time, the possibility of using military armouries as places of internment was also raised but rejected because of the prohibitive costs involved in providing proper heating, messing, and other sanitary arrangements.[169]

In the end, the plan was to have these detention centres serve as receiving stations where reservists and others could be delivered, processed,

1.4 Enemy aliens at receiving station, Montreal, Quebec

and temporarily held until more suitable, permanent facilities became available. In this regard, considerable energy was funnelled into refurbishing and improving Fort Henry in Kingston and the Citadel in Halifax, which were identified for long-term use as internment facilities. Both Fort Henry and the Citadel were selected because of their history and configuration as places of prisoner internment in the nineteenth century. The Citadel was also a natural and convenient location for those mariners either captured at sea or brought by ship to Halifax from other corners of the empire. Although consideration was given to transferring internees from western Canada to Fort Henry, a decision was made in early September to send all internees from British Columbia to the town of Vernon, located in the British Columbia interior, where a provincial jail with large adjacent grounds was made available by the BC government for the purpose of long-term internment in the province.[170]

All of the detention centres were retrofitted or upgraded to ensure that they would be satisfactory for the purpose at hand.[171] Adding iron posts and barbed-wire fences as well as installing new bars for the windows at Toronto's Stanley Barracks would take four weeks to complete. Retrofitting the fairground poultry building and constructing a barricade for an exercise area in Lethbridge would take slightly more than a week.[172] More extensive work, however, was required at Fort Henry and the Citadel in preparation for the arrival of internees. Although the buildings at Fort Henry had been placed in a sanitary condition and a new roof constructed over the prisoners' quarters in 1913, the eighty cells required additional work to accommodate the larger influx of prisoners. At the Citadel, the prison building on Melville Island needed to be rewired and the grounds made more secure.

The first arrivals at Fort Henry were reservists caught attempting to cross the border at nearby Gananoque, Ontario. Eighty-six others, who were transferred from Montreal, with additional numbers arriving from Windsor, soon followed them. By 31 August, there were 115 internees at Fort Henry. The total number increased to 200 by 21 September, including a group of thirty-nine from Toronto and twenty who had been brought by escort from Sault Ste Marie. Rumours that prisoners of war detained at Bridgeburg, Ontario, would be liberated by raiders from the United States prompted Canadian military authorities to relocate these and other prisoners from the Niagara Falls area to Fort Henry. The lower fort, however, could only hold 240 prisoners in total, and a discussion ensued about commandeering the nearby Tête du Pont and Artillery Park Barracks, together capable of holding over one thousand prisoners of war with minor modifications. The idea was rejected in favour of upgrades at the fort at a cost of $1,000, enabling the eventual accommodation of an additional 230 prisoners, or 470 in total.[173] As of 21 October, 223 internees were held at Fort Henry.

Elsewhere in the country, 380 were interned. At the Citadel, on 9 September, sixty-eight prisoners of war were turned over to local military authorities after the Spanish mail steamer *Montserrat*, en route to Genoa from New York, was intercepted by HMS *Glory*.[174] On 18 September, the first group of internees arrived at Vernon, British Columbia, where they were taken to a large institutional structure located on Lorne Street. The building had originally served as a provincial jail but had been converted in recent years to a branch hospital for the insane. Once the building was considered suitable for the purpose of long-term internment, the patients were relocated and the building and grounds prepared for the arrival of prisoners of war from all over British Columbia.[175]

All installations were under the direct authority of militia headquarters, which from time to time issued directives. These included an instruction to collect information on the reservists, which was to be compiled and turned over to the newly created Prisoners of War Information Bureau, an imperial body that would exchange information on prisoners through diplomatic channels with their German and Austro-Hungarian counterparts.[176] Orders were also issued to ensure that only reservists and those who demonstrated hostile intent were interned while all others were to be released after investigation determined they were not a security threat.[177] Most importantly, the administration and operations of the receiving stations and internment sites, falling under the authority of the military, would follow international rules and regulations governing the maintenance and treatment of prisoners of war. These rules were laid out in a royal warrant issued by the war office in London and circulated to all military authorities in the empire who were responsible for the welfare and security of prisoners of war.[178]

The royal warrant adhered to principles laid out in international conventions and law. These principles governed the conduct, expectations, and responsibilities relating to prisoners of war and were to be applied in order to lessen the burden of their captivity. In the crucible of war, the standards that were set protected such individuals from potential abuse, unnecessary hardship, and wanton attacks. As a matter of reciprocity, however, prisoners were to abide by rules that provided for security and order, the violation of which invited disciplinary action including corporal punishment. The protections extended to prisoners included an exemption from work, except for those jobs that were necessary from the point of view of maintaining the cleanliness of the facility and the health of the internees. Prisoners could work if compensated for at the rate of the standard daily military pay of one shilling or its national currency equivalent.

In the uncertainty and confusion during the early days of the war, the foundations of a policy were in place that would help guide and regulate the attitudes and conduct of those responsible for their welfare. It was a positive development with encouraging results. The initial accounts of conditions and activity at Fort Henry, for instance, were universally favourable, including official reports by the American consul in Kingston, Felix Johnson, who was locally assigned to represent German diplomatic interests – part of a larger diplomatic arrangement that followed from the neutral status of the United States in the global conflict. He communicated that the internees were well treated, while the conditions, although far from ideal, were described as adequate. "In point of daily conduct and disposition," the US consul reported, "the officers in charge at Fort Henry have no complaint against their wards, who are described as a happy, contented and clean-living lot of men."[179] There was little cause for complaint. Although order, discipline, and security were strictly enforced, prisoners were granted some freedoms within the rules. The internees who would not work were permitted to engage in personal amusements during prison hours, while those who wished to work were to be fairly remunerated. The funds, moreover, could be used to purchase sundry items for personal use at the local prison canteen.[180]

The issue of paying prisoner-internees for camp-related work at Fort Henry became an important consideration. There was much apprehension about the coming winter and the need for appropriate clothing.[181] The suggestion was made that it might be possible to prevent payment to the internees so that the monies earned could be put toward the purchase of cold weather items rather than frivolities from the canteen such as tobacco, sugar, and the like. The commanding officer at Fort Henry, Major H.J. Dawson, noted that the internees were under the impression the government would supply them with boots, socks, underwear, clothing, and other necessities. However, since many of the men refused to avail themselves of the original offer of parole by signing an Undertaking, Dawson concluded that the government would not aid them now by supplying the clothing as expected. Unless otherwise informed, it was Dawson's intention to withhold pay for the purpose of ensuring that they would be properly clothed for the coming winter.[182]

Dawson's suggestion, no matter how well intended, was troubling. The rules spelling out obligations and responsibilities were in jeopardy of being ignored. At the start of the war, it was not an encouraging sign, pointing to the likelihood of further non-compliance in response to whatever challenges might arise. Equally troubling was the information that a large number of internees, eligible for release if they signed an Undertaking, refused to do so. In large measure it was a reaction to the difficult employment situation in the country. Increasingly, there was no work to be had and freedom without work was meaningless. A number who did sign the Undertaking, such as former prisoners Mike Licik and Stephen Toich, having gained their liberty but facing hunger, would return to the fort asking to be re-interned.[183] In the choice between freedom and hunger, desperation made internment, in the early stages of the war, a likely, if improbable, source of relief and deliverance.

## THE ENEMY AMONG US

War brings with it much uncertainty: about the country, the future, and a nation's way of life. As a consequence, war is usually not entered into lightly. Naturally, victory is hoped for, but in equal measure invocations are offered up so that defeat might be averted and the people spared. The outcome is never certain, and for this reason fear often accompanies war. To allay the apprehension and anxiety, measures are frequently taken to reassure those called upon to sacrifice. But these only serve as a temporary reprieve. In the ongoing narrative that is war, fear prevails, never truly dissipating – merely channelled.

In Europe, as the war commenced, the question of who represented the enemy was clear, but in Canada with its multitude of immigrants from various parts of the world, the answer was not entirely evident. Could settlers hailing from countries at war with the empire constitute the enemy? For some like Captain C. Weaver, the officer commanding "A" Company, 19th Alberta Dragoons, who recommended a squadron be sent to the Clyde district of Alberta as a show of force, there was little dispute: the enemy was here and now. When T.J. Parkes wrote to the minister of militia insisting that the government's policy was too tepid with respect to individuals of German and Austro-Hungarian nationality, he too was convinced of the direction the government should take. At the heart of his complaint was that these people were enemies and should be treated as such. Men like Weaver, Parkes, and others were all similarly informed by a deep and abiding concern about the safety of the country. And why would they not? Rumours of sabotage and espionage were rife.

The problem, of course, was that these were rumours. There was little evidence to support the allegations and suspicions. Police investigations and other inquiries bore out no indication of enemy activity in the country. Yet rumours have a way of increasing the level of tension such that hearsay, supposition, and belief become reality. When reports were received by militia that an airplane was seen circling the government buildings in Ottawa, the soldiers of the Governor-General's Guards, a ceremonial regiment which paraded at the opening of parliament, were each issued ten rounds of live ammunition and instructed "to await the word before firing."[184] The speculation of a plane carrying a bomb, however improbable, translated into action that defied common sense. But this is, at times, the effect of rumour and the nature of fear and anxiety.

The mass psychology of fear is baffling. The cumulative weight of rumours and suspicions is suggestive, and conjecture serves as an easy substitute for convincing evidence. Rumours of an invasion from the US, for example, had the Canadian public on guard. Raiders were thought to have lined up on the border, awaiting the signal to strike. But the attack never came because there was no such plan and no such threat. Meanwhile, minor and seemingly innocent events were invested with meaning for which there was no basis. The 90-tonne gasoline launch held up by naval authorities on the coastal waters of BC, a purported spy ship, became the subject of an editorial by the *Calgary Daily Herald* which sermonized on the importance of acknowledging the legitimacy of the ubiquitous alien threat. "We have been disposed to take much of what we read and were told of the wonderful effectiveness of the German spy system with more than an average allowance of salt; such occurrences as this close at home, and others further away, should make us more believing."[185] That the alleged spy ship was discovered to be an unregistered fishing trawler mattered little. Whether true or not, every report was grist for the mill, escalating the level of public anxiety and paranoia.

Issues of sabotage, espionage, and treachery necessarily raised the question of loyalty. But what constituted loyalty or, for that matter, betrayal? Those who committed or intended to commit acts of a hostile nature were generally understood to be disloyal. This applied not only to citizens but also to unnaturalized immigrants, who by their settlement were part of the society and the body politic. But what did this mean precisely? Hostile intent connotes a purposeful act. Yet, in the case of the Polish and Ukrainian advocates of independence who made claims in keeping with Allied war objectives and principles, they were denounced for their political disloyalty and infidelity. Their activities touched only incidentally on the national interest, and not at all on national security. So how were they disloyal? In the words of the *Edmonton Bulletin*, this was Canada and no other allegiances would be tolerated. Divided loyalties were a sign of betrayal. This, of course, was not the position of Laurier and Borden, who acknowledged the deep emotional ties that made a break with the one's homeland a difficult proposition. However, their response was a political rejoinder framed by wider political considerations. For most native-born Canadians, the argument still stood: dual allegiances were unacceptable.

What this meant for the alien of enemy nationality was that the political and social arena in which they could operate was heavily constrained. Statements made by community leaders and activists were roundly condemned and viciously attacked as evidence of disloyalty, with the highly publicized case of Bishop Budka – the "Austrian mobilizer" – serving as an example to other miscreants. As for those who felt compelled to publicly justify or apologize for the activities and declarations of their colleagues and representatives, they were met with suspicion, derision, or doubt.

The statements made by Budka and others may have been inappropriate and possibly naive, but they did not represent a threat. This suggests that something more sinister was at work. When John Stover complained bitterly to officials in the Department of the Interior that one Mr Shaunessy [sic], a railway superintendent near Edson, Alberta, favoured German and Austro-Hungarian labourers at the expense "of our own Countrymen," he communicated a sentiment that was widespread. Believing him to be a German – "by the name he must be a German" – Stover not only denounced Shaunessy because of the preferential treatment accorded the non-native born but also because of who he thought Shaunessy was. More to the point, Shaunessy was condemned not for his actions, but because they were attributed to a presumed identity. In demanding that Shaunessy be investigated and the situation "corrected," Stover was insisting that he be removed because of his supposed origins.[186] That Shaunessy could have been someone other than of German descent was inconceivable because how, otherwise, could his actions be explained?

A similar rationale was at work when N.B. Walton called for the dismissal of the railway agent W.H. Bergman at Coblenz, Manitoba. Bergman was denounced not for his failure to communicate a malicious rumour – what was the point of communicating information that was patently false? – but because he was a German-speaker. It was felt that as a German speaker his allegiance lay with the alleged restless local enemy alien population, otherwise he would have forwarded any information based on his suspicions whether it had merit or not. Disloyalty was a function of birth or, as in the case of Shaunessy, perceived birthplace.

This was also the case for enemy aliens crossing the border, universally thought to be making their way back home to join the fight. There was some evidence to suggest that in certain instances this was in fact the motivation. But among a great many, especially the Austro-Hungarians, there was also much evidence to the contrary. Those attempting to gain access to the United States were doing so for ordinary reasons: work, personal security, and family. It confirmed what the RNWMP and dominion police already knew, namely that most immigrants from the dual kingdom did not feel particularly "warm" towards their homeland. From the perspective of Ukrainians, Croats, Czechs, Italians, Poles, Slovaks, Serbs, and others, whose minority status in a polyglot empire translated into political ambivalence at best, the draw of patriotism was weak. And yet the perception among the general population was that those heading for the US towards Europe were politically motivated because of their identity as Austro-Hungarians.

On a certain level, this perspective stemmed from the sense that blood ties and emotional attachments to the homeland were powerful influences. But, given the disfranchisement of minorities under Hapsburg rule, it was a leap in logic to suggest that this translated into a broader political identity, let alone the impulse to serve militarily a bankrupt autocracy. Rather, this perspective was informed by the idea, prevalent in early twentieth-century British Canada, that for a subject born under the flag of a sovereign, allegiance was pre-set. In the anarchy that was politics, subject status offered security in exchange for loyalty. Loyalty, owed the sovereign under whose flag the individual was born, was both natural and expected.[187] It was an imperial conception of political identity that had not yet been displaced entirely by notions of citizenship, serving as an important means by which duties, obligations, and rights were understood. But it also meant for some that loyalty could not naturally rest with Canada.[188] This had profound implications.

Subject status determined who belonged to the community. Those who were subjects of the British crown were part of the polity and enjoyed certain rights and freedoms. Those who had no relationship with the crown were on the outside looking in. More importantly, they would become marginalized and censured if they objected to their treatment. For example, the German-Canadian Alliance of Saskatchewan was harshly denounced because there was little tolerance and acceptance for a body that represented the interests of subjects of enemy states – so-called "enemy aliens." Enemy aliens had but limited rights and, in the context of a war fraught with fear and anxiety, they were entitled to even less say.

Public opinion about aliens of enemy nationality was generally unfavourable despite efforts by various ethnic communities to demonstrate their loyalty. The government's position was more cautious, however, based as it was on practical and political considerations. The war had put a halt to immigration from the European basin, and more particularly east-central Europe, the principal source of the great late nineteenth-century migrations. After the war, immigration from the region would resume. As a result, its future success would depend on the attitude and policies of the government toward east Europeans now.[189]

As far as actual threats were concerned, evidence suggested nothing was afoot. None of the reported incidents, rumours, suspicions, or allegations could be verified or substantiated. Moreover, many were simply false. The public may have been alarmed by the rumoured threats. The government, whose job was to be watchful, was simply uneasy. The uneasiness of the government was understandable; just because there was no evidence of a threat did not necessarily mean that a threat failed to exist. Memory of the Fenian Brotherhood persisted and was fresh on the minds of government officials. For this reason, Borden and others sought reassurance from those entrusted with the country's defence that necessary measures were in place. But there was also the problem posed by reservists of enemy states who were now resident in Canada. As registered combatants in their homelands, they posed a potential risk. The issue of what policy was to be adopted, therefore, was high on the list of security priorities.

But did reservists actually pose a threat? This hypothetical question needed to be answered. Generally, the inclination among officials was to remain cautious yet alert. On the other hand, with respect to those attempting to leave the country, there could be no doubt. Whether such individuals were homeward bound or simply going to the United States for work was hard to ascertain, but for those reservists who would find their way home they would be obliged to participate in the conflict and, by taking up arms, would directly menace the lives of British and Allied soldiers and the security of the empire at large. They were to be stopped. Hence, the Proclamation of 15 August made plain the prohibition against the departure of enemy reservists from Canada and allowed for their arrest and internment along with those civilian enemy aliens who violated the country's laws.

The issue of reservists as potential combatants also posed something of a conundrum. In an age of mass mobilization and military conscription, every able-bodied male within a certain age was a potential combatant. As government officials freely admitted, "practically everybody is a Reservist who is physically capable of bearing arms."[190] This meant that every enemy alien was suspect and their departure was to be prevented, given the potential risk. Moreover, they could and would be arrested and interned if required.[191] This would prove to be a herculean task and, at least initially, predictably muddled. It would also require legislation that granted special powers to the governor-in-council as the security operation ramped up with the militia in charge, ably assisted by the federal police, special constables, as well as immigration and customs agents.

The emergency legislation, the War Measures Act, enhanced the ability of the government to carry out the arrest, detention, and internment of individuals of enemy nationality. It further signalled to a restive population that the government was doing more to secure the country's safety. But perhaps most importantly, the 15 August Proclamation and the War Measures Act collectively served to address threats, whether real or perceived, current or future. Unfettered by parliament, the government now possessed extensive powers that enabled it to address danger in any form, from any quarter, with the help of a range of agents empowered to act on its behalf.

The initial arrests and the unrestricted nature of government powers unsettled those communities most affected. This was not the intention of the government. Wishing to allay their fears, the government issued a public notice on 2 September that reiterated its pledge, originally stated in the Proclamation, that those who went about their normal business would not be interfered with and that their well-being would be assured. The Proclamation and the 2 September Public Notice reflected the government's concern about maintaining peace and order. But it also made clear that it reserved the right to act against those who violated the laws and regulations.

In striking a balance, government officials demonstrated a cautionary yet considered approach towards aliens of enemy nationality. When Anthony Van Westrum of Brantford, Ontario, was arrested because he had openly and publicly expressed views on events in Europe that seemed to indicate pro-German sympathies, Prime Minister Borden interceded in the case at the behest of a number of prominent individuals who spoke favourably of the young man – "a fine fellow" and "a Hollander" – and who, they thought, had been mistakenly identified as a person of German origin. The Brantford city police chief and mayor both spoke privately to the youthful and impetuous Van Westrum with a view to correcting his impolitic statements. After a public disclaimer was issued, he was released with the knowledge and approval of the chief commissioner of dominion police, A.P. Sherwood.[192] Van Westrum was not above suspicion, but there was no point in indefinitely detaining a person on the basis of a verbal misstep, especially after the recantation. The Van Westrum case demonstrated a government attitude that was guarded yet temperate. It further pointed to the fact that, along with keen resolve, officials could show fairness and compassion, as was gestured in the cases of Erhard, Wadzka, Henle, Fanger, Einhorn, and others.

And yet it is also true that on balance the government was wary of those persons who originated from countries now at war with Canada. They posed something of a threat. It may not have been the peril imagined by the public at large but, as subjects of enemy states, they represented a danger nonetheless; hence, the official appellation "enemy alien." This was not a normative category as was understood by the public. It was a political and legal concept that was recognized in international law. As subjects of enemy states and potential combatants in the age of mobilization they were to be considered enemy aliens.

Although different from the public's understanding of what constituted an enemy, the underlying sentiment behind the legal-political category "enemy alien" was the same: the enemy was among us. This concept was evident in the statement of Undertaking which formed part of the 15 August Proclamation and the 2 September Public Notice.[193] Arrest was predicated simply on suspicion. Since subjects of enemy nationality had the potential of becoming enemy combatants, this meant that every alien of Austro-Hungarian and German nationality was suspect and prone to arrest, detention, and internment as prisoners of war. Only by signing the Undertaking, which committed them to disavow any hostile intent, could they granted parole. The presumption behind the Undertaking, however, was that such individuals were bent on doing damage to the country, underscoring their enemy status. That the government could conceive of individuals of German and Austro-Hungarian nationality as enemies would eventually have implications for the enemy alien generally.

Caught leaving the country and suspected of being a reservist, individuals were given the option of signing the Undertaking. Those choosing not to do so were interned, along with others such as naval reservists seized on the high seas and, more generally, enemy aliens who made clear their intention to join the colours or those who demonstrated hostile intent. The rationale for internment was in place. But because Undertakings were being signed in the majority of cases, there was no real urgency in setting up the operations or infrastructure for internment. This was fortuitous since the government was ill prepared to accept the thousands of enemy aliens who, between August and October 1914, were arrested and detained for questioning. By the end of October, only 603 were interned as prisoners of war; the rest were paroled under the condition that, having signed Undertakings, they would report regularly to a local magistrate or other person of authority.[194]

Internment, as it was initially conceived, was not meant to penalize. Indeed, some officials within government believed that those who broke parole should not be interned but rather imprisoned in penitentiaries and jails, where they would be forced to do hard labour. Compulsory labour by internees was forbidden under the covenant governing prisoners of war. The penal system, therefore, was seen as an important alternative in deterring and punishing those who would violate the conditions of their parole.[195] Moreover, diplomats representing the interests of the enemy states, such as the American Felix Johnson, reported that internment at this juncture was being fairly and humanely administered. All of this suggested that, with respect to the role and function of internment, the prevailing attitude among Canadian officials was benign. Internment was to be limited and measured, complementing the government's balanced approach in dealing with the issue of enemy aliens more generally.

Despite this attitude, the rationale, underlying principles, and framework for the internment and monitoring of enemy aliens were in place. And although no one could have conceived of internment as being other than a minor and incidental affair in the early stages of the war, the fact of the matter was that it could and would be used more widely should circumstances warrant it. With greater challenges lying ahead, and as fear persisted and the tolerance of the enemy alien diminished further, there surfaced a growing appreciation for internment and the role it might yet play.

## CHAPTER TWO

# Political Choices and the Prerogatives of State: Dealing with the Enemy Alien Problem

## THE THREAT OF POVERTY

In Canada, at war's start, embassy and consular personnel of enemy states were required to leave the country within a forty-eight-hour period. This instruction was part of a larger diplomatic arrangement that, in the absence of their own envoys, would see the interests of Germany and Austria-Hungary represented by US officials. American consular officers in Halifax, Saint John, Montreal, Toronto, Winnipeg, Calgary, and Vancouver were to assume responsibilities relating to immigrants from enemy states residing in Canada.

Of particular concern were the conditions facing aliens of enemy nationality. The growth that had driven the Canadian economy for fifteen years prior to 1914 had come to an end shortly before the war. The economy had contracted significantly such that by the spring of 1914 the country experienced both excess economic capacity and mass unemployment.[1] The effect on the itinerant immigrant labourer was devastating. But it would be the months ahead – particularly the winter months – that would prove most trying for the tens of thousands of enemy aliens out of work.

For the Austro-Hungarian consul general, Hermann Hann, who was still in place during the first few weeks of the war, the situation in Montreal was especially desperate. Among the approximately eight thousand Austro-Hungarian nationals who made the city their home, a thousand or more were out of work and hundreds were threatened with joblessness. Within this context, Hann issued a notice advising all Austro-Hungarians in Montreal to remain calm and to obey the rules of the local authorities, counselling as well that every person should, as a precautionary measure, live as frugally as possible. To the extent that it was practicable, he further entreated those who could help their less fortunate compatriots to protect them from "hunger and privations."[2]

Starvation was a real possibility, prompting Hann to approach Ottawa with a plan.[3] Underscoring the need for continuing representation, he suggested that, rather than completely shutting down the Austro-Hungarian consular offices in the city, the same premises might be used by the Americans under the sign "Austrian Section of the American Consulate," with interpreters available to assist in ascertaining the needs of those in the community left without guidance, information, or support. Hann also asked that he be allowed to communicate, under censorship of the Canadian government, with representatives of the community in Montreal and elsewhere with the object of forming committees to assist people during the winter. The point of his proposal was to relieve the distress of the unemployed and their families by organizing community groups capable of providing emergency relief.

Aware of the need to alleviate the fear and suffering among the growing numbers of the indigent and noting the sincerity of Hann's proposal, Canadian officials were prepared to consider the consul's petition. However, before granting permission, Ottawa sought the advice of the UK government. The secretary to the colonies, the Hon. Laurence Harcourt, had no objection to the proposed action. And so, prompted by a dispatch from the US secretary of state, who agreed to the plan, the Canadian government approved American consular efforts at advising "the poorer members of the Austrian colony." They would also permit Austrian correspondence with local contacts for the purpose of forming aid committees, albeit through the chief commissioner of the dominion police.[4]

Instructed by the American ambassador in Ottawa, the US consulate in Montreal would assume responsibility for the local Austro-Hungarian community, working in tandem with Hann, who departed for Buffalo but remained in contact, and the newly created Austrian Philanthropic Committee. The scale of the work was unanticipated and soon proved overwhelming. As the US consul general, W.H. Bradley, noted in dispatches to Washington, the situation was grim and threatened to become worse. Within weeks of taking control, four thousand had registered for assistance, including two hundred children. Of the group, two thousand were entirely without work and several hundred received a single daily ration of soup and bread from a recently organized relief kitchen.

To personally see the conditions, Bradley, bringing food and clothing, ventured several times with his own family into the community that was most affected – Ukrainians gathered around their local church. There he discovered widespread want and hunger, reporting that, on several occasions, he spoke to quiet crowds of a thousand or more begging for bread and relief. He said it was something that he had "hoped never to do again." "They do not seem evil-disposed, but cannot see why, after being brought here to work, they should be reduced almost to starvation for a war in which they are, apparently, not greatly interested."[5]

Bradley communicated with Canadian officials about the critical situation, but found division of opinion and uncertainty in government circles as to the measures that might be taken. Nevertheless, he held out hope that something might be done, especially since "the suffering among the poor will be greatly increased when the severe Canadian winter settles down upon us toward the end of the month."[6] He insisted that "preparations to meet it should be made now." To this end, Bradley praised the work of individuals associated with the Austrian Philanthropic Committee, which had originally been organized by Hann before his departure. Operating out of the Galician Financial Company building at 100 Antoine Street, they had, with the approval of the mayor's office, opened a soup kitchen.[7] But this was a stopgap measure. What was needed was a national policy that would create jobs for the thousands of unemployed enemy aliens or allow for their departure to the US, where they could secure work. As it stood, according to Bradley, the effective prohibition on travel to the US by enemy aliens had made of them "virtual prisoners of the country." It was a view shared by others.

The Hon. Sir Hugh J. Macdonald, a former interior minister and one-time premier of Manitoba, felt compelled to write a letter to Prime Minister Borden about the predicament of Germans not yet naturalized, having learned from the mayor of Winnipeg of the personal difficulties facing two young men of German origin.[8] Writing of their plight, he noted that because of their enemy alien status they had been discharged from a local branch of the Imperial Bank and, finding it impossible to secure work, were now without means. They could readily obtain employment in Minneapolis if allowed to leave the country but were prevented from departing because of their status. In Sir Hugh's view, they were "in a hole from which they cannot escape." According to him, this was a travesty. Since they had been invited to the country and were following the laws of the land, there was no excuse now for their mistreatment. Their fate, moreover, was shared by others, persuading the former premier to recommend to the prime minister that "they ... be

2.1 Slum dwelling, foreign quarter, Winnipeg, Manitoba

allowed to go to the United States or provided with work or means of living if they are detained here."

From Sydney, Nova Scotia, the Reverend M.C. Kinsale also corresponded with government officials, bringing to the attention of the secretary of state the serious situation at the local steelworks. Working at one-third capacity, the mills there had instituted mass layoffs, mostly affecting Austro-Hungarian nationals. Although recognizing that the 15 August proclamation prohibited enemy alien travel to the US, Kinsale urged a special allowance be given to them since the men and their families were in desperate need and there was but limited local assistance. He reported that the local American consul was besieged every day by large numbers of Austro-Hungarians pleading that they would like to work, if not in Sydney, then in the US, but were prevented from departing because they had signed the Undertaking that compelled them to stay put. Reverend Kinsale observed through his mission work that, in their desire to leave the country, they had no inclination to participate in the war;

they were simply motivated by the need for work. He asked the secretary of state, Thomas Mulvey, to "take this matter in consideration and find some way out of this difficulty, which, while guaranteeing the safety of the country, will help these men."[9]

Mulvey would, in fact, write to the chief commissioner of the dominion police, Colonel A.P. Sherwood, asking whether something might be done to meet the needs of the enemy aliens in Sydney. The police commissioner's response was that although he concurred with Reverend Kinsale's assessment – "he puts the facts fairly clearly and with absolute correctness" – the issue would have to be resolved politically. By placing the matter before the minister of justice, as he intended to do, the commissioner hoped that some government action would be taken. In the meantime, Sherwood noted there was some urgency in the matter insofar as "the condition of affairs at Sydney [was] similar to many other parts of Canada and some policy [would] have to be adopted to meet the situation."[10]

The effect of the travel prohibition to the US meant that enemy aliens would be forced to take a chance in crossing the border. Not all were successful. Mike Kitt, attempting to make the border crossing in order to look for work in the Dakotas, was arrested at North Portal, Saskatchewan, for stealing a ride on a freight train. Brought before Justice W.A. Neal, Kitt explained that without work and facing starvation he had no choice but to go to the US. The argument persuaded the judge to sentence Kitt to fifteen days of hard labour for violation of the Railway Act rather than internment.[11] John Spodarulek was similarly arrested at Brockville, Ontario, when he attempted to steal across the international line. He confessed going to Hammond, Indiana, only because there was no work in Ottawa where he had been a teamster at a box factory for two years.[12] Meanwhile, Tom Larivitch and Steve Vincovic could not offer a satisfactory explanation as to why they were on the Grand Trunk train heading from Toronto to the border. They informed the arresting officer, however, that there was no work to be had in Brantford, Ontario, where they lived. Arrested, they joined Martus Konekovitch of Fort Colborne, who also attempted to cross the boundary line in search of work.[13] A handful of cases, these revealed the desperation that compelled them to overcome their fear of imprisonment and cross the border.

The United States held out the promise of work, underscoring the difficult employment situation in Canada. Without the possibility of leaving the country, the personal circumstances of the enemy alien were severely tested. In Fort Henry, a number of the interned were prepared to be paroled. However, on learning they would not be allowed to depart for the US, they refused to leave the facility.[14] Prevented from travelling to the US, where they might find work, and lacking even the basic means to return to their respective homes, they were inclined to accept internment as an alternative to wandering aimlessly about the country, hungry and without hope.[15]

Although the recession of 1913–14 was of a cyclical nature, the war in Europe added to the economic crisis. Businesses were unwilling to invest, as were provincial governments. Given the economic uncertainty, all parties were scaling back on capital projects, but the retreat by government was especially criticized from a variety of quarters. Shaken by the turmoil in the grain markets as well as the interruption in commerce, the business community of Manitoba insisted on provincial action to help promote confidence and stability. They implored the government "[to] proceed along normal lines with respect to public works, thus setting, as far as possible, an example for the rest of the community."[16] The union movement in Manitoba was equally critical of the provincial government's withdrawal in the face of the economic challenge. Five hundred men were thrown out of work when construction in Winnipeg on both the parliament buildings and the new courthouse had stopped. Portrayed as a necessary austerity measure, the move came to be seen as short-sighted if not harmful, forcing the local Trades and Labour Council to organize a delegation that would visit Premier Rodmond Roblin with the hope of convincing him of the necessity of continuing government support for construction projects during this critical time.[17]

Governments on all levels were called upon to demonstrate resolve and leadership. That they showed neither proved unnerving, since official apprehensiveness not only was seen as adding to the ranks of the unemployed but also seemed to indicate that there was no plan. In the vacuum, suggestions were brought forward on how best to relieve, at least at the local level, the distress of the people. Citizens of Edmonton demanded the dominion government appropriate $300,000 for construction of a retaining wall on the riverbank.[18] Mayor Thomas R. Deacon of Winnipeg argued for a federally sponsored "Back to the Land" program, advocating government loans for those individuals who hoped to remain on homesteads but faced hardship or for those who might consider homesteading. With more individuals holding title to the land, "not only would much of the unemployment difficulty be settled," Deacon maintained, "but the country would be better off, owing to the increased number of farmers."[19] The approaching winter underscored the urgency of the matter, and across the country multiple proposals at the local level were actively discussed and considered. There was a palpable sense that something needed to be done, and soon.

Hardship was felt across a wide swath of the working population. In urban centres, a range of organizations and agencies sought to assist those most affected. Charities found it increasingly difficult to address the growing number of the indigent, particularly among the enemy alien population. For the enemy alien, the economic situation was especially trying. As the economy contracted, and employers had to choose between native-born and enemy subjects, it was the latter who bore the brunt of unemployment.[20] Preferential hiring, of course, had always been part of normal labour conditions in the country, but with war it assumed a more malign character. The employment practices of businesses and governments alike were increasingly scrutinized and held to account, with a growing chorus voicing the view that loyal British and Allied subjects were to be favoured because birthright mattered under the conditions of both war and need.[21] Governments and businesses were urged to support their own and to demonstrate their patriotism by hiring only those whose loyalty, a function of birthright, could be trusted.[22]

In Montreal, a group of English-speaking French and Italian waiters complained to the local major hoteliers that over four hundred individuals of German and Austro-Hungarian nationality held remunerative jobs that could easily be occupied by native-born men currently unemployed.[23] In Toronto, protesting that the management of the King Edward Hotel continued to retain Germans in their employ "in spite of our Canadian boys being bayoneted when lying wounded," a number of employees at the hotel, who described themselves simply as "British waiters," caustically asked the officer commanding Military District No. 2 to use his influence with management so that they could properly change the hotel's name to the "Kaiser Wilhelm."[24] In Calgary, the city commissioner, Adoniram Judson Samis, bowing to public pressure, gave instructions that single men of Austro-Hungarian and German birth working in the city's street-cleaning department were to be replaced by Britishers, as "it would be monstrous to employ members of a nation at war with the British Empire while men of the British race were unable to find employment."[25] The *Calgary Daily Herald* applauded the move, declaring that "there will have to be some discrimination used" since, as a matter of general principle, it should be the policy of civic authorities to employ first the native-born. As for immigrants generally, the *Herald* declared, after British subjects were all working, "If there is room for others ... [then] bring on the foreigners, married first."[26]

Pressured by discriminatory hiring practices, enemy aliens saw their situation worsen. Reports of near starvation and substandard living conditions were commonplace and widespread. In Hull, Quebec, municipal authorities were appalled after a health inspection of overcrowded rooming houses in which Ukrainians, Poles, and other Austro-Hungarian nationals resided. There they found 125 individuals huddled together in filthy squalor, with entire families living in rooms "no bigger than clothes closets." Eighteen individuals, including women and children, were crammed into one small house described as a sty.[27] To avert the spread of pestilence, the Quebec provincial board of health was instructed by the province's chief medical health officer to take action. The problem, of course, was that there was nowhere to relocate these individuals, let alone provide for their basic needs.

The situation in Ottawa/Hull was the result of the closure of the valley's logging mills, owing to the war's effect on the transatlantic commercial trade in timber.[28] It was expected all along that the closures would try the city's enemy alien population, who, in August, were already idle and penniless.[29] Without the prospect of employment – even temporary work – and with large numbers of enemy aliens released from the mills migrating to the city in search of jobs and aid, the months of September and October were expected to be difficult. The depth of the crisis, however, was unanticipated.

In early September the situation was described as unprecedented in the city's history, with approximately four hundred Austro-Hungarian nationals reported as being "absolutely destitute" and "starving." The *Ottawa Evening Journal* noted: "Many of the men are sleeping in fields surrounding the city, and are living upon scraps of food picked up at the back door of houses."[30] By early October, petty theft was reported to be pervasive. Immigrant children, street urchins, begging for alms, could be found on Parliament Hill, only to be chased away by the local police. Despite these conditions, the *Ottawa Evening Journal* declared that preferential treatment was being given to enemy aliens in search of work.[31] It was a false allegation, in no small measure animated by the gathering fear and resentment among the general public. It pointed to an awful yet recurring truth – that wars drew sharp lines between peoples. Notwithstanding the aliens' suffering and misery, in the view of most of the general public, providing for one's own took precedence over the enemy alien whose intentions and loyalties were suspect.

Still, the task of feeding enemy aliens and their families in Ottawa could not be ignored entirely. Distributing hundreds of loaves of bread daily, municipal authorities were concerned about the impact hunger would have on these unfortunates. With want and desperation rampant, the Ottawa police feared riots would soon break out – a concern that was voiced in other parts of the country.[32] In Vancouver, riots were fully expected. When they did not occur, especially after the cost of basic food-stuffs increased, there was genuine surprise and relief.[33] In Montreal, the board of control was particularly anxious about the possibility of distur-bances, recommending to the city council "that it was advisable to send a delegation to Ottawa to confer with the Federal authorities on the need for additional protection to property in Montreal on account of the foreign element here."[34] City councillors expressed no opposition to the move.

There was no opposition because there was a growing belief in Montreal that the city's enemy alien population posed a threat. It was estimated that between five and eight thousand enemy aliens lived in the city. Nearly all, according to the Charity Organization Society of Montreal, were out of work, without funds, and, prevented from leaving the country, in absolute want. As such, they constituted "a serious men-ace" to the city, one that would grow as the winter approached.[35] Entrusted with public safety, Montreal's chief of police, Oliver Campeau, reported to the city's Board of Control that police were helpless to deal with the situation. "Many hundreds of Austrians and Germans have been thrown out of employment because of their nationality," Campeau observed, and given that winter was close at hand, "these men will be ripe for all kinds of mischief." He concluded, "Robberies and outrages are sure to become daily occurrences," adding that the police service had few men and even less power to conduct house-to-house searches in the "foreign sections of the city."[36] At a public hearing held to address the issue, representatives emphatically declared that neither civic authorities nor charitable organizations were equipped to deal with the size and scope of the problem; the dominion government – "by whose act these men ... are prevented from leaving the country" – was called upon to take immediate action.[37]

The government was aware of the problem. As early as August, the minister of militia and defence, the Hon. Sam Hughes, in a letter to the prime minister communicated his worry about the unfolding situation and his concern for the future.

I am very much depressed over the question of foreigners in Canada, out of employment. Estimates vary as to the number of

these people unemployed, and it is an undoubted fact that there
are very many thousands of them practically destitute.

There is no hope of work for them for another year. The winter
will soon be coming on and destitution, if not starvation, will be
on every hand. Many of these are German and Austrian Reservists.
When people are fed they are, usually, contented. When people are
starving they are desperate.

Almost every offence committed will be laid at the doors of
these people and, of course, poverty will have a tendency to make
criminals of them.

If there are any means whereby they could be gotten out of the
country quietly, would it not be well? If they remain, I fear we will
have to take charge of them and establish large and expensive
camps all over the country to control and feed them. If they were
encouraged to go to the United States and were refused admission
there, as they doubtless would be, would it not have a tendency to
make them more law abiding in Canada?[38]

The importance of introducing a policy to manage the situation was
uppermost on the mind of Hughes. He acknowledged that the situation
required careful thought, but more directly he noted that with respect to
the enemy alien, "some lines must be laid out for their control and
maintenance."

The question of the control and maintenance of the unemployed
enemy alien population was also on the mind of industrialist Sir Thomas
Shaughnessy of Montreal. A prominent public figure and close confidant
of the government, Sir Thomas wrote as early as 28 August to the Hon.
Martin Burrell, minister of agriculture, about his concern over the looming enemy alien situation in the western provinces. He noted that the
German immigrant was in a better position to weather the growing
unemployment crisis, but among Austro-Hungarians the shutting down
of operations by government, corporations, and municipalities would, in
his view, have a negative impact. From Shaughnessy's perspective, "If
these men be permitted to reach a starving condition they will be dangerous, and, beyond doubt, some steps should be taken to deal with the
problem. They are practically prisoners of war, and cannot leave
Canada." He recommended that under the circumstances it might be
desirable to select suitable sites in each of the provinces, where "a
Detention camp could be located, and properly equipped, so that any
German or Austrian who applies for relief or is out of employment and
cannot take care of himself, may be removed there and held under

military supervision until the war is over, or employment offered."[39] The letter prompted the prime minister to direct Burrell to confer with the Department of Militia, the comptroller of the RNWMP, and other senior cabinet ministers for the purpose of bringing forward to cabinet council a recommendation "that was in the public interest."[40]

Arthur Meighen, the solicitor general of Canada, to whom a copy of the letter was sent, shared his views on the subject with the prime minister. He was personally opposed to Sir Thomas's suggestion to have jobless enemy aliens interned in camps, commenting that "such a camp would be looked upon as a lazy man's haven and men of all nationalities would be fruitful of expediencies to get there."[41] It would also affect the quality of free labour. Meighen recommended an alternative, an arrangement that would get the men on the land and set aside parcel lots that could be procured with little government assistance. "These Austrians," argued Meighen, "are workers as a rule and those I know would jump at the chance to acquire a small piece of land. They can live on very little." He urged the prime minister to give the plan serious consideration. "I realize that there are big difficulties in the way [but] the necessities are great and the goal is the correct one."[42] When the RNWMP comptroller argued for unemployed German and Austro-Hungarian immigrants to be interned in camps, Meighen reiterated his position that "by an extension of the homestead system under close Government supervision, a great many of these Immigrants can be better taken care of."[43] For Meighen, internment was a mistake. Moreover there were real alternatives to detention.

At the senior level of government, opinion was divided on what approach to take. The consequence of this disagreement was continued delays. Yet public impatience about what to do about the growing number of unemployed enemy aliens, combined with the prospect of an escalation in the crisis with winter approaching, made a decision inevitable. In late October, Prime Minister Borden wrote London. Outlining the severity of the situation, he noted it was estimated that some fifty to one hundred thousand enemy aliens would soon be without work, a great many of them having been dismissed by employers who felt the pressure of public opinion. Stating that they were prohibited from departing for the United States where they could possibly find work, Borden declared: "We must either let them go, provide them with work or feed them; otherwise they will become desperate and resort to crime." He communicated further that "our inclination is to relax measures preventing them from entering the United States, which is a neutral country, especially as

2.2 Overcrowded tenement housing, Toronto, Ontario, ca 1914

there is little probability of their reaching the enemy's country."[44] Borden wished to obtain the views and advice of the imperial government as quickly as possible.

Borden's communication was promptly circulated among various officials in London. In discussing the matter with the parliamentary secretary of the Foreign Office, Canada's high commissioner to the United Kingdom, Sir George Perley, impressed upon the former that this was "a very serious question in Canada."[45] Sir George noted that Borden considered it "a knotty issue" because of the underlying moral conundrum: the government had invited these people as immigrants to Canada. As such, the situation required sensitivity and an appreciation of the special circumstances. Sir Edward Grey, the British foreign secretary, in consultation with Laurence Harcourt, colonial secretary, took up the matter. Both agreed that despite the expense involved in keeping such a large number under the government's charge – "a serious burden" – the better course of action for the Canadian government was "to detain them within the limits of the Dominion." Citing the rationale behind the decision, Harcourt remarked, "This course, in spite of the expense which it will involve, will no doubt prove the most satisfactory and it will preclude the practical certainty of any Germans or Austrians drifting, by way of the United States of America, back to the enemy's firing line."[46]

The reply from London did not arrive until a full ten days had passed. The delay was an ominous sign, suggesting that the initial proposal of allowing the departure of enemy aliens for the United States would not meet with imperial approval. Everything was filtered through the prism of war, and since the imperial lead on war matters could not be ignored, the issue of dealing with the jobless enemy alien was now an internal Canadian affair to which Canadian solutions would have to apply. To this end, the government of Canada began to take what were perceived to be necessary measures.

## ORDER-IN-COUNCIL PC 2721

Pressure mounted on the government to deal with unemployed enemy aliens. Federal officials routinely received inquiries and petitions, and the press reported on the various efforts to ascertain the intentions and plans of the government. Curiously, several of the inquiries underscored the proposition, held by a segment of the population, that unemployed enemy aliens should be made prisoners of war. Albert Chevalier, director of the Philanthropic Society of Montreal, acutely aware of the difficulties facing the enemy alien population in the city and requesting from Ottawa some information on the government's strategy, raised the question whether the government was contemplating their internment as prisoners of war.[47] The proposition, although startling, was not hard to understand.

The War Measures Act, which had created the category of enemy alien, made synonymous in the public mind the idea of foreigner and enemy and provided for the internment as prisoners of war of those enemy aliens who contravened the laws of the land. The aim of the act, and of the immediate orders-in-council issued under the authority of the act, was to ensure that threats to the wider national interest would be addressed. Although formulated to counter specific threats – for example, the possession of explosives and firearms – the act was sufficiently broad based that it made for a wide interpretation of what constituted a threat. Hence, the unemployed enemy alien, presenting "a serious menace" by way of potential disturbances, fell within the range of a threat. The combination of would-be threat and enemy status – reinforced by speculative rumours regarding espionage and alleged treachery – made possible the notion that such individuals could be interned as prisoners of war.

This, however, was never the intent of the act. Indeed, Prime Minister Borden was clear in his assurance, made on several occasions, "that no arrests shall be made unless the persons in question evince an intention of leaving the country for the purpose of fighting against the British Empire, or otherwise assisting the nations with which we are, unfortunately, at war."[48] Moreover, release was all but assured for those who were prepared to sign Undertakings after their arrest. Thousands, who in the initial stages of the war had been arrested either for violation of the regulations or on suspicion, were in fact released in this manner. This was in keeping with the spirit of the 2 September Public Notice asserting that aliens of enemy nationality who went about their routine business would not be interfered with. It also followed from the argument, repeated publicly at times, that consideration was owed them not only because they had been invited to the country but also because the vast majority was law abiding.[49] The situation demanded empathy. In this regard, the superintendent of immigration, W.D. Scott, on learning of the desperate plight of enemy aliens in Vancouver, spoke against a proposal to make them prisoners of war. "If the only objection to these people is that they are destitute and unable to provide for themselves, I can scarcely see why they should be refused the same treatment as other immigrants would receive under similar circumstances ... I cannot see why they should be treated as military prisoners unless they have done something to bring them within the terms of Clause 2 of the Proclamation of the 15th ultimo."[50]

Nevertheless, the worsening employment situation for enemy aliens could not be ignored. This meant that dominion officials would have to address the problem while also acknowledging that special consideration had to be extended to them. They also, however, had to be ever mindful of the wider context: namely, maintaining security and preserving the country's obligations to the Allied war effort. The result was that on 28 October 1914, the Hon. Charles J. Doherty, minister of justice, submitted a report to the cabinet council outlining measures to be taken in managing the enemy alien situation. The proposal was adopted and approved the same day by the governor-in-council under the authority of the War Measures Act as order-in-council 2721.[51]

PC 2721 was carefully crafted, building on the powers inherent in the War Measures Act that sought to thwart espionage and prevent enemy aliens from rendering assistance by returning to the enemy's service. PC 2721 further provided for the "supervision and control" of enemy aliens as well as their detention as prisoners of war "under proper conditions

and maintenance." But it also made provision for the granting of exeats to those who had the means to leave the country if it could be
demonstrated they would not add to the strength of the enemy's forces.
In its aim, PC 2721 followed what was already occurring in practice.
Where it would supplement the standing emergency legislation was in
the specifics.

   Clause 1 of the ordinance called for the creation of a system of registration offices in cities and towns where large numbers of enemy aliens
were clustered. Specially appointed registrars were to operate under the
supervision of the dominion police (Clause 2). Enemy aliens were also to
be registered according to particulars that would assist in identifying
and monitoring their person and status (Clause 3). Clause 7 directed
enemy aliens to declare whether they would abide by the laws and customs of the land and had sufficient means to remain in the country, while
obligating them to report monthly to the local chief of police. On failing
to declare in the affirmative or report to police as required, they would
be interned as prisoners of war. Clause 7 further stated: "Any alien of
enemy nationality who in the judgment of the registrar cannot consis-
tently with the public safety be at large shall be interned as a prisoner of
war." Clause 10 authorized the Canadian militia to oversee the maintenance of enemy aliens as prisoners of war, requiring them to perform
work as was deemed fit. Recognizing that dependents of interned enemy
aliens might be placed in a precarious situation, Clause 9 permitted
dependents to accompany the prisoner of war into internment. Finally,
Clause 11 asserted that enemy aliens who had to register would not be
naturalized except under certain conditions.

   PC 2721 was soon followed by other ordinances. PC 2758, approved
on 30 October, identified cities in various provinces where registration
offices would be established: Sydney, Montreal, Ottawa, Fort William,
Welland, Winnipeg, Regina, Calgary, and Edmonton. PC 2817, approved
6 November, designated Major General William Otter, a professional
soldier with extensive military and administrative experience, as the officer commanding Internment Operations.[52] He would exercise executive
authority and have military forces placed at his disposal for the proper
carrying out of the operations. Other orders-in-council relating to registration and internment were to be introduced as needed. In the main,
however, it was PC 2721 that would shape conditions and have the most
effect on the greatest number of enemy aliens.

   The public announcement accompanying order-in-council 2721
stated that the ordinance had as its objective "the effective control and

supervision" of persons of alien enemy nationality. Although acknowledging that a majority were perfectly peaceable and posed no threat, the government noted that potentially there were those enemy aliens who had hostile intentions, and therefore it had an obligation to distinguish between them and the majority. In this regard, registration of enemy aliens and the internment of those who, in the interest of the public safety, could not be at liberty were seen as both a necessity and a duty. Curiously though, and almost as an afterthought, the announcement added that those who "would not be in a position to maintain themselves" would be treated as prisoners of war in accordance with the general rules of international law, more particularly those enacted by the Hague Convention.[53] The overall objective, therefore, was to intern those who should not be at liberty, which now included not only those who showed signs of hostile intent but also those who could not provide for themselves. Of significance was that the order-in-council collapsed two categories of individuals: those who potentially haboured ill will and hostile intent and those who could no longer fend for themselves. By treating both identically – either category of individual could be interned as prisoners of war – the government gave credence to the idea that the jobless enemy alien was, in fact, a security threat. It was an extraordinary development that would have enormous implications, changing the scope and character of internment.

And yet PC 2721 attempted, in the case of the unemployed alien, to alleviate the distress they faced. Clause 9, for instance, was an appreciation of the difficult circumstances that confronted not only the enemy alien but their dependents as well. The point was not to make their dependents prisoners of war but rather to aid and assist them in their desperate plight. The order-in-council was not to be used broadly. Indeed, although PC 2721 was in effect and the power to intern the destitute in place, the minister of justice, reacting to reports of absolute misery among enemy aliens in Port Arthur/Fort William and Montreal, recommended to the Privy Council that $1,000 be appropriated "for the immediate relief of the most urgent and deserving cases."[54] The rationale and preferred approach in both cases was to administer aid.

Not surprisingly, PC 2721 was interpreted as a gesture that sought to ease the plight of the enemy alien. It was reported, for example, that those interned would be provided with employment opportunities, giving the impression that internment was a make-work program. Internment was additionally described as a place of detention where enemy aliens would be fed and sheltered, suggesting that the motivation was animated by a sense of concern and fairness. Indeed, the argument, often repeated, was as follows: "To them a country owes a duty. They came here, some on the invitation of the Government, extended through the immigration service, and some at the suggestion of men who needed their labour. They are generally industrious and would not be idle if they had their choice. They cannot get work and they cannot return to their homes. Their detention under honorable restriction is the only apparent way of saving the most of them from risk of starvation and temptation to crime."[55] The statement would reflect the sense of obligation embedded in the 2 September Public Notice assuring enemy aliens that they would not be interfered with if they went about their normal business. But it was also true that PC 2721 had as its aim the surveillance and control of the enemy alien. Reports of suspicious activity and rumours of cross-border raids continued throughout the fall. And although much of it was dismissed as the work of mischief makers or cranks, PC 2721 served to address any worries on the part of the public.[56]

That the matter of supervision and control was to be taken seriously was reflected in the charge to the registrars. After making the necessary office arrangements, registrars were instructed to familiarize themselves with the protocol of registration and to make due inquiry of the persons brought before them. Questions of nationality, age, place of residence, current occupation, family, intention or desire to leave Canada, destination, as well as past military service were to be put before them.[57] These were to be carefully recorded in a registration book and similarly jotted down on a pass card to be carried by the registered enemy alien at all times and shown on demand to police, militia, or any other designated officer. More particularly, the registrars were instructed to use discipline and critical judgment in their assessment of the status and intentions of the enemy alien. "You will realize that the duties of the Registrar are not merely clerical," stated the instructions from the Department of Justice. "The proper discharge of duties demands that you should make due enquiry to ascertain the facts and exercise judgment and therefore it is necessary that you should personally consider the particulars of each case."[58] Furthermore, "you should communicate any other information which your enquiries may elicit and which you may think advisable to be considered in the public interest." Police duties were to be attended to by the chief of the local police at the registrar's request, while supervision of the entire operation would lay with the dominion chief commissioner of police. At its core, the registration of enemy aliens was a police operation that would employ the methods of and display the tempera-ment associated with policing.

Significantly, the instruction from the justice ministry, which directed the registrars to exercise judgment, offered them considerable latitude and discretionary power. It was insufficient to simply accept a declara-tion from an enemy alien at face value. The duty of the officer was to surmise, on a reasonable basis, whether the information offered was valid.[59] However, when the facts could not be ascertained, the conclu-sions drawn would depend on individual assessment and personal judgment. In this respect, the discretionary power of the registrar to recommend internment would follow the already existing wide powers of arrest that had been awarded police, militia, and others under the War Measures Act. As was the case with law enforcement and military offi-cers, the latitude given the registrar would have considerable bearing on the enemy alien, as would the system of registration itself.

Enemy aliens within a twenty-mile radius of the designated urban centres – that is to say, the area where the greatest number of unem-ployed enemy aliens were most likely to be found and, therefore, distur-bances most likely to occur – were required to register. Registration provided an effective means by which to assess and intercede before a problem could arise, principally by registrars posing pertinent questions to the enemy alien and gauging their response. The enemy alien response to inquiries would determine whether they would remain at large or be interned. Failure to register or report monthly as prescribed under the original ordinance became an immediate cause for arrest and intern-ment. This obligation to report became more stringent when PC 2721 was amended on 18 November requiring registered enemy subjects to report more frequently if deemed necessary. In keeping with the earlier provision of signing an Undertaking, the enemy alien was forced to sign an even more comprehensive pledge of loyalty and compliance.[60] The failure to report as instructed or sign the wide-ranging pledge served as grounds for internment.

A number of issues immediately faced authorities concerning the cat-egories of individuals to be registered. From Regina, an inquiry was made whether minors whose immigrant parents were naturalized but now of age were subject to the order-in-council regulations.[61] Also raised was the issue of whether Armenian and Syrian Christians formerly under Ottoman rule were subject to registration.[62] These and other questions were settled in favour of the individuals adversely affected, pointing to a willingness on the part of authorities to exercise prudence. And yet the power of discretion at their disposal meant that internment was largely a matter of personal judgment.

The registration offices, located where large numbers of enemy aliens were concentrated, ensured that measures were in place to help gauge and manage potential difficulties in areas that disturbances were most likely to occur. But it would also signal to the much-agitated public in these cities, where the native-born population was thought to be "vulnerable," that the issue of the enemy alien was being addressed. In those centres where registration bureaus were to be established the public was urged to exercise restraint with those enemy aliens who registered, as this "[would] greatly lessen the danger of any trouble."[63]

In towns or cities that had enemy aliens but were not designated points of registration, local officials were anxious about what steps were to be taken in view of the threat. The government assured them that the powers issued under the War Measures Act would suffice.[64] For some, however, nothing less than a registration bureau would do. When the municipal council of Brandon, Manitoba, passed a resolution demanding that the city be designated a registration site, the local member of parliament and president of the Canadian Bar Association, Sir James Aikins, approached Prime Minister Borden about the prospect of creating a bureau in the city. Citing the nervousness of the local inhabitants and a possible public backlash in this government stronghold, Ottawa obliged.[65] Also added to the list was the city of Victoria. This, however, would occur only after Major W. Ridgway-Wilson, an enigmatic figure who had ingratiated himself with provincial and municipal figures (securing the improbable title of "Director, Department of Alien Reservists"), convinced his provincial benefactors to nominate him for the federal position of registrar by emphasizing the local nature of the emergency.[66] With the addition of Brandon and Victoria, a total of thirteen registration centres were created.

The reaction to the process of registration in the targeted centres was varied. A few concerned citizens were offended by the developing situation and felt compelled to defend the enemy alien.[67] Still others were moved to suggest that registration had an unintended but beneficial consequence, since the process would "serve to free such people from distrust and so make their way easier in a strange land and under conditions which are necessarily more unfavourable for them than for others."[68] Among those resenting the presence of enemy aliens in the country, however, the steps taken were seen as futile if not pointless. Nothing would come of monitoring the enemy alien, so the argument went, since "the fact of having to report once a week is no deterrent to a man determined to vent his spite on the enemies of his country."[69] Martial law, they maintained, was what was needed, leading to the suggestion that the military and police be given "a free hand" in dealing with a problem that could otherwise prove to be a danger to the country.

Public talk of martial law, and more fundamentally the promulgation of PC 2721, had unnerved those cast in the role of enemy alien. Fearful of registering, significant numbers chose a watchful approach. Others, however, attempted to pre-empt the process by acquiring naturalization with the hope that citizenship might afford some protection. This resulted in a large number of applicants.[70] The rush towards acquiring citizenship did not go unnoticed. The British Imperial Association of Toronto, for one, objected to the granting of naturalization to Austro-Hungarian and German subjects during the war.[71] In the Canadian west, newspapers supported suspending naturalization for enemy subjects, despite the government's best effort to make the naturalization process more rigorous by introducing Clause 11 of PC 2721, which required several individuals with standing in the community to vouchsafe for each and every applicant.[72]

The requirement that a referee act as a guarantor failed to satisfy certain individuals whose outrage against enemy subjects applying for citizenship translated into legal action. In Ottawa, several prominent community figures intervened in the local naturalization proceedings.[73] In Vancouver, Justice David Grant rejected multiple applicants on the basis of insufficient documentation, unapologetically declaring in the case of two ethnic Poles that since there was "a two-to-one chance of their being alien enemies, they would have to establish without a doubt they were not [enemy aliens] or their applications would be laid over until the peace is declared."[74] In British Columbia's East Kootenay district, Justice George Herbert Thompson refused to grant naturalization certificates to Austro-Hungarian and German applicants on the grounds that during a state of war, as enemy subjects, "they had no status to apply for any civil rights in our courts."[75] But it was the celebrated case of Professor P.W. Mueller, dismissed from his teaching position at the University of Toronto, which underscored the unsavoury nature of the entire process. A resident of Canada for twenty years but never naturalized, Mueller hoped to be restored to his teaching position by acquiring citizenship. When asked "Whom do you want to win this war?" Mueller responded that it was an unfair question. The presiding judge rebuked

the good professor, sharply retorting that the query was well within the
purview of the court. He asked again: "Do you want to see Britain vic-
torious?" This time Mueller replied in the affirmative, only to have his
application for naturalization rejected.[76]

Clause 11 of PC 2721 imposed greater restrictions on those who
would apply for naturalization. The goal was to strengthen the proce-
dural aspect of acquiring citizenship and frustrate those who would
attempt to circumvent the process or look to outwit authority.[77] It also
denied, except in very limited circumstances, naturalization to subjects
of enemy nationality. Naturalization would guarantee civil and political
rights. In the absence of the guarantee, enemy aliens were left with very
little and what little they had was taken away. Indeed, shortly after having firmed up the naturalization process, Ottawa passed a ruling that
prevented enemy aliens from voting in municipal elections. Canadian
law had long held that it was unnecessary for a man to be a naturalized
before he could exercise the franchise in local municipal elections. With
the new order-in-council, enemy aliens, whether tenants or property-
holders, were now no longer eligible to vote. Deputy returning officers
were instructed to ascertain their status and turn away every alien of
enemy nationality who applied for a ballot paper.[78]

PC 2721 had effectively authorized the means to scrutinize systematically the status and welfare of the alien of enemy nationality, granting
extraordinary discretionary power to those who would oversee the process. It had also made provision for individuals deemed a public safety
risk to be interned as prisoners of war while limiting their access to
political rights afforded through the process of naturalization. Cumulatively, PC 2721 was a significant development in the succession of events
that would have bearing on the enemy alien. Not everyone was satisfied.
Some called for even harsher measures and penalties. Others, however,
warned against such irresponsible talk, arguing for common sense,
empathy, and tolerance. For them, this was not simply a war in the conventional sense of the term. Those who made the country their home,
but were most affected by the vicissitudes of war, needed to be reassured
that their decision to immigrate to Canada was the right one and that
the nation was both just and fair. Mindful of these larger issues, it was
thought to be both right and necessary that some basic if not fundamental questions be asked:

> While we are at war with Germany and Austria today and would
> misuse, persecute and deprive these people of their liberty while

they are peaceably going about their business, what impression are we going to make on the rest of the world that is now at peace with us; yes, and even our Allies today? What guarantee have the people of Denmark, Norway, Sweden, Russia and the United States or any other country that perhaps in the near future we will be at war with, that their turn will be next to receive from our hands the same treatment as we are proposing to give to the Germans and Austrians now because we are at war with their countries?[79]

By giving consideration now, Canada would create an impression. And this alone would be the guarantee reassuring future migrants that Canada was fair in its treatment of others.

### SUPERVISION AND CONTROL

Supervision and control of the enemy alien was the primary object of the ordinance (PC 2721) approved on 28 October 1914. Now the process of dealing with enemy subjects began in earnest. A sum of $20,000 from war appropriations was used to create a total of thirteen registration centres by the end of November. Within that month, 25,000 enemy aliens had registered. The number was far fewer than expected. However, with the obligation to register now in place, the police would be on the lookout for those who had not registered or, having done so, failed to report as prescribed.[80]

In the locations where registration centres were created, suspect aliens were routinely stopped by the local police and subjected to questioning and the demand to show their pass card. Those who did not possess the required document were immediately arrested and detained for processing as prisoners of war. But so too were those who failed to report. Reporting signalled compliance. Failure to report meant resistance and, therefore, became an important factor in the decision to intern. On 24 December, Mike Spycnka was escorted from Calgary to the Lethbridge internment facility for failing to report as required by the terms of his Undertaking. So too was Bill Spukie. Harry Krasij was interned at the Fort Osborne Barracks in Winnipeg on 2 January, having been given his parole six weeks earlier, but failed to present himself to authorities after that.[81] In Calgary, Stanley Copsh was arrested on 15 January and sent to Lethbridge as a prisoner of war for not reporting as ordered. Upon Copsh's arrival at the internment facility, the commanding officer, Major J.S. Stewart, observed the man was but four days late in reporting, had a

2.3 Enemy alien, police photo, Calgary, Alberta

steady job as a janitor at a CPR depot, and was not a reservist. Stewart could not see why Copsh was sent down and recommended his discharge.[82] Tardiness, however, was not at issue; rather it was what it signified that was of importance. Non-compliance implied defiance, for otherwise, why would an enemy alien, faced with the prospect of internment, fail to report on time? Copsh was not released.

The issue of hostile intent was very much on the mind of police officials. The commissioner of the RNWMP, Colonel A.B. Perry, sent special undercover agents to infiltrate communities to ascertain the names and addresses of those who refused to register and to learn what was afoot. In Calgary, where two such agents were sent, the RNWMP superintendent there, F.J. Horrigan, was of the opinion that "there was not a single German that could be trusted," convinced as he was that "they are playing the game to their own advantage."[83] Enemy aliens, he continued, "are not doing anything out of the ordinary, because they know that if they did, they would be put out of action in a hurry. They are waiting patiently, hoping and praying that the time will soon come." The statement revealed a deep suspicion and distrust, a sentiment not uncommon in the ranks of those entrusted with maintaining the security of the country. It also underscored the difficult circumstances facing the enemy alien: by acting they would be arrested and interned, but, equally, if they did not act, they could be arrested and interned since they were simply biding their time.

Not everyone was convinced of the inherent treachery of the enemy alien. From Edmonton, the RNWMP superintendent, T.A. Wroughton, communicated with the commissioner that he was somewhat baffled by the views of special agent Sergeant Brooks, who had been deployed in the area to carry out investigations. Wroughton had detected in Brooks an unbalanced and unhealthy attitude toward enemy aliens and felt that he was "obsessed" with the idea of spying and espionage. "He informed me that he had absolutely nothing that he could produce as direct evidence," Wroughton observed, "but from this, that and the other thing, he deduced certain results which, he in his own mind was satisfied, pointed to organized sedition among the Germans."[84] On the basis of Wroughton's knowledge of the facts, Brooks's hypothesizing about organized activity could not be substantiated. And yet Wroughton indicated that he was prepared to follow up, at any time, on specific information Brooks might provide. Intuitively, Wroughton was suspicious of Brooks and expressed reservations about the officer's dubious opinions. But he also felt obliged to consider information from this source. It hinted at the enormous pressure under which Wroughton and others like him operated. He did not wish to give the appearance that these supposed threats were all manufactured, so he was prepared to entertain Brooks's suspicions no matter how doubtful the evidence or absurd his claim.

The possibility of threat, imagined or real, meant that considerable effort would be expended in uncovering and rooting out potential enemies. Identifying them would depend on the circumstances. Onofruy Rozdolski, paroled in Winnipeg, was arrested in Yorkton, Saskatchewan. A travelling agent for the Western Canada Publishing Co., Rozdolski went about the countryside soliciting subscriptions for several foreign-language papers published by his firm. Moving about freely, he was also in a position to scout out information. As the arresting officer pointed out, "It appears that the object of registering these aliens is defeated if these parties are allowed to roam the country at will, even if they report to the Police at each town they visit monthly."[85] More stringent control over their movement and whereabouts was necessary; so was preventative action. The assistant registrar for the city of Toronto, for example, noting that a number of residences were suspected of harbouring enemy aliens, inquired whether the local militia could be called upon to help carry out house searches and arrest all those found. The basis for his suspicion was that the time for registration had passed. A large number of Austro-Hungarians, Germans, and Turks, therefore, were thought to be unregistered. Accordingly, "these are the ones that should be watched closely," the registrar argued, "and we must get after them immediately." The officer commanding Military Division No. 2 agreed, but with the caveat "within limits," appreciating the possibility of being drawn into an operation that would require enormous resources.[86]

Many of the arrests were spontaneous, and others were simply frivolous. C.E. Michaelis was arrested because he had in his possession a rifle, shotgun, and pistol. His arrest report, however, cited a series of other transgressions that appeared to be more consequential in his arrest. During the search of his premises, among his personal effects police found "numberless immoral pictures, statuettes and books." He was also described as being educated and obsequious in attitude: "On one day he would assume a smooth and cringing veil of partiality to the British nation, on another pass sarcastic remarks and talk in a bitter manner about the British." Described as "a degenerate," he was not released despite numerous petitions and appeals.[87] Reinhold Buchs, when taken into custody after applying for an exeat to the United States, similarly insisted that he be released because there was no cause for his arrest. The registrar for alien enemies in Toronto, Judge Emerson Coatsworth, explained to the commanding officer at the Stanley Barracks that Buchs had made a number of contradictory statements about his years of residency in Canada, but more importantly, as a mechanic it was thought that he would be of "considerable value" to the German army. Buchs, when applying for exit papers, also made the impolitic remark that he would proceed to the US regardless of whether authorization was granted, or, failing that, Canada would have to keep him. For Coatsworth there could be no release for an individual who might prove useful to the enemy and, since he was under arrest, Coatsworth could not see what possible cause Buchs had for complaint. Commenting on Buchs, Coatsworth added that from a personal point of view there was no reason to let him go.[88]

Other cases were equally hollow, including three Austro-Hungarian nationals arrested in Alameda, Saskatchewan, who were accused of military drilling. The arrest was based on the remarks of an eight-year-old child, who innocently inquired with his father why these men were pacing about in formation. Their supposed activity signalled a sinister motive. That they were unemployed did not help matters.[89] Jonathan Distram and Fred Klenzing were taken into custody on the word of an informant, who claimed they were spies. A neighbour, Mrs J. Doonen, on learning of their arrest, was sufficiently moved by their predicament to give testimony, identifying their accuser as their former employer, who, incensed by their unwillingness to work under his conditions, took revenge by filing false reports against them.[90] Although the testimony of Mrs Doonen was hard to ignore, Distram and Klenzing were interned. The case against Nikola Bodnar was apparently less complicated. Picking through a refuse heap that contained charred debris from a fire at the Edmonton armoury, Bodnar found discarded rifle parts. He was interned for having "weapons" in his possession.[91] Meanwhile, M. Besanthal came under suspicion after having made statements that were allegedly seditious in nature. His arrest was predicated not so much on what he said; rather, it was felt that in his capacity as a train conductor, he was in a position to drive a troop train and sabotage the transport. Since he was unmarried and with no ties, it was thought prudent that he be interned, "considering all the facts."[92]

Throughout this period, nothing was to be taken for granted and no stone remained unturned. But in order to carry out their policing duties, those tasked with supervision and control needed to demonstrate commitment and resolve. Not everyone was up to the job. Near Battleford, Saskatchewan, RNWMP Corporal T. Wiltshire, reporting to divisional headquarters, concluded there were no Austro-Hungarians or Germans who could be classified as enemy aliens in his district since most appeared to be naturalized. He also believed they presented no danger because they neither caused any trouble nor "by word or deed" had shown any sympathy towards the enemy. Wiltshire, however, was rebuked by his superior for his attitude, which was described as "certainly wrong from our point of interest."[93] Whether he believed the foreigners to be dangerous or not was beside the point. Lists and reports were needed as a preventative measure and he was instructed to get on with the job.

RNWMP Constable Fred Allan of the Radisson, Saskatchewan, detachment was also reproached for his naïveté after he attended a leisurely shooting match between local German farmers. Having spent some time with them, he concluded that they were all gentlemen. They were also said to be naturalized citizens. Chiding the trusting constable, Allan's commanding officer scornfully inquired on what basis he drew his conclusion. The commander admonished Allan, declaring that because they said they were naturalized citizens did not mean it was true; rather the onus of proof was with them. Since proof was not provided, they were obliged to hand in their arms. In the simplest of terms, the RNWMP superintendent clarified for Constable Allan what was expected of him:

"It is your duty to patrol your district and prosecute all alien enemies who have arms in their possession."[94] Constables Wiltshire and Allan were both reminded that only a steadfast approach to duty, not trust, would guide them in their responsibilities. This was war – not a time for neighbourly feelings – and they needed to show more gumption in their attitude toward the work.

When the first Canadian contingent was sent overseas and camped out on the Salisbury Plains in Britain, it was discovered that among the ranks were individuals with foreign-sounding names. Investigations led to forty-six men being identified as suspect, with the recommendation they be returned to Canada and discharged. The principal reason was their nationality. As subjects of states with which the empire was at war, the enemy had dangerously been brought into the ranks. Moreover, they were in a position to do harm. In London, the War Office suggested steps be taken to prevent their re-enlistment, and, if necessary, that they be interned as prisoners of war.[95] The colonial secretary, Laurence Harcourt, writing to the governor general, was more to the point. Expressing disappointment, he conveyed his "confidence" that, in the future, appropriate measures would be taken to prevent the recurrence of enemy aliens enlisting in overseas contingents.[96]

The arrests of suspected individuals in the ranks created enormous public interest, especially as it was reported that some of those detained had fought with the British in South Africa and elsewhere.[97] But the incident also sparked wild rumours. Tales regarding acts of sabotage by enemy aliens who had infiltrated the army contingent circulated, not least of which was the story of the attempted poisoning of Canadian troops. The source of the rumour apparently involved one W.R. Wagner of the Medical Corps, tasked with the job of chlorinating the water supply at the Salisbury camp. He was arrested as a suspected enemy alien whose "loyalty was in doubt." Wagner's position, however, gave rise to the report that a plot to chemically poison the troops had been foiled.[98] The Wagner case, as with others, highlighted the importance of duty and diligence. Danger lurked even in the most unlikely of places; if the country was to prevail, prudence and vigilance were required.

Stories of sabotage and espionage persisted throughout the fall and winter of 1915. Accounts regularly appeared in the major dailies, some more fantastic than others. The concrete foundation constructed by a German cement block manufacturer on the Île d'Orléans near Quebec City, for example, was rumoured to have been built in order to provide cover for German Americans who would attack Canada disguised as pilgrims on the way to the holy shrine at Sainte-Anne-de-Beaupré.[99] Meanwhile, the destruction of a railway bridge in Vanceboro, Maine – the act of a lone, deranged man – gave rise to the report that US secret service agents had similarly uncovered an alleged plot to blow up the Welland Canal.[100] It did not help matters that, in the aftermath of the Vanceboro bombing, the chief commissioner of dominion police, Colonel Sherwood, issued a circular to police forces about the need for extra vigilance. As the story was picked up by the newspapers, public imagination was ignited with talk of "assassins operating surreptitiously in the dark."[101]

The rumour-mongering added to the heightened sense of insecurity and put pressure on those in the field to search out and follow up on suspects, even if none were there. Many of the accounts, like the alleged Welland Canal plot, were found to be malicious and/or fictitious, including the most enduring one, the threat of a possible attack on Canada by raiders from across the border. Information gathered by Canadian secret service agents in the US, such as the number of hunting licences issued in the border states revealed there was no uptake in activity.[102] The border, nevertheless, continued to be the focus of attention.

Canadian immigration officials who were charged with stopping enemy aliens from crossing over to the US closely monitored border traffic. Several hundred, in fact, would be arrested in this way and turned over to the militia for internment as prisoners of war. But in the process it became increasingly evident that a large number were in fact residents of the United States (albeit of Austro-Hungarian or German nationality), moving from one US point to another, via Canada, in search of work.[103] Although the arrests were introduced as a preventative measure, the effect was to detain non-naturalized Americans, who, for the most part, were ambivalent about the war and, being in search of work, destitute as well.[104] The arrest and detention of American residents at the international border prompted US officials (and lawyers acting on their behalf) to intervene, calling attention to individual cases and prompting the question whether the arrests were necessary given that those seized were in transit.[105]

It was a question similarly asked by Canada's immigration superintendent, W.D. Scott. In his view, Canada was adversely affected by a policy that effectively arrested non-naturalized Americans. Once arrested and deposited on the border without means, they were now the responsibility of the Canadian government.[106] As Scott pointed out, these men were simply unfortunates in search of work. By bringing them under the authority of the government, through arrest and internment, Canada had effectively absolved the US of its role and responsibility. Scott asked to what end and for whose benefit did the policy exist? He was not alone in questioning the rationale and efficacy of the policy. The government had been mulling over the need for a policy revision for some time, at least since November, and would, in fact, communicate with London that it was inclined to allow such individuals to proceed through to the US without interference.[107]

The generosity of spirit displayed by Canadian authorities in this instance extended to other areas as well. Exit permits continued to be issued to persons who could show that they were not reservists, who pledged not to take up arms against Britain and its allies, and whose personal circumstances made it impossible for them to remain in Canada any longer. Sir Robert Borden personally approved an exeat for Stephan Schwartz, who was lured to Canada before the start of the war with a job offer as a chemical engineer for the Consumers Gas Company of Toronto.[108] Schwartz was released from his position without notice after the company, sensitive to bad publicity, took its cue from similar dismissals of enemy aliens in the employ of the city of Toronto. Being unemployed and without prospects or funds, Schwartz faced uncertainty and hardship. The prime minister, appreciating the difficulty of Schwartz's predicament, agreed to an exeat that would enable the unfortunate man to leave for the US in search of an opportunity there rather than remain in Canada in a state of misery and poverty.

The question of poverty and unemployment continued to vex officials as fall turned into winter and winter into spring. The threat of mass disturbances resulting from the crisis did not materialize as expected during the winter. In part, the problem was avoided by the extraordinary efforts of municipalities to provide relief and temporary work on public projects. In Vancouver, for those who could demonstrate long-term residency, work on a rotational basis had been provided, such as street cleaning, scavenging, and breaking rock for future planned roadwork. At Hastings Park a camp was created for single men, who were fed and given temporary accommodation in exchange for clearing parkland. Married men were also given food for removing trees and underbrush in Stanley Park.[109] Winnipeg and Edmonton introduced partial employment through local make-work projects, such as trenching for sewers and the like. Charities as well went beyond what was expected in their efforts to stave off hunger and despair among the homeless and indigent.[110] Nevertheless, there was no escaping the scale of want, and municipal officials looked to the provinces and the federal government to help the desperately poor, especially among the enemy alien unemployed whose predicament threatened to translate into greater difficulties.

Among other things, the order-in-council of 28 October, PC 2721, had provided for the arrest and internment of enemy aliens who were destitute. The intent of the ordinance was not to pursue such individuals per se. It did, however, have as its goal the control of such persons. In large measure, those who were arrested for being destitute were also the ones who failed to report. A correlation existed between the two categories. At a certain level, it highlighted the natural fear of the unemployed enemy alien: to register was an invitation to be discovered as being homeless and without work. Imprisonment in an internment camp would have been a foregone conclusion. With all the uncertainty that this posed, it was not surprising that significant numbers failed to report. From the government's perspective, however, the connection between the two categories underscored the value of introducing and maintaining a rigorous registration system. Registration helped identify individuals who, through a combination of their actions and status, were suspect. In effect, registration provided the means to identify those who were potentially dangerous, or if not dangerous, then a liability.[111] Either way, they needed to be controlled.

When Mike Kulik was brought before the police magistrate in Nelson, BC, he was sent to the Vernon internment facility, not simply because he was without work and destitute. Rather, Kulik was described as "an encumbrance on society" and, as a result, was said to be "a menace to the community and the nation."[112] Judge Emerson Coatsworth, the Toronto registrar, was more forthright in sending two penniless, unregistered enemy aliens to the Stanley Barracks: "A wretched lot, these enemy aliens enjoy the benefits of British institutions and traditions which they have done nothing in this war to earn. They are a stain on the national honor and should be removed."[113]

Regarded as a liability or a possible public danger, the enemy alien needed to be controlled. Organized meetings of the unemployed and public marches of the poor in Fernie, BC, and Toronto had been relatively peaceful.[114] Elsewhere, however, there was growing unrest. In Sydney, on Cape Breton Island, one hundred enemy aliens gathered together in protest, appealing to the city authorities for food. Their concerns not being heard, the crowd threatened to turn ugly. The protesters dispersed only after pleas for calm prevailed. Caught off guard, but perhaps as a warning, divisional headquarters sent a full military company to the city and announced that it was prepared to use military force in aid of civil power to prevent any further unrest.[115] There were no further disturbances.

At the end of March, in Cobalt, Ontario, it was reported that a cabal of enemy alien saboteurs had been discovered, purportedly planning to blow up the powder magazine at the Nipissing mine. The alleged conspiracy led to calls for the government to intern all enemy aliens in the north country.[116] Police investigation, however, revealed that there were no signs of extremism among the local enemy alien population. On the contrary, it was discovered that local agitators were behind the difficulties, organizing so that enemy aliens might be discharged from the silver mine and interned in order to be replaced by unemployed, native-born men.[117] Despite the evidence, calls for the wholesale internment of enemy aliens in the district persisted, serving only to heighten tensions and giving reason for further trouble in the district.

Throughout the winter, officials in Vancouver were pushed to their limits in providing relief for the mass of unemployed in the city. The strain eventually gave way, on 1 April 1915, to the decision to discontinue the municipal make-work program that had provided so much needed employment and relief to some 2,100 single men during the winter months. The decision, intended to force the hand of the province, had a direct, albeit unexpected, effect. Some four hundred foreigners, mostly enemy aliens described as "habitues of the breadline," took to the streets after they had been turned away from the American consulate, where they pleaded for help.[118] The crowd turned into a large mob of two thousand and rioting ensued. Although damage was minimal, the episode registered with provincial authorities.[119] Funds were at once approved for immediate use by the city to address the needs of the destitute. More importantly, assurances were given to city officials that "other arrangements" would be made for the care of the non-resident alien unemployed.

The allusion to "arrangements" spawned the rumour that internment authorities had been instructed to take charge of the enemy alien poor in Vancouver.[120] Interning so many at this time, however, proved problematic. Individual enemy aliens, a number of whom were destitute, had indeed been sent to internment facilities at Nanaimo and Vernon since the ancillary ordinance of 28 October came into force. But these were solitary arrests. That a large number of jobless poor would be arrested and interned as prisoners of war was never contemplated. This required resources that were not available. The difficulties demanded a bold solution.

On April 12, four days after the Vancouver riot, various representatives in British Columbia, involved in one way or another with the enemy alien issue in the province, met to discuss a remedy.[121] At the meeting a proposal was mooted to allow as many as possible of the Austro-Hungarians to leave for the US, a recommendation that was forwarded to Ottawa. On 24 April, contrary to the long-standing policy of preventing the departure of resident enemy aliens (except under extraordinary circumstances), an order-in-council was approved. Noting the difficult employment situation in Vancouver, the ordinance stated: "In these circumstances the Minister considers that exceptional provision may be made and recommends that labourers of Austro-Hungarian or German nationality at Vancouver who desire to go to the United States for the purpose of procuring employment, and who undertake not to engage in hostilities or otherwise to assist the enemy may be permitted to go if considered advisable by the District Officer Commanding at Vancouver."[122] The solution had its desired effect as a number of unemployed enemy aliens in the city immediately sought exit permits for the US.

Not all, however, were satisfied with the response. The riot in Vancouver had frightened local residents, creating resentment and bitterness in certain quarters. The *Vancouver Sun* was particularly vocal. The paper condemned the bedlam and chaos and challenged federal authorities to take charge of the problem rather than leaving it to municipalities to deal with: "There must be some remedy for the situation, even if they had to be placed in detention camps and put to work on the roads. The city has sufficient problems without taking on any due entirely to the war."[123]

It was a sentiment shared in Winnipeg, where an estimated ten thousand unemployed foreigners gathered in front of the city hall, clamouring for assistance and holding banners declaring: "We are not enemies of Canada" and "Give us bread or work."[124] The demonstration was orderly, if only because the police had taken precautionary measures. City officials, however, sensing the risk of future unrest, proposed a deputation of western mayors to meet with the prime minister and other cabinet members on how best to confront the problem. This was especially important given the growing protest among English-speaking workers in western Canadian cities against giving employment opportunities to enemy aliens.[125]

Grievances over employment created a natural tension between the native-born and the enemy alien, having the potential to escalate into violence at any time. The sinking of the passenger ship *Lusitania* by German naval forces on 7 May 1915, with the attendant loss of civilian lives, was just such a moment. In Victoria, British Columbia, gathering mobs attacked places of business considered "enemy-owned," while individuals believed to be enemy aliens were accosted in the streets. The attacks continued the following day, prompting the mayor to declare a state of emergency. Military authorities imposed martial law and eight hundred soldiers were soon patrolling the city.[126]

The tragic news of the *Lusitania* and the incendiary nature of the Victoria riot became the pretext, across the country, to confront "the enemy within the gates." Petitions demanding that enemy aliens be barred from civic jobs were ubiquitous, with British- and native-born workers insisting they would not work "alongside people whose countrymen have proved themselves to be 'beasts.'" Labour unions were also pressured to revise their statutes to block membership to enemy alien workers, thereby preventing them from seeking either union protection or redress after being dismissed from their place of employ. Most importantly, there were public calls for the mass internment of enemy aliens in Canada.[127]

Predictably, the public calls for mass internment, the attacks on individual enemy aliens, and job dismissals created considerable unease among those who were most vulnerable. Despite the improbability of their being granted exeats for the US, applications across the country increased markedly.[128] Others were not prepared to wait. On 14 May, some one thousand unemployed enemy aliens, mostly Austro-Hungarian nationals, started off from Winnipeg on a sixty-mile trek towards the US. Initial calls for a halt and attempts to stop them along the way were rebuffed, the militia being quietly pushed aside in the forward movement toward the border. However, recognizing the futility of their effort as well as being hungry and fearful of a confrontation with the military, the numbers slowly decreased with each mile. Only 192 arrived at the international line, where they were confronted by a contingent of Canadian militia supported by US deputies with rifles at the ready. Resigned and dejected, they were taken into custody and led away. Stragglers and others attempting to evade custody were eventually chased down and similarly arrested. All claimed they had no intention of forcing their way across the border but needed work. They also maintained that they feared internment. The total number finally arrested was 258.[129] Placed in boxcars under military guard, they were sent to the internment facility at Brandon. The march convinced the mayoralty delegation heading for

2.4 Aftermath, *Lusitania* riot, Victoria, BC, May 1915

Ottawa of the need to forcefully demand that the government do something nationally regarding the unemployment situation and the enemy alien problem specifically. There could be no further delay.

The seeming lack of political resolve earned Ottawa the ire of the unrelenting *Vancouver Sun*. Since British Columbia was the centre of unrest, the newspaper insisted that nothing short of the internment of all enemy aliens would do. Orchestrating a campaign, the newspaper encouraged citizens to demand government intervention or, failing that, to take matters into their own hands.

Although more than a week has passed since the sinking of the Lusitania, and the agitation for the internment of all enemy aliens in Canada, no official notice has been taken. Not only have the better-known public bodies remained quiet, but the authorities declare that they can say nothing because they are merely under orders and can voice no personal opinion ...

It then remains for the people of Canada to say whether or not they wish to expose the lives of women and children to these fiends in human form. The Sun is not seeking to take any credit for the agitation which has swept the city during the past week. We feel that it is simply a matter of duty which every man in this city and in this country should perform.[130]

Posturing by the *Sun* and other newspapers across the country created a permissive atmosphere. Enemy aliens were increasingly accused of seditious language and treason. Police investigations, however, usually found the cause to be the latent antagonism of British- and native-born toward the enemy alien, the former often goading the latter into making ugly comments. "A man would not be human if he did not have a regard for the country of his birth," RNWMP Inspector H. Townsend noted, "and when these German-born people are tormented by insulting remarks, which are usually made by men in an intoxicated condition, it is only expected that they reply with remarks which are not favourable to the British." Vocalizing his frustration with the number of complaints, he added: "Unless an Order in Council is passed making it an offence for anyone to utter words derogatory to the British cause, I think we are helpless, as I have heard nothing that amounts to sedition."[131] Edmonton's RNWMP superintendent, T. Wroughton, echoed his view. "The result of enquires into complaints of this kind is almost invariably the same as in this case. It is the foolish, unthinking and ignorant among the British themselves who are really at the bottom of all the trouble. They goad the aliens to such an extent that it is not to be wondered at that they reply in kind."[132]

A more disconcerting aspect of the public baiting, however, was the willingness of organizations as well as municipal and other politicians, many of whom were leading public figures, to support the call for mass internment. The South Vancouver municipal council passed a resolution urging the dominion government to intern all enemy aliens. A similar motion of the district council of North Vancouver followed this lead. In Calgary, after a local citizens' committee exerted pressure, the city council there passed a resolution to discharge enemy aliens from the employment rolls of the municipality, thereby facilitating their internment. Sir Charles Hibbert Tupper, a former minister of justice and solicitor general, went on record stating, "All Germans [who are] not British subjects ought to be interned. I would not trust one of them." Thomas Hedley, M.E., similarly declared: "The government ought to intern every one of them who has not been naturalized. I do not believe that [we] can be safe so long as the present arrangement is in force of having the enemy alien reporting to police headquarters periodically." F.C. Wade, K.C., also felt compelled to publicly assert, "All enemy aliens should be interned immediately. They are an active menace to the community." Meanwhile, in Vancouver, the Rotary Club, the Manufacturers' Association, and the Board of Trade all brought forward motions at their general meetings in support of the proposition to intern enemy aliens en masse.[133]

Within this toxic atmosphere, where public opinion favoured the wholesale internment of the enemy alien population, it was not surprising that when striking miners in the Nanaimo district on Vancouver Island insisted that enemy aliens be dismissed from their positions, the BC government obliged. The attorney general, the Hon. W.J. Bowser, had succeeded in convincing the dominion government to consent to the internment of enemy aliens in the coalmines of Ladysmith, South Wellington, Nanaimo, and Cumberland on the grounds that they were provisionally hired as replacement workers. Because the Vernon camp was filled to capacity and had to be enlarged before receiving the group, the enemy aliens were sent down the island to Victoria, where they were temporarily held in the unused portion of the new provincial jail. Once removed, British- and native-born miners stepped into their places, including those who initially went out on strike. The *Vancouver Sun* applauded the provincial government's move but noted: "While this is a step in the right direction, we feel that it should not be allowed to end here."[134]

The success of the miners at Nanaimo convinced a vocal minority in Fernie, BC, that a similar strategy might also effectively be used to force enemy aliens from the mines there.[135] Mobilizing the British, native-born, and Allied miners to lay down their tools, the agitators pressured the operators of the mine to dismiss all enemy aliens. The pretext was that they feared for their underground safety. As was widely noted, however, the real reason was that "if they can get 300 of these [enemy aliens] out of the way it will mean another day's work each for those left."[136]

Union executives counselled against the move, claiming that if there were specific allegations then these should be treated as a criminal matter; otherwise the attempt to force enemy aliens out of the mines was both illegal and morally wrong. Given the uncompromising nature of the protesters and fearing violence and loss of life, W.J. Bowser, the attorney general and acting premier, once again, relying on the Nanaimo precedent, ordered the internment of some three hundred miners of Austro-Hungarian nationality at Fernie.[137]

Although it was conceded that the attorney general "had exceeded his powers," the *Vancouver Sun* commended the move, contrasting it with the "milk and water" policy of the dominion government.[138] The fact of the matter, however, was that the arrest and detention of enemy aliens was illegal. As such, habeas corpus proceedings were brought against the provincial government for the release of the enemy aliens, creating considerable commotion and anger among the striking miners. The prospect of imminent violence forced Ottawa to act quickly. Although acknowledging that the detention of the men was illegal, the minister of justice, the Hon. Charles Doherty, instructed the director of internment operations, General Otter, to take charge of the enemy subjects already in police custody, interning them at once as prisoners of war.[139] The basis of his decision was the ministerial order PC 1501, hurriedly approved a day earlier, which stated that those enemy aliens who were competing with others for employment – the source of much of the consternation and public enmity – could be interned as prisoners of war.

It happens that many aliens of enemy nationality residing temporarily in Canada have retained or found employment in connection with various works, industries, trades or pursuits which are being carried on, and they should be protected in such employment according to the policy of said proclamation [15 August 1914], so far as may be compatible with the public interest.

The Minister has ascertained, however, that owing to the fact that in some cases these aliens of enemy nationality are in common employment with others, many of whom belong to the nationalities of the allied powers, or because of competition for their places by such friendly aliens, and in view of the hostility or animosity which has been aroused and excited by the war and the operations of the enemy, there is serous danger of rioting, destruction of valuable works and property and breaches of the peace involving the loss of life or personal injuries; and while in the view of the

Minister the dangers thus apprehended should, so far as may be practicable and expedient, be prevented by strict administration of existing legal means, he considers nevertheless that cases have arisen, or may arise, where in the general public interest, as well as in the interest of those concerned who are of enemy nationality, provision should be made, as a measure of expediency, for separating and detaining at the public charge those aliens of enemy nationality whose presence in any works, employment or community is a cause of such apprehended peril.[140]

PC 1501, retroactively, made legitimate the initial illegal arrest and detention of miners of enemy nationality at the Fernie mines.

News of the Fernie strike spilled over into other parts of the country. In Cobalt, Ontario, where the situation had long been festering, a petition for the internment of enemy alien miners was organized and presented to the minister of militia.[141] In the Frank district of Alberta, a citizens' committee petitioned for the removal of some 140 enemy aliens from the Hillcrest mine. Shortly after the company had rejected their demands, miners of British and Allied nationality indicated their refusal to work alongside the "enemy." As in Fernie, it was observed that "the movement against the enemy aliens is not prompted through any fear of their being a menace to the State or to the individuals with whom they labour, but is for the selfish purpose of getting them out of the way in order that more work be distributed amongst those left."[142] The situation was diffused only after an arrangement was made that just those enemy aliens who contravened the various ordinances would be dismissed from their jobs. A similar arrangement was made at the Acadia Coal Co. located in Stellarton and New Glasgow, Nova Scotia, where twenty aliens of enemy nationality were discharged and interned.[143] The selective removal of enemy aliens from the Hillcrest, Stellarton, and New Glasgow mines, it was felt, helped avert a catastrophe inasmuch as it was thought that the strikes would spread to other mines in parts of Alberta as well as across Cape Breton, affecting two thousand enemy alien miners in the first case, and six hundred in the latter. This did not come to pass, and enemy aliens continued to go about their business – albeit under the watchful eye of the local authorities.

That enemy aliens could continue to go about their normal affairs without interference was a complete mystery to E. Salmon of Qu'Appelle, Saskatchewan. In light of the danger and seeking assurance that something would be done to protect those most susceptible to the predations of enemy aliens, Salmon wrote the prime minister: "We are living in the midst of them in the country and know how little they can be trusted. There are many days, especially during the haying season, when the women and children are left entirely alone and unprotected on the farms. What assistance, therefore, could they get should these foreigners decide to attack or assault them during the men's absence, for they well enough know when they are away?" The prime minister replied that the proclamation of 15 August empowered local law enforcement to deal with disturbances and that the RNWMP had the situation well in hand. The letter, however, was passed on to Colonel A.B. Perry, the RNWMP commissioner, for comment. Perry observed that enemy aliens were reporting regularly to the police, and although suspicious activity was being closely watched, not every eventuality could be addressed. Suggesting that locals take some responsibility for their own safety, he cryptically added: "They should lock their doors." The remarks of both Salmon and Perry revealed feelings of distrust and ill will toward the enemy alien that were as deep as they were wide.[144]

## THE UNFOLDING OF INTERNMENT

When PC 2721 was approved, citizens and other groups immediately requested the government to establish internment camps in their respective communities. In Alberta, Henry Lyon, the mayor of Blairmore, wired the prime minister proposing that an internment camp be established for the purpose of building a national highway through the nearby Crowsnest Pass. He offered a building that, once fitted up, could accommodate a thousand men. The influential John Herron, former member of parliament, a cattleman, and the largest landholder in the province of Alberta, endorsed the proposal.[145] In Ottawa, the Valley Motor Association met with the minister of militia and defence, the Hon. Sam Hughes, to discuss the use of prisoner-of-war labour to break stones for highway construction.[146] The thinking was that the results would be of economic benefit to the area, but it also reflected a more basic attitude: being unemployed, the enemy aliens would appreciate the work and, now that they were prisoners of war, should be made to work. Reports from Europe alleging the abuse of Allied prisoners only reinforced in the public's mind that the labour of interned enemy aliens in Canada should be used.[147]

Government officials were not immune to the idea of putting prisoners of war to work. On the very day PC 2721 was introduced, F.H.

Williamson, deputy commissioner of the dominion parks branch, broached the subject with the deputy minister of the Department of the Interior, W. Cory. It was an idea that Cory himself had advanced. A few weeks earlier, he sought to convince Colonel Sherwood, chief commissioner of the dominion police, that since international law sanctioned the use of prisoner-of-war labour, such labour might be used in the national parks for the purpose of cutting down dead and burned timber. The idea met with sympathy by Sherwood, but the necessary legislation making jobless civilian enemy aliens prisoners of war was not yet in place. When PC 2721 was introduced, authorizing the use of enemy aliens as prisoner-of-war labour, Williamson resurrected the idea.[148] Arguing the merits of the original proposal in a memo, he emphasized the advantages that would accrue from the use of enemy labour in the parks: namely, the proposed work would give a return to the government for the cost of their upkeep, alleviate the suffering of the unemployed, and provide free fuel to the poor during the winter months. Other advantages included the fact that it would be practically impossible for the enemy aliens to escape (simplifying the guarding of the prisoners), while the prisoner labour would not compete with free labour, which would have generated the opposition of labour unions.

Distributed to the ministers of justice and defence, the memo soon became a matter for discussion and consideration. It also became the substance of press reports, with various newspapers eagerly awaiting information on how enemy alien prisoner labour might be put to use in light of PC 2721. It was speculated that prisoners would be deployed in the national and provincial parks. These included Algonquin Park in Ontario and the national parks of Banff and Jasper in the west. There was also conjecture that in Quebec internees would be sent to the northwestern Abitibi region. In all cases, it was reported they would be made to work, whether building roads or cutting timber or, as the *Edmonton Daily Bulletin* sarcastically put it, sent to the parks where "they will be enabled to work out their anti-British spleen upon good, tough Canadian stumps."[149]

The unsettling question of using internees as prisoner-of-war labour had been effectively resolved with the approval of PC 2721. Nevertheless, there was some trepidation in actually using interned civilians as POW labour. What made it palatable was that those arrested were also, in effect, reservists. Indeed, being able-bodied, they were subject to conscription, which meant that they were also potential combatants, to which the laws of war would apply, including being interned as prisoners of war and used as prisoner-of-war labour. In this regard, Canada's high commissioner to the United Kingdom, Sir George Perley, having conferred with a senior British official, cabled the prime minister that the view from London, although unofficial, was that "if the Canadian Government is forced to take charge of and feed Germans and Austrians, it would be quite proper under war conditions to make them labour at public works simply for food and lodging without paying them any wages."[150]

Yet the practical considerations of how to implement such plans still remained a perplexing question. Sir George Foster, deputy prime minister, acting for the prime minister, who was away in London at an imperial conference, asked the minister of justice to bring to cabinet council some definite plans "by which the interned are to be cared for, as regards employment and sustenance."[151] From Foster's perspective, it was "very important" that the matter be discussed and settled quickly in light of the escalating tension in the country. The final decision, however, would have to await the return of the prime minister. Without resolution of the matter, those directly responsible for the prisoners would reject requests to use their labour on local projects. Responding to an inquiry on the possible use of prisoner-of-war labour for road construction in Alberta, Colonel Perry, the RNWMP commissioner, for instance, denied the application.[152]

Indecisiveness did not mean that all matters concerning prisoners of war were held up. At the end of November 1914, an interim decision was taken to alleviate the most urgent problem that needed to be addressed – the existing internment facilities in Montreal, Toronto, and Kingston were operating at near full capacity. The Stanley Barracks held the maximum eighty-five internees.[153] Fort Henry, upgraded to receive 103 Turkish enemy aliens from Brantford, was now crammed with 413 prisoners in total.[154] As for Montreal, the committee of the Privy Council approved PC 2924, authorizing an expenditure of $5,500 for the retrofitting of an old jail in order to accommodate a further five hundred prisoners.[155] It was evident that more space was required given the numbers being processed.

The ultimate decision was to move interned enemy aliens from Montreal and Kingston to the Petawawa military camp located northwest of Ottawa.[156] In the first week of December, the first contingent of one hundred enemy aliens was relocated from Fort Henry and a similar number from Montreal. They were immediately put to work converting the summer camp quarters to winter-ready buildings and cutting trees to enlarge the camp area.[157] An additional six hundred were to follow, bringing the total there to eight hundred. The majority were of Austro-Hungarian nationality, the result of a decision to separate them from German prisoners because of controversies and conflicts over the war.[158]

The creation of an internment camp at Petawawa was but a preliminary step. Negotiations were also taking place between Prime Minister Borden, who had returned from London, and the premiers of Quebec and Ontario regarding the use of internment labour in clearing land in the north country for agricultural purposes. Once Quebec officials concluded an agreement with Ottawa, Ontario felt it needed to follow suit, wanting "its full share of German and Austrian prisoners of war for this work."[159]

In Quebec, land was set aside along the National Transcontinental Railway near the divisional point of Parent, but because of successful lobbying efforts this was changed in favour of a location – designated Spirit Lake – situated eight kilometres west of the colonization centre of Amos on the shores of Lac Beauchamp in the Abitibi region of Quebec. After consultation with the federal Department of Agriculture, a site was also selected in Ontario. Located ninety-five kilometres east of the railway depot at Hearst, where the railway intersected the Kapuskasing River, the site satisfied Premier Hearst's request that the facility be established at a distance from the proposed Quebec camp, which was to be situated near the border. The Kapuskasing station, as it was called, was to be set up alongside the Transcontinental Railway line and would comply with the federal demand that at least one thousand acres be made available.[160] At both Kapuskasing and Spirit Lake, the wood cleared from the land was to be sold to offset the costs of maintaining the prisoners.[161]

From the Ontario government's perspective, the benefit of the Kapuskasing proposal was that the internees would be fed, clothed, and equipped by the dominion government. Moreover, the labour would be free since it was the provincial government's belief that the federal authorities would pay the prisoners a nominal wage, officials noting that, "as they have to take care of these prisoners anyway, it practically means they get their work for nothing."[162] As for the number of prisoners that could be supplied, this "would only be limited practically by the ability to provide work and accommodation." Not just hundreds but thousands, it was understood, would be sent. But perhaps the most important benefit was that the resulting arable land would be offered to settlers, helping to inaugurate colonization in the region.

From the federal government's perspective, the establishment of the Spirit Lake and Kapuskasing camps addressed the problem of over-crowding at the existing internment facilities in Quebec and Ontario. But the camps also raised ethical questions, both political and social, about how to best deal with the mass of unemployed enemy aliens. In negotiations with premiers Gouin of Quebec and Hearst of Ontario, Prime Minister Borden communicated his desire that employment be given to the large number of destitute, interned enemy aliens.[163] There was consensus that the internees should work and, more particularly, should work for their own benefit.

By working, the internees were providing for themselves. In this sense their needs were being fairly met. But this was a short-term goal. Provincial authorities also expressed the idea that at the conclusion of the war and upon their release, the internees might be persuaded to take up settlement on the land they had cleared in Spirit Lake.[164] The plan did not end there. A further scheme championed by the US consul general William Bradley was to persuade some of the destitute enemy alien families in Montreal to relocate to Spirit Lake by providing a settlement opportunity there.[165] The offer of cleared land and cabins, it was thought, could effectively be used to encourage enemy alien families to settle in the Abitibi region. There was a real sense that both Spirit Lake and Kapuskasing would meet the immediate needs of unemployed enemy aliens and the long-term goals of both provinces.

The first contingent of ninety-three enemy alien prisoners of war was sent from Fort Henry to Kapuskasing via Toronto on 10 January 1915 and immediately put to work building barracks for other prisoners who were to follow. By 19 January, Major Clarke, the newly appointed com-mandant of the Kapuskasing camp, informed the officer commanding the divisional district that sleeping quarters for four hundred prisoners and one hundred troops were completed and an additional one hundred prisoners and guards could be taken care of weekly.[166] A total of 438 prisoners – most of whom were Ukrainians, Poles, and Turks – were on site by early March, relieving the overcrowding at Fort Henry. With a sizable workforce in place, it was not long before results were realized. In February, the federal Department of Agriculture received news that seventy-five acres had been cleared and a large amount of valuable tim-ber had been hand cut into logs and pulpwood.[167] Mills in the vicinity were notified that four hundred cords of pulpwood and three thousand logs were available for purchase, with the promise of more to come. In March, Commissioner J.E. Whitson of the Ontario government's northern development branch described the place as "a thriving lumber-ing village" and praised the work being done, noting it was "first-rate" and that the beauty of the place was slowly being revealed as the felling of wood progressed.[168]

On 14 December 1914, a party of prisoners was sent to Parent from Montreal and then immediately transferred to the proposed Spirit Lake site after the decision had been made to locate the camp there. These were soon followed by hundreds of others, and by mid-March 1915 some five hundred prisoners of war were preparing the ground as well as building log cabins. The internees were described "as taking kindly to the country" and warming to the idea that eventually they would be able to own and work their own farms.[169] By early April nearly seven hun-dred prisoners were clearing the land for both the experimental farm and the settlement area. In this regard, the first lot of twenty families from St Michael's Ruthenian Greco-Catholic Church, numbering ninety-two individuals, including women and children, had arrived, accompan-ied by a Ukrainian priest and a Byzantine icon of the Madonna (obtained by the US consul for their log chapel). Promised a cabin and one hun-dred acres of land at the end of the war, the families were to be "nomin-ally" considered prisoners of war until the close of hostilities.[170]

Overseeing the Spirit Lake resettlement effort, the US consul general William Bradley received applications from an additional fifty to one hundred enemy alien families who wished to leave Montreal. It high-lighted the difficult situation in the city. Clothing collected in the United States for Austro-Hungarian enemy aliens was being distributed through the US consular office in the city.[171] US officials also reported that even though road work was being offered to some registered enemy aliens in Montreal, thousands were still without jobs and scores of homeless had taken to living in the fields on the city's outskirts. Accordingly, the abso-lute destitute in the city were being arrested and sent to Spirit Lake as well as Petawawa, bringing the total number at the latter camp to 573 by the end of March.

The successful use of enemy alien labour in making improvements to the military facility at Petawawa suggested to officials that a similar effort might be used with respect to the military training grounds at Valcartier near Quebec City. The first overseas contingent had left Valcartier for Europe and the camp remained vacant. The grounds, however, needed to be enlarged for the training of the next intake of recruits. With barrack-style accommodations in place, the Valcartier military camp became a logical destination for the growing number of enemy alien prisoners in

2.5  Arrivals, Kapuskasing, Ontario


Quebec, especially since the nearby Beauport armoury, a facility where
enemy aliens were being held, proved inadequate in terms of space and
exercise requirements.[172] Enemy alien prisoners from Beauport, as a
result, would now be destined for Valcartier. The officer commanding
Military Division No. 5 was instructed on 29 March to make provision
for two hundred prisoners of war who were to be put to work clearing
bush and trees at the camp as soon as weather permitted.[173]

Petawawa and Valcartier helped relieve the crush of prisoners at a
number of existing internment facilities in Ontario and Quebec. So too
did Kapuskasing and Spirit Lake. But whereas the former were isolated
undertakings that served the interests of the militia – improving and
enlarging the military camps – Kapuskasing and Spirit Lake represented
an innovative means of offsetting some of the costs associated with
internment operations. Partnering with other agencies or provincial governments held the promise of reducing costs.

There was no question that the costs of organizing, administering,
and operating the camps were significant and mounting. Under the
authority of an order-in-council in November 1914, a credit in the
amount of $70,000 was extended to the director of internment oper-
ations and placed in the Bank of Montreal. A further $20,000 was

granted in December. At the same time, the Department of Justice expended $18,282, with $8,900 allocated to the registration of enemy aliens and $2,000 to relieve the distress of enemy aliens. On 22 January 1915 the internment director, General Otter, submitted a request for $100,000, which was amended to $150,000 on 18 February to meet all liabilities and requirements up to 1 March. Of this amount, $143,700 was spoken for: $89,378 for clothing and supplies; $25,764 for payroll, salaries, and camp expenses; $15,459.37 for the relief of families of prisoners of war; $7,049 for subsistence of prisoners before internment; and some $6,049 paid for the escort and transfer of prisoners. On 27 May, a request for an advance of a further $100,000 was approved on evidence that most of the existing funds had been spent and creditors were insisting on immediate payment for balances still outstanding.[174]

The escalating costs resulted in inquiries and criticism. Otter was forced to defend the strength of the guard at certain installations, the increase in administrative staff, and salaries of his senior officers.[175] By all accounts, however, censure of the director was unjustified for, as Otter noted, the duty assigned him "was an entirely new creation, of unknown possibilities, responsibilities or duration." Despite his "natural tendency to limit expense," costs were mounting because the operation was growing in scope and scale. Indeed, with each new camp and with the increasing number of internees, requests were continuously received by the internment directorate to authorize the purchase of camp supplies, clothing, equipment, and a multitude of other items for prisoners and guards alike.

A professional soldier, Otter complied with regulations. For example, he outfitted internees in the winter kit of a lumberman at a cost of roughly $15 to $20 each and soldiers were provided, as well as possible, with appropriate attire supplied through a local tendering process. Following regulations, however, would prove expensive and, given the pressure to limit expenditures, would invariably translate into major shortcomings. Where prisoners had good clothing of their own, no other was provided. Where soldiers had inadequate gear, they would have to make do until funds could be spared. The result was that soldiers were often ill-equipped and inconvenienced. The officer commanding the Kapuskasing internment camp complained, for instance, that the soldiers there were wearing fur caps in sweltering heat.[176]

In regard to assisting the families of those interned, PC 2721 permitted the wives and children of the interned to accompany them into the camps, but this was not always being done, resulting in many families left in want. Otter was tasked with providing subsistence in these cases and did what was necessary to ensure that starvation was averted. But he also looked to provincial agencies to assist, noting that his duty to the government was to administer his department "with all possible economy."[177] Indeed, the cost of relief for the destitute families of the interned was not insignificant, and Otter manoeuvred to reduce the financial burden of their maintenance. He would also not veer into areas that would compromise the operation or bottom line. For instance, when inquiries were made as to whether relief might be granted to desperate enemy aliens outside the camps who came to the attention of the military, these were universally turned away, with officers advised that such assistance was the sole responsibility of provincial relief agencies.[178]

The director of internment operations exercised prudence when it came to disbursements. And although costs could be trimmed, the initial underlying rationale behind internment – providing work for jobless enemy aliens – necessarily meant that a major outlay, wages, could not be easily controlled. Article 6 of the Hague Convention laid down that "work done for the State [was to be] paid for at rates proportional to work of a similar kind executed by soldiers of the national army."[179] Consequently, Otter was careful to ascertain the requirements of various projects, estimating the cost effectiveness of prisoner-of-war labour before such work was authorized. When the internment directorate was approached to approve the building of a promenade and road around the top of Glacis and to repair the Citadel Hill road in Halifax, the projects were rejected due to projected costs; the promenade required an estimated 2,500 days of labour and the Citadel Hill road the equivalent of 380 days. Constituting some 80 percent of the total value of the project, the cost of the prisoner-of-war labour was more than Otter was willing to bear.[180]

On the whole, the international regulation governing wages for prisoner-of-war labour constrained Otter in his ability to rein in expenditures, especially in view of the government's own commitment to provide employment to the interned enemy alien. Some reprieve occurred when the Justice Department decided that working pay for prisoners of war would not be issued until the conclusion of hostilities. They were also to be credited only twenty-five cents per day – the supplemental pay to soldiers for non-military-related work – and debited for the food, clothing, and everything else supplied them.[181] But this was simply delaying the eventual bill. Policy innovation was required if the problem of costs was to be fully addressed. Partnerships such as Kapuskasing and Spirit Lake had clearly shown the way in this regard. Because they benefited directly from the work derived from them, the governments of Quebec and Ontario were informed by the director of internment operations that the day-wage of enemy alien labour at both camps would be borne by the provinces. Although there was some initial resistance, the provinces finally agreed. As a result, wages for prisoner-of-war labour were now no longer the responsibility of the directorate. Partnerships were now seen as a way to reduce one of the largest expenditures – wages.

Partnerships became an early model for negotiations in both the creation of new camps and the use of prisoner-of-war labour. When London tentatively approached the Borden government about the possible internment of prisoners of war who had been captured at sea and were interned at Caribbean ports, the reply from Canada was that they could be accommodated but an expenditure of about four thousand British pounds was needed to erect buildings suitable for winter accommodation.[182] This expense, they argued, would have to be borne by the original interning power. Negotiations took place, and in late December 1914 it was agreed that the colonial governments of Jamaica and Bermuda (where prisoners were being detained) would cover the costs of quartering and maintaining prisoners transferred to Canada.[183] They were to be sent to Amherst, Nova Scotia, where E.N. Rhodes, a member of parliament for the federal riding of Cumberland and future speaker of the house, had lobbied for a proposed internment facility. The site chosen was the Malleable Iron Foundry located on Park Street. Altered at a cost of $12,000, the premises were fitted up to accommodate 650 prisoners. The new facility was ready for occupation by 1 April, and a total of 350 captured merchant marines that had been interned in Jamaica, including a number from the sunken auxiliary cruiser *Kaiser Wilhelm der Grosse*, were immediately transported there. On 17 April an additional three hundred prisoners of war, merchant marines seized in fighting off the Falklands, as well as a number of sailors from the destroyed light cruiser *Dresden*, were received from Bermuda.[184]

In the Canadian west, where the number being interned was overwhelming, the need for more space took on an air of urgency. The hundreds of destitute enemy aliens arrested after their march from Winnipeg to the US border were interned at the Brandon camp. Overcrowding at the facility prompted the suggestion that the Horse Show building in Winnipeg might be used once the 28th Battalion vacated the property. Close proximity to the enemy alien registration office and Osborne barracks (which served as a receiving station) made the pavilion an "ideal" place for an internment camp. That Winnipeg tradesmen would also benefit made the proposition all the more attractive to those campaigning for the proposal.[185] But in the end, the idea was rejected in favour of a more ambitious scheme that was taking shape.

In early February 1915, under considerable pressure from commercial mining interests to build a connecting road through the Monashee Mountains between Lake Okanagan and the Arrow Lakes in the BC interior (but for which a budget appropriation was unavailable), the British Columbia government approached the federal minister of militia, through an intermediary, to ascertain what might be done to support the project.[186] Forwarded to Otter for his consideration, the director replied on 22 March to the Hon. Thomas Taylor, BC minister of public works, that in connection with the proposed construction on the Monashee Mountain–Arrow Lakes Road, two hundred prisoners of war could be made available if the provincial government agreed to certain conditions: pay the prisoners at a rate of twenty-five cents per day per man, supply the requisite tools, and transport the men to the site.[187] Already the established practice at Kapuskasing and Spirit Lake, these precedents suggested to Otter a similar arrangement could be negotiated with the

B C government. Nothing, however, came of the offer, at least not until the Vancouver riot in early April 1915.

The enemy alien riot in Vancouver altered conditions. In the aftermath of the unrest, the provincial government gave assurance to civic authorities that something would be done to address the problem of the enemy alien poor. Since no more prisoners could be accommodated at the existing internment camps in British Columbia, provincial authorities brought a recommendation before the federal minister of justice to create a detention camp for enemy aliens ninety miles east of Vancouver on the main railway line. The plan was that the internees would be placed in tents under military guard and be required to cut and clear timber for their own maintenance. The estimated cost of the proposed camp was under $500.[188] The idea, however, was hastily conceived and naive in terms of both cost and implementation. It would necessarily lead to the reiteration of the idea originally proposed – a camp in the B C interior under the authority of internment operations, the financing of which would be shared.

There could be no equivocation on the issue of a new camp after the 7 May sinking of the *Lusitania*. The social and political circumstances had become increasingly volatile. Colliers on Vancouver Island had gone on strike, protesting the presence of enemy aliens in the mines. The mines in the Nanaimo vicinity were effectively shut down, and the only way to diffuse the labour tension was to intern the enemy aliens. With the prospect of more internees to come and hard-pressed to accommodate those already in hand, officials made the creation of a new camp, on the basis of the original offer made by the director of internment operations, a priority.[189]

On 18 May, after quick agreement between the B C minister of public works and internment officials, arrangements were made by the Public Works Department to receive twenty-five officers and soldiers and one hundred prisoners of war who would be put to work clearing a site for the new Monashee camp. These were to be followed by an even larger group of prisoners. Together they would begin the work of improving the road from Vernon to Richlands and constructing a new road from Richlands over Monashee Mountain to the hamlet of Edgewood located on the Arrow Lakes. At the time, the traverse between the two points was no more than a track that could only be negotiated by horseback, "and [could] not [be] improved without very great expense."[190]

News of the creation of the Monashee camp spurred interest among other communities in acquiring a similar camp so that prisoners might

NO FREE MAN

work on roads in their locale. Applications were forwarded to the attention of the Hon. Thomas Taylor, the B C minister in charge of roads, who, in turn, placed them before authorities in Ottawa. Of particular interest was a request by the citizens of Mara, who petitioned the government for a road between their town and Sicamous, connecting the Eagle Valley district with the outside world and providing settlers in the area with an outlet for their produce and livestock. It was noted in the petition that among the enemy alien internees at the Vernon internment camp a great many were miners by occupation and therefore accustomed to rock work. Taylor was enthusiastic about the idea, admitting that he was "extremely anxious to see this work undertaken as well as the completion of the road from Taft to Clanwilliam, thereby giving a direct road connection between Revelstoke and Vernon and all points in the Okanagan and Similkameen." He recommended that project, as well as a camp to be established in the area, to internment officials.[191]

After only a month of operation, difficulties with supply and access led to a decision by the minister on 28 June (with the agreement of internment operations) to close the Monashee internment camp. It was a regrettable decision but one that had to be taken in view of the unsustainable costs associated with the site. And yet the road was much too valuable to be completely abandoned. So, in addition to closing down the Monashee camp, there was also a corresponding recommendation by the provincial minister for roads, Thomas Taylor, to establish a new camp further down the trail at Edgewood, located on the Arrow Lakes, where it was estimated transportation costs could be reduced by one-third.[192] Once the recommendation was accepted, construction on the interior mountain road would resume mid-August after preparations for the new Edgewood camp were completed and some two hundred prisoners were transferred from Vernon to the site. In the meantime, the two hundred internees at the original Monashee camp were relocated at the end of July to a new camp on the waterfront of Mara Lake, where they were immediately put to work on the Mara-Sicamous road project, which finally had been approved.

The turmoil at Fernie was as instrumental as the unrest in Nanaimo in persuading the acting premier of British Columbia, Attorney General W. Bowser, to order the arrest and internment of the enemy alien miners there. Although the federal government opposed the move, having declared it illegal, Bowser would not relent, insisting that Ottawa deal with these men in a way that was consistent with the Nanaimo precedent.[193] Ottawa capitulated and passed order-in-council P C 1501 of

26 June, which legitimated the initial illegal arrest of enemy aliens at Fernie. The question of where to put them, however, remained.

Initially, Major Duncan Macpherson, the internment directorate's staff officer, thought that perhaps the internees could be taken to the Lethbridge camp. But this was impossible because of the large numbers there. The Vernon camp would also not do for similar reasons. The issue was finally resolved when, at a meeting of the Fernie district conservative association, it was argued that, since 350 to 400 enemy aliens would eventually be interned, the cost of transport of the whole lot to the coast would be excessive, and therefore it made eminent sense to keep them locally.[194] The nearby deserted town of Morrissey, where the Crowsnest Pass Coal Company owned the waterworks as well as a number of commercial and other buildings capable of accommodating over a thousand people, was available. That the internees could be put to work at the local Carbonado mine – abandoned in 1909 because of safety concerns – made the proposal all the more appealing. Internment officials took control of the prisoners, temporarily held at the Fernie skating arena, on 1 July. At the end of September, 164 of the men were sent a few kilometres down the road to Morrissey, where they occupied a three-storey hotel at the centre of a fenced-in compound. It was decided not to use the prisoners at the Carbonado mine but rather to employ them in cutting rock for a road that would connect the settlements of Elko, Fernie, and beyond.

Overcrowding proved challenging not only in British Columbia but also in the other western provinces, where the internment camps were just as full. When the interning officer for British Columbia, Major W. Ridgway-Wilson, manoeuvred to unload responsibility for enemy aliens arrested in the province onto the shoulders of Captain J.A. Birney of the Lethbridge internment camp – claiming the camps in BC could no longer accommodate any more prisoners – he was reprimanded, not simply for his failure to follow chain of command, but also for his presumption. Lethbridge was operating at full capacity and could not accommodate a single prisoner more, let alone others from outside Alberta.[195] The group rounded up in the trek to the US border from Winnipeg had added to the hundreds of destitute enemy aliens already arrested in Port Arthur and Fort William. As their numbers increased exponentially at various existing camps in the west, it became obvious that a new camp was needed.

First proposed by officials within the dominion parks branch shortly after PC 2721 had been introduced, the scheme to establish camps in the national parks was never far from the minds of internment officials, and

Major General Otter in particular. A meeting took place 12 March 1915 at the Banff railway station between the director of internment operations and the dominion parks commissioner, J.B. Harkin. There the two briefly discussed the possibility of creating camps in the national parks on a cost-sharing basis.[196] Otter wanted an arrangement like the one concluded earlier with the Ontario and Quebec governments. For Harkin, on the other hand, a zealot when it came to the issue of park development, the offer of internment labour was an opportunity. Financial austerity measures introduced as a result of the war had reduced the normal appropriation for park work by half. Internment labour, a fraction of the cost of day labour, could be used to make up for the shortfall.

Harkin consulted ranking representatives from Alberta in the Borden government about the idea of creating an internment camp in the Rocky Mountains National Park (later renamed Banff National Park). Both Senator Sir James Lougheed and R.B. Bennett, the local Calgary member of parliament, supported a program of utilizing enemy alien labour at the Banff Park in principle, but with the proviso in Bennett's case that the prisoners would work at a distance from the local population and not be coddled or indulged in any way. With their endorsement and aid, Harkin received approval of the plan from the minister of interior, the Hon. W.J. Roche, who stated that it was his preference to put the internees to work rather than "allowing them to eat their heads off."[197] Harkin instructed his supervising engineer, James Wardle, to provide information on possible projects that would enhance access to the park as well as its appeal, eventually deciding that work on the unfinished coach road from Banff to Laggan (Lake Louise) would be the most desirable. The road would facilitate public access and promote tourist interest in the natural wonder that was Lake Louise. As Harkin would later write: "It was felt that it was not good for the prisoners to live for months in a state of idleness; that it would be advantageous for them to have work to do and that, having to maintain them in any case, it would be good business for the Government to secure with such labour the construction of roads and other public works in the park."[198]

On 31 May, Otter informed the officer commanding Military District No. 13, Colonel E.A. Cruickshank, of his plan to transfer enemy alien prisoners of Austro-Hungarian nationality from the Lethbridge camp to the Banff park (leaving Germans and "other dangerous prisoners" behind) and to prepare for the new camp with troops and provisions supplied from Lethbridge. The order for Lethbridge guards would change in favour of a detail from the 103rd Regiment Calgary Rifles because most of the troops of the 25th Battery at Lethbridge were married. The new guard was to be supplemented with unmarried local enlisted men from Banff, specifically selected for the work by the Rocky Mountain park superintendent S.J. Clarke. Those not chosen, Clarke felt, would be "desperately disappointed," since many of them had been out of work for some time. Work at the new camp was the "only thing in sight," and he requested that those not selected might be taken on strength when the camp, or other camps, were in full swing, which, he understood, was the wish of the authorities.[199]

On 14 June, Colonel Cruikshank announced that a camp would be established at the foot of Castle Mountain, a terminal point on the unfinished Banff-Laggan road. Orders for supplies for fifty-three troops and two hundred prisoners, were placed on 17 June for immediate delivery. There was a delay however, when it was discovered the site proved uninhabitable. A new site was chosen a short distance away, and on 8 July a supply of barbed wire and staples for the prison enclosure was received. Once the prison compound was set up, the order went out for the enemy alien prisoners of war to be escorted to the place of their internment. On 14 July, with fresh snow on the ground (unusual for that time of year, even in the mountains), sixty prisoners arrived. A second contingent of equal size was carried to Castle by train 16 July. On the morning of 17 July the group was put to work cutting the coach road. An additional seventy-one prisoners of war arrived on the nineteenth, making 191 in total, all of whom were immediately gang-pressed into working on the right-of-way.[200]

Seeing this as a windfall, the ever-ambitious Harkin felt that internment labour could be utilized in other parts of the national park system. The newly created Revelstoke National Park was such a place.[201] A road to the summit of Mount Revelstoke, championed by local business interests, held out the promise of tourism and increased traffic to the area. R.F. Green, the area member of parliament, lobbied in Ottawa on behalf of the project, hoping to secure prisoners of war to work on the road. With the encouragement of Green, Harkin set about the process of identifying a location for an internment camp and in the company of deputy minister of the interior, W. Cory, selected a site. Shortly thereafter, Harkin wired Otter, requesting that the location be inspected for approval.

The director of internment operations, General Otter, was not opposed to the idea of an additional camp. The facility at Brandon was nearly full to capacity. Otter was also inclined to separate Austro-Hungarian prisoners – Ukrainians, Poles, Croats, and others of a labouring class – from German inmates at Vernon. Authorization, consequently, was granted to commence construction at Revelstoke on log buildings, which offered greater protection to the prisoners from the inclement weather on the mountain but which also could be built inexpensively.

During construction, Otter visited the camp and, having inspected the site, expressed his disappointment with what he found. The camp was badly situated and the space appeared to be too confining. The director nevertheless gave his approval to proceed with the opening of the facility, and the first group of fifty prisoners, followed by 150 others from Brandon, arrived 6 September 1915. They were immediately put to work on clearing and grubbing the land for the road right-of-way. Otter's criticism of the camp, however, was a portent of the problems to come. In little more than a month after it was established, inadequate water supply and disciplinary issues forced a decision to close the camp.

In their sojourn through the mountains in August, commissioner Harkin and deputy minister Cory had not only staked out a location for the Revelstoke camp but had considered other projects as well. Visiting Jasper National Park, they concluded that a road extension from the Maligne River to Medicine Lake would be invaluable to the park's development. With the prospect of using even more of the prisoner-of-war labour offered by Otter, Harkin suggested that some three hundred enemy aliens could be interned at Jasper. The idea had merit and was supported, but the difficulties encountered at Revelstoke demanded that all the attention and energy of the internment directorate be focused on resolving the problems there, thus delaying the establishment of a camp in Jasper Park until early 1916.[202]

As for Revelstoke, closure meant that a new place for the prisoners had to be found in quick order. Earlier on, Harkin had instructed his superintendent at Yoho National Park to identify possible projects on which prisoner-of-war labour could be put to use. E.N. Russell, the superintendent there, suggested enemy alien prisoners could be used to cut down a large stand of burned timber in the park at the junction of the Ottertail and Kicking Horse rivers, near the village of Field, BC. This proposal was of interest to internment officials because the sale of cut timber from the site had the potential of generating revenue. With winter closing in on the Revelstoke camp and with its close proximity to Yoho, two small groups of twenty-five internees each were escorted at the end of October from Revelstoke to the new site, where they hurriedly constructed the stockade and barracks to accommodate the

150 remaining prisoners who would follow in December. Here in the snowy reaches of BC's mountain interior, the internees were promptly put to work.[203]

Despite the initial missteps and the seemingly makeshift approach, by December 1915 a system of internment camps was in place across the country. The growing number of interned enemy aliens could be easily and readily accommodated. More importantly, the new camps were located and organized in regions of the country where the labour of the internees could be utilized in such a way as to reduce the cost of their maintenance. That valuable work might also be completed was a bonus. There were, of course, those who were skeptical about the use of internment labour, whether from a practical or ethical point of view. Others, on the other hand, were less than circumspect in their opinion as to how the interned enemy alien was to be treated. This followed from the understanding and belief that these were in fact prisoners of war. Indeed, on learning that a prisoner-of-war camp would be created in Banff Park, the *Crag and Canyon*, the local Banff paper, announced "alien enemies were coming here" and, although unsure of the enterprise, expressed "the pious hope that the authorities will make them work good and hard, with long hours, and guard them well."[204] It was a natural reaction, for how else would prisoners of war be treated?

### NO APPARENT REASON

Want was rampant throughout the country during the winter of 1914–15, as was apprehension and fear among the working class. Those who had jobs were anxious to maintain them and those without were desperate to secure one. Public officials were not impervious to the news of the suffering and plight of the unemployed. Municipal authorities, affected most immediately by the problem, sought to alleviate as much as possible the quandary of joblessness and homelessness. In a number of major urban centres, employment was provided in the form of short-term, make-work projects. A registry of unemployed, for example, was introduced in Saskatoon to identify, on the basis of length of residency and need, those who would be given a small allowance in exchange for breaking stones in the city's materials yard.[205] In Vancouver, it was thought that the relief fund for teachers might be better put to use in paying the destitute to clear city parks and thereby "saving the self-respect" of a wider number in need.[206] Charities were also supported in their relief efforts through the municipal rolls. In the end, however, the solution to the unemployment problem could only be resolved through a combination of provincial and national initiatives.

Those in greatest need were enemy aliens. Cast in the role of enemy subjects of a country at war with the empire, they became easy and frequent prey of suspicion and loathing. Society believed that the difficult circumstances facing the native-born should be given higher priority. Hiring practices were closely scrutinized with a view to assuring that only the deserving would be given jobs while employed aliens of enemy nationality were dismissed in favour of British and Allied subjects. This had serious implications for the federal government, which could not be seen to be in a position that contradicted the majority view that German and Austro-Hungarian subjects were to be treated as foes. Pressured to do something about the homeless and hungry enemy alien population, officials turned to a policy of internment.

PC 2721, which provided for the internment of destitute enemy aliens, embodied the government's attempt to solve the dilemma of helping the enemy alien while simultaneously not being seen as assisting them, certainly not at the expense of the native-born during this critical time. Some aspects of the ordinance – Clause 9 of the order-in-council, for example, which allowed family members to accompany their menfolk into internment – pointed to the government's ambition to alleviate their suffering and mirrored a wider concern about the precarious position of the children and spouses of internees. In this regard Internment Operations was specifically tasked with providing relief assistance in those cases where the need was greatest. As for those enemy aliens whose predicament attracted the personal attention of authorities, they too would be grateful for the consideration and leniency shown. None other than the prime minister granted Stephen Schwartz a reprieve. Schwartz was an engineer brought to Canada but dismissed from work because of his enemy alien status. In short, there was a sense among officials that, where possible, an effort had to be made to lessen the heavy burden experienced by enemy aliens.

This policy was demonstrated in the effort to have destitute enemy alien families in Montreal relocate to Spirit Lake, where, provided with a modest log cabin, they could eventually occupy one hundred acres of cleared land. It was a magnanimous gesture that also revealed the gravity of the crisis and the predicament faced by enemy aliens. That the government understood the level of despair facing the enemy alien was revealed in its willingness to contravene the standing policy (and imperial lead) on enemy subjects departing the country. In the aftermath of the

2.6 Women and children prisoners, Spirit Lake, Quebec

Vancouver riot, the government allowed the city's enemy aliens to leave for the United States in search of work. The initiative was a major policy reversal that showed the government's willingness to concede on even the most basic principles. Also prompting them to act was the fear that the situation in the lower BC mainland could escalate, resulting in unrest that would have been harder to control.

The federal government understood the effect of possible social unrest when it retroactively introduced order-in-council PC 1501, which legit-imated the initial illegal arrest and internment of enemy alien miners at Fernie. As long as they were employed, the enemy alien miners gave no grounds for arrest. Indeed, they provided no evidence of any wrong-doing or hostile intent. Rather, as was noted in several reports on the situation at Fernie and elsewhere in the mining districts of British Columbia, Alberta, Ontario, and Nova Scotia, the source of the trouble was the attitude and behaviour of native-born miners who agitated and orchestrated a campaign for the dismissal of enemy aliens from their workplace. The situation threatened to tear at the delicate balance of social order and jeopardize war work. This was to be avoided at all costs. From the government's perspective, workers were not to be dis-tracted from the war effort or their work and were to be dissuaded from

participating in actions that would threaten either. Indeed, when the passenger ship *Lusitania* was sunk and riots broke out, the government,
after much hesitation and misgiving, felt compelled to consider internment to prevent further disturbances and disruption.

By sanctioning the provincial mass round-up of enemy aliens at
Nanaimo and Fernie, federal officials demonstrated they were prepared
to sacrifice a part of society so that order might be maintained. It became
a guiding principle. When unemployed enemy aliens learned that some
three thousand jobs would be available in The Pas, six hundred of them
gravitated to the northern Manitoba town in the hope of securing
work.[207] It was a false report, however. After they had been turned away
in a desperate state, it was feared that they would migrate south to
Winnipeg, where thousands of their unemployed kindred had already
concentrated. As a result, some 350 of the group, who were living daily
on a single loaf of bread provided by the local RNWMP, were arrested
and interned. In the end, the government could ill afford to have them
add to the existing tension in Winnipeg. The public there was already
anxious and restless because of foreigners marching in the streets with
banners declaring, "We are not enemies of the country."

The fact of the matter, however, was that they were "enemies" of the
country, although not in the conventional sense of the term. The threat
they posed was existential in nature. The rumours and reports of sabotage and espionage that continued unabated from the outset of the war
were routinely shown to be false. Whether it was the report of the cement
manufacturer of German origin on Île d'Orléans allegedly conspiring
with German Americans in a planned invasion of Canada or the claim
that the fortress-like Strathcona Brewing Co. building commanding the
heights overlooking Edmonton was occupied by Germans, these were all
dismissed as being without foundation.[208] Enemy aliens *were* a threat,
however, because of who they were and what they represented.

When Mike Kulik appeared before a police magistrate in Nelson, BC,
he was destitute and homeless. Described as an "encumbrance" and
therefore "a menace to the community," Kulik – sullen, surly, and som-
nolent – represented all that was despised in the foreigner. Kulik was not
alone. There were many others like him, including Iwan Milan, whose
arrest report contained the damning remark that he had nothing save for
the clothes he wore.[209] For men like Milan and Kulik, there was no
promise and no future. They were, in effect, a disappointment if not a
disgrace – a sentiment perhaps best captured by Judge Emerson
Coatsworth, registrar of alien enemies in Toronto, when he passed

judgment over two indigent aliens of enemy origin brought before him. Contributing nothing and deserving of even less, they were, in his view, "a stain on the national honour" that had to be removed. It was an opinion that resonated in Winnipeg, where marching unemployed enemy aliens were denounced by onlookers who insisted they return to their homelands. The problem, of course, was that even if they wished to do so, they could not. Prevented from leaving, enemy aliens were, in the words of Sir Thomas Shaughnessy and Sir Hugh Macdonald, "virtual prisoners" of the country.

Some, of course, hoped to avoid being labelled an enemy alien by attempting to acquire naturalization. Others looked to enlist in the military in order to obtain relief from the hardship and reproach of being an "enemy." Many would not succeed, blocked by those who would deny them an escape. The naturalization process was made more stringent, while those who were incensed by the prospect of enemy aliens acquiring citizenship during a time of war challenged the practice of naturalization in the courts. As for those who volunteered and went overseas with the Canadian contingent, they not only risked being discovered and discharged as suspected enemy aliens, but also faced internment as potential saboteurs. The fate of W.R. Wagner, mentioned earlier, was one of those cases.

The enemy alien could run but not hide, and even those who had nothing to conceal would have much to fear. Therkild Therkildsen had enlisted in the Canadian Army under the name Thomas Ford.[210] He chose the name to help ease his way into Canadian society while avoiding the stigma of being identified as a foreigner.[211] Because of his military experience in the Danish Imperial Life Guards, Ford was given the rank of a non-commissioned officer. On the Salisbury Plains of England, Sergeant Ford was inexplicably arrested without charge. Put into civilian clothes, he along with a dozen other discharged soldiers of alleged enemy nationality were paraded under military escort through the streets of Liverpool to a waiting ship, where the local population denounced them as spies and encouraged the escort to kill them. On Canadian soil, Ford was interned at the Citadel in Halifax, where he would spend the next four months in a cell on a floor mattress before General Otter authorized his release.

After the Danish consul had interceded on his behalf, it was learned that Ford had been interned because he had admitted to his commanding officer that he could read German, which he had been taught in school along with English and French in his native Denmark. Knowing how to read German was suspicion enough, overriding any other consideration. German or Danish mattered not to those who stood in judgment. Therkildsen had hoped to blend into the fabric of the nation by changing his name and serving his adopted country. In the end, he could not escape mistrust and doubt, despite the fact that he was not an enemy alien and had nothing to hide.

It was against this backdrop of fear, resentment, and distrust that the government, in dealing with the issue of want among alien enemies, was forced to modify its actions and policies so as not to add to the uneasiness of an already unsettled public. Only within this context can the complicated and seemingly contradictory nature of PC 2721 be understood. Authorized under the War Measures Act, PC 2721 was no ordinary executive order. Although aspects of the ordinance aimed to alleviate the suffering of enemy aliens and their families (and were interpreted as such), it also outlined the conditions that pertained to the unemployed enemy alien and underscored their status as enemy subjects.

The introduction of PC 2721 was a watershed event. It established a system of enemy alien registration, declared destitute enemy aliens could be interned as prisoners of war, and resolved that, as prisoners of war, they could be put to work. A central aspect of the order-in-council was the creation of a system of registration. Registration would help monitor the status of enemy aliens, while the centres – placed in areas where enemy aliens were concentrated and therefore, disturbances, it was felt, would be most likely to occur – ensured that there was some means of control. Internment, if necessary, would apply to those who, in the judgment of registrars and others, constituted a threat. Indeed, failure to report to authorities was an important consideration in the rationale to intern, highlighting the supervisory aspect of registration. The enemy alien problem needed to be managed, and registration provided the means.

Registration arose from a concern about the enemy alien within the larger context of public anxiety and resentment and as such underlined the decision by government to craft a policy that would address and allay the public's unease. It was a momentous decision because it forced the government to reach for the solution of internment and gave credence to the idea that a civilian enemy alien could be interned as a prisoner of war. The implications were profound. Organizationally, it led to the expansion of internment facilities across the country. But perhaps most importantly, as prisoners of war, enemy aliens would be subject to the laws of war that governed captured military combatants. That the government would treat civilian enemy aliens as captured combatants was made evident in PC 2721, in which the government declared that the internees could be made to work. The Hague Convention made legal the use of prisoner-of-war labour, which necessarily led to the understanding that the internees would be treated as nothing other than prisoners of war.

Within this climate of anxiety, doubt, and hostility, it fell upon the government to instruct those responsible for dealing with the enemy alien that they be given the necessary powers to carry out the functions of surveillance and control. Since the status of the enemy alien (whether unemployed or not) was paramount, it necessarily followed that discretionary power would be granted to interning authorities. This power was already available under the initial 15 August proclamation, but now it was tied to registration. Those who would report to authorities within the framework of PC 2721 could be assessed while those who did not report, largely because they were without work, would be immediately interned. Internment, however, was predicated on the ability of registrars and others to make an assessment. This required considerable latitude and would result in arrests and internment largely based on personal judgment and discretion. Registrars and others were charged to establish the facts, but the point of the exercise was also to assess the level of threat and to maintain control. The instructions and objectives, therefore, worked at cross-purposes. Combined with the discretionary power awarded to interning officials, it was not surprising that the process would be abused and exploited.

Countless numbers of enemy aliens were arrested and interned for no apparent reason other than the trouble they might pose. Both Nikola Bodnar and M. Besenthal, for example, fell victim to the worst fears of those who would decide their fate, demonstrating the serendipitous nature of the process of arrest and internment. But these and other cases could also reveal the glibness and mean-spiritedness of those in authority.

Among such cases was that brought forward by the Imperial Russian Consul, S. de Likhatcheff, who wrote to Sir Joseph Pope, the undersecretary of state for external affairs, that eighteen Poles, all Russian subjects, had been illegally arrested and detained in Toronto. The problem was that the court interpreter, J. Goodman, acting for the crown, identified them as Germans and Austrians. Goodman, whose family had migrated to Scotland from Russia when he was a child, claimed to know both Russian and Polish, yet, according to Likhatcheff, he "neither understood what these people told him nor did he make himself intelligible to them." Despite his limited skills, Goodman apparently had been hired because of government policy that gave preferential treatment to British subjects when it came to jobs in the public service. The detained Russian immigrants were released after they had produced their passports and the consul intervened. But Likhatcheff was not impressed. He alerted Pope to the obvious: for the accused men to be heard, they needed be understood. In the future, in a matter that carried such personal consequence, the government had to ensure that those in its employ possessed the requisite language skills – otherwise "a braying ass would do just as well in the position." As he would later put it more delicately and simply: "Much depends in dealing with the problem of immigrants on having a good interpreter."[212] Then there was the case of Thomas Koch who was arrested for "acting in an ugly and suspicious manner." The RNWMP superintendent of the Regina district recommended that Koch be interned, since a neighbour would be able to look after his farm, and stated: "I do not see that he would be put to any trouble, while he might give us trouble."[213] Koch would spend more than a year in a prison camp on the basis of suspicion and, more significantly, because it was thought that he would not be too terribly inconvenienced.

As for Mike Bundziock of Cobalt, Ontario, he appealed his internment, claiming his only transgression was that he had innocently remarked that the Italians would not be able to stand up to the Austrians in the Alps.[214] The comment apparently gave Constable William Church reason to vent his fury, calling Bundziock a "Damned Pollack," while repeatedly kicking and punching him about the head during his arrest. Bundziock appeared before the local magistrate with blackened eyes and, not knowing the English language, "did not understand much of what was said," let alone why he was being persecuted by the constable who had beaten him twice before without cause. He unsuccessfully appealed his internment. Meanwhile, Partenio Giovanbattista of Fernie, BC, was suspected of entertaining and cavorting with the town's womenfolk.[215] Incensed by the idea that a foreigner was defiling the honour of British women, Constable Harry Hughes forcibly entered Giovanbattista's home, accused him of being a German, and threatened the man with six years' imprisonment. When Giovanbattista showed him his Italian passport, the constable declared the document to be of no value, tore it up, and proceeded to beat him with his truncheon. Under arrest as an enemy alien, Giovanbattista was brought before a police magistrate, where as an Allied national he would avoid internment but not before being charged and fined for "disturbing the peace." The Italian consul, on learning of the incident, was so infuriated that he insisted the chief of the dominion police investigate since he planned to take the matter up with the Italian ambassador in London.

The latitude given to officials ensured there would be abuses. The unfettered power given to such individuals, enabling them to stand in judgment, violated some basic principles of justice and natural law. Indeed, for the sake of administrative convenience, they were vested with discretionary powers that allowed them to dispense with the principle of legal compliance. It was not the role of the police and militia to determine whether people were guilty or innocent of crimes, or to punish those who broke the law. Rather the power of arrest was given for the purpose of properly administering justice. Yet, the powers awarded were frequently used to supplant the law and to execute justice unilaterally. Whether knowingly or unwittingly, in either case, the untrammelled powers being exercised reinforced the need for police and other officers to be governed by the rule of law; for it was only in this manner that their conduct could be regulated.

The importance of these basic notions of justice was not lost on Fred Henion.[216] An American citizen who had settled in the Ontario town of Atikokan northeast of Fort Frances, Henion was arrested for allegedly having expressed anti-British sentiments. The complaints made against him were accompanied by a demand that he be interned as an enemy alien. Henion, an active community member, was released only after he was able to convince military officials in Winnipeg that he was in fact an American and had made no such statements. Henion, however, hoped to gain satisfaction by launching legal action against the officer commanding the 98th Regiment at Fort Frances, Lieutenant Colonel D.C. McKenzie, who had orchestrated his arrest and detention. It was discovered, during the investigation, that Henion and his wife, who were teetotallers, had organized a petition to block the renewal of the local hotel's liquor licence, a business in which McKenzie had an interest. The colonel, it would appear, had hoped to eliminate the threat to his business by initialling Henion's arrest and detention.

Under investigation, no evidence of wrongdoing could be attributed to McKenzie, and he was acquitted. Meanwhile the action was defended by no less than the deputy minister of justice, E. Newcombe, who argued, "It is regrettable that Mr. Henion should have been arrested, but in these times of war and of public danger the officers charged with the duty of protecting the general safety do well to neglect no reasonable precaution." Avoiding altogether the issue of the intentions of the senior commander, Newcombe blithely added, "I am satisfied that he acted upon his view of duty and not from any improper motive." The decision to delegate unlimited powers to the police, militia, and others made abuses such as that experienced by Fred Henion inevitable. These incidents were all too common and would persist throughout much of the war.

After PC 2721 was introduced, the arrest of the destitute and others resulted in a sharp increase in the numbers being detained. Several hundred were interned prior to the ordinance, but by the end of February 1915, the number had increased almost fourfold, with 2,294 enemy aliens behind barbed wire and an additional 36,620 reporting in the major cities. By the end of June 1915, the number of internees had nearly doubled, totalling some 5,088.

The growth in numbers spawned a series of new internment camps. A key motivating factor in this increase was the pressure to rein in the costs of the operation. Initially, an annual allocation of $100,000 was approved, quickly supplemented by an additional $250,000. But the expenses were mounting and the director of internment operations, General William Otter, soon looked to offset some of the costs by partnering with provincial governments and other agencies. Partners were chosen on the basis of a cost-sharing arrangement and the proviso that work be found for the internees. As prisoners of war they would be compensated for their labour, which was of importance to Ottawa, satisfying as it did the official desire that some sort of "employment" be given the destitute enemy aliens. But this also meant that the camps for the interned would be created with the needs of the partners in mind, for there was every expectation that they would benefit from the labour of the prisoners and a return would accrue from their investment. The result was that camps were created according to economic criteria, which determined ultimately where the camps would be located and what projects would be selected.

With an eye to developing the north, the Ontario and Quebec governments saw the possibility of using internee labour on experimental farms that would help promote colonization in these remote areas. It was an innovative scheme that could be made to work if there was adequate planning and oversight. Much the same could be said of the proposal to use prisoner-of-war labour for the construction of difficult roads in the BC interior and the national parks. In the climate of austerity and with limited budgets for non-essential public work, the availability of a large pool of inexpensive prisoner labour proved to be an opportunity that was hard to pass up. That it also addressed the problem of the jobless enemy alien was simply a plus.

It was not long after the decision to form partnerships that the infrastructure for a system of internment began to take shape. The original internment facilities – Fort Henry, the Citadel, Montreal, Vernon, Brandon, and Lethbridge – were supplemented by camps at the Petawawa and Valcartier military training grounds as well as a host of receiving stations across the country. There was also the newly created Amherst internment camp that served primarily as a place of detention for naval merchant marines caught on the high seas and transferred to Canada. All of these would operate throughout the war in varying capacities but mostly as holding and transfer stations. What was really novel, however, was the series of camps established in the Canadian hinterland – in Kapuskasing, Spirit Lake, Castle Mountain, Edgewood, Mara Lake, Revelstoke, Jasper, Morrissey, and others. Far from view, these camps would have enormous implications for the interned enemy alien. Indeed, sent into the vast expanse of the Canadian wilderness, the enemy alien would labour under military guard with few witnesses and even fewer who cared about what was taking place. It was an extraordinary situation that would become even more incredible as the process and practice of internment began to unfold.

# CHAPTER THREE

# Behind Canadian Barbed Wire:
# The Policy, Process,
# and Practice of Internment

## POLICY, PARAMETERS, AND CONSTRAINTS

John Kondro, a suspected enemy alien, was brought before a police magistrate. Since the young man had no registration papers and no evidence of gainful employment, the justice determined that Kondro should not be allowed to roam free. He ordered him interned. Jacob Kondro, John's father, working away from home as an itinerant labourer, learned about his son's internment and, writing in February 1916 to Brigadier General Edward Cruickshank, pleaded with the district commanding officer for the boy's release. The elder Kondro pointed out that he was a naturalized Canadian and, as such, found it inconceivable that "Canada would take their own people and put them in an internment camp." He ended his appeal with the plea: "Please let him go."[1]

Captain Peter Spence, the commander of the Banff/Castle Mountain internment camp, headed an inquiry regarding the conduct of the lad. Spence noted that, on the whole, Kondro was well behaved and by all accounts a good worker. He added, however, that since the boy was but seventeen years old (and therefore under age) and his father naturalized, it meant the young Kondro was a British subject.[2] That a British subject was behind Canadian barbed wire did not appear to carry much weight with the operation's staff in Ottawa. Kondro's file remained dormant. At the end of his tether and sensing no reprieve from his situation, John Kondro, while working on a bridge gang near the Spray River, made a dash for the bush with four other associates. Hoping the bullets from the guard would not find their mark, he succeeded in escaping his captors.[3]

The Kondro case was important on a number of levels. It demonstrated the arbitrariness of arrest and internment and, more generally, the extent of the desperation among those who desired to be free. Since internment was a military operation and the consequences associated with escape potentially fatal, it was a telling sign that Kondro and the others chose to flee. It gave evidence that the conditions, on balance, were intolerable. But on another level, and perhaps more importantly, when Jacob Kondro, the father, conveyed his disbelief and astonishment at Canada's actions, he gave expression to his feelings of disillusionment and betrayal. Kondro had accepted Canada as his adopted country. His expectation, reasonable by any standard, was that Canada would reciprocate by respecting his rights and, by extension, those of his family. Anything less would have been a betrayal of the trust he had placed in the country.

Brothers John and Philip Marchuk were arrested and interned for crossing the international boundary in search of work. John Marchuk pleaded for clemency for his brother and himself.[4] He claimed not to have known that crossing the border was prohibited. He also stated that the arresting officer, RNWMP Constable M. Waston, had taken $300 worth of collateral in order to guarantee their security, but having received the property, he placed them under arrest. Waston was tried and convicted of extortion. Marchuk felt this offered sufficient cause for their release. But more to the point, John Marchuk thought there was an initial mistake in the brothers being sent to an internment camp. Internment, as he understood it, was for those who were hostile to the country or who had committed treachery. He insisted they were not traitors nor did they contemplate doing anything that would harm their adopted homeland. Marchuk's petition failed to impress. It was rejected, as was the request for the return of the extorted collateral.[5] A number of other appeals were also dismissed, and the brothers Marchuk remained interned until 1917.[6]

The brothers' misfortune was accentuated by bewilderment. Why did they deserve internment? From Marchuk's perspective, they had done nothing to warrant punishment that was more appropriately applied to individuals who had committed treason. They were loyal and it was expected that they would be given the benefit of doubt. In this regard, the brothers shared with the elder Kondro the same sense of shock and incredulity. There must have been some mistake. What Jacob Kondro and John Marchuk failed to understand, however, was that internment was not about loyalty or disloyalty. Rather, it was about the existential threat that the enemy alien posed. Internment was a policy used to address the core problems of enemy alien unemployment and destitution, as well as the anxiety and resentment of the broader population.

Those who were caught in the net would be subject to internment
from which there was little possibility of escape. This was because
internment was being driven by external factors. Even for those, like
John Kondro, who were naturalized, it would prove extremely difficult
to extricate themselves from detention. Release would depend not only
on the particulars of the case – whether the prisoner was well behaved
– but also on the employment situation and the tenor of public opinion
in the country. As a result, there was a bias against discharging anyone,
except under extenuating circumstances and only if some employer provided a guarantee of work. This would profoundly affect the lives of
individual prisoners.

Joseph Leskiw, a prisoner of war at the Banff/Castle internment camp,
wrote to newly promoted Brigadier General E. Cruickshank, the officer
commanding the Alberta military district, pleading for his release. He
claimed that he was a naturalized citizen of Canada. His papers, obtained
by writing to the courts for a copy, lay on the desk of the camp commandant. These, Leskiw stated, were ignored – the commander of the
camp insisting that, in addition to his naturalization papers, he was
required to produce an offer of work from a prospective employer. He
begged the general: "Do not forget of me [sic]."[7] When Mary Mikela, the
spouse of Brandon prisoner of war no. 879 Zoka Mikela, wrote to the
RNWMP requesting the release of her husband on humanitarian grounds,
Laurence Fortescue, the RNWMP comptroller, inquired of General Otter
whether this might be approved. The family, it was noted, was not coping well with Mikela's absence of over a year. Otter replied that there
was nothing to be gained from his release. The director rhetorically
posed the question, since Mikela was destitute when arrested, "if
released now what has he to do? And is it not likely that he will soon be
on our hands again?" Otter indicated that he would consider release,
but only on condition that "some responsible party" guaranteed the
prisoner work.[8]

That internment was unrelated to loyalty was demonstrated more
generally by a policy, originating in London, which distinguished
between so-called "friendly" and "enemy" aliens.[9] It was felt that the
Allied war effort would benefit militarily from making a distinction
between the various nationalities of the Austro-Hungarian and Turkish
empires, many of which were restive and opposed to imperial rule.
Individuals of a minority status, whose opposition to Austria-Hungary
or Turkey could be cultivated, were to be given the benefit of the doubt
and treated charitably. Consequently, the category of "friendly alien"

came into being. Whether resistance to imperial rule would occur was unknown, but at least there was the possibility of a revolt, and the minority populations needed to be convinced that their interests lay with the Allied cause.

In principle, the idea of attracting "friendly" national minorities to the cause was accepted by Canadian authorities. Initially, there was some confusion as to which nationalities should be considered "friendly," but clarification from London helped to identify these groups. In Austria-Hungary, these included the Czechs, Croats, Italians (from Trieste and the Trentino), Poles, Romanians, Serbs, Slovaks, Slovenes, Ukrainians, and in the Turkish Empire, the Armenians, Greeks, Macedonians, and Christian or Chaldean Syrians.[10] National committees in the United States – the Bohemian National Alliance and Relief Committee, Polish Relief Committee, and National Croatian Society – immediately seized upon the opportunity to make representations and/or send representatives who could vouchsafe for their ethnic kindred in the Canadian camps.[11] However, in the case of Ukrainians – comprising the majority of those interned – a great many remained prisoners, notwithstanding their status as "friendly" aliens.

Lack of political influence was in part the reason for the Ukrainians' continuing predicament. But for a community deeply affected by the economic crisis, and whose members were disproportionately represented among the unemployed in the country and in the camps, there could be no avenue for release. This was also the case with ethnic Poles in Canada, whose continuing internment and status as "enemy" aliens prompted Polish organizations in the US to protest what was described as both a "painful affair" and a "misunderstanding."[12] The representations, which aimed broadly for a change in the enemy alien status of ethnic Poles, did not appear to impress authorities and were generally ignored. The issue was not whether Poles or Ukrainians collectively were "friendly" or "enemy." Rather, they represented a threat as unemployed foreigners and, as such, would bear the stigma of societal rejection and the burden of continuing internment until the conditions in the country improved.[13]

Work became a metaphor for anything that had to do with the interned enemy aliens and the filter through which decisions were being made. Lack of employment opportunities in the country meant that interned enemy aliens would not be easily or readily released. The political commitment to provide relief to enemy aliens, as was originally intended by Prime Minister Borden, meant that the experience of internment would be fundamentally tied to the question of enemy aliens working. But because they were without work and destitute at the time of arrest, attitudes toward the interned enemy alien were being shaped in a very specific way. Indeed, being unemployed at the time of arrest meant that interned enemy aliens should and would accept whatever work was given them.

Various parties were persuaded that this type of labour was an opportunity. It was presumed that prisoner-of-war labour, by its very nature, was relatively inexpensive and compliant. Furthermore, it was thought, because of their status as prisoners of war, they could be made to obey and forced to work. Indeed, by compelling them to work, the relative cost of the labour could be reduced. All that was required was discipline and resolve in ensuring that the enemy alien as prisoner of war would not only work, but also work hard. This would have bearing on the attitude toward interned enemy aliens as prisoners of war and the type of work they would be expected to perform.

Much of this was made possible because of order-in-council 2721. Clause 10 of PC 2721 was explicit in its charge that the Canadian militia would oversee the maintenance of enemy aliens "as prisoners of war" and that they would perform work as required. This suggested that the work would be quasi-compulsory. Those interned would be put to work, a requirement that derived most immediately from their status as military prisoners of war. Laws governing land war, stemming from the Hague Convention, had sanctioned the use of the labour of military prisoners, primarily for their own upkeep, but also as long as it was unrelated to the war effort.[14] This was an attempt to regulate the behaviour of belligerents during conflict. In the process, however, it provided the legitimacy needed for prisoner-of-war labour to be used. Canadian officials who, faced with the challenge of providing some sort of relief to the unemployed enemy alien, seized upon the possibility of using the measure as a means to address the problem. Indeed, as was the case in The Pas, the labour situation was fairly chaotic throughout the country and enemy aliens seeking employment were often left without options.[15] Internment introduced some order and discipline into what was a muddled and precarious state of affairs. Its success depended, however, on the idea that the interned civilian enemy alien was in fact a military prisoner of war.

Being a prisoner of war had serious implications. Internment, after all, was a military operation. As such, it was a highly regulated regime, and those interned would be subject to a variety of military strictures and

3.1 Internees in enclosure, Monashee, BC

conditions.[16] This had to do with the rules governing the treatment of prisoners of war. These were applied so that security and order might be maintained, not only for the benefit of the military guard but for the prisoners as well. In this regard, regulations prevented prisoners from being exploited, tormented, or abused. It also introduced an element of respect into the relationship between captor and prisoner. Guards were obligated to follow the international covenant governing the treatment of prisoners, and prisoners were equally obliged to abide by the ordinances governing their conduct. Only in this way could calm and stability be attained, a condition that benefited both parties. The failure of any prisoner to follow the rules carried with it severe consequences. This included corporal punishment, a reduction in diet, and other penalties. Lethal force could also be used against those who attempted to escape or physically resisted their captors.

The conditions of detention were carefully managed by way of standing orders that were regularly amended to ensure compliance with both international practice and the diplomatic agreements concluded between the belligerents.[17] Prisoners of war were to be properly fed so that their health and welfare would not be compromised. This would apply to accommodations as well. Provision was also to be made for daily exercise. Meanwhile, the prisoners were to be protected from public humiliation and retribution. Prisoners could work, but could not be coerced into doing so.[18] Prisoners were to provide for their own maintenance, and if required to work for the state, this was to be in a limited capacity. Moreover, the work was to be neither excessive nor dangerous, nor could it be related to the conduct of the war. As prisoners of war they were to be compensated at the going rate of standard military pay. Those who chose not to work would receive no funds. Finally, a distinction was also to be made between so-called first- and second-class prisoners, that is to say, officers and persons of an officer class and those of a lower socio-economic standing. Overall, the conditions and treatment accorded prisoners of war would be guaranteed by neutral powers. These were entrusted with representing the interests of the belligerents and they would routinely send out diplomatic personnel on fact-finding missions to various camps and stations. In Canada, the interests of Germany and Austria-Hungary were initially represented by the United States and later, after the US entry into the conflict, by Sweden and Switzerland.[19]

Canadian authorities were careful to exercise caution in their administration of the camps and to follow the precepts of international law as it applied to prisoners of war. Furthermore, General Otter, the director of internment operations, was a professional soldier who, by all accounts, sought to maintain a standard of military professionalism and conduct. Internment was a military operation after all. Perhaps it was for this reason that he was mystified and dismayed with the situation at the Lakehead, where local officials in January 1915, faced with a large number of unemployed and destitute enemy aliens, organized the arrest of some eight hundred to be processed for internment.[20] Turned over to General Otter, they were now his responsibility. As civilians, their internment did not fall under the rubric of military necessity. But this was a political decision and he a military man. His job was simply to ensure that the operation was carried out according to the regulations set down in the Hague Convention regarding the treatment of prisoners of war.

The administration of the camps and the decisions taken depended on the quality of commanders and soldiers alike. Command appointments were based on experience, education, and professional credentials. Lawyers, accountants, businessmen, ranchers, even a professor of French could be counted among them. Prior military service or some experience with policing was valued, but in the end this was outside their control. The officers appointed were a queer mixture of professionals and ambitious types with varying degrees of ability. This was especially so since a number of the appointments had been injudiciously made or, in fact, had been foisted on internment operations.

Those who desired the status associated with a command position eagerly sought the rank of a commanding officer. Soliciting promotions either for themselves or family members, men of influence applied enormous political pressure in the bid to secure appointments. The parliamentarian T.J. Stewart, for instance, hoped to secure the command of the Banff/Castle Mountain internment camp for his brother Barnard Stewart.[21] The chief constable of Edmonton, George Hill Sr, sought to have his son – described as "strong and athletic" – appointed an officer at the Jasper Park camp.[22] Meanwhile, Lieutenant Colonel J.C. Scott, a man who "possess[ed] considerable influence in Quebec," exerted pressure to have his son Louis G. Scott appointed to a military command, again at Jasper.[23] As a result, all sorts of individuals with suspect ability were imposed on internment operations. The placement of Barnard Stewart was circumvented only when it was discovered that he was fifty-four years of age and equipped with a truss for his hernia that would have made it impossible for him to even mount a horse.[24] The appointment of George Hill Jr, on the other hand, could not be avoided. He was given the position of lieutenant at the Jasper camp despite the fact that, when action was taken to have him join the expeditionary force, it was noted he was unlikely to pass the medical examination for overseas duty because of his "abnormal corpulence."[25]

It was only with great effort on the part of senior command that officers of questionable physical ability and emotional character were replaced.[26] But this also meant that the administration of the camps tended to be uneven. A number of the camps – Vernon and Petawawa for instance – offered no cause for concern as to the manner in which they were being administered. Others, however, gained notoriety – Kapuskasing, Spirit Lake, Banff, Lethbridge, Edgewood, and Mara Lake – as places where discipline, control, and organization were in short supply. The commanding officers at these camps cited a number of problems that made difficult the job of command. The problems included managing an internment camp in the wilderness, exercising both jurisdictional authority and control over prisoners, and dealing with the quality of the guard assigned.

The majority of the internment camps were created in areas that were removed from urban centres. This ensured that the work of the prisoners would not compete with free labour in populated centres, where the labour situation was volatile and the native-born population excitable. Working prisoners on the frontier, however, posed a significant security challenge. Work parties, whose movements were only partially restricted, meant that flight was a real possibility, despite the prospect that escapees could be shot. The makeshift nature of many of the camp enclosures was a further invitation to escape, by tunnelling or other means. From the perspective of the camp commandants, who were held personally accountable for any security lapse, prisoner escapes had to be prevented at all cost. Tremendous pressure, therefore, was applied on guards to ensure that security would be maintained, ratcheting up the levels of stress and frustration between officers and soldiers, guards and prisoners.

The partnership between the internment directorate and other government agencies, a way to reduce the cost of the operations, created a symbiotic relationship. The various entities depended on each other for their success. But these partnerships worked only as long as their respective institutional objectives were met. The problem was that the goals for each were different and not easily reconcilable. As a military operation, internment was to provide for the safeguarding of prisoners of war. For the provincial governments of Ontario, Quebec, and British Columbia as well as for the federal Department of the Interior, in which the dominion parks branch was located, internment offered development and growth opportunities. The institutional goals and needs of the two – security versus development – were not simply at variance; they were largely incompatible. This would necessarily lead to friction and disagreement between officials regarding the expectations and conditions under which the prisoners would work.[27] Parks officials were adamant that monies apportioned for prisoner wages depended on the quantity, quality, and scheduling of the work received. To the extent that employment was being provided for the prisoners, this was acceptable to internment officials. But such arrangements also had to fall within the strictures governing internment operations, placing constraints on what both the prisoners and military officers could and would do.

Additionally the frontier work camps were difficult to manage because of the particular physical and mental demands of guarding prisoners in an extreme environment. Many of the camps were located in the mountains or the Canadian bush. The harsh conditions and strain associated with isolation in these places tested even the most physically hardy and psychologically prepared. It was for this reason that commanding officers insisted on having experienced personnel. This was not always possible.

The commandant at the Kapuskasing camp, Lieutenant Colonel G. Royce, complained bitterly that in response to a telegram urgently requesting "four good husky military policemen," he was delivered men who had no policing experience, two of whom had no military training at all.[28] He explained: "a military policeman here has charge of 100 prisoners, and is responsible that order is kept, and that the prisoners are turned out for duty, and it requires men who have experience in order to intelligently handle the prisoners as a great deal depends on how these duties are performed." As for the draft of the supplementary twenty-five men he had requested, Royce despaired at the class of individual he might receive, noting "these men cannot be too smart for this work and we have no facilities for training them owing to the present weather conditions."[29]

The heart of the problem was that the best eligible men were being recruited for active service overseas, and those that could be spared were of an inferior calibre. Enlistments for frontline duty were a priority, and every available man who showed potential was called upon to volunteer, even the guards at the camps.[30] Commanding officers of internment camps, therefore, were instructed to permit and encourage guardsmen to join battalions being prepared for the battle in France. These were to be replaced by returning soldiers who, their nerves frayed, were no longer suitable for frontline duty, or by recruits deemed unfit for active service.[31] From the perspective of maintaining a professional and competent corps of soldiers, the result was disheartening and demoralizing. Although he offered an apology – "I am doing my best for the returned soldiers and for all those who have been in the Expeditionary Force who are not really fit for service in the trenches" – Major A.E. Hopkins was clear that a number of those sent to Jasper Park from France were not well and consequently unsuited to undertake the difficult work at hand.[32] The nerves of Sergeant F.W. Holmes, formerly of the Princess Patricia Canadian Light Infantry, were "completely broken down." One returned soldier, Private D.J. Mellon, according to Hopkins, "does not seem to be quite right in his mind," while Private C.H. Royal was described as having great difficulty coping, even blowing a bugle.

Tension coloured the relationship between camp commandants, the officers commanding military districts, and recruiting officers who "grabbed men on furlough," persuading them to join units going overseas. The district military commanders were exhorted to put a stop to this "wholesale exodus," but pressure to secure recruits for overseas duty took precedence and very little was done in this regard.[33] Not surprisingly, various camp commanders took unilateral steps to curb the poaching of their men. Lieutenant Colonel G. Royce, the commandant of the Kapuskasing camp, declined all overseas applications and cancelled furloughs in response to the plundering of his ranks.[34] But this was only part of the ongoing dispute between the commandants and senior officers. Internment required more men than expected. As a result, requests for additional personnel were frequently made. The men were expected to be well trained, physically fit, and mentally sound. Known for his forthright views, Colonel Royce declared there was no point in having men who were unprepared or incapable of handling the travails of guarding prisoners on the frontier – they simply would "not be able to stand the work."[35]

The insistence of the camp commanders for quality personnel followed from the difficult circumstances involved in managing an internment camp on the frontier. The only way to have a functioning and well-run operation was to maintain discipline. Discipline among the guards, consequently, was a major concern, and detailed standing orders for camps were routinely and widely broadcast among the troops.[36] These were to be carefully followed and executed. Failure to do so carried with it severe penalties including courts martial and other forms of punishment.[37] But an orderly camp also depended on discipline among the prisoners. It was expected that they would follow the rules and accept their lot as prisoners of war. Among the internees this was neither evident nor necessarily accepted. They were, after all, civilians who happened to be interned.[38] There was an expectation that they would be treated fairly and certainly not as military prisoners. The problem, of course, was that the designation prisoner of war sanctioned the government's desire and need to remove them from the comfort of society and to put them to work in a manner that, at the very least, alleviated the problem and, so it was presumed, their suffering as well.

MAKING INTERNMENT WORK

A number of nationalities were represented among those interned. Although they were to be treated equally as prisoners of war, ethnic tension and class distinctions made this a difficult proposition, especially in the context of detention. Internment brought together, in close proximity, a diversity of humanity who felt poorly treated and hard done by. The frustration and resentment, barely contained, affected relations among the different groups and classes. Disputes between German and

Austro-Hungarian inmates concerning the causes of war, for instance, became a regular occurrence and required the separation of the two. Differences in social class, a source of friction and bitterness under normal conditions, also required the partitioning of men of property from members of the working class.[39] This was especially so since the military practice, sanctioned under international law, of differentiating between officers and regular servicemen resulted in individuals of property being shielded from the common workingman.

The internment camps in Canada reflected these divisions. So-called "first-class" prisoners would enjoy better messing, be housed in separate quarters, and be entitled to certain privileges and freedoms, including the hiring of "second-class" prisoners as servants or batmen to satisfy their personal needs.[40] "Second-class" prisoners were responsible for the camp's maintenance and provided for their own needs by cutting firewood and drawing water. As for the separation of the nationalities, an enormous effort was made to consolidate the camps and internment stations along national lines.[41] By June 1915, for instance, Fort Henry was the place of internment for 210 Germans, twenty-two Austro-Hungarians, and one Turk. At Petawawa, a total of 583 were interned, all of whom were of Austro-Hungarian origin.[42]

National and class distinctions were seized upon by Canadian authorities for additional reasons. The majority of enemy aliens interned were destitute and unemployed. By definition these were labouring men. As labourers they also represented the great wave of immigration recruited from east-central Europe in the late nineteenth century, principally from Austria-Hungary. A large number of the interned enemy aliens were, in effect, both working class and of Austro-Hungarian origin. The second-class prisoner-of-war designation (that allowed for this type of individual to be put to work ostensibly for their own maintenance) meant that these individuals could be placed at working camps being created on the frontier. This simultaneously solved the problem of separating Germans from other internees while also putting to work enemy aliens of Austro-Hungarian origin who were previously unemployed and in need. The ability to separate German nationals from the others would also become important as the government in Berlin began to show growing interest in the treatment of German subjects in Canada interned as prisoners of war.[43]

Austro-Hungarian nationals, notably individuals from among the minority groups located on the periphery of the old empire, were overwhelmingly represented in the frontier camps. They were there because the intention was for them to be put to work; those who were considered medically unfit "to stand the bush life" would be screened out.[44] German internees, on the other hand, remained in or were transferred to permanent internment stations – Amherst, Halifax, Kingston, Toronto, Lethbridge, and Vernon – where work for the most part was not obligatory. At Fort Henry, an internment station reserved for "first-class" prisoners, stone repairs to the buildings in the lower square and the road leading to the fort were approved and the work carried out.[45] But this was an exception to the rule. The primary purpose of Fort Henry, and similar permanent installations, was to hold German prisoners of war, some of whom were captured merchant marines, until a decision would be made regarding their disposition. These facilities were not meant to be work camps.[46] In fact, a small number of internees of non-German descent who were incapable of working were also sent to these installations.[47]

Not everyone was pleased with the fact that German prisoners were idle at the permanent stations. At Lethbridge, it was reported that German internees were being allowed all manner of privileges, not least of which was being permitted to go about town under escort as well as play golf. The camp commandant, Captain J.A. Birney, answered the reports by claiming that ordinary prisoners were allowed no privileges, while only two officers were given such concessions. These privileges, he explained, were granted under the regulations that governed the treatment of men of an officer class.[48] That German prisoners of war were permitted "such indulgences" was declared unacceptable and a public call was made to do away with the rules.[49]

From the point of view of the general public, whose anger was fuelled by reports from Europe of the abominable treatment of British prisoners at the hands of the Germans, enemy alien prisoners of war were expected to work, not dawdle. On this point, officials in the dominion and provincial governments, as well as in the militia, were inundated with requests and recommendations regarding the use of the prisoners in the camps. Informed that prisoners were deployed in Ontario on roadwork, the Automobile Association of Nova Scotia was anxious to secure internment labour from the Citadel for use on provincial roads in Nova Scotia and inquired with the military how this might be done.[50] As well, negotiations were reported to have taken place between the director of internment operations and the municipality of Amherst on procuring prisoner-of-war labour for that city.[51] In the BC interior, the citizens of Nakusp petitioned for the creation of a road to be built by prisoners of war from the Vernon camp, connecting the town to a nearby mineral hot spring, which it was hoped would enhance local tourism and open the region to settlement.[52] The mayor of Kelowna, BC, also urged the provincial government to take enemy prisoners from Vernon in order to establish a Kelowna camp, insisting that Kelowna deserved its "share" of the business that would result from both a prisoner-of-war camp and the advantages "that would come to us from public works."[53] Meanwhile, from Malakwa and Solsqua, also in the BC interior, requests were received for the construction of a road between Revelstoke and Mara.[54]

In principle, federal officials, and specifically internment operations, were not opposed to such requests, but insisted that two conditions be met. The proposals had to be supported by their respective provincial governments, and, from the perspective of the director of internment operations, the security of the prisoners had to be assured. When the commissioner for public works in Nova Scotia, for instance, requested that prisoners be used on the roads between Halifax, Chester, and Mount Uniacke, and Bedford to Dartmouth, the reply from the internment directorate was that, aside from the fact that there were few Austro-Hungarian second-class prisoners at the Nova Scotia camps, the woods bordering these roads made guarding them a difficult matter.[55] The request was denied.

A great many of the requests from British Columbia failed to receive the support of the BC provincial government. To deflect public criticism in these instances, BC officials claimed that approval of projects ultimately rested with the military authorities.[56] This, however, was only partially true. In fact, the BC government was very interested in road development in the province's interior and made every effort to secure federal agreement on projects it considered a priority. The Vernon to Edgewood road, which led initially to the creation of the Monashee camp, was of particular importance. When the Monashee camp proved unsustainable because of cost overruns and was closed in September 1915, the project was not abandoned. Rather, a new and more accessible camp at Edgewood was established not far from the original camp in order to continue with the project.

The Sicamous–Mara portion of the Revelstoke road was also a priority consideration.[57] Given the heavy rock-cut work involved, it was felt that this could be done economically with prisoner-of-war labour. As regards the internees at the Morrissey camp, they could be used effectively on the Elko–Fernie section of the road that made its way through the Crowsnest Pass, a potentially important transportation corridor. But this would have to be done carefully in view of the agitated state of the local population. Indeed, when the camp was established and the internees put to work on the road, the Elko Board of Trade petitioned the minister of the militia, Major General Sir Sam Hughes, that since the prisoners were competing with local free labour they needed to be confined to the camp or alternatively their prison wages taxed at a rate of 10 per cent.[58] The BC government would seek to balance its interests with local and wider concerns, although it would be a source of some friction.

From the perspective of the provincial governments, the most important factor determining the value of the camps was whether there was a net benefit. They had to be useful, efficient, and viable. This would be determined by keeping an accurate account of the hours of labour performed, the cost of the labour, and the value of the work. Meticulous reports were prepared, either weekly or biweekly. These accounts were checked and double-checked. Any discrepancy required explanation and all costs had to be justified before auditors would sign off on invoices and payment released. Plans and work schedules also had to be closely followed. All of this required a high degree of coordination and cooperation between those responsible for the security of the prisoners and those entrusted with ensuring that value for money was being met. This was not always possible because of differences in views and objectives such as who should pay for incidental costs.

The agreement that led to the establishment of the Mara Lake internment camp in BC was concluded, for example, only after negotiations between internment and provincial officials had taken place. The basis of the arrangement was much the same as elsewhere. The province would provide the tools and blasting powder, hire horses and wagons, transport supplies, and pay the prisoners of war.[59] The problem with the agreement, however, was that not all the details were finalized, leading to disputes over other charges and expenses incurred. For example, which party was responsible for the cost of clearing land for the encampment was never fully discussed. Nor was it established whose responsibility it was to bring in equipment and tools or what labour was expended in constructing the prison enclosure.[60] Paying bills was a learning experience for internment authorities. Costs had to be closely monitored and assessed. Subsequent internment camps, such as at Yoho and Jasper, as a result, were built by the prisoners themselves.

Attention to expenses at Mara Lake also extended to the work performed by the internees. Biweekly reports, showing the finances and progress made on the road, were prepared by the supervising superintendent and sent to the deputy minister of public works for his approval. Between September and November, for example, prisoners cleared an estimated 18,200 feet of right-of-way (fifty feet wide) – constituting 20.66 acres – for the sum of $286.00. A total of 17,800 feet (twenty-five feet in width) was grubbed and a further 17,300 feet of the new road graded at a cost of $866.10. This work also entailed excavating by hand some 2,400 yards of earth and 2,128 yards of rock as well as constructing eight culverts and one bridge, costing $1,250.90. There were additional material expenses – dynamite, fuses, caps, exploders, and stumping powder – as well as the salaries of cooks and the supervising engineer. The final outlay for the construction of slightly more than three miles of finished road was $5,963.98, a significant saving because of the nature of the labour.[61]

The biweekly reports on the Mara Lake road showed enormous progress being made through difficult terrain.[62] But the reports also intimated that there were problems. Work, for instance, was only undertaken intermittently during the month of December; only 700 yards of earth and 920 yards of rock were excavated and 340 feet of road graded in the period from 1 to 15 January 1916. The reduced output was officially attributed to the extreme cold weather.[63] Unofficially, however, it was pointed out that the prisoners lacked proper attire for the weather.

Although a special warrant of $5,000 was issued by the BC government to meet some of the expenditures in connection with the Mara Lake road – helping among other things to cover the cost of footwear – the road superintendent, R. Bruhn, expressed his dismay that more was not being done to provide for the prisoners. From Bruhn's perspective, valuable work was being needlessly lost because of questionable decisions. He was especially critical of the directive from internment operations that two pairs of light socks were to be issued instead of a single lumberman's pair. Bruhn alerted the BC deputy minister of public works that "if General Otter, in giving this instruction, is looking at this matter from a financial standpoint, I consider the point is very poorly taken, as one pair of good lumberman's socks will last all winter when two pair of the socks now provided are only good for a very short time. With the socks now in use, it is impossible to keep the snow out of the shoes and rubbers, causing the men's feet to be cold and wet. This again causes dissatisfaction; it is impossible to get the men to work as they should and the cost of a pair of suitable socks is lost in a few days work."[64] Subsequent reports noted additional problems: prisoner discontent with

3.2 Roadwork, Mara Lake, BC

food; a shortage of sentries, resulting in smaller numbers of prisoners being sent out; and, perhaps most importantly, increasing resistance among internees toward their work assignments.[65]

In the months that followed, progress was made despite the shortcomings and interruptions to the work schedule, at least until mid-July 1916 when General Otter decided to reduce, by half, the allowance prisoners could draw on their POW earnings.[66] The intention of the initiative was to force savings among prisoners so that at the time of their eventual release, they would have funds to begin their life anew.[67] His decision, however, did not go over very well with the prisoners. A complete cessation in work resulted. Tied as they were to a schedule, however, provincial overseers insisted the work needed to proceed, regardless. R. Bruhn, the supervising engineer on the Mara Lake road, noting that the military authorities were unwilling to employ sterner measures against the prisoners who refused to work, made clear to the camp commandant that unless there was a change, the arrangement at Mara Lake would end.[68] According to Bruhn, the purpose of using prisoner labour was defeated if discipline was not enforced. Eventually, a number of internees were transferred out and the work continued with a smaller contingent once the camp was relocated farther down the road. This helped to address some of the logistical and disciplinary problems associated with the original camp. But it also meant that the work would proceed slowly.

At the Kapuskasing camp in Ontario a similar concern arose about keeping costs to a minimum while making certain a maximum effort was being extracted from the internees. In this matter, officials in the northern land development branch were guided by the instructions of Ontario's premier.[69] The premier, William Hearst, was adamant that no claim for work received before the date of the agreement between the province and the militia, 23 February 1916, would be paid. Further, he made clear that "we will only take labour when we want it, and that we will not be compelled to retain any labourers on the work that are not satisfactory to us." Hearst also asserted: "We could not afford to pay 25¢ per day in the winter time, nor would we want to pay for any class of men they might want to send to us." From the premier's perspective, the work had to be accounted for and the expense justified.

Both provincial and internment officials kept detailed accounts of the completed work and associated costs separately.[70] Invoices for work received would be paid only after the figures were reconciled. The records would show that the work at Kapuskasing was indeed substantial. Trees felled in clearing the one thousand acres for the experimental farm as well as the adjacent forested areas provided logs that would be milled into lumber at the camp sawmill. Between 1 May and 20 July 1915, 8,818 logs were cut. During the period 20 July to 1 September, 4,810 logs were cut, and between 1 September and 13 November, 6,911 logs were cut, resulting in 1,567,605 board feet of lumber destined for the market.[71]

Roadwork was also undertaken in and around the camp. The northern development branch reported in December 1915 that some 35.3 miles of roadway had been grubbed, ditched, and graded.[72] In January 1916, a total of 124 acres were also cleared along the railway line. Meanwhile, the value of the roadwork completed by internment labour for the month of February, as reported by branch officials, was $1,536.25, or one-quarter of the projected normal cost. The figure, a significant savings, attracted the attention of internment officials, who claimed the actual value to be $2,253.50, a discrepancy of some 2,869 man-days of prisoner labour. The difference was attributed to the number of religious holidays (which authorities were bound to respect) and sickness (real and imagined), but since the prisoners, for whatever reason, were not working, provincial officials insisted on the accounts being adjusted.[73]

In the end it would not matter, since the work fell outside of the terms of the intra-agency agreement and all of the work completed before 23 February 1916 was done at no cost to the Ontario government. After 23 February, however, the Ontario provincial government would pay only for work received.

To take maximum advantage of the inexpensive pool of labour, the work at Kapuskasing was planned out. Logging – cutting trees into six-, ten-, and twelve-foot lengths – and roadwork – slashing, grubbing, grading, and bridge construction – entailed gangs of prisoners being sent out daily, under guard with government foremen in charge. Each gang was given a work assignment, whether cutting a designated stand of trees or grubbing a section of roadway, and was expected to fulfill a day's quota. The routine continued in this manner until the job was done. Once the supply of forest on the experimental farm had been exhausted, and with roadwork completed in the vicinity of the camp, tent camps were established farther afield, not only in the O'Brien but adjoining Owens, Fauquier, and Williamson townships as well.[74] The scale of the operations required a sizable staff and guard, which were periodically supplemented as the demands increased and an appreciation for the scope of the work developed. With over 115 buildings (constructed by the prisoners for various uses), the camp was a veritable beehive of activity where some 1,200 prisoners and nearly 400 military personnel and government staff worked at a variety of jobs. Writing to the adjutant general in Toronto, the commandant, Lieutenant Colonel George Royce, spoke glowingly of the quality and amount of work being done: "I can assure you that this camp is worth seeing, and it would surprise you, the magnitude of the operations here."[75]

But not all was as well as it appeared in the northern Ontario camp. Production dropped off after March 1916. From a monthly average of 5,600 man days of work, only 3,086 days of work were reported in April and 1,767 days in May.[76] As was the case at Mara Lake and other internment camps across the country, interned enemy aliens were beginning to protest both their conditions and treatment by resisting and refusing to work. In May the matter came to a head at the camp in the form of a full-scale riot.[77]

The Kapuskasing riot was brutally suppressed, and although it gave pause to internment and government officials, the future of the camp was never in doubt. It was much too valuable an enterprise. Investments, both financial and political, had been made in seeing that the experimental farm project was a success. For the dominion government, the camp provided a way to determine the agricultural potential of the region while serving as a demonstration farm.[78] The Ontario government, on the other hand, recognized the value of the scheme as a catalyst for colonization in the area. There was also the matter of removing interned enemy aliens from the urban centres, where idle confinement was viewed as problematic and undesirable; in the north country, they could at least be put to work. And finally, there was the question of revenue being generated from the sale of felled trees, a potentially significant source of income that could help defray the costs of the operation. There was too much at stake. Kapuskasing would not be abandoned despite the setbacks.

Arrangements had been made with provincial governments – British Columbia, Ontario, and Quebec – regarding the use of internment labour. But the agency with which internment operations would have extensive dealings was the dominion parks branch in the Department of the Interior. The question of how the interned civilian prisoners of war might be used was never in doubt. Their primary function would be to undertake roadwork. Developing roads in the national parks was of utmost importance because of the predilection and drive of the commissioner of the dominion parks, J.B. Harkin. Harkin, a man of no small ambition, saw the national parks as a boon and a bounty for the country.[79] National parks were places to which Canadians could retire, relax, and rejuvenate. But for this to occur, roads allowing visitors access to destinations in the parks had to be created. In light of the reduction in appropriations for his department, Harkin was drawn to the opportunity presented by internment labour.

A priority project in the parks was the Banff–Laggan coach road that would have opened up access to Lake Louise and surrounding area with its fantastic views. The internees who arrived from Lethbridge were immediately put to work at the terminus of the uncompleted road located near the foot of Castle Mountain, an imposing natural wonder. By the end of August 1915, within a month and half of their arrival, the internees had cleared and grubbed four miles of right-of-way. The supervising engineer, J.M. Wardle, was satisfied with the progress, although he complained that the pace was slow.[80] More, he claimed, could have been done if the prisoners had been experienced. Nevertheless, the results were encouraging, suggesting that a road planned for the summit of Mount Revelstoke might proceed.

The Revelstoke road had been championed by the local member of parliament, R.F. Green, who, in his efforts to secure government

contracts and work for Kamloops and Revelstoke, approached the
minister of justice, the Hon. Charles Doherty, about completing the
unfinished motor road in Revelstoke Park.[81] Green managed to convince
the minister, arguing that the work would benefit both the enemy alien
and the town of Revelstoke, which, with the completion of the road to
the summit, "could get tourists." After a site was identified and log buildings constructed, Austro-Hungarian prisoners were brought in from
Vernon and Brandon in early September. With pick and shovel, they
were put to work clearing, grubbing, and excavating the right-of-way, as
well as cribbing and building culverts to help shore up the roadway.
Sections of the road were also graded. Although there was disagreement
between the guards and foremen "as to who should make the prisoners
work," by 5 October, the supervising engineer, J.M. Wardle, pleased with
the results on the road, could report, "A good showing for the time left
should be made, as the aliens up to the present time have worked well."[82]

Wardle, however, had spoken too soon. Pressed to work even harder
in order to get ahead of the winter, which on the mountain summit was
fast approaching, the prisoners began to protest the conditions and their
treatment. The blacksmiths refused to dress the tools, and on a number
of days road gangs simply would not leave the camp.[83] Adding to the
pressure, the inclement weather, in combination with the altitude,
threatened the camp. A decision was taken to get off the mountain and
close the facility. The unfinished work, however, did not sit well with the
local business folk, who feared that the internees would not come back.
Their suspicions were confirmed. Despite the best efforts of local
Revelstoke officials to secure internment labour the following year, the
situation in the country made it so that their request for prisoners would
not be fulfilled.[84]

The prisoners who came down from the summit on Mt Revelstoke
were sent to Yoho National Park. Yoho was nearby, and an accessible
CPR line made the transfer of prisoners and supplies an economical
proposition. The site was also selected because the park superintendent,
E.N. Russell, was convinced that timber from a recent fire in the area
could be harvested, thus making the camp revenue producing.[85] In his
view the material could be got to market at a reasonable price and "by
this means these prisoners, instead of being a burden on the Government,
could be made to pay for their own keep, or at all events assist towards
their maintenance."[86]

Russell strongly advised that this be the direction, especially in light of
the severe winters in the area that prevented other types of work. Logging

would give the best results, while roadwork on a nearby planned scenic route connecting the Otterhead River to the Natural Bridge on the Kicking Horse could be postponed until the following spring/summer. However, J.B. Harkin, the parks commissioner, personally partial to the road project, was convinced the internees could be made to work on both.[87] In the end, Russell and Harkin both proved to be wrong; extreme weather – fierce winds, low temperatures, and blizzard conditions – soon made any kind of work impossible. From mid-January to mid-February, the prisoners, paralyzed by the weather, were only able to work three days on the motor road. Enduring harsh conditions, they did all they could simply to survive, fetching firewood from the bush and removing snow that threatened to inundate the camp, which with the spring thaw would have made the site uninhabitable.

Weather conditions at the Otter internment camp improved in late February and early March 1916. But with the improvement in weather, the prisoners, sent out to cut the new right-of-way, were pressured to make up for lost time.[88] To reduce the walking distance, a direct trail was cut in the forest between the camp and the worksite on the Kicking Horse River where the prisoners were tasked with building a major bridge. The working time of the prisoners was also extended from seven to eight hours so that greater advantage could be taken of the longer daylight hours. Meanwhile, the park superintendent, E.N. Russell, insisted that the prisoners not only work longer but walk faster to their jobsite. The internees resisted the pressure to accelerate the pace of work and in time became increasingly non-compliant. When a decision was made to relocate the camp at the end of the April to a summer site at the confluence of the Boulder and Kicking Horse rivers, military authorities expressed genuine relief. Spring flooding threatened to cut off the original camp from its supply base, and it was felt the move would also improve the prisoners' attitude.[89]

The new camp, in place by June, offered no reprieve, however. Work conditions were impossible and life at the camp was made miserable by the sweltering heat, insects, and the spring run-off that was compounded by torrential rains. Flooding at the new site forced the two hundred prisoners to higher ground. It also threatened the nearby settlement of Field to which the internees were rushed over to help save.[90] As they became increasingly ragged, wet, and worn out, a foul mood developed among the internees by August, many of whom refused to work. The prisoners began to argue against their internment, claiming they failed to understand "why they should be interned while hundreds of other alien enemies are allowed not only to go free but to earn their living in the country."[91] Major General Otter rejected their grievance. Fearing a return to the original camp site in the coming winter and learning through uncensored letters that inmates at the Morrissey internment camp were no longer working, the internees remained resolute in their decision not to work.

The month-long prisoner strike showed no signs of abating, even after rations were scaled back and privileges withdrawn. No further work could be secured from the prisoners "unless strenuous measures were resorted to." The camp commandant, Lieutenant Brock, however, expressed unease with this course of action.[92] The park superintendent, E.N. Russell, was equally doubtful about the prospects of the prisoners returning to work and concluded that if they were unwilling to work or could not be compelled to work, then the camp needed to close.[93] Believing the problem lay with the command, the director of internment operations, General Otter, changed out the officers and ordered the return of the camp to the original winter site.

By this time, however, the prisoners busied themselves with a plan to escape. Using a shovel and kitchen cutlery, they were well on their way to tunnelling out of the compound. The plan was foiled at the last minute when the passageway was discovered.[94] The prisoners' use of crudely fashioned weapons in their attempt at escape forced officials to reconsider the plan to relocate the camp. In early October, the decision was taken to shut down the camp completely. By the end of the month, the majority of the prisoners were herded onto a train destined for Quebec and Spirit Lake, where the "unruly" bunch would await their future.

Winter in the mountains was a generally trying affair, but for those encampments set up with tents for accommodation it was especially arduous. The prospect of enduring the extreme temperatures in canvas tents was not to be contemplated and the prisoners at Castle Mountain, who had been making progress carving the coach road out of the forests, were on the move in November 1915. In the hopes of beating the fast-approaching winter, a retreat to Banff was chosen as the best alternative. Huts, built earlier for construction workers at the Cave and Basin site, could be used by the troops, while long-house-styled barracks could be constructed easily and quickly for the original two hundred prisoners of war from Castle Mountain plus an additional two hundred Austro-Hungarian prisoners, for whom, Harkin proposed, "we have got work to provide."[95]

That there was work to be done in the vicinity of the Banff townsite was indisputable.[96] No sooner had they arrived prisoner work gangs were set to work making local improvements and additions: clearing land for the new St Julien subdivision, filling and draining the land at the recreation park, brushing the buffalo paddocks, building the retaining rock wall at Bow Falls, and repairing sidewalks and streets in town. They were also put to work on a variety of projects in and around Banff for the amusement and leisure of the locals and visitors alike: building a ski run and toboggan glide, an ice palace for the winter carnival, and hiking trails for the Alpine Club of Canada; clearing land for horse pastures, tennis courts, and a shooting range; extending the golf links and constructing an access road to the golf course at the Banff Springs Hotel.

As was the case with their work at Castle Mountain, the principal effort of the internees at Banff was road building during the winter of 1915–16 (and once more in 1916–17, when they would return again to their winter quarters). The roadwork in and around Banff included building a connection between the Cave and Basin site and Middle Springs, eliminating the corkscrew turns on Tunnel Mountain, constructing a major bridge across the Spray River, and cutting a carriage road to the Upper Hot Springs through Sundance Canyon. The internees worked with the "rock-crusher," a machine located at a quarry on the Spray River used to provide crushed stone for road material. Work on a road to nearby Lake Minnewanka, a project of some importance to the local business community, was not undertaken. To appease local interests, however, a satellite camp was established there for the purpose of completing remedial work on the lakeside wharf as well as tidying up the area while also shaping the existing trail to the lake so as to make it more traversable.

The value of the work done by the internees was not lost on Commissioner Harkin, who was anxious to secure as much labour as he could from internment operations. During the discussion on relocating the Castle Mountain camp, he not only proposed an additional two hundred prisoners for Banff (bringing the total there to four hundred) but also requested three hundred more to be taken on at Jasper.[97] The Jasper camp would not materialize until mid-February 1916, the difficulties at Revelstoke and Banff serving to postpone the decision.[98] But once those problems were resolved, some two hundred prisoners were transferred from the Brandon internment station to Jasper with the prospect of being immediately put to work.

With their arrival at Jasper Park, there was a sense of satisfaction and optimism that long-standing plans for the park might now be realized and various projects completed. The *Edmonton Journal* reported that it would not be "one continuous round of sightseeing for the prisoners," but rather they would be working on "an ambitious program of work" that had been laid out for them.[99] Within the week, 125 internees were cutting fence posts to be sent to the buffalo parks at Wainwright and Elk Island and twenty-five prisoners were digging the water main in the Jasper townsite. An additional twenty-five were sent out to repair the Athabasca River Bridge and cut ice around the piers.[100]

Aside from cutting fence posts (eventually numbering 5,500) and working on the town waterworks, it was also planned that the internees would string telephone lines in the park and construct a golf course for the use of residents and tourists. Most importantly, however, they would build roads, significantly elevating expectations about the work that could be done and the benefit derived: "The amount of work to be accomplished is only limited by the duration of the war," the *Edmonton Journal* reported, "but at any rate Jasper Park will see the biggest development this year that has yet been undertaken."[101] There was some credence to the claim. The plans for the park, which identified possible road projects for the internees, included a road up from Pocahontas near Punchbowl Falls to the Miette Hot Springs, an automobile road along the west side of the Athabasca River to the falls, and a road from Maligne Canyon to the Medicine and Maligne lakes.[102]

Expectations, however, would depend on whether the internees would submit to a regime of heavy roadwork. This proved optimistic, for within a few short weeks of their arrival the interned enemy aliens, protesting their food as well as their treatment, staged a hunger strike.[103] This was eventually followed by a complete work stoppage. Parks officials urged the camp's military authorities to exercise greater authority and discipline. Although work would resume under threats and other forms of intimidation, the consequences of the applied pressure were escapes, both from the main camp at Jasper and from a satellite camp at Maligne Canyon, where a gang of prisoners had been sent to work on a road connecting the canyon and Medicine Lake. Escapes, however, were a costly venture. Significant resources were expended in the various attempts to recapture the fugitives and the work consequently was delayed. With mounting escapes and the growing obstinacy of the prisoners, the viability of the Jasper camp was reassessed and the decision was taken to close it down in August 1916, no more than six months after it had been established.

The various projects on which the internees laboured were regularly covered in the press. The accounts were a combination of staid reporting and elemental optimism. Whether through roadwork or other projects, the prisoners of war were often described as making steady progress. But along with such confidence also came the conviction that more could be done. In Calgary, for example, the local Horticultural Society, embarking on an ambitious scheme to plant fruit-bearing and other trees throughout the city in the spring of 1916, was convinced that internees from the Banff camp might be used to good effect on the city-wide project and persuaded the city's Board of Trade to jointly submit a request for the use of internment labour for this purpose.[104] "For a work so desirable," the *Calgary Herald* foresaw no great difficulty in granting permission.[105] In Saskatchewan, the bumper harvest required additional hands in the field. There was considerable worry that hired help in sufficient numbers might not be found. The proposal that prisoners of war from the Brandon camp might be used to bring in the crop was welcome news.[106]

It was a widespread belief that internment labour could be used profitably and effectively. The prisoners were a ready source of available labour that would benefit the country, if properly deployed. For this reason, the president of the Dominion Steel Corporation, Mark Workman, in a private letter to the prime minister, suggested that consideration be given to the idea of bringing three or four thousand additional prisoners of war from Britain so that they might also be put to good use.[107]

The confidence of Workman and the public at large was misplaced, however. For although progress was being made on a number of important public works projects and much accomplished, the use of internment labour was not without setbacks and challenges. Those who had intimate knowledge of internment operations knew there were serious difficulties, obstacles, and surprises that made the effective and economical use of internment labour problematic. They were aware that much of what had been achieved had been brought about through force and resolve that tested not only the men's strength but their spirit as well.

THE TRIALS AND ABUSES OF INTERNMENT

A warrant for the arrest of William Wysk and two of his companions was issued after it was reported bushels of wheat had been stolen from a farm near Two Hills, Alberta. Wysk was arrested 11 February 1915 and taken to Vegreville, where he was confined to an enclosure at the local fire hall. Theft of grain was a common enough occurrence given the hardship in the area. But for Wysk, who admitted his guilt, the problem was that he had been previously interned. Wysk was not prepared to accept imprisonment once again. Alone in his cell, Wysk placed a strap around his neck, fastened it to a joist above his cell, and jumped from his bunk bed. Found swaying from the beam, Wysk was quickly cut down. It was too late to save him. An inquest investigating the cause of death delivered the verdict that the act was premeditated, the deceased having arranged for the disposal of his worldly possessions just before he took his life. A rider accompanied the verdict that no blame whatsoever was to be attached to any person or persons.[108]

William Perchaliuk had been an internee at the Lethbridge and Castle Mountain camps for over a year before his release on 26 June 1916 when he and twenty-five others were paroled to work for the Canmore Coal Company. Coal mining was hard on Perchaliuk, who suffered from a respiratory ailment. Seeking an alternative, he enlisted in late November as a private with the 211th Infantry Battalion, being mobilized at Calgary as part of the Canadian Expeditionary Force. A shortage of recruits resulted in a push to bring the battalion to full strength. The hurried nature of the campaign, however, meant that new recruits were inadequately screened. As the battalion was preparing to depart for Europe, an officer from the Castle camp recognized Perchaliuk. Perchaliuk was thought to be an escaped prisoner. Speaking "broken English," he confessed to being a prisoner at the camp, but stated that he had been paroled. The explanation would not matter. By joining the Canadian military, Private Perchaliuk had contravened the order prohibiting the enlistment of enemy subjects in the king's army. Hauled from the ranks, he was taken to a Calgary police holdover, where he awaited the judgment of a police magistrate.

For Perchaliuk, there was no doubt as to his fate. Being in violation of his parole, he was destined to return to Castle Mountain. The prospect of doing so, however, was too much for him to bear. On the evening of 5 December, alone in his cell and still in uniform, Perchaliuk removed the military puttee from his leg and made a loop of it. Tying it to the cell bars, he pulled himself up and, slipping his neck through the improvised noose, let go. Despite efforts to revive him, Perchaliuk did not survive. The autopsy report identified strangulation to be the cause of death, with the deceased suffering from respiratory congestion – his lungs "darkened from coal smoke and dust." The jury at the inquest further concluded the rash act appeared to have been committed during "a fit of despondency." With no one to claim the body, the corpse of William Perchaliuk remained at the undertaker's, the departments of Justice and Militia squabbling over who would pay for the burial.[109]

Wysk and Perchaliuk had both experienced internment, and the idea that they would be imprisoned a second time proved overwhelming. Seeing no future other than hardship, privation, and humiliation, they lost hope. And once hope was lost, they were not long in succumbing to their deepest fears and anxieties. Their actions were those of desperate men who saw in suicide an escape from captivity and torment. Faced with the unpalatable alternatives of internment or death, they chose the latter.

Wysk and Perchaliuk, however, were not alone in their visceral reaction to the prospect of further captivity. A large number of the detained or imprisoned in the internment camps were just as determined and unwavering in their desire to be free. Moreover, so personally unbearable were their circumstances that they were prepared to risk everything, including their lives. Not all were successful in their attempts at freedom. At the Brandon camp, fifteen Austro-Hungarians planned a breakout by pulling up the floorboards of their barracks and escaping through the boiler room underneath. Making their getaway, they were discovered by an alert sentry who gave the alarm. In the confusion and excitement, eighteen-year-old Andrew Grapko rushed one of the guards and was shot with a bullet that passed through his body behind his lung. Mike Butryn was also shot, but in the back, as he ran fifty yards down Tenth Street. Two others were bayoneted, forcing them to retreat. Taken to an infirmary, Butryn would survive the shooting; young Andrew would not. Interviewed in the aftermath of the affair, the internee Simon Konrat stated that before the incident, the prisoners had been denied exercise for several weeks. But more importantly, he claimed that monotony and isolation were getting to the inmates, driving them "crazy." Konrat declared that, frustrated and discouraged, many "[were] willing to make another dash for freedom when opportunity offers itself even by taking the risk of death from a bullet."[110]

Freedom had a price, and a number of prisoners were willing to pay it. Not surprisingly, attempted escapes with deadly consequences would occur across the country. Scheduled for transfer under guard by train from Montreal to the internment camp at Spirit Lake, some 106 Austro-Hungarians were marched to the city's railway station. Approaching Windsor Station, the prisoner Bauzek bolted from the ranks, running down a side street. Pursued by soldiers, he was ordered to stop. Ignoring the command, Bauzek was fired upon, a bullet hitting him in the back, going through his right lung. He would later succumb to his wound.[111] In early June 1915, at Spirit Lake, an Austro-Hungarian prisoner escaped along with three others, successfully making his way to the adjoining province only to be shot dead at Whitefish, Ontario.[112] Two weeks later, in another incident at the facility, an internee was mortally wounded when a local farmer, carrying provisions by hand car near Amos, Quebec, came upon an escaped prisoner and, feeling threatened, fired two shots. It was reported the farmer was accustomed to carrying a rifle, as in fact were all the inhabitants near the camp, because they were afraid of travelling unarmed.[113] Elsewhere, prisoner John Stigess was being transported by train from British Columbia to a camp in the east as part of the effort to consolidate prisoners by nationality and class. Some 125 kilometres east of Port Arthur, travelling along the north shore of Lake Superior, Stigess took a chance at freedom by leaping from the train. Fleeing into the thick bush, he eluded a party sent out in pursuit. For Stigess, however, the decision to exit the train and make his way without basic wilderness skills was an unfortunate one. His body was found some time later in the bush. A coroner's jury returned a verdict of death from exposure and starvation.[114]

The bid for freedom was a regular occurrence at virtually every internment station and camp. Success depended on the watchfulness and quality of the guards as well as opportunity and circumstance. But cheek, nerve, and grit, of which there was no shortage, also played a major part. Twelve prisoners would escape en masse at Amherst. Choosing a night of inclement weather, when a blizzard and severe cold ensured the guards would seek shelter, the group passed under the wire unnoticed.[115] At the Lethbridge camp, six men escaped when the first-class prisoners, using kitchen utensils, tunnelled 110 feet from their bunkhouse to the city nurseries adjacent to the camp. A mine fan had been built by one of the prisoners as had a tiny sled used to remove earth. No suspicion was raised during the tunnelling despite the fact that tons of earth had to be disposed of. That all forty of the first-class prisoners in the compound did not escape was a relief to the officers at the camp. When another tunnel was discovered days later, constructed by the second-class prisoners and near completion, everyone was left dumbfounded. Had the tunnel not been discovered, the whole camp would have emptied. Exasperated by the incompetence of the military command at the camp, the Morning Albertan (Calgary) declared, "Something should be done to some person, soon and plenty."[116] Meanwhile, at Fort Henry, located on the banks of the St Lawrence River directly across from the United States, a motorboat needed fixing. Prisoner Babel and two other inmates were called upon to look at the engine. Completing the repairs, the group, supervised by an unarmed escort, set out on the open water for a trial run. Travelling a distance, they were ordered to return. Instead, they seized the officer, tied him up, and made for Cape Vincent on the American side. Once there, they left both the boat and the bound officer behind as they made their way inland.[117]

Escape, among other things, was a form of defiance. It not only signalled a deep desire to be free, but also represented a response to internment and everything that was wrong with it. Objecting to the very premise that they should be held and made to work, the prisoners claimed that internment was unfair. Frustrated, resentful, and reaching the limits of their patience and endurance, internees at various camps reacted by collectively resisting and challenging those immediately responsible for their condition and plight. At Fort Henry, suspecting that soldiers were pilfering inmate food, the prisoners there engaged in a battle of wills with camp officials over control of the kitchen. The tension soon escalated into an open confrontation, requiring a contingent of guards, using fixed bayonets, to subdue the mob. Two prisoners were injured, with one receiving a wound over the ribs and the other to his chest.[118] Commenting on the incident, the local paper described the discipline at the fort as lax, arguing that a portion of the guard should have been chosen from the permanent force, since only men who were used to strict discipline could control others.[119] But also at fault, according to the newspaper editorialists, was the fact that the interned enemy aliens were not working, "and that is the pity of it." Work would have had a salving effect on the prisoners, whose idleness disposed them to complaining. But since the prisoners at this first-class prisoner facility could not be compelled to work, which was "regrettable," they should at least "be made to behave themselves."[120] The message was understood. Within days, several prisoners at the fort, having been found guilty of minor misdemeanours, were subjected to a round of punishment consisting of solitary confinement and a reduced diet of bread and water.[121]

The situation was no better at the Amherst camp. Prisoner Fritz Klaus had assaulted a guard while being escorted to the exercise compound. The trouble escalated, with others joining in, at which point camp police and additional guards were called out "to quell the mutiny." Resisting, Klaus was shot dead, while four others were critically wounded. The reports would attribute the disturbance to a planned escape attempt.[122]

At Kapuskasing, frustration and anger mounted when some three hundred newly arrived prisoners from Petawawa refused to do manual labour, claiming that this was within their rights. The attempt to isolate the protest leaders resulted in an outbreak of violence that soon spread across the entire camp. Twelve hundred rioting prisoners were engaged by three hundred troops who used their bayonets freely. Those who rushed the fence in a failed attempt at freedom were shot. The casualties included one killed, nine critically wounded, and four others requiring medical attention.[123] The incident startled camp authorities, who, in the aftermath of the riot, responded by issuing an order announcing the internees would not be forced to work. But as a precautionary measure, the commanding officer, Lieutenant Colonel George Royce, also quietly recommended that the camp be equipped with a heavy machine gun: "It might never be required, but it would certainly have a moral effect on the prisoners."[124]

Cumulatively, the escapes, resistance, and suicides pointed to the underlying truth of the matter: internment was an unbearable affair. It exacted a heavy toll on the internees, whose psychological and physical limits were being sorely tested. The travail of confinement was not easily borne and did much to make the lives of those detained intolerable. But it was in the work camps, on the frontier, where the ordeal of internment was the most demanding and the endurance of the interned enemy alien especially tried. The Canadian wilderness was foreign and unforgiving. For those who would be forced to work arduously in the bush it was inconceivable that this was their lot. Whether at Castle Mountain/Banff, Edgewood, Monashee, Revelstoke, Mara Lake, Yoho, Morrissey, Kapuskasing, or Spirit Lake, the prisoners were compelled not only to work, but to work hard under trying conditions. They had to contend with the deep snow and bitter cold of the high altitude. In other cases, supplies and provisions were made unavailable or wilfully denied. And then there was the endless, gruelling nature of the work, with which the prisoners had no experience. In short, internment was an impossible situation from which many sought to escape.

The prisoners at Castle Mountain complained greatly of the conditions and, receiving no hearing and expecting no relief, fled either singly or in company with others from the camp. In August and September 1915, escapes in the double digits from the Castle camp occurred. When, five prisoners escaped at once on 18 October, the officer commanding, Major Duncan Stuart, was asked to explain. The troops, he pointed out, had been under considerable stress as they were overworked and daily rations had been cut back (in line with an official directive). After he assured headquarters that the matter was in hand and would not be repeated, the escape of five more prisoners three weeks later led Stuart to admit the problem was more deep-seated. The prisoners, he argued, were induced to flee because of the cold and inadequate attire. Stuart indicated that he had appealed on ten different occasions for clothing to be issued, but was ignored. In the meantime, the situation had become desperate. "During October," he wrote, "the prisoners complained bitterly of want of boots and overalls, and having to sleep without fires; one prisoner who escaped left a letter to a friend saying he preferred to take the chance of being shot escaping than live under the conditions." Stuart added: "In the face of this lack of clothing and boots there is 5 inches of snow on the ground, wet and slush in the middle of the day; some prisoners have boots with their soles half off. Their feet are soaking wet every night, and nearly half of them are in rags. I am ashamed to meet them."[125]

Prisoner Dmytro Tkachyk described in a letter, which somehow escaped the notice of the camp censors, that the conditions at Castle Mountain were inhumane. Those who were sick but diagnosed as fit were forced to work after being prodded with bayonets, while the internees who feigned sickness were placed in a dark cell on a punishment diet of bread and water. Shackled and confined in a cold cell for fourteen days on bread and water with a blanket, one prisoner, Tkachyk claimed, emerged crippled with rheumatism.[126] Prisoner Nick Olinyk, writing to his spouse in a letter that would be censored, also spoke of the ordeal. "As you know yourself there are men running away from here every day because the conditions here are very poor, so that we cannot go on much longer, we are not getting enough to eat – we are hungry as dogs. They are sending us to work, as they don't believe us, and we are very weak."[127] That Olinyk and the others were weak from hunger was not surprising. The number of calories in a standard Canadian internment ration was 2,595.52. It was estimated, however, that the energy required for a man at work was 2,903 calories. Although the prisoner food allotment – costing 5 1/5¢ per meal – was theoretically the same as that issued for troops, it fell far short in terms of caloric sustenance, if only because food provisions could not always be supplied and substitutions were routinely made: unleavened flour or pancake substituted for bread, fermented cabbage for vegetables, and rice or rolled oats for meat.[128]

The situation at Castle Mountain/Banff paralleled the conditions at other work camps on the frontier. Relocated in October 1915 from Mt

3.3  Rock cut, Edgewood, B C

Revelstoke, where the snow threatened to overwhelm the camp, the internees were brought to Mara Lake. By November, the new camp at Mara Lake was also in the grip of severe weather that could only be addressed with proper winter attire. No arrangements, however, had been made to secure the necessary clothing, and although subsequent requests were made stressing the urgency of the matter, mismanagement and indifference meant the bulk of supplies would not arrive at the time when it was needed most.[129] The situation at Edgewood was no better. The road superintendent there, John Black, declared that although the prisoners were prepared to work, it was too much to expect of them to be working in −20° Fahrenheit weather clothed in light gear.[130] They were, according to Black, clad exactly as they were in the summer, with only a sweater over a cotton shirt and no coats or mitts. They also had been without a change of underwear for almost half a year.

Whether it was on the Mara Lake–Sicamous or Vernon–Edgewood road, work slowed down considerably because the necessary attire was unavailable. At Edgewood, it was admitted that using force would have been counterproductive inasmuch as it would have hindered future work. But more to the point, the cold was such that the internees were simply concentrating on gathering wood for fires in order to stay alive and nothing else. Force would not have made a difference.[131] The problem, however, was that eleven days of work at the camp were effectively lost in December. For provincial officials, this was a matter of concern. The benefit to the province was commensurate with both the quantity and quality of the work performed and whether it was on schedule. Delays added to the costs, particularly with respect to the salaries and supplies for the overseers. That the delays were caused by disregard or negligence was, therefore, unacceptable. Accordingly, the BC minister of public works threatened to shut down the work at the camp.[132] By late December, supplies would arrive, but not without further problems – General Otter having rescinded the order for heavy winter lumbermen socks in favour of two pair of summer socks that were on hand.

The austerity measures exercised by internment officials were in keeping with the goal of keeping expenses to a minimum. The cost of supplying internees with winter clothing amounted to three-quarters of the budget appropriation for internment operations at this time.[133] Cost cutting, consequently, was the order of the day, and every measure was taken to achieve the objective of reducing expenses. When General Otter learned that prisoners at Mara Lake and the other internment work camps in BC were being given a meat and bread allowance of one-half pound each above the normal military ration, he ordered it stopped.[134] The reduction affected the work output of the internees, who, when reproached for not working as they should, responded by claiming that "they [were] hungry and unable to work as hard as when they were properly fed."[135] The superintendent at Mara Lake, R. Bruhn, argued that "although the rations they are now getting may be enough for a man not working, they are hardly satisfactory to a man expected to do a good day's work." J. Griffith, the BC deputy minister of public works, again filed a protest with internment officials, claiming that he would have to shut down the work "unless the men are fed like human beings."[136] Although the objection received a sympathetic hearing from Lieutenant Colonel Ridgway-Wilson, the BC liaison with the internment directorate in Ottawa, the matter was left to General Otter, who was not inclined to change the policy, which applied across the country.[137]

From the perspective of the BC officials, the issue was fundamentally one of ensuring that nothing would impede the work of the internees. Although the Mara Lake road superintendent, R. Bruhn, and the deputy minister of public works, J. Griffith, acknowledged there were considerable savings using internment labour – the Mara Lake project cost less than one-quarter of the normal expenditure – they firmly believed that more could be done without the seemingly unnecessary delays and obstacles. "We are not unmindful of the fact that we have had the opportunity of obtaining cheap labour," wrote the deputy minister to General Otter, "but we would have liked to make the best use of it."[138] On this point, where possible, General Otter was prepared to make concessions. When the superintendent at the Yoho camp complained that interned aliens were not working the same length of time as at other camps and the time spent walking to and from the worksite ate into the seven hours designated for work, instructions were received from Ottawa to extend the working day to eight hours. The order was issued despite the fact that "the great depth of snow ... made it impossible to make rapid progress." Indeed, as was admitted with respect to the situation in Banff, walking in deep snow "amount[ed] to practically a day's work in itself."[139]

It was a hopeless situation for the internees, many of whom appealed to their friends and family for help.[140] Mrs F. Munsche of Toronto wrote to the justice minister, pleading for the release of her husband Frank Munsche, a chef on a CPR train, who was removed from the train travelling between Toronto and Winnipeg and interned at Brandon. She argued that he was a naturalized Canadian and had lived in Britain and Canada for sixteen years as a peaceful citizen, but more directly she and her three small children depended on him as the family's sole supporter. She asked that he be restored to the family as "I am entirely without means of support."[141] Maria Marchuk of Bienfait, Saskatchewan, also did her best to free her husband, Philip Marchuk. Unable to understand why he was interned and confused as to when or if he would be released, she claimed that, with winter coming on, "the children and myself are suffering greatly, and what my fate will be God only knows." She begged for her husband's freedom, "so that he should come back to his children, for we are in great need."[142]

Thoughts of home were not far from the minds of the internees. Internment deprived them of their liberty, but, removed from their families, they were also in no position to assist those left behind.[143] The fate of their families weighed heavily on their consciences. When prisoner Nick Olinyk wrote to his wife, whose health was failing, he acknowledged the effect his absence had on the family. "Please try to find somebody to help you," bid Olinyk; "I am sure you are very weak, and I would advise you to write a letter to the camp commandant asking for support." "If they refuse to give it to you," Olinyk counselled, "ask them to release me, and I could support you as you need."[144] Dr J. and Mrs E. Allen, who knew of the plight of Mrs Tymczuk (Demchuk), whose husband was interned at Banff, applied for his release, claiming that her health and personal circumstances had placed her in a position of considerable distress. The application was sent to General Otter, who, although expressing sympathy, declined it on the grounds that "should this man be discharged and not be able to obtain employment, his family will be worse off than ever, as the subsistence allowance is stopped." Moreover, without employment, it was thought that more than likely he would have been rearrested and again interned.[145]

Mrs J. Mudry of Calgary was also in desperate need. Having nowhere to turn, she asked in a censored letter to her husband, a prisoner at Lethbridge, what remained for her to do.

My condition here is very poor. You know very well that they do not want to support me with food and fuel, and I am in trouble in regards to the rent. I haven't any money to pay the rent, and the landlord doesn't want to keep me any longer in the house. In such condition I am here my husband.

I received your letter. I received $1.00 from you for which you will accept my thanks, and also I am very glad to hear from you that you are in good health.

That is all the money that I have, what you have sent me. I don't know what I shall do. I was in the City Hall asking for support, for myself and for my child. They sent me to the Government Office and they told me to go to work and give my child to the crèche.

Now I write you to ask you what I shall do. Shall I give our dear child to a crèche – or not. Also I write you that those men, who were

released at Lethbridge, have told me that perhaps you could be
released too. Why don't you ask for it? If you don't want to come
home I will come to you, because I cannot stand any more.[146]

Among families of those detained, some support was given. Annie
Dandys, whose husband John was interned at the Morrissey camp, was
reported to be destitute. An investigation by the RNWMP detachment in
Coleman, Alberta, concluded she and her three small children, ages five,
three, and one, were in fact near starvation. The last remaining chickens
had been sold and all that remained were five pounds of flour and six
ounces of coffee. As with others, internment officials referred Annie
Dandys's case to the Salvation Army.[147] The needs of those in want,
however, could not always be met. The consequences sometimes resulted
in tragedy. In Vancouver, Constable Ricketts was called to the Powell
Street residence of Katie Fedych. There, in squalid surroundings, he
found a woman sobbing uncontrollably over the body of her six-month-
old child. With her father interned at Morrissey and no food or money
in the home, the baby had died of starvation. In broken English, the
bereaved mother attempted to communicate her fear for her remaining
four children. With no money to bury the child, her case was referred to
the Associated Charities.[148]

Internment touched the lives of many, and in unexpected ways. For
soldiers who served as guards at the camps, the experience was not
something they had bargained for. Many, animated by patriotic feelings
and the desire for glory, were now thrust into a situation that seemingly had nothing to do with the war. Moreover, the tasks they were
asked to perform were tedious and endless. Guarding the prisoners at
the working camps, in twenty-four-hour shifts with eight hours of rest,
was exhausting, requiring immense perseverance and concentration.[149]
Not everyone was up to the job of maintaining the necessary levels of
alertness. The effect, at times, was a breakdown in discipline, which
resulted in tension between commanders, soldiers, and administrators
alike. Where this happened, military justice would be applied, exacerbat-
ing the problems and ratcheting up the level of underlying resentment
and frustration.

Castle Mountain/Banff, in particular, gained a reputation for the substandard performance and unruliness of its personnel.[150] The original
commander, Major Stuart, was relieved of his duties after scores of
escapes had taken place and camp guards were charged in separate incidents for public drunkenness, providing liquor to prisoners, and for

allegedly having fired their rifles in the town of Banff. Despite the introduction of measures that would help with the discipline, the situation failed to improve under the new commander. When Private Beale was found sleeping at his post, Major Peter Spence recommended he be "severely dealt with ... as an example to the other soldiers." Inquiring whether the maximum sentence could be applied after Beale was found guilty (which was expected), Spence further asked whether the trooper might be sent away from the camp to the military jail in Calgary, since he felt "the moral effect [on the others] would be greater."[151]

Predictably, in a climate full of spite and ill will, the guards at Castle Mountain/Banff resisted or ignored orders, including several that banned soldiers from liquor stores and local bars.[152] Complaints about the unreasonableness of the Castle camp officers were registered with military headquarters.[153] Others not wanting to make trouble for themselves would seek relief from their predicament by simply applying for overseas duty. When a recruiting officer came to the Castle camp in search of volunteers, a full one-quarter requested transfers, despite their knowledge of what awaited them on the European front. But perhaps it was the words of Private George Lomax that best captured the mindset of some of the guards. When denied transfer by the camp commander (who feared the loss of his most able men), he pleaded with the officer commanding the Alberta military district that he be "liberated" from the camp.[154] His wish granted, Private Lomax would be killed on the western front a year later.

Personnel at other camps also protested the treatment accorded them by their superiors, who often came in for criticism and attacks on their character. At the Lethbridge camp, the medical officer objected to the "irksome and absolutely unnecessary" regulations with which he declared he "[was] unable and unwilling to comply."[155] At Jasper Park, the camp commander, Major J. Hopkins, abruptly dismissed Lieutenant A.C. Bury ostensibly for having failed in his duties at overseeing the satellite camp at Maligne Canyon. The real reason, later revealed, was that Bury had been colluding with parks officials in an attempt to remove the officious Hopkins from his command.[156] With few exceptions (Fort Henry being one), guards and officers at the camps were often at odds with each other.

The criticism of the administration of the camps was not strictly an internal affair. Outside sources were equally disparaging of the way in which camps were being managed. When prisoners escaped from Amherst, it was thought that the camp commander had facilitated their escape. "It is bad enough," declared Senator Henry Cloran of Montreal (who had received reports of the "treasonous" affair), "to send our flesh and blood to fight the enemy in a foreign country without being betrayed at home." He demanded the government should see to it that "there are no traitors in our midst and that the enemy is not replenished from our own internment camps."[157] At Lethbridge, the new commander, Major Date, came increasingly under fire for his handling of the camp and especially for not being able to stem the tide of escapes from the facility. Rather than accept responsibility, Date expressed dissatisfaction with his men whose characters he felt made them unfit to serve. He was adamant that only those who were "steady and reliable" be picked for duty at his camp in the future.[158]

This corrosive atmosphere took its toll, hardening the hearts of those responsible for the well-being of the internees. With discipline at many of the camps in short supply and increasing pressure to use prisoners to maximum effect, abuse of power would occur. The abuses included the harsh treatment of the prisoners, notably to extract work or to enforce compliance. But it also extended to other "irregularities" at the camps, highlighting the issue of professional misconduct as well as the poor judgment and motives of those in charge.

At Toronto's Stanley Barracks, for example, Christmas presents destined for the internees were pilfered. Although an investigation was conducted, nothing was done at the facility to discipline the soldiers who were widely believed to have stolen the items.[159] Theft of personal possessions, in particular cash, also occurred where opportunity presented itself, most notably at the start of a prisoner's detention. Requiring that they relinquish their possessions, enemy aliens were issued receipts, but not in every instance. Without a voucher, the grievances of those affected were left unaddressed and what little wealth they had would disappear.[160] The opportunity to take advantage of the predicament of the enemy alien also took other forms. The commandant of Spirit Lake, Lieutenant Colonel William Rodden, owned land adjacent to the camp. Putting the prisoners to work on his property, he had them cut 1,100 cords of pulpwood, which he endeavoured to sell. Only a close audit by provincial authorities discovered the fraud. Although Rodden contended this was done "in error," he was relieved of his command by the minister of justice.[161] What distinguished Rodden was that he was found out. But in this matter he was not alone. Internees were frequently used for personal or private gain at other camps – with or without permission.[162]

The private struggles of prisoners of war Mytro Couch and Fanny Priester underscored the coarseness of petty indifference that would cause so much unnecessary hardship and distress. Mytro Couch, suffering from a debilitating ailment, had with him medicine that helped him cope with his pain. The medical NCO at the Morrissey camp where Couch was interned, Sergeant Oughton, destroyed the pills. The sergeant explained that acting as the camp censor he was under instructions to destroy "foreign printed matter" no matter what the source. Although the pills were produced in the United States and described in English, Oughton's actions were excused insofar as he was said to have been following instructions. After Couch requested that some other form of medication be substituted, the request was denied and he was left on his own to deal with his illness.[163]

Fanny Priester was interned as prisoner of war no. 5003 at Vernon. The BC facility (along with the one at Spirit Lake) served as a place of detention for women and children who, unable to fend for themselves, followed their menfolk into internment.[164] After almost a year at the Vernon station, Priester asked to be released. A domestic dispute apparently triggered the request.[165] She claimed that her brother in Kamloops could provide for her, adding that "I am a girl and have nothing to do with the war ... [and have] never had the slightest idea of harming anybody and don't see how I could." Although he was initially inclined to release the woman, Otter refused the application, claiming that she was too familiar with the operations of the station in which she was interned. He also contended that there was "strong extant prejudice" in the province regarding the release of enemy alien prisoners. The arguments seemed specious, however, especially in light of the release of others.

Priester insisted that she be heard. Her case would eventually come to the attention of the minister of justice some eight months after her initial application. After careful deliberation, the minister approved Priester's discharge but not before Otter, in an effort to forestall her release, stated, "I have personally seen the woman, who is decidedly a German, young, and to my mind a cunning, determined type." "It is possible," the general conceded, "that I am wrong in my estimate of Miss Priester and consequently over-cautious," but as he also noted, "she is now as well housed as others of her class, and therefore has no cause for complaint on that score." This, however, ignored the issue. As one of Fanny Priester's defenders pointed out: what information could an innocent charwoman possess that would so threaten the security of the country? It was a reasonable question and one for which no answer was given.

The challenges encountered by internees were numerous, but none more so than the physical abuse which was to become so much a part of prisoner life. The rules governing the treatment of military prisoners of war were explicit in that punishment was to be used under special circumstances and only to maintain discipline and order in the camp. For instance, prisoners charged with "conduct prejudicial to the good order and discipline of the camp" were to be brought before a tribunal and evidence entered so that an appropriate judgment might be made. Although a concerted effort was made to adhere to military procedure, this was not always the case. Sentencing at times was seen as a formality and punishment a means to an end. Moreover, it went beyond military protocol.

Indeed, the use of punishment was widespread at all of the camps. It was used increasingly as a way to extract work from the internees. At Castle Mountain, the district officer commanding, in the company of the American consul who was sent to report on the camp, acknowledged in a communication to General Otter that the internees had registered numerous complaints regarding their treatment by the guards.[166] Prisoner Chiskolok complained that he was forced to work when he was sick. When he refused, the guard struck him with his rifle and called him a son of a bitch. Prisoner Demchuk objected to being handcuffed and confined in a solitary cell after he refused to work. Prisoner of war no. 12, who went by the name of Harris, protested that Private Little pointed his rifle and shot at him after he and other prisoners (citing the bad condition of their boots and clothing) refused to work. Prisoners Bilak and Botha were also both threatened with shooting when they refused to work. A revolver, for instance, was pointed at Botha's head after he had been struck with the butt end of the pistol. On learning of the brutal treatment from the military district commander, General Otter replied, "The various complaints made to you by the prisoners as to the rough conduct of the guards, I fear, is not altogether without reason, a fact much to be regretted and, I am sorry to say, by no means an uncommon occurrence at other Stations."[167]

The situation elsewhere, indeed, was no better. A letter of a former inmate describing the conditions at the Lethbridge camp was published in the *Chicago Tribune*. Relaying in detail the undisciplined behaviour of the guards, the letter created a stir. The claims – serious and disturbing in their import – led to an investigation that aimed to establish whether the allegations were true. General Otter dismissed some of these as "trivial," stating that the punishment meted out was "easily understood as being necessary as well as legitimate."[168] He was dismayed, however, by information confirming that strappado was being used on the prisoners. In this method of torture, prisoners are handcuffed with their hands tied behind their backs or above their heads and lifted up by a rope with toes barely touching the ground. As Otter put it, this went beyond the limits of the Army Act or British custom, and he advised the military district commander: "How any palliation can be offered for these punishments I am at a loss to surmise, but of this I am certain that a repetition must not occur, and I would trouble you to notify Captain Birney [the camp commandant] – That if a more close supervision cannot be exercised over the officers, non-commissioned officers and men of his command in their treatment of prisoners, the object of their present duties are rendered valueless, and the good name of Canada brought to a level with the Huns."[169]

Officers in the field, whether in the camps or overseeing the work parties, were pressured to maintain discipline and order among the prisoners. Furthermore, the use of disciplinary measures was expected and even encouraged by provincial overseers, who insisted the work not fall behind schedule and that maximum advantage be taken of the available labour. Internment administration was also urged to adopt needed measures to move work projects along. Both Commissioner J.B. Harkin and his assistant James Wardle, for instance, asked General Otter, after enemy alien blacksmiths at Revelstoke refused to dress tools and the commander, Captain Rose, showed little willingness to enforce discipline among the prisoners, to take action "to have this matter satisfactorily adjusted."[170] The captain was relieved of his command shortly thereafter on the orders of the general, who claimed Rose had failed to meet the requirements of the position, "besides which the Dominion Parks Commission, for whom work is being done by the prisoners under his charge, greatly complain that results are not being obtained by their labour commensurate with the expenditure entailed, through the lack of energy, and indifference of this officer."[171]

Where Captain Rose lacked energy and demonstrated indifference, others did not. At Edgewood, the prisoners refused to work, complaining of the quality and insufficiency of food. From the perspective of the supervising road engineer, John Black, the problem rested with the commandant, Captain Harvey, who "petted" the prisoners, allowing them to have their own way. According to Black, Harvey had lost control of the camp and could not be expected to reassert his authority "without a much firmer stand than he is taking, which is, he claims, all he can do under the regulations." Black, however, was buoyed by the actions of a junior officer at the camp, Lieutenant Brooks, who, in the absence of the commandant, employed a six-day punishment diet of bread and water and threatened beatings as a way to force prisoners back to work. The "stringent measures" employed resulted in an all-out strike. Writing to the B C deputy minister of public works, Black nevertheless commented, "Brooks is handling the situation in the proper way and if left alone will get the results we want." He added, "Can you support him for commandant of this camp?"[172]

The deputy minister of public works in B C, J. Griffith, was uncomfortable with actions that went beyond regulations and which compelled the internees to work. Time and again, Griffith received reports, whether from Mara Lake or Edgewood, that prisoners refused to work for a variety of reasons and any advantage was therefore lost unless there was a change in attitude.[173] This could only come about through coercion. On this point, however, Griffith would not concede, for, as he pointed out, the internees were civilians and could not be forced to work if they objected to it.[174] Griffith was not alone in his reservation. J.B. Harkin, commissioner of the dominion parks branch, also had occasion to reflect. He was quoted as saying in the *Mail Herald* (Revelstoke) that internees were not criminals. Moreover, as citizens of countries at war with the empire and Canada, they simply found themselves in an unfortunate predicament. Accordingly, "Under international law they may not be treated as ordinary prisoners but are entitled to certain consideration."[175]

There was an implicit understanding that these were individuals who warranted empathy, and in the case of Griffith, this was because they were civilians. They were non-combatants and, therefore, deserving of greater consideration than if they were simply military prisoners. In effect, they were to be treated in a manner that was in keeping with their civilian standing. And yet, despite this recognition, it did not entirely dissuade Harkin, or for that matter Griffith, from using internment labour on public works, nor did it fundamentally change how the workers were being treated. The use of internment labour was an opportunity not easily passed up.

Interned enemy aliens believed that they were civilians – and needed to be treated as such. At the Yoho camp, the internees there claimed that they did not understand why they should be imprisoned while other

3.4  Grubbing, road construction, Monashee–Edgewood, BC

alien subjects were allowed their freedom and able to earn a living in the country as well. There was no answer to these and other questions. The reaction of the frustrated internees to the seemingly callous indifference of officials was predictable. At Yoho, the refusal of the internees to work turned into a month-long strike, despite the use of harsh measures by camp authorities to break the collective resistance of the group.[176] At Kapuskasing, they took matters into their own hands by driving railroad spikes into the logs, badly damaging the mill saw.[177] For others, less equipped physically or psychologically to deal with the pressures of their incarceration, the stress was simply too much to bear.

At Castle Mountain, while under guard, Mike Penziwiater slipped away on several occasions from his work gang, only to return voluntarily to the camp at night. During his last escape, he did so under a hail of bullets; five shots fired in his direction all missed the mark. On his return, Penziwiater was confined to the compound where, increasingly, he wandered about in a state of agitation. Suspecting that he would attempt to climb the fence (at which point he more than likely would have been shot), officials recommended that Penziwiater – as well as prisoners L. Baran and H. Andrusak who were also suffering from mental breakdown – be committed to the provincial asylum at Ponoka, Alberta. No action, however, was taken. Only when Penziwiater violently attacked another prisoner, beating him nearly to death with a stave in a fit of uncontrolled rage, was he charged with delusional insanity and taken away.[178]

Then there was the case of George Luka Budak, who arrived at the Banff internment camp from Regina on 6 December 1916, though no charge had been laid against him. At the time of his arrival, he persisted in his loyalty to the Allies. Harmless and quiet, Budak kept to himself. From the outset of his incarceration, however, Budak showed signs of depression and nervousness. On 19 December, anxious for his personal safety, he asked to be quartered at night in the guardroom cell. The request was granted. On Christmas Eve a commotion was heard in the guardroom. Entering, the guards found a quantity of blood on the cell floor and Budak under a bed. Pulling him out, they discovered his throat had been cut through the larynx. His abdomen was also slashed open with his bowels spilling out. A bloody razor lay next to him. With no recognizable pulse, but still conscious, Budak, nodding in response to questions put to him, indicated that he alone had committed the act. A coroner's inquest delivered the verdict, George Luka Budak "came to his death by wounds self-inflicted, cause unknown."[179] In point of fact, it was internment that killed him.

OUTSIDE, LOOKING IN

Reports concerning the treatment of Canadian and British prisoners of war in German POW camps during 1915–16 appeared with frequency in the press. Most of it was negative, some of it sensational. British prisoners were said to have been whipped by guards at the Niederzwehren camp, and Lord Kitchener stated in the House of Lords that British prisoners were being shot down by their German captors. Sensationalism aside, there was ample evidence to suggest that the conditions experienced by Allied prisoners were indeed difficult. Information provided by the American ambassador to Germany, James Gerard, indicated that the conditions of captivity in Germany were arduous and demanding. Such reports confirmed the rumours of suffering among captured Allied soldiers, whose fate was never far from the public mind.[180]

Not surprisingly, one element of Canadian society demanded retribution when it was discovered that prisoners in some Canadian camps were being dealt with leniently, certainly with far greater consideration than was shown Canadian prisoners in Germany. The *Calgary Daily Herald*, commenting on the apparent lax situation at the nearby Lethbridge camp, declared that the interned Germans there should be given no special favours.[181] Meanwhile at the Vernon camp, on learning that Germans of an officer class were granted day passes, the local paper queried, "Why are some of the aristocratic German prisoners at the Vernon internment camp treated with such sickening deference and consideration? Why are they given all manner of privileges which renders their confinement a farce?"[182] Challenging the practice, the *Vernon News* demanded that tougher measures be applied. This was war and no quarter was to be given the enemy, whether at home or abroad. "Do the authorities responsible for the affairs of the internment camp realize this? Are they merely playing at being at war, or are they not seized with the supreme gravity of the situation? It is not pleasant to refer to these things, but the souls of many of us are consumed with burning and well-justified bitterness these days against our brutal foes, and the questions above set forth are forcing themselves home upon our minds with a strength that makes silence no longer a possibility." A year and a half later, when tunnels were uncovered at the Vernon camp and twelve prisoners managed to escape, the newspaper once again pressed its point that camp administration needed to be tougher in their approach, mocking officials by proposing that prisoners "be furnished with gloves and knee pads so that in future the somewhat arduous labours connected with constructing tunnels may be made as easy as possible for these gentlemen who in every other respect are treated with such consideration and respect."[183]

Others, more charitable in outlook, suggested that standards defining civilized behaviour had to be maintained, especially in light of the reports of enemy wrongdoing. The treatment of prisoners was a mark of civilization, and although the barbarism of war had the potential of being at its worst in a prisoner of war camp, humanity was not to be disgraced or discredited by primitive brutishness or prejudice. Humanity would be redeemed by the tolerance and compassion shown to those who depended on the mercy of others. In this sense, British civilization was justified in the midst of the horror that was war and every effort was to be taken to ensure that the principles of humanity would extend to prisoners of war.

Canadians, it was argued, could take real satisfaction in the knowledge that standards and principles were, in fact, being upheld by Britain and its allies: "Canadians, even in the thick and sorrow of the war, thank God they are not allied with brutish tyrants, but with men whose humane instincts are proof against the most debasing influence of war."[184] Whatever was transpiring in Germany, the claim was made that the treatment of prisoners of war in Britain, and the empire more generally, was exceptional. Britain and Canada could point to the positive commentary of diplomatic observers and of prisoners themselves, who reportedly sang the praises of Allied captivity.[185]

Not everyone, however, was willing to accept, at face value, self-serving statements averring that the rights of prisoners were being respected or the principle of British fair play was at work. A number of groups and individuals conducted their own investigations to verify whether prisoners were being accorded treatment that was in keeping with international precepts and law. The activist Emily Murphy, for one, as convenor of the Committee on Peace and Arbitration for the National Council of Women of Canada, inquired about conditions at the Lethbridge camp, reminding the commander there that his position was one of national service in the highest sense of the term. It was a position of extraordinary responsibility, she declared: "The opportunity thus afforded you of lightening the bitterness of the men's incarceration and of showing the true meaning of human brotherhood cannot fail to have its effect on these, who will, in all probability, remain to form the German element in Canada when the war is over. In this connection it is unnecessary to add anything further, in that the honour and good conscience of the British are, and have always been, inseparable from a generous treatment of their hostages." The letter was passed on to the director of internment operations, General Otter. The general, irritated by Murphy's prying and sermonizing, voiced his pique by tersely responding to her questions regarding sufficiency of food, space, exercise, and the like.[186] Otter did not have to be reminded of his duties and responsibilities. He was well aware of them, and of the pressures that accompanied the job.

Murphy was not alone in expressing an interest in the welfare of the prisoners. The Ukrainian community of Manitoba did what it could to ease the burden of internment at the Brandon camp by seeing to the spiritual and basic needs of the internees. The community leaders also harnessed the goodwill of Florence and Fred Livesay (the dominion press censor), both of whom actively campaigned on behalf of the prisoners for their release.[187] They claimed that the internees were largely ignorant of the law and harmless and inoffensive in their disposition. Fred Livesay was told through an intermediary, however, that the director of internment would not discharge of prisoners without an offer of employment. In the camps they would stay until circumstances warranted otherwise.

As a military operation, internment in Canada remained for the most part out of public sight. This was possible because the majority of the camps were located on the frontier and access was limited. But certain camps did offer a chance opportunity for a visit. Castle Mountain, an encampment not far from Banff and Calgary, was just such a place. Those who came included royalty (the Duke and Duchess of Connaught), newspaper reporters, as well as the adventurous and mildly curious. When Major Stuart was commander of the camp, Mrs Stuart treated the visitors to tea and light fare. They could stay overnight as well to enjoy the full experience of being outdoors and, of course, take in the views. Curiously, however, their interest did not extend to the prisoners, who were paraded daily and sent out to work under armed guard. With the stunning beauty of the mountains about them, visitors chose to see what they wished to see and ignored the rest. Returning from one such outing, an anonymous traveller to the Castle camp wrote in rapturous terms about their experience:

Three miles further along the trail an internment camp, a veritable white city, is reached. The camp is ideally located beneath the shadows of the Castle mountain, laid out with all due attention to the laws of hygiene, and cleanliness is one of the watchwords. Pure water is piped down from a stream up the side of Castle Mountain and every attention is given to the health and well-being of the inmates of the camp, in fact the sick bay at the time of the visit contained not a single inmate. The officers from Commandant Major Spence down to the non-coms have a conception of the true meaning of the word hospitality, which they dispense with lavish hands, and a dinner in the officers' mess tent leaves nothing to be desired by the most fastidious epicurean. To reach the very limit of enjoyment the night should be spent at the camp, if one is fortunate enough to receive an invitation from the officers. The evening can be most pleasantly spent in watching the fantastic shadows which play over the heights of Castle Mountain – and in other agreeable ways. And when one turns in for the night, one should offer up prayers to Allah, the all-merciful, for a shower of rain, for if there is anything in this world more delightful than listening to the patter of rain drops on a tent roof the writer has yet to find it. And to be awakened in the morning and introduced to a plate of hot buttered toast and a huge cup of steaming coffee with the request or command to partake of it before arising to the acme of hospitality. A substantial breakfast in the officers' mess, followed by the run to Banff in the fresh, cool air of the morning makes one think that this old world is a mighty pleasant place to live in.[188]

That the life of the prisoners did not appear to concern visitors, or for that matter the wider public, highlighted a general acceptance of the idea that internment served a purpose. Although the degree to which internment was needed was not fully understood, at a certain level, there was a willingness to defer to officials, who, being in a position to know, were thought to be acting appropriately. But perhaps more importantly there was ample evidence that unemployed enemy aliens faced want and hunger and internment offered a form of relief from their predicament. In this sense, there was no reason to dispute the apparent need to send these people to the camps. What went on there was of less concern than the fact the problem of the enemy alien was being dealt with.

In part, it was an attitude cultivated by the government, which maintained that its efforts were aimed at relieving the distress of those who could no longer provide for themselves. It was a position that was formally conveyed to the American government (representing German interests) in response to a German diplomatic protest, which alleged that German civilian prisoners were subjected to compulsory labour at the Kapuskasing internment camp.[189] Regarding the specifics of the allegation, the Canadian authorities officially replied that the prisoners were not compelled to work. Rather, they did so of their own free will and were clothed and fed at government expense, receiving twenty-five cents a day in accordance with regulations. Moreover, it was declared that none of the prisoners were Germans, but Austro-Hungarians and a few Turks, while only one hundred German civilians were interned in Canada, of whom ten were employed as cooks and rendered their services voluntarily. After the governor general's adjutant, Lieutenant Colonel Edward Stanton, personally observed that several hundred prisoners were working in the vicinity of the Petawawa military camp,[190] the claim was made that it was the employment situation in the country which forced the government to introduce measures leading to the internment of those who were without any means:

> It was ... directed that those who had not the means or intent to remain in Canada conformably to the laws and customs of the country, and subject to the obligation of reporting monthly in their registration district, might be interned. It is true that the Order in Council provides for their internment as prisoners of war, but the intention of this was that as no provision had been made for the maintenance of these people by the country of their allegiance, and as they would, therefore, have to be supported by the authorities of Canada, the status of prisoners of war, and the regulations governing their custody and maintenance, might be accorded and applied to these unfortunate aliens of enemy nationality who necessarily became a public charge.[191]

As for their labour, it was declared to be of little value. Its purpose was simply to afford "some occupation for people who must necessarily, in the interest of humanity, be maintained at the public expense." But more to the point and in defence of its position, the government emphatically asserted that the actions taken "were in accordance with our domestic system to employ at such labour as they are qualified to perform, persons whether native or foreign who are cast upon the charity of the State ... And that neither the state of war nor any rule sanctioned by international convention or practice requires that destitute people of any nationality when seeking relief from the State should be immune from a similar requirement." It added: "The provision, so far as it goes, that they should be accorded treatment as prisoners of war, obviously works to the advantage of these distressed people rather than as a hardship."[192]

From the government's perspective, interned enemy aliens were deemed military prisoners of war and as such could be put to work. Although government action was depicted as altruistic and benevolent, the default argument was that it was both legitimate and justifiable, being in accord with international understandings and domestic provisions. That there may have been some uncertainty, however, was intimated by the statement made that there were only one hundred German civilian prisoners, of whom only ten were working and voluntarily at that. As there were hundreds more of German origin in Canada who were interned, mainly reservists, a distinction was being made between military and civilian prisoners of war. It reflected a latent skepticism about classifying interned enemy aliens as military prisoners of war. This skepticism had been clearly articulated when an application was referred to the judge advocate general to convene a district court martial against two internees at Fort Henry caught in the act of trying to break through a stone wall. The application was refused principally on the grounds that the men were not prisoners of war but merely "interned enemy aliens."[193]

The opinion of the judge advocate general compelled General Otter to seek clarification from the minister of justice, fearing as he did that "we may be acting illegally."[194] Defending the government's position, the deputy minister of justice, E. Newcombe, invoked the ruling in the British case of *The King v. Superintendent of Vine Street Police Station, Ex parte Liebmann*, (1916) 1 K.B. 268: "An alien enemy resident in the United Kingdom, who, in the opinion of the Executive Government, is a person hostile to the welfare of this country and is on that account interned, may properly be described as a prisoner of war although not a combatant or a spy."[195] Newcombe also cited the Manual of Military Law, 1914, which, referring to an enemy alien being taken as a prisoner, stated: "Such individuals are not civil prisoners; they are taken into captivity for military reasons, and they are therefore prisoners of war." Interned enemy aliens were, according to the Canadian government, military prisoners of war to whom the laws of war applied.

Notwithstanding the Canadian position, Germany rejected the idea that interned civilians were prisoners of war as was conventionally understood. Although they were prisoners, interned enemy aliens were in fact civilians and not military combatants and, therefore, were to be treated as such. It was a principle that Germany was prepared to defend and from which it would not retreat. The distinction between civilian and military prisoners followed from the German concern regarding the treatment of its nationals in foreign lands and the German law on imperial citizenship, which maintained that Germans abroad, naturalized or not, continued to be subjects of the emperor. A political and moral obligation, therefore, fell on the German government to intercede on behalf of its subjects residing elsewhere and to defend their interests.

A major impetus in the German calculation to act on behalf of its citizens abroad was the diplomatic manoeuvring between Britain and Germany on the issue of the treatment of prisoners of war. Allegations of German atrocities were widespread in the British and Canadian press, including reports on conditions at the POW camps of Wittenberg and

Doeberitz and the prison camp for civilians at Ruhleben. It was imperative that German authorities counter allegations of barbarity and inhumanity by pointing out irregularities in the British and Allied treatment of German prisoners. The camps in Canada became a point of interest in the German effort to offset British and Allied reports regarding German brutality.

The principal claim in the German diplomatic protests related to the compulsory work of civilian internees on public projects. The claim was animated by American reports detailing the treatment of prisoners at various camps. Kapuskasing and Spirit Lake were initially singled out as facilities where German civilian prisoners were subjected to compulsory labour such as clearing the land, felling trees, and sawing wood, for which, according to German officials, they received "the disgracefully low pay of 25 cents per day." Germany demanded that the British government instruct Canadian officials to put a stop to the activity, iterating that only volunteer labour could be used and that they be paid the average local wage of free labourers as was done on the German side. It was further conveyed that if the reply were unsatisfactory, the German government would "feel justified in adopting counter measures with regard to the subjects of Great Britain detained in Germany."[196]

Canada rejected the claim. The Canadian response was informed by the notion that since no provision had been made for the maintenance of the internees by their country of origin and to avoid having them become a public charge, the status of prisoner of war would apply.[197] Citing Article 6 of the Annex to the Fourth Hague Convention, Canadian authorities claimed that Canada could employ the labour of prisoners of war according to their rank and status. Furthermore, they could be authorized to work for the public service and the work was to be paid proportional to the work of a similar kind executed by soldiers of the national army. German authorities rejected the Canadian response, and the threat of retaliation was raised once again, especially after information became public regarding the alleged ill treatment of German prisoners at Amherst and Nanaimo.[198]

The Canadian treatment of enemy alien prisoners was of concern to British officials because of the wider implications for Allied prisoners in Germany and Austria-Hungary.[199] Consequently, Britain pressed Canada into accepting in principle that Article 6 of the Hague Convention would not apply to civilian prisoners. This was subsequently conveyed to German authorities, but with the proviso that interned civilians in Canada, working voluntarily, would not receive the customary local pay associated with "free labourers" because they received food and lodging gratis.[200] Moreover, given that the pay scales in Canada and Germany for the same class of work were far from equal, it was felt that anything other than the military rate of pay would involve inequalities in remuneration. Twenty-five cents a day for the labour of an interned civilian was deemed to be "sufficient."[201] As for the question of compulsory labour, the principle was accepted that civilian prisoners would not be forced to work. But if there were issues, it was for German authorities to identify these since it was impractical, if not impossible, to investigate charges of a general nature.[202]

German officials vigorously clung to the proposition that interned enemy aliens were civilian prisoners whose civil status had to be respected. In this regard, they were to be neither viewed as military prisoners nor put to work without their consent. Coercion was also not to be used to elicit obedience or acquiescence. In short, there were standards that needed to be met and officials in Germany would hold the Canadian government to account. They were not alone. When, in February 1916, the minister of interior, W.J. Roche, replying to a parliamentary question, declared that the nature of the work performed by internees was not voluntary (since this was the only way "we could get a lot of work done"), Bonar Law, the colonial secretary, asked for an explanation. "It appears to be difficult to reconcile this statement," wrote Law, "with the assurance that has been given to the German Government that no civilian prisoner is compelled to work."[203]

It was difficult to reconcile because, in practice, the dynamics at work led to the use of civilian enemy aliens on road-building and land-clearing projects in Canada. A number of the reports by neutral American representatives, sent to investigate conditions at the various camps, alluded to the use of compulsory internment labour. There was no ignoring it. There were those, however, who were prepared to hide the fact. When Foreign Office officials received a report on the situation at Banff, and it was observed that the internees were forcibly engaged in work, one of the officials furtively advised that nothing should be said about it because the prisoners did not appear to complain.[204] The use of civilian internment labour was recognized as running counter to the arrangement between the belligerents – but would anyone notice if no one confessed and would anyone care if no one complained?

This attitude was due in part to the seminal belief that the majority of interned enemy aliens were of the labouring class and therefore accustomed to the work. A large number of the US reports noted that, in general, the prisoners were being well treated. But the reports were also punctuated by the belief that the prisoners were not being unnecessarily burdened because they were already habituated to the work. Indeed, the American consul, Harold Clum, having visited the camp at Banff, declared that the work was not arduous since there were "no officers or men of officer class among them."[205] The point for Clum was not whether they were being forced to undertake the work or that it was too hard, but that it was in line with their station in life. What else would the prisoners do? If idle, would they only hurt themselves?[206] It was a problematic attitude, giving credence to the idea that interned enemy aliens should be put to work while ignoring their real grievances.

The reports of US consular officials helped to serve the German interest in alleging Canadian maltreatment of civilian prisoners in its camps. German diplomatic protests were numerous and unremitting. Adding to the pressure were the remonstrations of the Turkish and Bulgarian governments, which were equally adamant about protecting the rights of their co-nationals abroad and holding Canada to account.[207] Decidedly absent, however, was any protest by the Austro-Hungarian government. Austria-Hungary did file complaints against the alleged mistreatment of Austrian officers in Canadian camps,[208] but it was conspicuously silent on the matter of second-class prisoners who were Austro-Hungarian subjects. Since they represented a range of national minorities on the margins of the empire and had little interest in the European conflict, their pre-war exodus as economic migrants gave sufficient reason for the Austro-Hungarian government to surrender any claim to their allegiance.

In most cases, defending the interests of the internees was left to the various ethnic communities and their representative organizations. The Polish Relief Committee of Chicago, for example, urged the Canadian government to put a stop to the abuses in the camps and improve conditions that faced some three hundred interned Poles. The eminent Polish pianist and composer Ignacy Paderewski, a member of the Polish National Committee, also requested the discharge of interned enemy aliens of Polish origin, a request that was repeated by the Serbian War Mission in New York, acting on behalf of Serbs, Croats, and Yugoslavs generally.[209]

Internment officials in Canada addressed specific charges and allegations that were based on information contained in American reports, foreign newspaper accounts, and public allegations. These were met head on, often dismissed as fabrications or gross exaggerations of the circumstances. The shooting death of the inmate Fritz Klaus at the Amherst camp, who was allegedly murdered as he lay on the ground, was flatly denied, despite the evidence. A charge that the internees at the Lethbridge camp "had to work like convicts" was dismissed on the grounds that the person who made the accusation, an alleged former prisoner, was unknown to internment officials. Regarding the disposition of interned Turks at Fort Henry, General Otter declared that they, as well as others, were far from living in "miserable conditions" as was alleged by the Ottoman Porte, but rather they were "being fed the same as our own soldiers, well-clothed and in comfortable surroundings." After one Otto Mueller had made an affidavit that enemy aliens were subjected to "rude and inhuman treatment" at a camp located twelve miles from Montreal, it was pointed out that no such camp existed in the vicinity. The allegation that prisoners in the frontier camps were stripped naked and deliberately exposed for several hours to the attacks of mosquitoes was also dismissed by General Otter as an exaggeration; mosquitoes in the Canadian bush were ubiquitous. As for the series of allegations contained in letters published by the *Chicago Tribune* and the German American press, which caused the British emissary to the US to strongly advise that they be publicly refuted, these too were rejected as hysterics.[210]

Not all of the accounts or allegations of ill treatment could be so easily explained or dismissed. Complaints of abuse and mistreatment, corroborated by incriminating statements made by camp officers, peppered the reports of US consular officials who were obliged to record prisoner complaints. There were a significant number of such protests, some of which were trivialized. At Banff, for instance, the prodding with bayonets (resulting at times in blood being drawn) was described as mere "pricks," and at Mara Lake it was dismissed as "punishment a man would be able to tolerate." But other complaints, such as excessive discipline, punishment, and unprovoked beatings, could not be ignored. Where the evidence proved incontrovertible, such as at the Lethbridge camp, where prisoners were strung up and stretched by their wrists, Canadian officials acknowledged the maltreatment and explained what adjustments had been made.[211] Where it was demonstrated that soldiers had exceeded their authority or officers failed in their duty to ensure the well-being and safety of the prisoners, internment officials communicated that such individuals had been either censured, relieved of their duties, or reassigned to other units.[212]

In the main, internment officials felt they were doing all they could to ensure that the operation was being run within the provisions set out in the military manual and the various army acts governing the treatment of prisoners of war. They could also take great comfort in the reports of some of the American representatives who praised the work of the military authorities in providing for the health, hygiene, and general well-being of the prisoners. US consul Felix Johnson, for one, having visited the Kingston internment facility in May 1916, reported that "the prisoners speak in glowing terms of the treatment accorded them in Fort Henry," and again, in August, he observed that the prisoners were so well treated at the fort that there was difficulty in having them removed from the facility.[213] Johnson, however, may have been overstating the case. Others were less inclined to suspend their judgment on what amounted to the imprisonment and forced labour of civilians and excoriated the operation for its unjust treatment of interned enemy aliens.

US Consul Gebhard Willrich of Quebec City, tasked with reporting on conditions at Spirit Lake, was not impressed with what he saw, having visited the camp in November of 1916.[214] Spirit Lake, a place of internment for some 1,300 enemy aliens at the height of its operation, saw a significant reduction in the number of its inmates. Those who remained, however – some 250 – were in an agitated state. Sent to investigate and given permission by General Otter to privately interview the prisoners, Willrich was surprised by what he heard and observed.[215] Huddled together in shacks that scarcely sheltered them from the cold and harsh weather, without heat and deprived of rations for refusing to work, the internees complained of beatings, confinement, insults, and neglect. The contempt in which officers and soldiers held the enemy alien was also in evidence, the consul noting: "The man charged with police authority at this camp ... had exercised his authority in a rather brutal way, under the mistaken notion, that these prisoners were criminals rather than unfortunate solely through circumstance. Petty annoyances, loss of small liberties, even physical punishment had thus resulted solely to gratify the petty officer's rather brutal instincts." Among the prisoners, forced to labour, a sense of hopelessness and despair prevailed. A number claimed they no longer cared what happened to them, refusing to obey orders despite being punished. Others looked to Willrich as an advocate, pleading for their release, citing their families' desperate situation. Willrich could not have been other than moved when the prisoner H. Domytryk handed him a letter, written in English,

3.5  Clearing wood, Spirit Lake, Quebec

received from his nine-year-old daughter, Katie, which told of the child's
fears, anxieties, and hurt:

> My dear father:
>   We have nothing to eat and they do not want to give us no food.
> My mother has to go four times to get something to eat. It is better
> with you, because we had everything to eat. This shack is no good,
> my mother is going down town every day and I have to go with
> her and I don't go to school at winter. It is cold in that shack. We
> your small children kiss your hands my dear father. Goodbye my
> dear father. Come home right away.

From Willrich's perspective, it was inconceivable that people could
be treated this way. It was morally wrong. The problem, according to
Willrich, was that these were civilians, not military combatants, who
had demonstrated neither disloyalty nor hostility toward the country.
As immigrants, they had further shown their commitment to Canada by
leaving their past behind them. Now, however, according to Willrich,
they were being treated as "quasi-criminals." This ran counter to the best
instincts and interests of the country. How the government could approve

this conduct in good conscience was simply incomprehensible: "The temporary saving, which may be affected by the payment, or rather allowance, of such a pittance as 25 cents per day for a full day's work, not even payable to them or their families in full, seems to be inexpedient and unjust, the former because men will not render a day's work for that amount, even when pretending to do so; unjust because most of these men had good profitable work prior to their internment and families to support, which now are more punished than they are." Willrich argued that Canada should not treat these men as enemies, having invited them to Canada, but rather conduct a policy that was both "just to the prisoner and the Dominion." He called for their release: "There is no doubt in my mind, that at the present moment, the great majority of the prisoners at Spirit Lake could safely be returned to their homes and families, and that such return would be more profitable to Canada in the end than their retention in the camps as unwilling workers and strikers."

Consul Willrich's views were unwelcome. It was not for the consul to pass judgment on policy, nor was his obvious empathy for the internees appreciated. After Willrich's visit, the camp commander at Spirit Lake, Lieutenant Colonel J. Rinfret, quickly telegraphed the director of internment, General Otter, informing him that the consul's report, which followed from the diplomat's pronounced anti-British and pro-German views, was certain to be unfavourable. He recommended that it be intercepted.[216] The prime minister, Robert Borden, apprised of the situation and alarmed by the possible political and diplomatic repercussions, requested that an application be made to Washington to obtain the services "of a reliable official" who would be able to reassess the conditions at the camp.[217] As for Willrich, the undersecretary of state for external affairs, Sir Joseph Pope, suggested that he might be removed, "either by quietly arranging for his transfer to some other sphere of usefulness, or procuring the withdrawal of his Exequator." Days later, on learning that the US government was about to recall the consul, Pope alerted General Otter of his suspicions that Willrich was carrying with him letters from the prisoners. Such an act would contravene the censorship laws and was thus punishable. He advised Otter on bringing the matter before the postmaster general for his action. According to Pope, Willrich's duplicitous behaviour should not go unanswered. He needed to pay a price for such behaviour, which had been carried out under the cover of diplomacy.[218]

Among other things, Willrich was opposed to compulsory labour. But this was nothing new. A long-standing criticism of Canadian internment policy was that civilian prisoners were compelled to work. And although Canadian officials explained that the labour was not compulsory, Germany, ever watchful, persisted in its demand that under no circumstances should German civilian prisoners be forced to work and that only those who willingly gave their consent should be used.[219] To this end, German authorities offered subsidies to interned Germans in the Canadian camps so that they would not have to work unless they so wished.[220] As for Austro-Hungarians and others, increasing access to US officials, who at the very least were obliged to report their complaints, provided them with the resolve to resist. It proved problematic insofar as the internees by the end of 1916 and early 1917 began exercising their right to refuse work and conducting strikes when pressure was brought to bear on them. It thus became increasingly apparent that the operation, as it was initially conceived, was unsustainable. If internment were to play a continuing role, it would have to be different from what was originally planned.

## CIVILIAN ENEMY ALIENS AS POWS

The modern condition of war, in which every able-bodied man capable of bearing arms is a potential combatant, would force technological and strategic innovation as a response to the phenomenon of nations at war. One of those responses was to designate resident subjects of enemy states as "alien enemies" and impose upon them a number of conditions, including the possibility of interning them as prisoners of war if they acted in a hostile manner. This was a significant development because it meant that, once interned, enemy aliens were to be considered prisoners of war and treated as such. The notion that interned enemy aliens could be put to work was now effectively legitimized. Indeed, the convention governing the laws of war provided for the possibility of prisoners of war being put to work as long as they were not coerced and the work was unrelated to the war effort. But more importantly, by equating the status of interned enemy aliens with that of military prisoners of war, officials in Canada believed they were now in an enhanced position to address the twin problems of enemy alien destitution and unemployment. Once they had been interned as prisoners of war, it was felt that unemployed and destitute enemy aliens could justifiably and rightfully be put to work. The practice was also described as a positive development, "affording occupation for people who must necessarily in the interest of humanity be maintained at the public expense."[221]

There were a number of difficulties, however, with this line of reasoning as it was expressed in Canada. First, the majority of enemy aliens arrested showed no evidence of hostility; nor were they necessarily thought to be hostile. On the contrary, as Canadian government officials openly admitted, they were interned because many were simply paupers and no longer able to care for themselves. Second, it was a leap in logic to equate the status of interned civilians with that of military prisoners to which the laws of war would apply. The argument, originally articulated by the deputy minister of justice, E. Newcombe, was that order-in-council 2721 provided for the internment of enemy alien poor, but that "the status of prisoner of war and the regulations governing their status and maintenance" would apply because "no provision had been made for the maintenance of these people by the country of their allegiance."[222] It may very well have been that PC 2721 allowed for the internment of civilian enemy aliens as prisoners of war in keeping with their enemy subject status, but it did not necessarily follow that they should be treated as prisoners to which the laws of war would apply. They were, after all, civilians who showed no signs of hostility.

Interned enemy aliens were civilian prisoners, not military prisoners of war. It was a fine distinction but an important one in light of the implications for those interned. But why was that distinction neither formally recognized nor followed? At a certain level, the problem resulted from the lacunae in international law that remained silent on the rights of interned civilians as prisoners of war. It was also, however, a function of political and military calculation in which the various warring states cautiously approached the issue as one that had to be shrewdly negotiated within the framework of reciprocity; both Britain and Germany as well as other belligerents were careful not to make concessions without equal gains.[223]

And yet there was an underlying sentiment, implied in the negotiations, that interned enemy aliens were to be recognized and treated as civilians. This followed from an appreciation of the fact that interned enemy aliens were non-combatants, at least those who were non-reservists. Therefore, they were entitled to greater rights and protection than captive soldiers. In this regard, the convention governing prisoners of war applied to bona fide military prisoners. But to civilian prisoners more than the military code of conduct was owed.[224]

In Canada, this view was held by the military judge advocate general, who, when asked to convene a military tribunal to try enemy aliens for an attempted escape at Fort Henry, refused to do so on the grounds that they were interned enemy aliens and not military prisoners: military law did not apply to them.[225] The deputy minister of justice responded (citing the Manual of Military Law) by claiming that interned enemy aliens could not be classified as civil prisoners because they had been taken into captivity for military reasons. But he was wrong on this point. The primary reason behind their internment was not military necessity; rather, on the contrary, the motives were economic, social, and political.

The distinction between civilian and military prisoners was aggressively defended by Germany. Strategic and political reasons informed the German decision and action, but this in no way detracted from the principle that interned enemy aliens were civilian prisoners. On this point, German officials not only remained defiant but also threatened retaliation. The threat of retaliation persuaded Britain to accept the principle; Canada, given its imperial connection, did so as well. But until that time, interned enemy aliens would be recognized and treated as conventional prisoners of war.

The distinction made between civilian and military prisoners was not a mere abstraction. It had real and serious consequences for those interned. As prisoners of war to whom the laws of war applied, enemy aliens were to be put to work. Although they could not be coerced, they were required to work for their own maintenance and on public works authorized by the state. Furthermore, they were governed by a military code of conduct and subject to a regime of military discipline that elevated the level of tension in the relationship between captive and guard and which enemy aliens as civilian prisoners would have to endure.

Not everyone connected with internment operations agreed with the idea that civilian prisoners should be treated as conventional prisoners of war. The BC deputy minister of public works, J.E. Griffith, for one, expressed his consternation over the matter. When pressured on the issue of using force to expedite the work, he objected, claiming that these were civilian prisoners and could not be compelled to work. J.B. Harkin, the parks commissioner, was also charitably predisposed toward the enemy alien prisoners, noting that they were not "criminals" and were owed a certain amount of "consideration." Nevertheless, despite acknowledging their status as civilian prisoners, both Griffith and Harkin were not above using internment labour – when needed. Internment labour proved much too alluring to give up and could profitably be used if properly managed.

Among a certain segment of the population, the use of internee labour was predicated on the idea that these were bona fide prisoners who needed to be treated accordingly. They believed that the difference between civilian and military prisoners of war was largely immaterial. As subjects of a foreign sovereign, the prisoners' loyalty was believed to rest elsewhere. Therefore, these were enemies and, in the context of internment, were to be treated as such. In this regard, there were a great many public calls for the internees to be handled in a manner befitting their status as enemies, including at the Lethbridge station where antagonism toward the prisoners ran high after a series of escapes exposed deficiencies at the camp and, by extension, the Canadian military. "Prisoners at the camp have been treated with too much leniency," the *Lethbridge Telegram* declared, "a leniency which the recent escape shows has not been appreciated. If the outcome of the escape of the German means severe measures and stricter vigilance in dealing with the interned it cannot be said that it comes too late."[226] Interned enemy aliens were prisoners of war and needed to be treated in a manner that reflected their status. At Lethbridge and other camps where they were idle, the prisoners, it was declared, needed to be put to work not simply as a matter of principle, but because these were enemies who would go to extraordinary lengths to make good their escape and do harm. Putting them to work would occupy them. But their status as enemies would also be firmly established in this way, making indisputably clear how they were to be dealt with.

For those who were either more cautious or inclined to accept the idea that these prisoners were civilians and therefore entitled to greater consideration, the issue of their use as prisoner labour was mitigated by the circumstances facing the enemy alien – these were individuals who were without employment. They would work because there was no other choice. The economic situation in the country was difficult and there was no work to be had. Under the circumstances, therefore, it was the best that Canada could do and it was the least disagreeable among possible alternatives. Internment certainly was not to be interpreted as punitive. Indeed, since many of the enemy aliens were common labourers, it was felt that they were already accustomed to this sort of work. Because they were habituated to physical labour, the work they were asked to perform was seen as neither out of the ordinary nor especially burdensome.

This particular view was widely held, including among diplomats entrusted with the welfare of the internees. American representatives, for example, believed that, as second-class prisoners, the internees were already accustomed to the type of work expected of them and, therefore, it was not particularly taxing. It was an attitude that helped mask the central issue, which was whether the internees as civilian prisoners should be made to work at all. It was an attitude shared by some officials in the Foreign Office who thought the work to be not only straightforward from the perspective of the enemy alien, but beneficial as well. As one official in London commented, clearing the parks of brush wood and the like was "not unduly onerous," and "serves to provide them with fresh air and exercise, conducive to health."[227] It was a regrettable sentiment, since it would help reinforce the isolation of the prisoners, who, by virtue of their internment, already felt alone and abandoned.

From the perspective of military officials overseeing the internment operation, the civilian versus military distinction was theoretically important, but until such time as the matter was diplomatically resolved the difference was largely moot. The internment of enemy aliens was being filtered through an operational lens. Specifically, as a military operation, internment administrators were expected to perform their military duty. Indeed, although there was some concern among internment officials as to how and why enemy aliens were being rounded up and interned en masse, as was the case at Port Arthur, Ontario, and Fernie, BC, their duty was not to question why, but to carry out their orders. Moreover, when senior government officials, such as the interior minister, made clear that the point of internment was to have those interned working (which followed from their prisoner of war status), it simply reinforced among internment officials the idea that military regulations and expectations would apply.

The agreement reached in due course with German authorities on the civilian designation of enemy alien prisoners would place constraints on the operation as a military affair. But even so, it proved difficult to treat the internees as anything other than conventional prisoners of war. This was because there was enormous pressure to make internment work. Internment was not strictly speaking a military-security operation. Its purpose was to deal with the distress of the unemployed enemy alien and, after June 1915, with those enemy aliens who were competing for jobs with the native-born. Enemy aliens would be provided with work, albeit in a controlled environment. In this way, it was thought they would be helped. However, assistance, even in this qualified form, did not mean that it would be at any cost. It was both counterintuitive and counterproductive to have unemployed enemy aliens interned and remaining idle. For the operation to succeed, it would have to be financially viable and therefore sustainable. Hence, the enemy alien prisoners would not only be put to work, but also, as much as possible, pay for the cost of their internment.

An important feature of the internment operation was to have the labour of the prisoners contracted out to parties willing to pay their wages. What made this proposal attractive was that the wages were set by internationally sanctioned rules governing the treatment of prisoners of war. Prisoners of war would be paid a military wage. More particularly, they would be paid the supplementary military wage for non-military work, or twenty-five cents a day. It was a boon to those agencies that entered into negotiations with internment operations. A key consideration, however, in making the proposal viable was that nothing should impede the work. On this point, the contracting agencies were firm. Whether it was the parks branch in the federal Department of the Interior, the northern development branches in Ontario and Quebec, or the Department of Public Works in British Columbia, all of the concerned parties insisted that nothing interfere with the progress of work; otherwise there was no economic benefit to be had.

The implications of this were enormous. Internment officials were in effect obliged to make the prisoners work. And although those in the field were prohibited from using coercive measures, discipline was still used as a way to move the projects along. Indeed, officers were encouraged by road superintendents and other overseers to use all necessary means to achieve results. Despite this pressure, military officials were careful to follow protocol and generally applied only those disciplinary measures that were regulated. Some would go beyond the rules, committing egregious breaches of protocol to which General Otter would voice his objection. But there was no mistaking the intent. The prisoners would work. Even when a diplomatic agreement was reached between Germany and Britain, the use of civilian prisoner labour in Canada continued. Although Canadian officials denied German accusations of compulsory labour, in practice, they did apply pressure – withdrawing privileges, for example – in the hope that prisoners would capitulate.

By mid- to late 1916, those administering the camps were acutely aware that progress on projects would be limited if they did not apply harsher measures. The major impediment was the growing resistance among the internees to the idea that they should be made to work. For example, the officer commanding Military District No. 2, Brigadier General W.A. Logie, observed that at Kapuskasing, "the basis of the discontent seems to be that the interned aliens are compelled to work."[228] Logie declared that it was "unfair" to the camp commander "not to give definite instructions on this point" and intimated that without adequate punishment the entire program was in jeopardy. If the prisoners were to be compelled to work, what punishment should the commander impose on those who refused, Logie would ask? The director of internment operations, General Otter, cautiously responded: "With respect to the cause of discontent on the part of the prisoners, viz, their obligation to work; the question is one that it has not been considered advisable to promulgate any definite order upon, as there is no regulation compelling them to do so, while on the other hand it is better both for themselves and the public that they should. Therefore, the matter has been left to the tact and judgment of Commandants."[229] Control, with a view to achieving results, was a discretionary matter to be handled within reason by local commanders.

Entrusting the camp commanders to exercise judgment in the management of the prisoners was both natural and expected. But this also opened up the prospect for abuses to take place, made possible because of the unevenness in the quality and composition of the command and guard alike. Internment was not a military priority, certainly not with respect to the events in Europe. As such, all sorts of individuals were being appointed and promoted within the ranks. Some were more capable than others. A few, however, were simply ill equipped to command under what were decidedly frustrating and demanding conditions. For instance, the constant rotation of qualified personnel underscored the difficulty of command, especially as the camps became places to which men with all sorts of shortcomings were frequently sent. Lieutenant Colonel W. Ridgway-Wilson, for one, complained bitterly of the quality of the guard furnished to the camps in the BC interior, protesting that officers and men were being shifted about without any regard for the special needs of the operation. Expressing his dismay with the situation, Ridgway-Wilson openly declared the camps were made "the dumping ground for all the misfits."[230]

What this would demonstrate was a general lack of appreciation for the requirements associated with the job being asked of both the officers and men. The operation demanded fortitude, especially among the guards. Not everyone, however, was up to the task. In some respects, this had to do with expectations. When recruits were taken on strength, many were animated by a passionate desire to participate in the glory that was war. Being sent to the frontier to oversee a motley crew of unfortunates was not what they expected. The resentment was channelled toward the internees. The prisoners would be subjected to all sorts of abuses, ranging from patent violations to petty offences. The use of violence was commonplace.

Regardless of the severity of the injury or offence, the complaints received were often dismissed as incidental or inconsequential.[231] At the Banff camp, after he had been jabbed with a bayonet after a soldier commanded him to move faster, prisoner P. Shymanski was observed to have suffered "no harm." Meanwhile, complaints of being forced to work while sick were dismissed as frivolous. When prisoner S. Fortyniuk asked that he be excused from work, pleading that he did not have enough strength, the camp medical officer, Captain R. Brett, dismissed his request. There was "nothing wrong" with the man, wrote the physician; he was simply "tired of work." It was believed that Fortyniuk and others like him, feigning illness and fatigue, were hoping to shirk their duties.

An intense adversarial relationship existed between prisoner and overseer. This would necessarily define the prisoner experience but also, more generally, infuse the temper of the camp with a profound sense of insecurity and anxiety about the future. This had little to do with the routine of camp life that was known and unchanging, but rather spoke to a deeper concern faced by those who continued to languish behind barbed wire: would there be any end to their misfortune? In the ambiguous context that was internment – where decisions affecting the individual lives of the prisoners appeared to be haphazard or motivated by enmity – the answer was not immediately evident. But for those affected, they still had to cope somehow.

The reaction to a seemingly endless period of internment was varied. Some steeled themselves against the prospect of a long imprisonment. Others would try to escape, and, like John Kondro and many more, they would succeed. A few, however, were not so fortunate. During a camp transfer from the west to the east, for example, several internees leaped from a train onto an adjoining track near Broadview, Saskatchewan, and were hit by an oncoming locomotive. Taken to a hospital in Regina, it was reported that one of the prisoners would succumb to his injuries.[232] As for Peter Konowalczuk, shot twice in the back and abdomen while attempting to escape from a work gang at Castle Mountain, he would survive his wounds, but not before the local paper, the *Crag and Canyon* (Banff), crowed that it was a "deserved lesson."[233] And then there were those like prisoners Mike Penziwiater, L. Baran, and H. Andrusak, who, under the stress of internment, suffered emotional trauma. In the depths of despair, the experience of internment also got the better of George Luka Budak, William Wysk, and Bill Perchuliak, who ended up taking

3.6 Wounded prisoner, Castle Mountain, Alberta

their lives. For them, it seemed there could be no other escape from their misfortune.

The abuses, the grind of endless hard labour, as well as the harsh conditions of working on the frontier all took their toll. What was surprising, however, was that despite the difficulties and obstacles, steady progress was made on many of the projects to which the prisoners were assigned. As it was often stated, more could have been done if there had been fewer disruptions and less interference. Be that as it may, much of value was accomplished and at a significant saving.

At Kapuskasing and Spirit Lake camps, the internees were made to labour on projects that aimed to further the settlement and economic development efforts of the Ontario and Quebec governments. The experimental farm station also gave dominion authorities an opportunity to assess both the potential of the region and the methods learned for possible future application elsewhere. The success of these experiments was yet to be determined, but the groundwork had been laid. In British Columbia, the prisoners were put to work on difficult sections of roads, where it was felt that the greatest benefit could be derived from their labour. The heavy rock-cut work that had to be done by hand could be undertaken at a fraction of the cost of traditional methods. Finances were a real impediment to developing the network of roads needed to open up the promise of the provincial interior, but with internment labour, the future was now made possible. This was also true of the national parks, where development had suffered a setback because of reduced appropriations. Work in the national parks would continue despite the war, or, perhaps, because of it.

Overall, the results were significant, substantial, and certainly cost-effective. When the Vernon-Edgewood road was completed in August 1916, the road superintendent, J. Black, praised it as an outstanding piece of work. When the BC minister of public works, Thomas Taylor, assessed the newly constructed auto road, he approvingly pronounced judgment on the work, claiming it was "money well spent."[234] Although the road at Mt Revelstoke was never fully completed, it was estimated that the cost for the section of road constructed by internment labour on the summit was but one-third the outlay for similar day labour.[235] In Yoho, the large stand of burned trees, which resulted from the Wapiti fire, was cut, shaped, and sold as railway ties and mining props, leaving a positive balance of more than $16,000 on the books.[236] But it was the roads in the national parks that mattered most, especially in Banff and Jasper, where new throughways held the promise of even more tourism. Visitors and Ottawa officials who inspected the new and improved roads were impressed. The commissioner of the parks, J.B. Harkin, was impressed by what had been accomplished and stated that, after the war, jail and penitentiary labour could be put to use for similar purposes elsewhere in the parks.[237]

All of these projects were made possible because the internees carried out much of the work under pressure and duress. Although internment officials denied accusations of compulsory labour, the issue continued to dog them. The rationale behind their denials was that this form of employment provided the interned enemy alien with an opportunity that otherwise would not be available. Moreover, it was animated by a genuine concern for those left without means, reflecting the best of intentions borne of a basic humanitarian impulse. Of course, in certain quarters this may have been the case, but there was no denying the fact that the internees as civilian prisoners were being put to work and that a benefit was derived from their labour. It was no wonder then that published news that the government benefited from the labour of some five thousand indentured enemy aliens in the amount of $1.5 million was considered not only embarrassing but harmful since "in all probability it will be brought to the attention of the German authorities." The point of concern was not that the information was false or inaccurate but rather the political effect this would have. Avoiding the issue of how the government benefited from internment labour, the prime minister argued that in explaining the benefit derived, the social and economic context of internment needed to be considered.[238]

From the perspective of US consul G. Willrich, no explanation could excuse what he found at the Spirit Lake camp. His outrage at his discoveries alarmed the camp commandant, who sought to minimize the diplomatic damage that would result from what would undoubtedly be a critical report. Although the damage was contained and Willrich removed, the report revealed an unspoken truth. According to the American representative, there was insufficient reason for these people to be kept behind barbed wire, let alone maintained in deplorable conditions. On the contrary, he claimed, they were legal immigrants who had made a commitment to Canada and no good would come from a policy that treated them as enemies.

Willrich was treading on delicate ground, going beyond his prescribed role. He was not in a position to judge policy but to report the facts. To his credit, he was voicing concerns that appeared to be widely held among the interned enemy aliens but were not heard. For them the issue was not whether they were civilian or military prisoners of war but the fact that they were being held in a prisoner of war camp. For many of them, the war was distant and had no personal meaning. They had come freely and openly to Canada, without malicious hearts. That they were now in a prisoner of war camp was inconceivable to them. In the words of the Marchuk brothers, "there must have been some mistake." For Jacob Kondro, whose son in desperation would escape and disappear in the deep forests of the Rocky Mountains, it was incredible to think that Canada "would do this to its own people."

Jacob Kondro and the brothers Marchuk were not alone in their bewilderment. Countless others similarly claimed they failed to understand why they were in a prisoner of war camp. Brandon prisoner of war O. Rozdolski claimed that his arrest and internment were an obvious misunderstanding. A travelling publisher's representative, he asked his employer, the West Canada Publishing Company, to intercede on his behalf. Rozdolski stated that he had reported as a registered enemy alien for eight months, but now for some reason the chief of police in Wilkie, Saskatchewan, stated that his registration papers were not in order. He wrote:

This is the crime shown to me as "breaching of parole" of which I was declared guilty; otherwise I would not know why I was treated as the greatest criminal during my investigation at Wilkie, South Battleford and during my transportation to Brandon. What I have suffered in these five days and the disgrace during my transportation to this place I could not describe. I would have felt happier had they shot me right-away at Wilkie ... It would be terrible if there was no possibility at all of getting out of here before the end of this damned war, which is not the fault of we foreigners. I hope, however, that your company will not desert me at the present after my ending the fourth year of service and will try to annul my arrest which is simply based on a misunderstanding. I have always done my duties strictly. I am no traitor or spy. I have not talked about the developments of the war. Why should I suffer unjustly?[239]

The matter of justice also weighed heavily on the mind of Erwin Kohlman, an alien of enemy origin. Working for the city of Toronto as an administrator, he had been released from the municipal service. He was considered a "busybody," and it was deemed expedient that he be arrested and interned. From his confinement at Toronto's Stanley Barracks, Kohlman pleaded his case, maintaining that he was no spy. But he was also pragmatic if disillusioned about the prospect of his own release:

I have been taught a cruel lesson in this last month. I had in my righteousness considered the orders of the Premier of the Dominions as supreme, but I had not taken into account that there could be political intrigues. One of your own officers has told me that the opinion prevails I should not be freed, even if a ransom of $10,000 might be offered. This remark explains sufficiently the current of opinion. However, when anybody thinks that I have committed anything detrimental to the law of this country, I demand the penalty for such crime or misdemeanor. I am perfectly willing to suffer punishment for it, but give me the chance of clearing myself from insinuations, do not keep me locked up like a criminal who knows what he at least is interned for. I want fair play and justice![240]

For Kohlman, there could be no justice. He was an enemy alien and now a prisoner of war. He would be treated as such.

## CHAPTER FOUR

# The Alien as "Enemy": Questions of Acceptance, Belonging, and Fit

## CIRCUMSTANCES AND CONDITIONS OF RELEASE

On the prairies in the spring of 1916, there was considerable worry as to whether enough farmhands would be available to help with the seeding. Enlistments in the military from the western provinces were heavy, resulting in a dearth of men for agricultural work. George Bury, the vice-president of the Canadian Pacific Railway, characterized the situation as "the most serious problem confronting Canada today," leading him to believe that Canada's economy was in peril.[1] To address the shortage, the government undertook a series of measures. Advertisements were placed in over five thousand American newspapers in an effort to bring in thirty thousand seasonal labourers from the United States. A policy of granting servicemen month-long furloughs to help with the ploughing and seeding was also introduced. The newspaper campaign, however, failed to attract the necessary numbers and fear of loss of pay dissuaded soldiers from applying. Within this context, the issue of putting interned enemy aliens to work on farms – an idea that had been mooted for some time in Ottawa – was soon discussed in earnest.[2] Originally assigned to public works projects, internees could now, with little effort, be mobilized to work on Canada's agricultural lands. The prisoners would have little reason to complain, given the opportunity to come out from behind barbed wire.

Rumours of the government's plan to use prisoners of war in a farm support scheme led to speculation about the number of enemy aliens that would be made available and the conditions under which they would be employed. It was reported, for instance, that the total interned was ten thousand, 60 per cent of whom were to be placed on farms.

Other sources estimated that there were nine thousand at the Jasper camp alone and thousands more at internment stations in Brandon, Lethbridge, and Vernon, all of whom could be used as farmhands. However, the idea of prisoners of war at liberty, uncontrolled and unsupervised in the Canadian countryside, proved disconcerting and triggered criticism. Calgary's Board of Trade, for instance, was opposed to any policy that would see interned enemies widely dispersed, arguing that it was a "risky procedure."[3] The *Morning Citizen* voiced a similar objection when it expressed concern about the difficulty of preventing escapes after prisoners were distributed across the vast expanse of Canada's wheat region.[4] But the agricultural problem was serious, and in Ottawa the government was increasingly convinced that the use of internees for farm work was indispensable.[5]

With spring seeding imminent, Prime Minister Borden called upon his officials to bring forward a proposal that would address the agricultural labour shortage using war prisoners. A meeting in Winnipeg brought together those whose interests and abilities were needed for the successful planning, implementation, and execution of a farm support scheme, including the director of internment operations, the commissioner of immigration, and executives representing the Grain Growers Association, Grain Exchange, Canadian Bankers Association, and the railways. The deliberations resulted in a plan that would see prisoners made available from the Brandon camp, which was centrally located in the seeding area. Prisoners of war were to be drawn from a prepared list that identified those who posed little or no threat, while other likely candidates for work on the farms were also to be transported on special trains from two camps in the east, Kapuskasing and Spirit Lake. Regarding risk, it was stated that the majority of those who would be discharged were "Ruthenians or Ukrainians born in Galicia, but of non-Teutonic origin and with little, if any sympathy for the Austrian cause."[6]

Not all of the details could or would be settled at the meeting. It was unclear, for instance, whether the federal government would cover the cost of the rail transport for each released prisoner (set at 1¢ per mile to a maximum of $2.00), or if farmers would pay the up-front cost of transportation to be recovered from the internee's first month's wages. Nor was it established how applications for enemy alien labour were to be made, although it was suggested that farmers would apply directly to the camp commandants. But on many points there was agreement, primarily related to the obligations that were to be met by both farmer and prisoner. Farmers were to employ the enemy alien prisoner for no less than seven months, pay each a standard monthly wage at current rates (board and lodgings inclusive), and commandants were to be informed on a monthly basis of the conduct of their enemy help. Escapes were to be reported immediately. Prisoners were to abide by the terms of their parole and honour their contracts, the failure of which would have legal and other consequences.

Initially, there was uncertainty about whether farmers would accept the proposal. In advance of the plan's implementation, Major D. Coleman, the commander at Brandon, the camp at the centre of the proposed scheme, attempted to set an encouraging tone, assuring the local farming community and the general public that there was nothing to fear. As he pointed out, the men at the Brandon camp were there "solely on the ground that they could not obtain work on account of their nationality, and it is only men who can safely be trusted that will be allowed out."[7] Such assurances were not enough for the *Vancouver Sun*, which was unequivocal in its opposition to the publicized plan, especially as regards the government's intention to pay the prisoners market wages. Invoking images of long-suffering British and Canadian prisoners of war in Germany, where "dogs are encouraged to bite and worry them, while the slightest attempt at self-defence is followed by chastisement at the hands of the Germans," the *Sun* questioned the government proposal. How was it that the Canadian government was prepared to employ enemy prisoners of war in the harvest field at the rate of $2 a day? Allied prisoners, the paper reported, were being paid 2½¢ for road building and other hard manual work. If enemy prisoners were to be given a wage, then the paper mockingly suggested they be remunerated at the rate of double the daily prisoner wage in Germany, or 5¢ a day, which was "eminently fair."[8]

The scornful attitude of the *Vancouver Sun* belied the deeper problem of a labour shortage, which already in late 1915 had shown worrying signs. The shortage threatened to cripple not only Canadian agriculture but a range of other industries as well. Some companies, turning in desperation to the government for assistance, suggested the possibility of strategically using paroled enemy aliens to help alleviate the situation. In Minto, New Brunswick, a coal region experiencing a severe labour shortage, operators of the local mine inquired with the Justice Department whether enemy alien miners on parole in Springhill, Nova Scotia, might be transferred to Minto, where, it was argued, they were needed much more. In an effort to strengthen their case, company executives assured officials that there was no security risk since the enemy aliens would be

4.1 Field work, Amherst, Nova Scotia

practically isolated at Minto "as if they were interned."[9] Quick to quash the proposal after it was made known to them, the Dominion Coal Company at Springhill, fearing the loss of their paroled enemy-origin labourers, raised objections with the government, pleading that they were no less affected by the acute shortage of workers.[10]

The rivalry between these and other companies over enemy alien labourers highlighted the scarcity of workers generally and served as a catalyst for innovative thinking in the search for solutions. Looking toward the possible use of alternative sources of labour, and bolstered by news of the Farmers Employment Scheme, companies soon began to petition the government not only for the use of paroled enemy aliens but for the release of actual prisoners of war to help address the deficit. The Georgian Bay Lumberman's Association, for one, citing competition from neighbouring mining companies, asked their member of parliament and minister of railways, the Hon. F. Cochrane, whether Austro-Hungarian prisoners of war interned in Canada might be put to work for the company. Since other lumber companies were expected to make similar applications, the minister of railways queried, "Would there be any objection on the part of the government, or is there anything in international law which might prevent our utilizing the services of the prisoners of war to supply this shortage?"[11] The matter, initially directed to the prime minister, was forwarded to the ministers of labour and justice for their consideration.

The minister of labour, the Hon. W. Crothers, observed that the question was not without merit since firms seeking application for the use of prisoners of war had approached him as well. But he had real and serious concerns. Crothers was especially suspicious and fearful of the possibility that the applications for the prisoners were prompted "by the thought that their services can be secured at lower than the ordinary rates for such work."[12] This, in his opinion, would undercut the existing labour market and had the potential of creating additional difficulties. From Crothers's perspective, the use of prisoner-of-war labour was a workable idea, but only if the men were offered and paid free market wages. If they were to be released, Crothers insisted, "we should have a statement from the employers undertaking to pay certain stated rates of wages and to provide other reasonable conditions for the men." He also freely admitted that there were other dimensions to the question: "Many of these men were interned simply because they were unable to maintain themselves and not because of any offence that they had been guilty of or might thereafter be guilty. If they now say to us that they are prepared to support themselves I think we might properly give them the opportunity of doing so."

Consulting with other cabinet colleagues and following Crothers's lead, the justice minister, the Hon. Charles Doherty, instructed General Otter, the director of internment, to contact the firms that had made initial inquiries and inform them of the government's intention to make prisoners of war available, "upon being satisfied that they had obtained employment at current rates of wages; that such employment has some permanency; and that other labour was not available for the purposes for which it is desired to employ these aliens."[13] The instruction led shortly thereafter to a spate of applications, including from the Standard Chemical, Iron and Lumber Company, the Minto Coal Company, Dominion Coal Company, and McLachlin Brothers Ltd (manufacturers of sawn lumber), all indicating that company representatives would be at the camps to interview and make selections from those prisoners made available.[14]

By mid-May 1916 the first batch of internees was released from Petawawa to work in industry. These were subsequently followed by a group of twenty-five from Spirit Lake to work on the Canadian National Railway. At Amherst, twenty-five internees of Austro-Hungarian nationality were released for work with the Minto Coal Company. After an application had been made, a nominal roll of forty-one prisoners from Kapuskasing was prepared for the consideration of railway companies in northern Ontario. They would be discharged along with seven others. In Alberta, the Canmore Coal Company asked for the reinstatement of five prisoners from the Castle Mountain camp who had been previously employed with the firm, citing that their manner and conduct had never been an issue and their loyalty never in doubt. They further requested a dozen more men, claiming there was an urgent need to meet the growing demands placed upon the company.[15]

The numbers discharged were relatively small, at least until 2 June, when F.L. Warrington, a general executive of the Canadian Pacific Railway, made application for the release of one thousand Austro-Hungarians to work as track labourers on the north shore of Lake Superior in the railway's Algoma/Lake Superior division.[16] Warrington offered to employ the prisoners at $1.90 a day as long as the season permitted. On 12 June, General Otter informed the commander of the Brandon station, Major Coleman, that his request would be fulfilled and that, in addition to those being released under the Farmers Employment Scheme, as many men as possible were to be discharged to the railway, including Austro-Hungarian reservists – provided, of course, there was no serious charge against them.[17] Three hundred discharge forms and a similar number of Undertakings were immediately delivered to Coleman for his use once it was determined that this was the number who could be prudently freed.

When it was learned that sixty-one from the pool of three hundred chose not to be discharged (some claiming they were physically weak and unable to perform heavy railway work), Lieutenant Colonel D. Macpherson, the internment staff officer in Ottawa, conveyed to Coleman: "They must either accept employment offered or be turned out of camp as non-dangerous prisoners who refuse their liberty and employment."[18] The staff officer stated to Coleman that the internees could not be permitted to remain a public charge. On 22 July, acting on Macpherson's orders, Coleman divided a group of 116 prisoners who were considered non-dangerous but who refused to sign the Undertaking, into batches of twenty, drove them to the railway station at the point of a bayonet, and gave them each a free ticket. The tickets entitled them to be transported to their original point of arrest, or, in the case of those seized at the border, to Winnipeg.[19] The seemingly rash decision to be rid of the prisoners pointed to the undeclared intention of internment officials to close the Brandon camp. Within a week of the departure of the internees at Brandon, the last group still held there, ninety-three prisoners of mainly German origin, was transferred to Morrissey in British Columbia.

The action which saw the turning out of prisoners at Brandon was consistent with a policy decision, taken April 1916, to systematically discharge all prisoners deemed "non-dangerous" while transferring to designated facilities those considered incorrigible, untrustworthy, or held for strategic diplomatic reasons. As a result of the decision, in the course of six months, not only would the Brandon camp close (29 July) but a series of other camps, made redundant, would soon end operations as well: Petawawa (8 May), Beauport (22 June), Jasper Park (31 August), Edgewood (23 September), Toronto's Stanley Barracks (2 October), Halifax Citadel (3 October), Yoho (23 October), and Lethbridge (7 November).

A number of immediate factors were instrumental in the closure of several of the camps. These included the opposition of prisoners to their work regime at the Jasper Park and Yoho camps, the numerous escapes at Lethbridge, and the end of construction on the Edgewood Road project. At Beauport and Stanley Barracks, the declining number of arrests in Montreal and Toronto meant that these facilities were no longer necessary and would serve in the future simply as transit stations for enemy alien prisoners being arrested and sent en route to other destinations. But it was pressure from industry, pushing for even more prisoner-of-war labour, which resulted in even greater numbers being released and, concomitantly, in the closure of some of the other major camps.

Hundreds of prisoners were systematically released during the summer and fall of 1916. These were sent individually to farms and in groups of ten or more to either railways, collieries, or other companies and corporations, including Algoma Steel, Dominion Iron and Steel, International Harvester, Canada Cement, Abitibi Pulp and Paper, the Asbestos Corporation, National Steel Car Company, and Brewster Transport among others.[20] Both Canadian agriculture and industry would benefit, securing large numbers of workers who were obliged to remain with their employer until the conditions of war affecting their status changed.

With increased demand, the number of prisoners at the larger work camps also diminished. In August 1916, 172 prisoners were released to employers from Spirit Lake. The following month, applications from railways resulted in an additional 319 men being discharged from the same camp. By December 1916, from a peak of 1,312, all that remained at Spirit Lake were 275 individuals.[21] When the Castle Mountain camp was moved to Banff in mid-November 1916 for winter quartering, the numbers there dwindled to 250. By the end of the month the camp was further depleted when twenty-eight Galician Ukrainians were released for work and seven Hungarians transferred to the Morrissey camp. Three months later, an additional 133 individuals were released from Banff, leaving but eighty-two prisoners in total. From Kapuskasing, in February 1917, the Dominion Iron and Steel Co. received 110 prisoners. In March, the company requested and received a further 140 men from the northern Ontario camp, followed by an additional 132 in April.

The quick and successive reduction in numbers soon forced the issue of consolidating some of the remaining camps, with groups of prisoners being transferred to a few select facilities. When Spirit Lake closed 11 January 1917, 178 prisoners were transported to Kapuskasing. On 3 May 1917, the day that Fort Henry was shuttered, the last of the internees at this facility were also transferred to Kapuskasing. The Banff internment camp closed 15 July 1917, when the remaining forty-seven prisoners were shipped to Kapuskasing – but not before they were hurriedly put to work by the parks branch on one last project, extending the golf greens at the Banff Springs Hotel. This project was deemed an "imperative" by Parks Commissioner J.B. Harkin, who observed: "If we do not have it done by them there will be little chance of getting it done by day labour."[22]

The release of prisoners did not always result in camp closures; exceptional circumstances in British Columbia forced officials to adopt a more calculated approach. In BC, requests for the release of enemy alien prisoners from camps situated in the province were no less urgent or pressing than elsewhere in the country, but the mood was different and the anti-alien sentiment sufficiently powerful enough to give pause to any suggestion that enemy alien prisoners in the province might be released in response to requests. Federal politicians from BC (in particular, members of parliament R.F. Green, H.S. Clemens, and H.H. Stevens) as well as a number of provincial officials, including Premier W.J. Bowser, were careful to take into account the public's contempt and long-standing suspicion of the enemy alien, making known their opposition to any possible release of the prisoners in the province. Replying to a CPR request for prisoners of war to be used on summer track work in the BC provincial interior, General Otter denied the application because of the directorate's commitment to the BC government not to release internees from camps within the province for fear of public reaction.[23] In the end, despite the economic rationale and impetus for the majority to be set free, the fate of the prisoners in British Columbia would be determined by political considerations. Without provincial approval, the release of prisoners could not be authorized. As a result, prisoners in BC were not discharged as a rule, and those few released were freed on condition they would accept assigned work away from the province.

Decisions relating to prisoner release were being shaped by domestic concerns, but the issue was also framed by external politics. Interned civilian enemy aliens in Canada were treated as prisoners of war and as such became objects in the wider discussion and negotiation between the warring powers on captured personnel. Prisoner rights were paramount during the negotiations. But so too was the issue of their status and future, which necessarily touched upon the possibility of their exchange. In August 1916, diplomacy led to an initial agreement between Germany and Britain (applicable to the colonies) that called for the repatriation of civilian prisoners unfit for military service.[24] News of the arrangement in October triggered applications for repatriation from a number of eligible German internees in Canada. But as the process moved along, the fear of being "disadvantaged" increasingly governed the response of the belligerents.[25] German internees in Canada were being held as bargaining chips in the diplomatic seesaw, accounting for the relatively large number of German-origin prisoners who would remain behind Canadian barbed wire for the duration of the war.

Parallel negotiations also took place between Britain and Austria-Hungary involving the possible repatriation of civilian prisoners of war. But these negotiations posed a different set of challenges for Canada. In contrast to interned Germans, a great number of whom were captured merchant mariners, Austro-Hungarian civilian prisoners, by and large, had migrated to Canada as settlers. Having adopted Canada as their home, what, if any, obligation was owed them? Moreover, in the context of international convention and understanding, could they be repatriated given that they were settlers?[26] If not, then what possible rationale existed for their continuing internment? The political and ethical conundrum that their continuing internment posed, which the negotiations served to highlight, forced Canada to choose either to repatriate those it did not want or release those it had once welcomed to its shores. It was an awkward dilemma. Either way, the issue pointed increasingly to the untenable nature of Canada's continuing policy of internment and served as an important stimulus in the decision to release those Austro-Hungarian civilian prisoners who gave no cause for worry.

The public reaction to the release of so many enemy alien prisoners of war was generally negative. The prospect of alien competition in the labour market, especially in British Columbia, was of immediate concern. But so too was the risk. On this point, as was often repeated, it was confounding to think that enemy aliens interned as prisoners of war now posed less of a threat than they did a few months ago. Circumstances had not changed. So why were these enemies now considered sufficiently harmless to be let loose in the country? The *Calgary Daily Herald* questioned the wisdom of releasing interned Austro-Hungarians and Germans: "It is just the antithesis of what Canadians might reasonably expect in the interests of the country. It is really inconceivable that such a state of conditions should exist in face of the elaborate precautions that have been taken since the outbreak of the war to safeguard our railways and other public utilities."[27] From the wider public perspective, the release of prisoners of war, civilian or not, was both a perplexing and unwelcome development. It would require the government to cautiously manage the ongoing process of prisoner release, to secure, if not acceptance, then at least public forbearance of its decision to discharge prisoners of war.

To this end, managing the process meant that only those enemy alien prisoners who were classified as "non-dangerous" would be paroled. The designation was chosen precisely for its ambiguity. It was normally understood that enemy alien reservists, if repatriated, could be deployed on the battlefield, therefore providing sufficient reason not to release such individuals. And yet it was accepted that if they signed an Undertaking and committed to follow the restrictions outlined in the 15 August 1914 Proclamation, they could be released and remain free. What would matter, then, was not whether an interned enemy alien represented a conventional security threat (although this was a concern where individuals actively expressed anti-Allied sentiments); rather, the case for each prisoner would have to be assessed on its own merits. In practical terms this meant their personnel files would be vetted before the director of internment operations, who would determine whether they could be released based on the cause of their initial arrest and an assessment of their attitude and behaviour while interned.[28] Continued internment, consequently, was tied less formally to traditional notions of security and more directly to personal conduct, specifically their disposition toward formal authority while interned.

In part, this emphasis on conduct followed from the need to ensure that the internees would abide by the conditions of their release. Once discharged, it was expected that they would accept and respect the terms of their parole and employment. For those released to the railways, for example, this meant complying with regulations governing their service, which among other things stipulated that ten hours would constitute a minimum day's work.[29] If internees objected to the conditions of their employment and became vagrants, they would be turned over to civil authorities.[30] Former prisoners, of course, could be re-interned if they violated the restrictions of the August Proclamation, but there was general agreement that if due diligence were exercised – identifying malcontents and others of similar ilk in the release process – then such problems could be avoided.[31]

The internee's record of conduct was considered important because it was thought that this would help gauge the character and disposition of those being considered for release. It did not mean that problems could be entirely averted. There was no accounting for how former prisoners would respond to their freedom. But the provision requiring prisoners to carry parole cards with them at all times and register with local authorities encouraged compliance if not acquiescence. These were important measures of oversight. And yet it was felt that the best assurance of good behaviour was the opportunity of employment upon their release. Although they would have to abide by certain rules and regulations, it was thought they would be grateful for both their employment and liberty.[32]

In view of the measures taken to ensure an easy yet secure transition, internment officials felt they were no longer responsible for the welfare or conduct of the discharged prisoners. Once the decision had been made to remove prisoners from the authority of the internment directorate, there was now no longer a binding administrative obligation to have anything further to do with these former inmates. When it was learned that several released prisoners had left their employers and were re-interned at the Citadel in Halifax, Otter instructed the commandant to discontinue the practice:

I observe that several Aliens released for employment have been re-interned at your station, a contingency that it was never contemplated should occur, as those released were not considered dangerous, but only interned for the reason that they were "destitute." Consequently, when provided with employment, they have no further claim on our sympathy, and if not willing to work though able, must take their chances of living the same as any other lazy individual. You will therefore, having previous knowledge, please refuse accepting any such man.[33]

Since a growing number of prisoners who had been released to various employers were now leaving their service, it was unclear who was responsible for their conduct and welfare. Although there were restrictions on the mobility of the released prisoners, the reality was that they were on the move, resulting in problems for which someone or some agency needed to be responsible.

The movement of the released prisoners was prompted by a number of factors. In an increasingly tight labour market, advantageous rates of pay were being offered as a lure to attract recently discharged prisoners.[34] There was also the natural tendency for former prisoners, released to employers at a distance from their families, to quit their work in order to return home.[35] And then for a small but significant minority, flight was a reaction and predictable response to the avariciousness of employers who sought to take advantage of the vulnerable position of those recently released by either not paying them for their work or threatening re-internment should they object to the conditions of their employment.[36] In such cases, internment was followed not by freedom but continuing hardship.

Those who were being taken advantage wondered who if anyone would intercede on their behalf and where could they turn for justice. Mistreated or feeling trapped in their situation, they sought assistance, ironically, by appealing to internment officials, turning in particular to General Otter as the individual who approved their initial discharge and authorized their parole cards. Considered their benefactor, he alone, they felt, would be able to assist.

Otter was careful, however. When evidence pointed to maltreatment of recently released prisoners, he would sometimes intervene – but only if the situation was acute and if it appeared to offend his personal sensibilities. When the case of former prisoner of war no. 1056, A. Cherumachzynsky, was brought to the general's attention, he made an effort to assist. Cherumachzynsky had worked for six months in the employ of one Thomas Naylor under the Farmers' Employment Guarantee Scheme and was owed $136.30. Naylor refused to pay. It was unclear to Otter whether Naylor, who had a "habit of avoiding his liabilities," could be brought before the courts by an enemy alien. Citing the urgency of the matter (since the former prisoner had no means of support), Otter inquired with the Justice Department on a course of action. Justice officials replied that Cherumachzynsky was well within his rights to sue, upon which Otter conveyed this information to the former internee who had asked for his help.[37]

In most other cases, Otter was unmoved. Sent to work in the Canadian bush far away from their families, former prisoners petitioned that they be granted amnesty from their place of work and be permitted to go home. There was little that Otter could do. They were employed, and in contrast to their situation a few short years back, where want and hunger were rampant, they now had no reasonable claim on the government or its agencies. Nevertheless, they would write:

> We beg you humbly; kindly let us to know can we go to work to any other company in Canada? ... We was so many months locked in the Fort Henry, now we are in the bush. Instead of solid walls in fort, we see only solid bush and heaven ... We have our families and friends in Canada where we can work with them in the same places ... Our health conditions are too bad to stay longer in the bush ... We can rapport ourself by the police same as our friends. So we beg you Hon. Sir, very much kindly let us know how goes this matter and how about our parole cards as we need them to rapport us after our arrival.[38]

In their opinion, Otter's officials would give no further counsel other than that they should show their release orders to the local police chief, who would authorize their move – if he could be so convinced. This callous indifference, so commonplace, was underscored by the frank statement of disavowal to those who appealed for help: "The Internment Department has no further jurisdiction over you after your release."[39]

For officials at the internment directorate, the fate of those released was a matter for which others were now responsible. More precisely, it was officially left to the dominion police and the RNWMP to deal with any problems that might arise. But it was not the role of the police to address the needs or concerns of former prisoners. Their role was to ensure that laws were observed and the public order maintained. To this end, the police dutifully carried out arrests with a view to punishing former prisoners who threatened either the peace or the established order. When eleven prisoners released from Kapuskasing refused to work on the Welland Canal, they were arrested, fined, and sentenced to six months' hard labour in the Guelph Ontario Reformatory. The chief commissioner of the dominion police, Colonel A.P. Sherwood, expressed satisfaction with the ruling, believing that the fate of the eleven (along with thirty-nine other former prisoners sentenced to hard labour at the Burwash Industrial Farm for having refused work) would serve as poignant reminder to other potential shirkers.[40]

In a few cases, however, internment officials did agree to the re-internment of several former prisoners who had all served short prison sentences for minor criminal offences. Steve Fortyniuk, for example, convicted for a petty offence, was immediately sent to Morrissey at the end of his sentence. His crime and misfortune, the theft of warm socks, had marked him as a person to be deported – an objective, it was felt, that could readily be achieved by his re-internment as a prisoner of war.[41] But Fortyniuk's case was rare. Prisoners of war who had been released from internment were now the concern of others and, if at all possible, were not to be re-interned. Otter's attention remained focused on the 2,620 prisoners of war who as of late November 1916 continued to be held in one of the several remaining camps – Morrissey, Vernon, Mara Lake, Banff, Kapuskasing, and Amherst. As for the prisoners who had been paroled, they would have to find their own way. What they would soon discover was that life outside the internment camps would be no less difficult.

REJECTION, RESENTMENT, AND REFUSAL

Prisoners of war continued to be released with regularity at the start of 1917. The de-commissioning and consolidation of camps expedited the process, with lists being prepared of those who could be discharged without issue. Prisoners were released in groups, at times in numbers of a hundred or more, such that by 2 May 1917, a total of some 2,300 prisoners remained interned.[42] Mara Lake would close in May of 1917, leaving the Amherst station as the largest remaining facility, housing approximately 850 internees – Kapuskasing followed with 500, Vernon 350, and Morrissey and Banff at 300 apiece.[43] On 20 June, 2,032 prisoners were reported to still be interned, a total that was reduced further in July when the internment camp at Banff closed.[44] Although Halifax's Citadel and Toronto's Stanley Barracks continued to be used as holding stations for enemy aliens in transit, the overall operation was gearing down as the directorate sought to fill requests for labour from across the country. Only in British Columbia, where the government was concerned with public opinion, were prisoners not released locally, but rather paroled to employers in the east.[45]

   With their release, former prisoners were confronted with a host of problems. Lack of funds was the most pressing, and requests were often made at the time of release to internment officials for access to monies earned. Cheques in small amounts were issued, but, generally, funds were not to be dispersed until the end of hostilities. This also applied to property that had been seized, for which applications were being received. From Sturgeon Falls, in northern Ontario, Alex Ostapchuk and four others, while expressing their gratitude to General Otter as their emancipator, pleaded for the return of $368.35 which had been taken from them years earlier.[46] The ex-prisoner J. Alexandruk also wrote for the return of funds confiscated in the amount of $42, but for which he had only been given a receipt of $35.25. He further hoped to receive the $4.70 from the $10 his brother had sent to him while in camp, and still on account with camp authorities, as he had no idea what became of it.[47] That some of the confiscated funds and valuables could no longer be accounted for tended to complicate their situation.[48]

Without resources, many former inmates found themselves at the mercy of their employers. Recruited from the camps and given employment and transportation, prisoners were under contract. From the employer's perspective, however, measures were needed to ensure that their effort and investment would not be lost. Pressuring the former prisoners to work under trying conditions, employers often colluded with local authorities to prevent their departure. Parole cards were withheld, registration certificates went unsigned, and the threat of arrest was widely exercised.[49] Without food or money, hundreds, setting aside their fears, took to the road hoping either to reach home, family, and friends, or to simply leave their predicament behind.[50] Whether they received what was owed them was of less importance than their desire to get away.

The measures used to extract work from former prisoners or restrict their movement also applied, more generally, to the enemy alien population. This weighed heavily on those affected. George Werenka, for one, wrote the minister of justice asking for assistance for himself and his co-workers. Suffering from a debilitating ailment, he stated that the Canadian Copper Company of Sudbury, with whom he was employed, had not only refused him sick leave to recuperate, but also threatened him with arrest and fines should he decline to work. He indicated that several of his colleagues, enemy aliens all, had already been arrested and sentenced to six months' imprisonment for refusing to work. "Was this justice?" Werenka asked. He appealed to the minister "to do something for us poor people," adding, "It's not our fault that Canada is at war with Austria."[51]

Companies who employed enemy aliens used the threat of arrest as a deterrent against flight. But it was largely a rearguard action that could not hope to mitigate the problem, as countless enemy aliens, including paroled prisoners, abandoned their employers to go home or to seek better pay elsewhere. Labour was in short supply and the competition fierce as companies tried to attract alien workers who might be lured away by higher wages. Although industry complained bitterly about the practice – claiming that the competition between companies promoted flight, encouraged insolence, and drove up wages – very little would or could be done. When the CPR complained to General Otter that the prisoners sent their way were "deserting" and inquired whether the militia might help to apprehend them, Otter's response was unequivocal – they were not deserters in the military sense because they were no longer prisoners of war; rather, they were under civil contract "amenable to the penalties for breaking such."[52] When the minister of labour, W. Crothers, was asked about how to control the movement of enemy aliens, he quipped that a good start would be for industries to curb their hunt for enemy alien labour, which encouraged them to leave.[53] When the president of Wood-Valance & Company suggested that the military take over the mines "and make these foreigners work at the point of the bayonet," the correspondence was politely acknowledged without comment.[54]

Increasingly, the question of the role and place of released internees, as well as enemy aliens more generally, was being debated within the context of the country's war objectives and the sacrifices being made. Tens of thousands of Canadian lives had been lost on the battlefields of France, and those who returned were scarred by the conflict. The Great War forced distinctions that in the mind of the returned soldier made clear who represented friend or foe. The sacrifices also necessarily moved them to close ranks against threats, real or perceived, and to ferret out those who insulted or took advantage of the struggle's cause. They felt that there was no greater injustice than enemy aliens in Canada, who fraudulently stood to gain while the Canadian soldier and his family sacrificed all.

It was not surprising that when recuperating soldiers were sent to the Stanley Barracks in Toronto to be disciplined (having complained of their treatment at the Whitby Hospital), they protested at having to serve their sentence alongside the enemy aliens also being held there. Recently returned from the front, they felt it was an insult to share a prison with enemy aliens.[55] Veterans were equally incensed at the prospect of having to work alongside enemy aliens or that enemy aliens were being employed in munitions and other industries vital to Canada's war effort. It was seen as a travesty and an affront to those who had served king and country that so many of them were occupying plum positions. Conducting impromptu raids on a dozen or more factories in Toronto, veterans sought to identify all enemy aliens for the purpose of their removal.

4.2  Exercise yard, Stanley Barracks, Toronto

These tactics ended only after municipal officials agreed to meet with a committee of the returned men, who insisted on the creation of a civic bureau (under the authority of veterans) that would serve as both an employment registry and a clearing house for their complaints.[56] As for the principal demand that "all aliens found in places of employment should be interned and should be used on city jobs and farms under supervision of a returned soldiers' guard at a small wage," there was no official endorsement, although the mayor of Toronto, Thomas Church, and several aldermen personally expressed solidarity with the views and opinions that were voiced.

Veterans' concerns registered with officials because of the group's growing influence. Their numbers, organization, and energy were helping to galvanize public opinion in support of issues that were beginning to emerge and shape the political discourse of the day. Questions regarding franchise, compulsory labour, conscription, the military vote, and employment for the returned soldier were key concerns that increasingly informed the thinking and actions of the veterans and their supporters.[57]

They were a force to be reckoned with, and those who questioned or opposed the brotherhood would garner their loathing and ire.[58]

As the carnage on the European front continued to exact a heavy toll, the question of how to best support the troops was pivotal. More men were needed, and conscription – an issue championed by the Borden government – was viewed as vitally important for Canada's war effort and, more immediately, for those still fighting in the trenches. Help would be on its way. But the government faced a dilemma: how to ensure the measure would be adopted if franchised aliens of German and Austro-Hungarian nationality voted against it in an election that would be called on the issue of conscription.

Disfranchisement – the process of retracting citizenship – was discussed as a possible solution, and yet for the government it was a complicated affair. Disfranchisement was, after all, an extreme measure, one that would not sit well with the parliamentary opposition. And then there was the ethical dimension to the issue as well. Was it possible for citizenship to be revoked when individuals who had extended their loyalty and sworn allegiance already held that right? This was a puzzle to which an answer was not readily available. Although the government distanced itself from the more radical statements and actions of its members and supporters – the conservative Colonel J.A. Currie, for instance, sought to introduce a private member's bill in parliament to amend the criminal code by making the candidacy or support of an enemy alien for public office a criminal offence – it could not entirely rule out the possible disfranchisement of recently naturalized enemy aliens.[59]

The argument for disfranchisement was premised on the idea that aliens of Austro-Hungarian or German nationality, although naturalized, could not reasonably discharge the highest duty of citizenship because it was unnatural, cruel, and even dangerous to ask them to take up arms against their kindred. Since they could not fulfill the duties of citizenship, it was argued that they should not be allowed to pronounce on issues concerning the war.[60] It was felt their origin, language, upbringing, kinship, and natural sympathies prevented impartial judgment and that they would oppose being forced into military service – to choose in effect between blood ties and their adopted country. It was a troubling scenario and from this perspective alone Prime Minister Borden was inclined "to exclude men of enemy nationality [from voting] who had not resided in Canada for a considerable time."[61] Still, Borden was unconvinced, at least until other events took place that overshadowed any misgivings he may have had.

In Toronto, encouraged by the growing anti-alien public sentiment and fuelled by the local veterans' branch and sensationalist press, the mayor, Thomas Church, put forward before the municipal council a motion recommending the disfranchisement of aliens of enemy origin who had not lived in Canada for twenty-five years. The majority in city council passed the motion. Endorsed by a variety of local conservative papers and picked up by the press countrywide, the actions of the Toronto politicians touched off a national debate on enemy alien loyalty and the government's position on "enemy franchise."[62] Inadvertently drawn into the controversy, the government could not postpone making a policy decision, a situation that was underscored by troubling political news from the west.

In Alberta, reports had identified conscription as the reason behind the defeat of the Conservatives in the recently held provincial election. The foreign-born electorate, acting on the fear of conscription, was identified as a critical factor in the rout. There was a clear lesson to be drawn. If a conscription bill at the federal level were to be successfully implemented, then the issue of alien franchise had to be addressed. Indeed, it was felt that without pre-emption, the enemy alien electorate – described as a "Trojan horse" by the prime minister's closest confidants – would threaten the government at the polls.[63] Considerable weight was brought to bear on the prime minister, who by this time was increasingly convinced there was no way to avoid the issue.

For members of the Great War Veterans' Association, on the other hand, there was no vacillation or doubt on the question.[64] At a July general executive meeting held in Winnipeg, the association passed a resolution and forwarded it to the government declaring that all aliens of enemy origin should be prevented from registering as voters in the federal election, except those who had managed to enlist for service in the war with the Allies. The decision garnered the support of veterans' branches across the country. The stakes were raised further when the Conservative member of parliament Colonel Currie, during a discussion to amend the Land Act, took exception to the idea that both full citizenship and dominion lands could be granted to aliens of enemy birth, stating that it was an insult to the men in the trenches. Naturalization was a privilege, not a right, he asserted, and certainly not to be bestowed on enemies of the land. This was especially the case, he argued, since the intent of the enemy alien was treachery, which had to be stopped – an opinion, Currie affirmed, that was shared by every man who had returned from the front. Invoking the support of the veterans, Currie declared that those who opposed denying the enemy alien naturalization were simply pandering to the "German vote" in the west, which was all the more cause to disfranchise the alien of enemy origin.[65]

Currie's outspokenness was lauded by other Conservatives, who, fearful of the consequences of an election gone wrong, sided with the parliamentarian's candour while deprecating the government's tepid stand. There was everything to gain and much to lose, and any hesitation on the part of the government was a sign of either impotence or indecisiveness. The *Calgary Daily Herald* argued:

The worst that can be said of the Currie proposal is that it is a breach of faith in a matter that is of minor moment to the people concerned for the time being. And in answer to that criticism it may be added that the breach is not altogether one-sided. Many Germans and Austrians, naturalized citizens of Canada, have acted since the commencement of war in ways that are the opposite of patriotic or loyal. In their cases there is no obligation on the part of the government to keep faith. If the disqualification were made general it would only mean that the rule was being made to apply to those whose loyalty is of unknown quality as well as to those whose conduct gives proof that they are not loyal. If loyal citizens suffer as a result it will be their misfortune; nothing worse.[66]

Under the circumstances, the government's decision to disfranchise citizens of enemy origin naturalized after 1902 was inevitable. Not everyone was pleased. The War Time Elections Act, introduced in parliament on 20 August 1917, was met with howls of protest and disapproval from the liberal press, which denounced it as "a cheap party trick" devised to bolster the electoral success of the Conservatives. From other quarters, criticism went much deeper. By passing the legislation, it was argued that the government not only violated the trust of those invited to Canada's shores, but also through its rank cynicism and disregard for the rights of citizens undermined the moral standing of the country in its ongoing struggle against autocracy and tyranny:

No country or people can take a short cut to victory by wrongdoing without suffering moral loss and damage. The proposal to disfranchise naturalized citizens of the Dominion is legally indefensible and morally wrong. Canada cannot hope to be moral victor in the fight against Germany by adopting the immoral code of

German militarism. Canada is out to destroy autocracy in Europe, not to establish it on the free soil of the New World.

Let those who will attempt to tear up Canada's "scrap of paper" by breaking the nation's solemn obligations to those whom she invited to settle in the Dominion, but the day any party in the country, by *force majeure*, carries a law to deprive the stranger within the gates of the rights of citizenship, that day Canada steps down from her high position which is warring against Prussian tyranny and for democratic freedom ... To disfranchise the naturalized immigrant who came to Canada trusting in promises made, and relying on the honor and integrity of the Canadian people, would perjure the Dominion in the face of the world and give the lie to her proud boast that Canada is the land of freedom.[67]

Passed in August 1917, the War Time Elections Act, along with the Military Service Act authorizing conscription, would become central issues in the December federal election, called by the prime minister, who hoped to receive a mandate. Not surprisingly, the political opposition denounced both pieces of legislation as "Hunnish" measures that threatened to bring "Kaiserism" to Canada. The political divisions ran deep. In Quebec, opponents of conscription broke up scores of meetings in support of the government's position. In Kitchener, formerly Berlin, Ontario, the prime minister, campaigning on the issue of conscription, was shouted down and a riot was narrowly averted. The protesters in Kitchener, with its large German-born population, were said to be enemies, akin to the Bolsheviks fomenting revolution in Russia.[68] The agitators in Quebec were denounced simply as hooligans.

One proposed solution to the Kitchener protest was to "isolate" the city by way of a boycott.[69] Although nothing came of it, the public reaction to the developments in Kitchener was visceral. Opponents of conscription were described as either *agents provocateurs* or enemy aliens who were taking advantage of "Canadian liberality." The mood was such that in Toronto when seventy-four enemy aliens were arrested in a crowd debating conscription, they were identified as having "abused the liberty allowed them by participating in public discussion of Canada's Governmental affairs." There were calls for maximum punishment. After a short period of detention, however, the seventy-four were released from custody on orders from Ottawa, but not before being warned that their attendance at any meeting "hostile to the country" would be followed by internment.[70]

Across the country, aliens of enemy origin became increasingly uneasy with the public's growing anti-alien sentiment and accusations of disloyalty. How could they ever demonstrate their loyalty, if there was no opportunity to do so? Prevented from serving because of their "enemy" status, how could they respond to those who would now denounce them as benefiting from their exemption as "enemies"? The issue of conscription, defined in terms of service and sacrifice, gave the franchise to those women whose husbands were serving overseas – their marital status conferred upon them political standing and the recognition of a grateful nation – but there was no such opportunity in the case of enemy aliens who were prohibited from enlisting. On the contrary, commanding high wages, they were frequently described as "living off the fat of the land."[71] For enemy aliens, there was no clear way of escaping their situation.

From the public's perspective, the possibility of enemy aliens taking advantage of the country was not to be countenanced. As Canada's best sons were fighting and dying on the battlefields of Europe, it followed then that the enemy alien should not be allowed to live freely in the country without some form of recompense or atonement. In this sense, it was seen as both right and natural that enemy aliens be forced to work according to terms that reflected their status as enemies. As a result, in the caustic debate on franchise, there was added the issue of compulsory labour.

The labour shortage in the country by the fall of 1917 was acute. The demands of war increased the need for coal, timber, iron, and food. Production increased exponentially, but demand outpaced supply. Various schemes had been introduced, including attracting migrant workers from the US, releasing all of the remaining prisoners of war from Canadian camps, and even the proposal, raised on several occasions, of transporting tens of thousands of prisoners of war from Europe to work in Canadian industry and on Canadian farms.[72] These plans were less practical than a policy that would simply ensure that everyone was working, including enemy aliens, at wage rates that did not negatively impact production or output. Others, however, had a less charitable outlook. They demanded that measures be taken to alleviate the pressure. Calls were soon made for enemy aliens to be conscripted, to have them forcibly put to work at jobs when and where needed and at wages that reflected their enemy status.

The public call for universal conscription of enemy alien labour was persistent. The *Lethbridge Telegram* wrote: "As for reaping the advantage, the bulk of it goes to the enemy foreign element. If these men, by

reason of their standing, cannot be conscripted, and, as stated, are taking advantage of the situation which their predominance gives them,
then it is high time that this class of labour should be conscripted, and
contribute to the war by working at a wage, in true measure of the
value received, without being placed in an envious position in the eyes
of those who have already of their free will been called away to war."[73]
In Manitoba, with its ongoing shortage of agricultural labour, the desire
to see alien labour put to work translated into a full-blown campaign
to pressure the government into adopting a measure that would see all
alien labour conscripted, placed on farms, and paid at the rate of
Canadian soldiers overseas.[74] The newly appointed minister of militia,
Major General S.C. Mewburn, caught up in a moment of unbridled zeal,
echoed this sentiment at a public gathering in Hamilton, adding that any
earnings over $1.10 a day should be seized.[75]

Mewburn's pronouncement aside, the government was cautious about
taking any premature action on compulsory labour, resisting pressure by
citing the need for a thorough review. Government reluctance to move
on the issue was met with derision and scorn.[76] Bolstered by mass meetings, the Great War Veterans' Association met with the prime minister
and other cabinet officials and pressed their case that the enemy alien
question had to be dealt with in an appropriate manner. They insisted
that in addition to conscripting alien labour, the government should
adopt other measures, namely denying enemy aliens from holding public
office, seizing all of their firearms, supressing their newspapers, and compelling them "to wear a badge, or token, prominently displayed, designating that he is an alien of his class."[77] The government responded by
insisting that the conscription of enemy alien labour would impede production in western Canada while organized labour was sure to oppose
it. The government also pointed out an international dimension to the
question that was difficult to ignore: Germany was bound to take
umbrage with the negative treatment accorded its nationals abroad.

The government position was informed by confidentially sourced
information regarding the state of labour in western Canada and its own
critical assessment of the situation. The leadership of organized labour
in the west was said to be increasingly in the hands of "the foreign alien
element, if not even the enemy alien element," and any untoward actions
had the potential of leading to large-scale strikes and perhaps even civil
unrest.[78] For instance, reports circulated about disturbances at the
Federal Coal Mines in Lethbridge, where the local union with its many
foreign-born workers went on strike after an enemy alien had been

discharged and the mine operators refused to reinstate the man.[79] Other miners in the vicinity, it was reported, were also prepared to weigh in on the matter unless the situation was satisfactorily adjusted. Given the potential explosiveness of the labour situation, it was understandable that the government would exercise caution. But in the end it was the government's own calculation about the relative gains and costs that would guide its approach.

Loring Christie, legal adviser and special assistant to the prime minister on international affairs, was tasked to draft the government's position on the conscription of enemy alien labour in Canada, and to outline its advantages and disadvantages.[80] While acknowledging the widespread public demand for the conscription of enemy alien labour and the appropriation of their wages, Christie argued there were considerable disadvantages to pursuing this line of action. The public, as he pointed out, would have been appeased, but the discriminatory legislation would invariably lead to reprisals that would be visited not only upon Canadians but upon all British subjects on enemy territory. Christie argued: "We cannot hope to engage successfully with the enemy in a competition of atrocities." On this point alone, there was much for Canada to lose.

But there was also the question of benefit to consider. Christie asked: What gain was to be had in compulsory labour? The value of the work produced by conscripted labour working under protest would not compare to voluntary work and the loss would be considerable. The suggestion often raised in petitions that the entire enemy alien population be interned Christie dismissed as unrealistic. The cost of feeding, clothing, lodging, and guarding the prisoners was neither practical nor viable if recent experience was any indicator. As Christie noted, internment in Canada (and in the United Kingdom) had demonstrated that without careful planning and organization any work obtained would be "negligible." If internment were to be viable, at least on the scale proposed, Canada, in his opinion, would have to establish national factories or situate internment camps near such factories. But even if this were the case, despite a mix of inducements and compulsory measures, the prisoners, Christie felt, would refuse to work, negating any advantage that might be obtained.[81]

The minister of justice, the Hon. Charles Doherty, in a wide-ranging debate in parliament on the issue of conscripting enemy alien labour, repeated many of the same arguments made by Christie.[82] Doherty also disabused Conservative house members of the idea that coercion might be used against those remaining prisoners who were reported to be resisting the work in the camps. In particular, he claimed there were legal and moral aspects that needed to be considered. On the issue of forcing the remaining prisoners to work, would Canada "stoop to the inhumanity of the Hun?" he asked. In a surprising admission, he explained that these men were civilian residents of the country and not prisoners of war, at least not prisoners of war in the strict sense of the term. If they were prisoners of war in the conventional sense, then the Hague Convention would apply and they could be made to work. But they were largely indigent and unemployed men to whom an obligation was owed, especially since they had been invited to the country and were prevented from leaving. Doherty also made clear that there would be retribution if the remaining prisoners were compelled to work and that such a policy would not sit well with Britain. As for conscripting enemy alien labour more generally, the minister argued that nothing profitably would be gained from it, certainly not without using force. Was it the intention of parliament, Doherty queried, "to send a slave driver out with the alien armed with a whip to keep him working, [because] short of that what course could you pursue?" It was a rhetorical question. Internment, at least the way it was practised, had run its course. There was no turning back.

And yet the policy and practice of arrest and internment continued, albeit in a modified form. The assistant commissioner of the RNWMP, J.A. McGibbon, instructed members of the force not to be too strict in enforcing the law.[83] Indeed, greater leniency was being demonstrated with respect to those arrested for minor infractions, such as failure to report. This, however, did not mean that officials would turn a blind eye to matters that merited action. When enemy aliens came under suspicion or demonstrated a rank disregard for political authority, they were still to be treated in a manner that underlined their enemy status. Werner Vent of Saskatoon, for instance, employed as an attendant with the CNR in a dining car, was arrested and sent to Kapuskasing for possessing German documents. These included certificates of birth and confirmation, a certificate of guardianship, a police permit, and, most importantly, a list of names of prominent Germans living in Chile and the United States, the purpose of which he could not satisfactorily explain.[84]

But it was for enemy aliens engaged in political activity, such as Leon Mechnavech of Sudbury, that arrest and internment would be especially reserved. Initially charged under the new Idlers Act, but released by a magistrate, Mechnavech was re-arrested and interned under orders of the chief dominion police commissioner, Colonel A.P. Sherwood, for having objectionable material found in his possession: the anti-war Ukrainian pamphlet *Komu Potribna Vina* (Who Needs War).[85] Also interned were Nick Yawney, Joseph Harasym, and Pete Stefaniuk, who had been found guilty of a similar offence.[86] Internment still had a role to play, but it became more defined in purpose.

The shifting nature of internment reflected changing conditions in the country. Political radicalism was afoot, and enemy aliens who were participating in activity considered harmful to the interests of the country became targets of arrest and internment.[87] At the Occident Hall in Toronto, police broke up a meeting of the Social Democratic Party of Canada. Naturalized aliens at the meeting were unmolested, but eighty enemy aliens were taken into custody on grounds that they were discussing government policies. At another meeting of socialists at a private Royce Street residence in Toronto, ten enemy aliens were arrested after they were accused of uttering statements critical of the government.[88]

From the government's perspective, these and other arrests were regarded as necessary. Potentially seditious activity was cited as the principal reason for exercising police measures.[89] But there were other pressing concerns as well, notably maintaining peace and order. With multiple strikes occurring, the tense labour situation (allegedly being fomented by "Hun propaganda") was adding to both nativist pique and disturbances that threatened the peace. The public's intolerance bordered on fanaticism, with numerous reports of aliens being set upon by crowds of angry citizens. In Vancouver, a gathering turned riotous after being whipped into a frenzy by demagogues and mercilessly attacked several nearby individuals with "foreign accents." Days later, a mob called for a rope to hang a seventeen-year-old boy whose inopportune anti-war remarks cast him in the role of an enemy alien sympathizer. He was spared only by the timely intervention of the police.[90] In Montreal the public rage that followed from a fire which levelled the Montreal Biscuit Company and thirty other buildings lessened only after one of the witnesses was arrested because he had a German-sounding name.[91] In Toronto, where anti-alien sentiment was running at a fever pitch, an eight-week-old baby, born of Austro-Hungarian parents and designated an enemy alien by municipal authorities, was denied assistance at a city hospital.[92]

These and other incidents pointed to a breakdown in civility and common sense. It also led to the collapse of law and order in Toronto on 3 August 1918. After an inebriated veteran had been physically removed from a Greek family restaurant, two hundred returned soldiers and one thousand sympathizers ran amuck in the city, destroying alien-owned eating establishments.[93] The police were hard pressed to put down the rioting veterans, who rallied behind the call for the denaturalization of aliens and the internment of all enemy aliens. The events were repeated the following day when veterans and sympathizers returned to the streets to do battle with the police. Although this incident was described as a disgraceful affair, the principal demand of the returned soldiers could not be ignored entirely, namely, "that immediate action be taken to repress disloyalty and sedition in Toronto among the foreign element."[94] For the government, it was clear that it still had to manage the enemy alien question carefully in the face of a hostile and susceptible public.

### EXERCISING CAUTION, MANAGING THE PROBLEM

With America's entry into the war in April 1917, the diplomatic interests of the Central Powers were assumed by Switzerland and Sweden, including responsibility for the welfare of enemy alien internees. A division of labour was arranged, so that the internment camps would be visited regularly and matters relating to the health and welfare of prisoners could be addressed in a timely and responsible fashion. The frontier camps, however, proved difficult to access. Visits were periodic and irregular and more often than not would occur only after complaints were received from prisoners. There were no such complaints from prisoners at Morrissey, which led the Swiss consul general, Samuel Gintzburger, charged with overseeing German interests in B C and Alberta, to believe that it was a "happy camp." After a long-delayed visit to the facility, he was surprised by what he discovered there. Although the physical space was well maintained and hygiene observed, it was the relations between guards and prisoners that he found wanting. Prisoners complained of being routinely abused and beaten, usually for refusing to work, followed by a round of aggravated punishment – solitary confinement accompanied by a diet of bread and water for prolonged periods. Although they had previously petitioned the consul, their letters had been suppressed. For the Swiss consul, this was unacceptable, placing him in a position to protest the conduct of the officers and soldiers at the Morrissey camp and declaring that further visits would be forthcoming.[95]

Gintzburger, whose official report was forwarded to Berlin, came in for personal criticism and attack.[96] The undersecretary of state for external affairs, Sir Joseph Pope, maligned Gintzburger, a respected Vancouver businessman, declaring that his antipathy towards the British cause disqualified him as a neutral observer.[97] The censor at the Morrissey camp,

Constantin Babij, when asked to comment on the diplomat's report by the internment director, declared the complaints were "petty imaginations," no doubt animated by the consul's telling the prisoners "they might write anything they choose."[98] However, Gintzburger was not alone in his assessment of what was taking place at this and other internment camps in the country. A visit to the Amherst camp by the Royal Swedish consul general, David Bergstrom, independently confirmed that, from his point of view, the whole system appeared to be "very defective."[99] There were problems and there was no disguising the fact.

These problems were openly and freely admitted in correspondence between camp commanders and the director of internment operations, General Otter. At Kapuskasing, citing the ongoing insubordination of prisoners, the commandant, Lieutenant Colonel W.E. Date, reported on the actions that had been taken to control the prisoners.[100] Prisoner S. Konrad was given a two-day punishment diet of bread and water for refusing to obey a lawful order. W. Knittler was assigned to 168 hours of solitary confinement for insubordination and using insulting language toward an officer. E. Hoyer was sentenced to seventy-two hours of solitary confinement for using profane language in the presence of an officer. Those who attempted to flee or were suspected of flight were subjected to a combination of solitary confinement and punishment diet. The prisoner A. Derouet was given twenty-one days for cutting a hole in the bunkhouse wall, while J. Druzovic and P. Radloff were each punished with fourteen days of solitary for leaving the pump house without permission.

These and other incidents at Kapuskasing all pointed to the contest of wills that was shaping up between prisoners and camp officials. For the officers and guards, order and compliance could only be obtained through the threat or use of force. When, at Kapuskasing, a group had refused to turn out for roll call, Lieutenant Colonel Date, reaching the limits of his patience, took matters into his own hands:

I decided to call their bluff right there and then. I called for about twelve men, posted armed sentries over the other bunkhouses, in case their inmates attempted a mix-up, went into No. 1 [bunkhouse] with Capts. Gibson and Kirkconnell and ordered the prisoners up for roll call. A few hesitated, but an automatic six-shooter poked in their faces made them step lively. They stood up like sheep and answered their names. Afterwards, I had them counted, then told [Prisoner] Baffin to roll his blankets and come out, which

he did most obediently. Furthermore, I told [Prisoner] No. 2232
Policardo to follow suit, seeing he was so mouthy just previously.
He came like a child. After we left there was not a sound in No. 1,
and the whole thing was done so quietly, and they cowed down so
completely.[101]

When prisoners at the same camp went on strike in November 1917, the
guards fired upon them, shooting one prisoner. Delighted with the outcome, Date wrote to General Otter after the incident: "At the time of
writing I am pleased to say that all the Departments are working and
running smoothly. Besides, there were 114 out in the slash piling wood
yesterday. I think they have had enough of strikes, and that prisoner
being shot by a sentry yesterday has made them realize what they are up
against. It has been their boast that we were afraid to shoot, and that
orders to that effect [were] bluff – 'American bluff' as they termed it."[102]

Camp authorities were prepared to use violence to intimidate and
coerce the prisoners, highlighting the ongoing tension and discord in the
camps.[103] Although a semblance of order prevailed, it was an altogether
uneasy affair. The prisoners complained frequently about their treatment
and insisted on their rights. When Austro-Hungarian internees at the
Vernon camp felt they were without adequate diplomatic representation (believing the Swedish consul general in Ottawa and vice-consul
in Vancouver were representing Canadian interests and not their own),
they turned to the Swiss representative asking that their grievances be
placed before the German Foreign Office for transmission to the Austro-
Hungarian government.[104] When no satisfaction was obtained and news
was inadvertently received of the escalation in brutality toward Austro-
Hungarian prisoners at the Morrissey camp, they appealed directly to the
Imperial German Foreign Office, petitioning for intervention and assistance.[105] Internment officials, on the other hand, were largely unsympathetic, downplaying the grievances and protests of the prisoners.

The dynamics of the relationship fuelled the perception among internment officials that the remaining prisoners were not simply incorrigible
but dangerous as well. Their defiance underscored the opinion that they
were a menace and not to be trusted. It also reinforced the view that the
remaining prisoners should not be discharged. When Sir Thomas Tait of
the Minto Coal Company applied for the parole of six prisoners to assist
with work at the mine, General Otter informed him that he could not
reasonably free them. Tait, however, would not be denied, applying
pressure through the Office of the Fuel Controller, citing national

importance. Unwilling to appear obstinate, the director finally agreed to supply fifty men to the company, but only on the condition that they be supervised under armed guard. Since the cost of accommodating and feeding the guards fell to the companies, an attempt was made to modify the proposal. Otter, however, insisted that the men were a danger and needed to be guarded and he would not provide them under any other condition. It was a principle Otter would adhere to in the months to follow.[106] Indeed, successive requests for prisoner labour were met only after the contracting agency accepted the provision that a military guard accompany the working parties.[107]

The railways became the major recipients of prisoners under this arrangement. Working parties of prisoners were allocated primarily from Kapuskasing to the CNR in northern Ontario (Folyet and North Bay) and from Amherst and Kapuskasing to the Canadian Government Railways in Atlantic Canada (Sackville, Moncton, New Glasgow, Edmunston, Port Borden, Campbellton, and Truro).[108] From Morrissey a group of sixty-five was sent to work on the Goose Line Railway near Munson, Alberta, effectively leading to the closure of the Morrissey camp in October 1918. In each case, one guard was assigned to every two prisoners and was provided with food and accommodations. Prisoners on the other hand were paid 20¢ an hour and fed a soldier's daily ration for which a charge of 50¢ per diem was deducted from the prisoner's wages.[109] Not all prisoners were eligible to participate in the supervised work details. Camp commandants were instructed to discharge only those who could be expected to work and who would dutifully follow the orders of guards once outside the camps.

Although the prisoners who remained behind barbed wire expressed a desire that their torment would end soon, everything pointed to their continuing internment. As for those responsible for their keep, it was fully expected that the prisoners would remain interned until the end of the war because their release was seen as harmful if not dangerous. With radicalism and social unrest threatening society, "the time," according to the internment director, "was not safe to release them."[110] Moreover, there was a growing belief among officials – an idea that was circulating and never fully disputed – that the remaining enemy alien prisoners would not be released but, in fact, would be repatriated along with others who might yet be arrested, interned, and deported for engaging in political agitation.

The political situation in early 1918 was difficult throughout the country, and government officials were guarded in their approach to the

4.3  Enclosure, Morrissey, B C

enemy alien question. In addition to the disputes over military conscription, service, and franchise, there was growing conflict over labour rights.
Enemy aliens were perceived to be at the centre of many of the difficulties encountered. Not surprisingly, their involvement or interest in labour
issues, whether real or imagined, was regarded negatively especially in
light of their status. Their activity, including their unauthorized movement from one jurisdiction to another, made them targets of official concern and interest at this critical time.

   The supervision and control of paroled enemy aliens derived not only
from the requirement to register under the 1914 order-in-council P C
2721 but also the requirement to report to authorities in designated
centres on a monthly basis. The requirement to report expanded on
20 September 1916 under order-in-council P C 2194 and applied to every
enemy alien in Canada who had no permanent place of residence. This
ensured that transient aliens of enemy origin (thought to pose the greatest risk) could be closely watched and dealt with should they violate the
terms of their parole. The measure enabled the police to maintain extensive records and conduct investigations where necessary, as in Halifax

where a so-called "Black List" was compiled.[111] Despite this effort, it was determined that more extensive record keeping was required, especially since the existing order-in-council failed to take into account those enemy aliens who had a permanent residence. In May 1918, 81,144 enemy aliens were registered, of whom 2,087 were interned. But this number did not include the countless tens of thousands who fell outside the provisions of PC 2194, most notably enemy aliens of German nationality, the majority of whom had permanent places of residence in Canada.[112] The need for greater vigilance of these individuals became an important stimulus in the government's decision to amend the existing orders.

More immediately, the move to amend the orders was motivated by the large number of letters being received. Some warned the government that the unauthorized movement of enemy aliens was an invitation to trouble. Correspondence from Freeman Harding, a barrister and active local Conservative in Kamloops, for instance, was brought to the attention of the minister of justice. Explaining that police officials were handicapped in their efforts to properly handle the local enemy alien problem, Harding called for a more comprehensive system of registration and monitoring of all enemy aliens. Harding believed there was some urgency in the matter since anti-Allied propaganda was being circulated among the enemy alien population, "with I.W.W. [Industrial Workers of the World] principles somewhere hidden in the operating machinery."[113]

Other correspondence more routinely emphasized the economic costs of enemy alien movement. The cost to companies, whether in terms of manpower shortage or lost training, was enormous, the petitioners complained. As it stood, enemy aliens were relocating without permission and little interest was taken "to follow them to see that they are punished for breach of the regulations." Only a policy that restricted their movement and made "the right to travel on the part of alien enemies a matter of grace rather than a matter of right" could help correct the situation.[114]

Pressure by industry and growing concern over radicalization among the foreign-born led justice officials to recommend the general registration of all enemy aliens, regardless of whether or not they had a permanent address.[115] On 5 August 1918, PC 1908 was approved, amending the original September 1916 order. It required every enemy alien between the ages of sixteen and sixty to register whether or not they had a permanent address. In addition, they were required to carry a parole card with them at all times, remain within the jurisdiction in which the parole card was issued, seek permission in the case of travel or departure, report monthly to a chief of police or designate (including at the point of arrival should they be given permission to travel or depart from their residence), and abide by all other existing rules and regulations that applied to enemy aliens.[116]

The 5 August order-in-council authorizing the general registration of all enemy aliens had a chilling effect on those who had a permanent residence. Unsure of what to make of the new requirement, Reverend C.F. Christiansen, a Lutheran pastor from Debigh, Ontario, wrote to the minister of justice for clarification. Speaking on behalf of his parishioners who had turned to him for counsel, Christiansen stated that many considered themselves Canadians and did not wish to declare that they were enemy aliens by signing the required Undertaking. They feared that this would affect their status and property holdings both during and after the war and negate the rights they enjoyed. Moreover, the measure was unjustified, in his opinion, given that these were a peaceful and law-abiding people whose sons were loyally serving in Canada's military. He argued that it was inconceivable to think that they would be treated as anything other than Canadian. He ended the letter by offering his characterization of the situation: "They do not feel bound to Germany in any way, consider Canada their country, and wish to be counted citizens of Canada."[117] The reverend's correspondence was acknowledged with the customary response – those who abided by the laws of the land would not be adversely affected.

Order-in-council PC 1908 was designed to further curtail and actively monitor the unauthorized movement of enemy aliens. In this way, radicalism would be held in check, deemed all the more necessary given the growth in membership of radical organizations, including the anti-war Ukrainian Social Democratic Party of Canada (USDPC). With forty locals across the country, Ukrainians of both alien and enemy alien origin (subjects of Russia and Austria-Hungary respectively) were being drawn to its ranks. PC 1908, consequently, proved an important instrument to limit the travel and cooperation between the leaders of this organization and its adherents.

From the perspective of the chief commissioner of the dominion police, the threat posed by the USDPC and other organizations suggested this effort may not have been enough. It was his view that "unless some action is taken to deal with these people, before they get too strong, it may eventually lead to general strikes throughout the country."[118] However, Colonel A.P. Sherwood, the commissioner, was already ahead of the situation. Eighteen individuals, all members of the USDPC, were arrested in Montreal under order-in-council PC 915, an order that had been introduced to deal more authoritatively with seditious libel. Sixteen of the group responsible for printing and distributing circulars deemed seditious were interned under the order. Meanwhile, the press, plant, and machinery were all seized under a censorship warrant with the intent of making it impossible for the printing of seditious literature to resume. For good measure, the authorities expressed their preference and desire to melt the lead type, sell the press and motor, and deposit the amount received for credit until after the war.[119]

From an official perspective, it was imperative that not only these but other militants be warned and held to account. As was soon made evident, this would also apply to anyone suspected of engaging in "prohibited activity." The issue of what constituted prohibited activity was addressed in a special report commissioned by the government and authored by Charles Cahan, a businessman and active Conservative Party supporter from Quebec who managed to capture the attention and support of the prime minister.[120] Cahan was unyielding in his opposition to socialist and labour leaders, recommending that the 5 August executive order be extended more broadly to include Allied aliens originating from the Russian empire as well. "Thoroughly saturated with socialistic doctrines which have been proclaimed by the Bolsheviki faction of Russia," these people, Cahan believed, were no less a danger than enemy subjects of Germany and Austria-Hungary. Because they were being led by a variety of associations that induced them to strike and engage in otherwise "treacherous" behaviour, Cahan claimed that these individuals needed to be monitored and tightly controlled along with the traditional enemy alien. In this regard, Cahan asserted:

> It is absolutely necessary for the preservation of peace and good order in Canada that this propaganda should be strictly supervised and controlled; and as a first step to attain that end, all these foreigners should be compelled to register, and to report to the Civic Police ... No valid objection can be made to the registration of these foreigners. In England and in France, all foreigners, even those of allied nations, are compelled by law to register and to report to the local police at stated intervals, and whenever they change their places of residence. The Aliens in Canada particularly mentioned above should register in Canada under the same conditions as Enemy Aliens.

Cahan recommended that a number of socialist organizations be declared unlawful and that membership in them be designated a criminal offence. He also proposed that public utterances of a socialist nature be punished, censorship more rigorously enforced, and wider powers relating to search and confiscation introduced. Finally, in keeping with policy developments in the United States, Cahan suggested that the police force be reorganized and a central public security branch, much like the Federal Bureau of Investigation (FBI), be formed in the Department of Justice to help coordinate and lead the fight against sedition in the country.

The prime minister and justice minister enthusiastically accepted Cahan's recommendations and directed that his proposals be immediately implemented.[121] In response to the issue of registering Allied alien Russian, Finn, and Ukrainian subjects from the Russian Empire, the Canada Registration Board was instructed to quickly make available relevant information that had been previously compiled under its mandate, especially with regard to where such individuals lived.[122] Cahan's other recommendations were also put into practice. On 24 September, order-in-council PC 2381 was approved, banning the publication, use, and distribution of enemy alien–language material.[123] This was followed by PC 2384, which outlawed organizations identified by Cahan as seditious in nature. Finally, on 2 October, a Public Safety Branch was created under executive order with Cahan appointed its director.

As the director of the Public Safety Branch, Cahan went about the business of proposing and outlining new ideas and strategies to combat the threat of political and labour unrest, quickly interfering in matters that ostensibly related to law and order but which in fact reflected his own prejudices.[124] When correspondence was received from a Ukrainian cultural organization inquiring whether concerts and theatrical plays in the Ukrainian language could be held, Cahan, on behalf of the government, notified the petitioners that no meeting in a foreign tongue of any kind, except religious services, could take place in Canada during the war.[125] When Finnish community leaders requested permission to create a representative community organization, Cahan warned them that any hint at socialist activity (which he detected in the organization's proposed charter and membership) would come in conflict with Canadian laws, "obliging" the government to deal with them "in a summary manner."[126] As for those individuals that Cahan, through his investigations, suspected of harbouring or fomenting anti-government sentiment, he privately denounced them to police and justice officials, recommending that steps be taken to silence their activity.[127]

Cahan's energetic if obdurate approach won him admiration and thanks within certain quarters. It also garnered criticism. A sweeping ban (order-in-council PC 2384) was placed on a number of political associations, including the Social Democratic Party of Canada (SDPC). The effort to bar and silence the SDPC, however, was opposed by several cabinet ministers who criticized the executive injunction, insisting on an amendment that would lift the ban on the SDPC. Ministers T.A. Crerar and N.W. Rowell, in particular, argued that the sanction against the SDPC was counterproductive and unjustified given that the goal of the organization was constitutional change not revolution.[128] Banning the party negated the first principles of democracy, they argued. The government was also criticized by the liberal element in the country, which was inclined to see the measure as punitive and unjust. Bowing to pressure, an amendment restoring the right of SDPC association, resisted by Cahan, was introduced.

In the end, however, it was not Cahan's views that caused concern about him as much as it was his abrasive approach, which raised questions about his suitability, especially after he criticized the Justice Department and dominion police for not having adequately addressed the radical threat among the foreign-born. He openly suggested more could be done to contain enemy alien radical activity by reorganizing policing in the country. Cahan sought greater power to hire special investigators and soon began to assign police for such purposes without authorization.[129] It proved to be Cahan's undoing. Rebuked by senior government officials for both his public comments about policing in Canada and his intrusion in police matters, Cahan tendered his resignation. It was accepted.[130] Cahan's resignation led to the dissolution of the branch after four months of chaotic operation. In its brief existence the agency did much to increase the level of anxiety and tension in the country, especially among the foreign-born communities.

Cahan's resignation in early November 1918 was fortuitous. Coinciding with the signing of the armistice, his resignation provided a context for the dissolution of the Public Safety Branch. Initially declared indispensible, the branch was now no longer needed. And yet the challenges associated with the war lingered on. There did not appear, for example, to be an effective solution to the ongoing problem of enemy aliens, whose "simple presence," the superintendent of the Ontario

Provincial Police observed, "upset" the English-speaking population.[131] There was also the issue of what to do with civilian prisoners of war who were either still interned or working in small groups under military guard on the railways. Hostilities may have officially ended, but the fate of the interned remained unresolved.

In late October, several weeks before the cessation in hostilities, the long-awaited agreement negotiated between the German and British governments regarding the exchange of prisoners of war, combatant and non-combatant, had finally been submitted to parliament.[132] The settlement assigned a quota regarding the number and quality of prisoners to be repatriated, with emphasis placed on the return of civilian prisoners to their countries of origin. It was evident to all at the time that their repatriation was both desirable and needed. Now that the hostilities had ended, the importance of proceeding expeditiously with their exchange was underscored. But the political question of their removal was a thorny one. Most of the prisoners in Canada were legal immigrants and as such were owed a certain amount of consideration. Having been invited, could they now simply be expelled without their consent? How to sort out those who should or could stay in the country was yet to be determined.

From the perspective of the director of internment operations, whose business it was to oversee all aspects pertaining to the care, welfare, and disposition of the prisoners of war, the question of their future was uncertain. Nevertheless, it had to be planned for. On 18 November, one week after the signing of the armistice, General Otter communicated with the commanders at the three remaining camps, as well as officers overseeing the few outstanding railway work details, requesting them to send him "the names and numbers of such prisoners in your charge as have been very troublesome or shown decided antagonism to British or Canadian rule."[133] The communication was further followed by an order for a listing of those they considered "undesirable," as a preview to their being possibly deported from the country. The commandants quickly replied.[134]

Major N.E. Nash, commandant at the Vernon camp, reported that of the 354 prisoners of war at his camp, eighty-six were well behaved while the rest were identified as "undesirable, troublesome, or unwanted." The "undesirables" were said to be either pro-German or pro–Austro-Hungarian in their views or bitter against Canada and Britain. Others were described as politically suspect. He labelled the remaining to be either feeble, insane, or "decidedly eccentric." At Kapuskasing, the "undesirables" were identified as those who were considered to be difficult characters or who had been incarcerated for petty offences. The majority, however, either were thought to be IWW or had been interned for congregating at secret meetings. An additional twenty-two were identified as being responsible for fomenting strikes at the camp. At Amherst, sixty individuals were said to be members of the IWW, a consequence of the activity of Leon Trotsky, who, according to the camp commandant, did much to encourage them when he was briefly interned at the facility and before his release as an alien subject of an Allied country, Russia.[135] As for the one small railway work detail that continued to operate, Major G. Anderson sent news from Munson, Alberta, that there were no troublesome prisoners in his party. He indicated that when his detail was formed, all the difficult personalities had been sent to Kapuskasing, and "the only trouble that I have had has been of a petty nature and the threat to re-intern the offenders [sending them back to the major camps] has had the desired effect."[136]

From Otter's perspective the armistice signalled the need to prepare for the possibility of expelling the prisoners from the country. For the prisoners and their families, on the other hand, the armistice held out the promise of a long-awaited release. Joseph Kaminecki of Ethelbert, Manitoba, petitioned the minister of justice, requesting that his children, John and the Reverend Peter Kaminecki, finally be set free. The former, a teacher, had been arrested in 1916 and interned at Kapuskasing as a result of his insolent attitude toward authority while reporting. The other son, a Ukrainian Catholic priest, had been arrested and sent to Vernon on information received from the American FBI, which accused him of suspicious activity while travelling in Cuba on missionary work. The elder Kaminiecki, in failing health, pleaded with the minister to intercede with General Otter, who had denied them their release in the past: "I pray You Sir, have mercy over me and try to do your best by writing the Director of Internment Operations. I am heartbroken. Consider please, my age being 72 years. I am sick at present. I am waiting the hour of my death. Consider please, the expenditure of my last cent for my children's education and now instead of having their support I am left alone depending on the mercy of strangers."[137] Reverend Peter Kaminecki was released, but only after the Ukrainian Catholic Vicar General, Fr Ambrose Redkevich of Montreal, a respected and trusted figure, offered his personal guarantee that the interned cleric would not pose any further trouble. John Kaminecki, on the other hand, would have to wait for his fate to be determined.

Katherine Przycylska also appealed for clemency on behalf of her husband, Harry Koruna, who had been arrested for using profane language with a railway constable. Przycylska pleaded for Koruna's release, claiming that his internment was unwarranted in view of the nature of the offence and the fact that she and her three children, including a boy left limbless because of an accident, were entirely dependent on him. That Koruna was Ukrainian, she argued, also had to be taken into consideration: "Ukraine is a biggest part of Russia, which is Ally of Great Britain. It is true that he was born in Eastern Galicia, which was a part of the now Defunkt Austrian Empire, but it is not his fault or mine or yours that he was born there. The Ukrainians were and are pro-Ally always and were at all times strongly against their persecutors." She concluded by asking that Koruna be paroled, "if not for good, then only for a time or a couple of months so he would be able to straighten out his affairs here, for which I will ever pray."[138]

Mrs Thomas Leubetich of Montreal was no less fearful for her situation. Hearing the rumour that deportation awaited all interned enemy aliens, she became increasingly agitated about what was to become of her and her family. Panic setting in, she wrote to the prime minister, pleading that her husband be spared from deportation and released:

> I beg you for the love of God and for my three poor little children
> to give to them their poor father for since nearly 7 months we have
> been in great misery, for as for me I am incapable of working and
> if you send my husband to Europe that would be to send us to the
> cemetery, all four of us, my children and myself, but I do not
> believe that the Prime Minister of Canada will act so, for he ought
> to have more justice than that.
>    You understand that after having very little and having worked
> for 12 years to earn his living and to assure that of his children, to
> see his money stolen, to see his family on the road [homeless] and
> in misery, to imprison him ... is that not strange? My husband
> arrived in Montreal 15 years ago and he is now 34 and he has
> always worked in Canada which he prefers to his country and now
> to send him to the other side to that country which he no longer
> remembers and when he would prefer to remain here. As for me,
> I prefer Canada and I do not wish to leave my native country.
> I would beg you do not send me to that distant country for as I
> tell you, in sending him so far, you will drive us to the cemetery,
> my children and me.

To prove to you that my husband is not an undesirable man in the country, I am sending you some letters of reference to give to the Chief of Police Sherwood of Ottawa and who has sent them to me to show to Captain Carter and I am sending them to you to prove to you what kind of man my husband is. He is not a traitor for it is quite the contrary. He is a man, sober, honest, and working. That is the reason why I beg you not to send him to the other side of the World for we have enough misery as it is.[139]

The deputy minister of justice, E. Newcombe, acknowledging her dire circumstances and distress, assured Mrs Leubetich that her application would be put before the minister of justice for his consideration. But he also revealed to her that he was "unaware of any intention to deport your husband when released."[140]

It may have been true that it was not the intention of the government to deport anyone who had been released. But this said nothing of those who were still interned. Indeed, while the deputy minister was assuring Mrs Leubetich that it was not the government's intention to deport internees who were paroled, he was quietly investigating immigration regulations pertaining to expulsion and how these might apply to some of those still interned.[141] A government decision, in fact, was in the process of being made regarding who among the remaining prisoners would stay or go.

PRESSURE

The signing of the armistice on 11 November 1918 was a time of joy, but also of profound relief. The seemingly endless conflict had at long last run its course. For those behind Canadian barbed wire, the moment had come none too soon. A number of prisoners had been held captive from the very start of the war. Their liberation, long awaited, now appeared to be at hand and with it the anticipation that their personal struggles had finally come to an end. They were to be disappointed. The armistice conditions did not provide for their immediate release. Rather, the discharge of prisoners of war, combatant or civilian, would depend on the terms of a treaty of peace. This was yet to be finalized.

Although unhappy that immediate steps were not being taken to repatriate the remaining prisoners, the public could take some comfort from the idea that with war's end they would eventually be gone. Still there was unease. As weeks passed, the rumour circulated that the

internees would be released back into Canadian society. With no information forthcoming, the rumour gained traction and a growing segment
of the population became increasingly agitated as a result. Would these
wilful enemies of Canada be allowed to walk freely among those who
bore the sacrifices of war? Would they now become fellow citizens?
"Persons who were too dangerous or too objectionable to be left at large
while the struggle was going on are not the best sort of material for citizenship in the Canadian democracy," declared the *Vancouver Daily
Sun*.[142] It stood to reason that as a menace to the country all enemy
aliens still interned needed to be removed now that the war was over.

The question of their removal was a delicate matter for the government, whose policy was still unclear at this point. Although negotiations around repatriation of prisoners of war had been largely concluded,
the issue was complicated because of the prevailing norm that maintained settlers could not be repatriated without their consent. On this
score, the Hon. J.A. Calder, minister of immigration, conceded it was
entirely possible that the civilian prisoners were entitled to their release.
Although he did not favour letting them loose all at one time, believing
the public would not countenance such a move, Calder was guided to
recommend, "We might adopt a plan whereby they could be released
gradually." But to the degree that public opinion mattered, he also suggested prisoners were to be carefully assessed in terms of "desirability." Accordingly, General Otter was instructed to gather information
on the internees.

Anticipating such a request, Otter had already collected statistical
information on the prisoners. The numbers had been fluctuating, but
he was able to report that 2,222 prisoners were still interned as of
1 December 1918. Among this number were 1,700 Germans, 469 Austro-
Hungarians, 11 Turks, 7 Bulgarians, and 15 others. All of the prisoners
were located at four remaining camps: Munson (63), Vernon (388),
Kapuskasing (1,007), and Amherst (764). On their status as possible
candidates for release, Otter was able to state with "a fair degree of reli-
ability" that there were 516 individuals who were hostile to official
authority and British rule, 134 agitators, 54 insane, and 5 incurable with
tuberculosis. He estimated the total number of "undesirable residents"
to be 709. Among those of German nationality, 800 were merchant marines transported from the West Indies and held by Canada at the request
of imperial authorities. They were to be sent back to Europe as a matter
of course, since the government of Jamaica and the other Caribbean
islands refused to accept their return. The director also made it known

that nearly all of the prisoners expressed a desire to remain in Canada (or else go to the United States), underscoring deportation as the approach to be used in ridding the country of this element. Otter acknowledged the government's instruction that no discharges would be authorized until a policy had been formulated.[143]

The rumour that interned aliens might remain in the country elicited a strong reaction, with petitions from organizations and individuals who sought to pre-empt their release. In December 1918, the Toronto branch of the Council of Women resolved that all interned enemy aliens and their families were to be deported – a resolution that was passed unanimously by the executive of the national council. Similarly, the South Vancouver Soldiers and Sailors Mothers and Wives Association petitioned for the deportation of interned prisoners and their families. Lieutenant Colonel R.C. Cooper, commander of the 11th Battalion, Canadian Garrison Regiment, stationed in Vancouver, endorsed the petition. Writing to the Hon. Thomas White, the acting prime minister, Cooper expressed incredulity at the thought that interned enemy aliens, still held and presumed treacherous, might be set free. "I consider it inconceivable that men [who] were interned as dangerous to the country could, at any time, be allowed to obtain any rights here. It is a matter of course to be thoroughly discussed before any action can be taken but in the best interests of the country, and, speaking from a local point of view, I hope no action will be taken until the Government has at least heard the views of the B.C. [caucus] members."

These and scores of other similar protests persuaded the government to proceed with the removal from Canada of those prisoners considered menacing or otherwise judged to be disagreeable. On 23 January 1919, a report was submitted to the Privy Council and approved by the governor general as order-in-council PC 158.[144] The order authorized the minister of justice to deport from Canada those interned aliens of enemy nationality considered "dangerous and hostile" or who would make for "undesirable citizens." On 24 January, the deputy minister of justice, E. Newcombe, instructed General Otter to ready for transport a small trial group of 100 prisoners. The outcome of the experiment would help determine the logistics for the future transfer of the remaining number. Within weeks of the order, overseas passage was secured and arrangements made for the reception of the prisoners in England and their eventual relocation to the continent. Shortly thereafter, under guard, a contingent of one hundred prisoners was quietly mustered onto a ship bound for Liverpool from Saint John, New Brunswick.

As a government measure long overdue, news of the order-in-council was welcome. But why stop there? A resolution passed by Vancouver's city council urged the government to widen the scope of the order so that all enemy aliens in the country might be deported, so as "to be freed of a menace that sooner or later will have a demoralizing effect upon the country and militate against the rehabilitation and repatriation of the thousands of men who suffered and who have bled to make this country possible."[145] The Vancouver declaration was one of many similar resolutions passed by urban and rural municipal councils across the country, including Toronto, Victoria, Hamilton, and Ontario's Victoria County.[146]

Sundry other organizations, associations, and private individuals also felt compelled to join in the chorus calling for mass deportation. In Brantford, Ontario, where anti-foreigner sentiment was at a fever pitch, the Brant Avenue Methodist Church demanded the removal of all enemy aliens from the country.[147] Meanwhile, John Bassett, publisher of the *Montreal Gazette*, insisted that the government deport 150 Russian Canadians who had honourably served with the CEF in France but who, declaring their sympathy for the revolutionaries in Russia, refused to be sent to Siberia to fight Bolsheviks as part of an Allied expeditionary force. For Bassett, deportation not only was seen as an appropriate and deserving punishment for such treachery but also would serve as an example to others. Endorsed by the minister of the militia, Bassett's idea, however, was dismissed as impractical. As the deputy minister of justice, E. Newcombe, observed: "If the Justice Department is to deport these Bolshevists, it follows they must deport all Bolshevists and indeed it follows also that they must deport all other Bolshevists ahead of these very men in as much as these men are returned soldiers."[148]

From Newcombe's point of view, there may have been a hierarchy in the type of "Bolshevik" the government was prepared to deal with. But from the viewpoint of the returned solider, a Bolshevik was a Bolshevik no matter what and they wanted them all out. In late January 1919, veterans in Vancouver, four hundred strong, gathered to pass a resolution demanding the deportation of suspected radicals.[149] In Alberta, the veterans who had assembled for their provincial convention also vociferously condemned Bolshevism, "whose pernicious doctrines are well-known to be of the made-in-Germany brand." They demanded that all enemy alien agents of "Bolshevism" be deported while those of British nationality be imprisoned and deprived of their franchise.[150]

On 26 January, in Winnipeg, on learning that a meeting of social democrats was being held, enraged veterans marched on the hall where the conclave had gathered and brutally attacked the individuals there.[151] The mob next set out for the Austro-Hungarian Club in the north end of the city where, turning riotous, they savaged the building's interior and severely beat suspected enemy aliens in the vicinity. Numbering 2,500, the mob was dispersed when, approaching the central police station (where it was rumoured that one of their own was held), they were confronted by a company of soldiers with rifles and bayonets at the ready. A potential riot the following day was averted only after the Winnipeg mayor, Charles Gray, was able to convince the veterans, who had gathered at the local meat processing plant where large numbers of enemy aliens were said to be employed, of the practical wisdom of placing their concerns before provincial officials and business interests in the community.

The veterans' prejudice and hostility toward the enemy alien were ubiquitous. Nothing less than their expulsion would do, especially those suspected of seditious activity. The connection between the enemy alien and alleged sedition had evolved as a result of the challenging labour situation, which had once again elevated the level of resentment and antagonism in the country toward the alien. In the intervening years, when labour was in short supply, jobs had been filled by enemy aliens and other foreign-born workers. However, the steady return of soldiers from the battlefields of Europe now placed enormous pressure on the labour market. Jobs were scarce, and veterans, facing unemployment, demanded the dismissal of enemy aliens and others from the workplace. Immigrant workers who insisted on fair play and equality were soon identified with foreign political intrigue. For many veterans, this helped to establish that the enemy alien was indeed a threat in both theory and practice. Enemy aliens not only were seen as tacit supporters of a foreign ideology that needed to be rooted out, but also occupied jobs of which they were undeserving. The solution was for employers to dismiss enemy aliens and for the government to finally deal with the problem of their removal from the country.

On this point, a riot in Winnipeg had been averted by the efforts of the city's mayor, who encouraged veterans to lobby businesses to have enemy alien labour replaced with returned men. It was a suggestion taken up at once by the veterans, who set about organizing delegations to meet with employers, large and small.[152] Representatives were immediately sent to discuss with company executives the replacement of enemy aliens employed with the Canadian National Railway. Another group met with the local Swift packing plant, extracting a concession

4.4 Great War Veterans' Association protest, Winnipeg, Manitoba, 1919

from the company management to provide five hundred jobs currently held by allegedly disloyal foreigners. Elsewhere in the country similar steps were taken as the demands of veterans prevailed. In British Columbia, when it was reported that 8,500 enemy aliens were holding positions that could easily be filled by returned men, various manufacturing, retail, and other associations announced their support for such a move.[153] T.F. McDowell, president of the BC Board of Retail Merchants, for one, believed "that 300 returned soldiers could be employed in the grocery business alone in the province of British Columbia if the foreigners were not in competition with the white man."[154]

The issue of replacing enemy aliens with returned soldiers was embraced by the *Vancouver Sun*. But it was also imperative that industry not be disrupted, as this would have an adverse effect by reducing job opportunities for the returned men. The *Sun* argued that a measured approach was required in order to rid the province of its alien enemies while preserving existing jobs. To this end, the *Sun* was firm in its position: "We need have no compunction about using the alien enemies for our own advantage and discarding them as soon as there are more worthy men ready to take their places."[155]

The *Morning Leader* of Regina, on the other hand, expressed skepticism. Although a case could be made that returned soldiers had first claim on employment, the abrupt dismissal of so many enemy aliens simply deflected the problem. Would not the burden of maintaining them in idleness be shifted onto the country, the veteran included? By suddenly throwing aliens of enemy nationality out of work, would it not be an invitation to trouble, leading to those conditions that "[have become] the veritable hotbed for the breeding of Bolshevism and all that this term has come to mean in this unsettled world"? Deporting enemy aliens was an option, but this would have been an enormous undertaking – "an almost insuperable one" – according to the *Morning Leader.* As for the idea, frequently cited, that the government should inaugurate a program of public works where the majority of enemy aliens in the country would be forced to work, this could not be achieved without great effort. Among the editors of the paper there were no easy answers except that during this difficult period of postwar transition, sober government leadership was required.[156]

The debate in the press mirrored the movement to pressure government into formulating a comprehensive policy that would address the public's interest in dealing with the enemy alien question more generally. In Brantford, Ontario, a regional conference was convened to discuss the future of the enemy alien in Canada. A strong resolution was passed favouring the internment of all enemy aliens in the country.[157] At an Ontario provincial meeting of the Navy League, a sweeping resolution was unanimously passed seeking to disfranchise enemy aliens for a period of fifteen years, deport all who had proven dangerous, confiscate any surplus wealth they had made during the war, restrict immigration from enemy countries for twenty years, and compel all aliens to take an oath of allegiance within the year.[158] In B C, a member of the provincial legislature, G.S. Hanes, introduced a motion before the assembly that called for the expulsion of enemy aliens from the province and their further exclusion from the country through a prohibition on their immigration.[159] Expressing its approval of the order paper and noting the public's support of the initiative, the *Vancouver Sun* declared:

The matter is one that, of course, falls entirely within the jurisdiction of Dominion authorities. If they have been rather slow in taking action, the explanation may be that they are waiting for public opinion to get behind them and urge them along. The process of making up their minds will be aided by the knowledge that the attitude of the province is emphatic. No argument should be needed to show that this country has neither the room nor use for men who were considered so dangerous as to necessitate their

being interned during the war ... It is not a problem of statesman-
ship. No particular ability is required to tell these people to get out
and stay out. As long as they are allowed to remain they give rise
to a feeling of insecurity and discomfort.[160]

The extraordinary pressure placed on the government from a wide
range of sources induced it to appease its critics. Acknowledging "the
force of feeling" which had been gathering in the major cities, order-in-
council PC 332 (14 February 1919) was introduced under the authority
of the War Measures Act. The executive order approved the internment
and deportation of any enemy alien judged to be either hostile or
undesirable. This was to be carried out by summary judgment in specially convened courts. Further, the order made it possible not only for
municipal and local authorities, but for any person who was "sufficiently representative of the feeling of the community" to lay a complaint. In those centres where the numbers proved exceptionally difficult
to administer, the order authorized the formation of citizen committees
to help review cases and assist the appointed local magistrate, thereby
expediting the process. The government's position was: "To the extent
that deportation can be availed of, it will be carried on until all the Alien
Enemies, who have shown hostility or become undesirable as citizens,
are gotten rid of."[161]

Enthusiastically embraced by those who had vigorously advocated
for decisive action, the order had the effect of invigorating those interests. Almost immediately, private individuals offered their services to sit
on citizens' committees, while municipal officials inquired about what
steps were needed to constitute and activate the commissions. Veterans'
groups were equally quick to submit names of those they felt should be
brought before a magistrate. In Vancouver, D. Grout of the BC County
Court Chambers informed the deputy minister of justice that the local
veterans' association had compiled a complete list of names and residences of some five thousand alien enemies considered suspect. Grout
explained that the veterans were anxious to receive support from the
Justice Department to hire a staff of four in order to prepare charges
against them, assuring the deputy minister that "the money would be
exceedingly well spent."[162] Meanwhile, the Alien Investigation Board
of Manitoba, independently organized under the authority of the
Manitoba premier, sought to cooperate with federal authorities "in
procuring evidence and prosecuting undesirable aliens" with a view to
their deportation.[163]

The movement to deport enemy aliens from the country necessarily raised questions about immigration. The presence of so many "undesirables" in the land highlighted, according to some, the failure of immigration policy. In their opinion, those who had engineered the large migration of newcomers to Canada in the past had engaged in a foolish and irresponsible exercise.[164] The country was now full of enemy aliens who were neither wanted nor needed. It was felt that decades would now have to pass before Canada could fully absorb them and their children. It stood to reason that no more enemy aliens should be allowed into the country. Assurances were sought from the government that the practice of immigration would stop for at least twenty years or, alternatively, diligence should be administered in the type and quality of immigrant let in. Veterans' groups, Orangemen, and Canadian Clubs were particularly incensed by the prospect of Hutterites and Mennonites (reportedly on the move from the United States) being allowed in, insisting that they be barred from entering the country. Doukhobors, already present in the country, were to be forced to leave.[165]

When the government announced that, according to international custom, it could not debar entry to Canada of anyone because they belonged to a particular religious sect (some of whom also happened to be American citizens), the public and especially veterans' groups were furious. The issue of immigration was soon taken up in the House of Commons. H.H. Stevens, member of parliament for Vancouver, was especially vocal in his opposition to a policy that failed to acknowledge the problematic aspects of a liberal immigration, which, he claimed, had blindly allowed for groups of people to enter into the country too ill-equipped to understand or appreciate the advantages and subtleties of Canadian citizenship. "It became quite clear during the war," Stevens asserted, "that, in the main, masses of ignorant immigrants forced from their own lands by oppression and poverty, cannot be made citizens, for they know nothing of our institutions and system of government, and what little they do learn is impressed in hostility."[166]

The government was skeptical, however, about placing a wholesale stop to certain categories of immigration. Canada was in need of future immigrants, and a policy of exclusion that applied to different classes of people could only harm the country's national interests. The candid remarks of the *Morning Leader* of Regina were more to the point: "Those whom we style foreigners have been doing the rough, disagreeable work in our slaughter house, steel mills, and to some extent in our lumber camps. Women of foreign birth have become our charwomen.

Are all these kinds of work to be done in the future by men and women of Anglo-Saxon birth?"[167]

The arguments advanced by the *Morning Leader* were rejected by those who persisted in their opposition to immigration. They were firm in the belief that as long as the alien (and enemy alien in particular) remained in competition for jobs with returned men, there could be no room for them in the country. Thus, the campaign to identify any enemy alien considered objectionable and therefore deportable continued. To this end, the quasi-judicial citizen tribunals, which had been created to investigate aliens of enemy nationality, continued to collect names of enemy aliens, making a determination on the basis of the information brought forward. In the course of three months, in Winnipeg alone, 1,200 cases were heard before the Alien Investigation Board. So-called "loyalty cards" were granted to nine hundred individuals. But three hundred were also classified as "undesirables" – their future pending.[168]

The ongoing effort to pressure employers to replace alien workers with returned soldiers, the telling public debate on immigration, and the tribunals' hunt for so-called alien undesirables weighed heavily on newcomers. The life of the immigrant was trying at best, but now it was simply unbearable for some. A town hall meeting was called in St Catharines, Ontario, bringing together seven hundred workers of different nationalities – Poles, Italians, Finns, Ukrainians, and Russians. As they pleaded for fair play, a resolution was unanimously passed that condemned the agitation directed against them as aliens. Those in attendance also appealed on behalf of their Canadian-born offspring, so that at the very least the rights of their children might be respected. Being ever practical however, they additionally sought permission to leave the country: "Let us leave Canada as free agents, just as we came, to go where we will."[169] In Toronto, the Ukrainian Presbyterian community urged the Great War Veterans' Association to join with them in persuading the government to allow Ukrainians "to depart in peace," a call that was supported by a thousand other Ukrainians gathered in Hamilton who passed a similar resolution.[170] Meanwhile, Ukrainian community leaders brought forward a petition, adopted at meetings organized in Oshawa, Toronto, and Montreal that appealed for the restoration and extension of full civil rights for Ukrainians in Canada. On the basis of the community's contribution to the development of the country and commitment to Canada, the petitioners asked that a number of their grievances be addressed. They requested among other things that the "enemy alien" label be lifted, full privileges of citizenship be restored to those from whom it had been taken away, freedom of movement permitted, families reunited, and naturalization allowed. They also asked that the deportations cease.[171]

Concerned citizens within the German community sent an open letter to the government highlighting the recent difficulties. They claimed that the destruction of property in Winnipeg during the recent riots and the assault on individuals of foreign appearance by returned soldiers had alarmed the foreign-born in the city. There was no protection, and officials failed to give any assurance that these disturbances would not be repeated. They urged the government to put a stop to these "intolerable conditions" and to take measures that would help educate the public. In this regard, they offered to do their share, but "if the Government, or the Parliament respectively, do not desire our co-operation, we would greatly deplore such an attitude as not compatible to the interest of our commonwealth, and we assure you that our people, as opportunity presents itself, will seek other fields for their industry."[172] The open letter was not meant as a threat; it was a sincere statement reflecting feelings said to be widespread among Germans living in Canada. Concluding their appeal with the declaration, "We had no part in bringing about this terrible war and have regretted it no less than any other nationality in this or any other country," the petitioners pressed the point that Canadians of German origin were innocent of any wrongdoing and undeserving of the treatment accorded them. Government officials acknowledged the receipt of the memorandum with the terse statement "Your concerns are duly noted and will be brought to the attention of the minister."[173]

In the camps, reactions to the rumour that the remaining enemy alien prisoners would be deported were varied. At Vernon, a few wilful and defiant men sought to put on record their claims and grievances.[174] Others, anxious and fearful, asked for clarification regarding the reported statements that all internees would be either repatriated or deported "without exception."[175] The majority insisted that, months after the armistice, a decision was needed one way or another. Petitioning the new minister of justice, the Hon. Arthur Meighen, for their repatriation or release, the prisoners at the Vernon camp claimed that the anxiety and stress associated with their continuing internment were no longer tolerable. If the stories of mental anguish suffered by Canadian prisoners of war in Germany were to be believed, there had to be a similar level of appreciation and sympathy for their situation. "You have personally stated in the Commons," wrote the authors of the appeal, "that 54 of the prisoners have become insane, which is an awful percentage ... what is the reason for their insanity?" They claimed that rations had been reduced – "getting just too much to die and too little to live" – while abuses at the camp had not let up. They implored the minister of justice to observe the basic principles of humanity and release them from their ordeal.[176] The situation in Kapuskasing, reportedly no different, also resulted in prisoner appeals to the minister requesting their rapid release, repatriation, or deportation.[177]

The internees were clearly in an agitated state, providing some credence to the rumour that the Vernon prisoners were preparing to engage in unrest and a possible escape. The rumour prompted justice officials to suggest closing the Vernon camp as a precautionary measure and relocating the prisoners to either Kapuskasing or Amherst where the facilities were more secure.[178] This suggestion followed the example of the Munson internment station, whose relocation earlier to a railway siding at Eaton, Saskatchewan, proved unworkable, resulting in the closure of the Eaton camp and the transfer of prisoners there to Amherst.[179] General Otter, however, was of the opinion that their immediate expulsion from the country offered "the most feasible and economical mode of meeting the possible difficulty."[180] Consequently, Otter recommended in early May that all the unmarried males at the Vernon camp, numbering two hundred and considered hostile, be sent back to their countries of origin. Another two hundred or three hundred from other camps, "of whom the country would be well rid," were to be added if arrangements for transportation could be found.[181]

Operational difficulties encountered four months earlier during the transport of the initial group of one hundred prisoners – passage from England to the Continent had been nearly impossible to obtain – meant that Otter's recommendation, conditionally accepted, would have to wait. Nevertheless, the possibility that prisoners from the Kapuskasing camp, like the Vernon internees, might also be finally expelled from the country came as good news to Lieutenant Colonel W.E. Date, the commander at Kapuskasing, who pointed out that the camp had become a repository for agitators who were "more or less a nuisance to us" and "the type of man found around city pool rooms, making an easy living." He pronounced them all to be "a loafing, good-for-nothing lot, and the sooner the country is rid of them the better."[182]

By May 1919, there was a decided lack of progress in dealing with the deportation of enemy aliens who had been brought before the tribunals, fuelling the frustration of veterans, who insisted that the government was not doing enough. In Winnipeg, 150 veterans petitioned the

Manitoba premier, urging the immediate internment, confiscation of property, and deportation of enemy aliens, now numbering seven hundred, whom the Manitoba Alien Investigation Board had found to be "undesirable." Citing the growing anti–enemy alien sentiment in Winnipeg, subsequent deputations professed they were apprehensive for the safety of the city and insisted that the provincial government either do something about the seven hundred or resign. Expressing sympathy for their demands, the premier responded that authority over enemy alien deportation rested with the federal government and that the provincially organized Manitoba Alien Investigation Board was not empowered to deport – it could only examine the cases. The power to deport, ultimately, was reserved for specially appointed courts.[183]

Judges had been specifically assigned to expedite matters, but among veterans it was felt that the process of deporting enemy aliens was much too cumbersome and inefficient. Cited as the reason for the backlog in the number being processed, the slow progress served as a major source of complaint among veterans and the basis for conflict with government. Yet, despite the criticism, the process had been sufficiently streamlined to help establish the grounds for deportation against those enemy aliens deemed "offensive or undesirable." The Manitoba Alien Investigation Board, for example, identified Peter Get as an undesirable for having demonstrated an obnoxious attitude toward authority during questioning by members of the board. Acting as the complainant, the board sought to obtain a court ruling on the obstreperous Get. Brought before Judge S. Myers, Get was refused legal representation. With no witnesses called, Get was immediately ordered interned, with Justice Meyers declaring that "to allow this man to remain at large in the City of Winnipeg was a menace to the peacefulness of the City, as the Returned soldiers threatened to take the law into their own hands unless this man was interned."[184] The same rough justice also applied in the cases of Wasyl Plaszyaski, Nick Skotniski, and others who were sent to Kapuskasing, where they would await their fate.

Order-in-council PC 332, issued 14 February 1919, defined the powers and duties of the specially appointed magistrates and was intended as a quick and easy manner by which the problem might be addressed. Moreover, its purpose was perfectly understood by the justices, who were already predisposed to accept the proposition that dangerous and/or objectionable foreigners needed to be deported. The order facilitated the removal of this "undesirable class," offering the opportunity to demonstrate unequivocally that any subversion, political or otherwise, would not be tolerated. It was seen as an absolute necessity, according to the Hon. Justice H. MacDonald in a letter to the minister of justice, "that an example be made to show them that law and order must be maintained and that all attempts to interfere by revolutionary means with our form of government, whether Federal, Provincial or Municipal, will be sternly repressed."[185]

The importance of dealing with undesirables was especially apparent to federal officials after the escalation of labour troubles in Winnipeg in June 1919.[186] Moreover, order-in-council PC 332 was seen as a mechanism by which enemy aliens allegedly involved in the protests could be readily deported. Indeed, during the height of the Winnipeg General Strike, when two enemy aliens were killed and dozens more wounded, some thirty-one "foreign rioters" were arrested and interned under PC 332 and the amendments introduced in June 1919 to the Criminal Code and the Immigration Act (Section 41), which made involvement in anti-government/disorderly activity a deportable offence.[187] The arrests would become part of a larger RNWMP initiative, undertaken during the summer, to rid the country of hundreds of labour militants, alien and enemy alien alike.[188]

Earlier in May, General Otter had recommended unmarried male prisoners from the Vernon camp be returned to their countries of origin. But it was the Winnipeg protests and General Strike that finally served to rouse officials in Ottawa, impressing upon them the importance and efficacy of removing from the country those still held in the camps. Their removal would signal the government's resolve and intent to meet head-on those who would seek to disturb the peace and public order. It was not a coincidence that the move to expel the internees assumed a sense of urgency and resolve.

On 19 June, General Otter was instructed to prepare immediately a list of prisoners and secure overseas transport by any means possible. He replied that 450 prisoners could be made available at once, adding that information had been received stating a direct European connection could be obtained with the assistance of Dutch authorities, thereby bypassing Britain, where the bottleneck in transportation was occurring. Among the 450, Otter proposed to include fifty-two men who were insane, whose costly upkeep – twice that of a regular prisoner – warranted their early expulsion. To this number interned German merchant marines were also to be added. A dispatch had been received from the secretary of the colonies indicating that German prisoners, transferred from the West Indies and interned in Canada at the request of imperial authorities, could now be repatriated, since arrangements with German officials had been made for their receipt in continental Europe. With the quick approval of the minister of justice, Otter put in motion the removal of a large contingent of prisoners. Within a matter of weeks, on 24 July, 872 prisoners were herded onto a chartered ship that set sail from Montreal bound for Rotterdam. The number included 575 German mariners interned at Amherst, 105 prisoners from Kapuskasing, 163 from Vernon, and twenty-nine insane who could be readied in time for the journey. Accompanying the prisoners were fifty-three officers and guards who were supplied with one thousand rounds of ammunition, "as a pre-cautionary measure."[189] The move was widely reported in the press, eliciting expressions of public support, relief, and satisfaction.

There now remained 1,308 prisoners: 270 in Amherst, 899 at Kapuskasing, and 139 at Vernon. Twenty-two women and thirty-three children – families of some of the male prisoners – were among those interned at Vernon, all of whom Otter proposed to deport, since the women, in his opinion, "[were] as a rule even more disloyal than the husbands."[190] The cost of maintaining these prisoners was approximately 90¢ per head or roughly $1,200 a day. Given the expense, Otter suggested that the outlay be reduced as quickly as possible. Noting that 340 could be safely released, having been identified as non-dangerous or inoffensive, the director awaited instructions. On 13 August, Otter was ordered to release the 340 prisoners, exercising "due regard" with respect to each case.[191] To reduce expenditures, he was further instructed to shutter the Amherst camp and eliminate staff elsewhere. Otter immediately gave orders to close the camp at Amherst, which would formally cease functioning 27 September. The director proposed to keep open the Vernon camp to accommodate the families still there, at least until arrangements could be made for their deportation. He also wished to oblige the RNWMP commissioner, who was convinced that "a large number of troublesome aliens in the West" would still be interned.[192]

The commissioner's concern was misplaced, however. After the initial roundup of radicals during the summer raids, the arrests in the fall were fewer than predicted. Moreover, with the promulgation of the Treaty of Peace – expected any day – the political and legal foundation for internment had all but vanished. The push was on to quickly remove as many as possible from the camps. Of the one thousand prisoners who remained, Otter was asked to prepare a further list of those who could be sent to Europe immediately. The cooperation of authorities in Germany meant that prisoners of German nationality were in the best position to be sent back. As a result, prisoners of German origin, totalling 436, were readied, to which six Austro-Hungarians and one "miscellaneous" were added. Gathered together in Quebec City, 443 enemy alien prisoners eventually boarded the SS *Pretorian*, which set sail for Rotterdam 4 September.

The activity led to petitions by those who sought to prevent the removal of their loved ones from the country. Family members of some of the interned – mothers, fathers, and wives – appealed to the government, pleading for clemency. From within the camps, a number of internees also applied for amnesty. Applications would be heard, but only rarely were the circumstances such or the appeal convincing enough to override the initial assessment and decision to deport.

J. Bieber's request for permission to remain in Canada, for instance, was declined. Though he was officially charged with suspected espionage, it was in fact Bieber's sale of illegal liquor to troops stationed in Kentville, Nova Scotia, that initially led to his internment and for which there would be no pardon.[193] Martin Shweig's application was also turned down, ostensibly for travelling without a permit, but in actuality because of his previous convictions under the Ontario Temperance Act.[194] As for the appeal of prisoner Carl Vohwinkel, it was rejected on the grounds that his wife allegedly was leading "an immoral life."[195] This also appeared to be the reason behind the denial of Adolph Hundt's application. The original complaint against Hundt, which led to his arrest and internment, had emanated from Mrs Hundt, who allegedly "wished her husband out of the way so she could carry on with other men."[196] Immigration officials recommended to General Otter the deportation of the Hundts, feeling that there could be no room for families of this type in Canada.[197]

Not all the applications were treated in so callous a manner. George Hamann was released largely due to his wife's entreaties. Immigration officials felt it would have been a considerable hardship for Mrs Hamann, a woman of British birth, and her Canadian-born children to be sent to Germany.[198] Mrs A. Tudali also successfully appealed for the release of her son who, at nineteen years of age, had been interned for attempting to enlist despite being an enemy alien, pleading that she needed the help of her eldest son to raise her other four young children.[199] Meanwhile, Mary Bihun, in a simple letter written in broken English, was able to convince authorities to release her son. Consideration was given to Bihun in view of her poor circumstances and elderly status.[200]

4.5 Enclosure, Vernon, BC

Individuals who did not have the confidence of internment and immigration authorities and were judged to be misfits or miscreants would be removed from the country. But it was the political agitator and mischief-maker who was the real object of official attention in the final decision to deport. Expulsion awaited those who had demonstrated a hostile attitude toward authority or were suspected of engaging in political unrest, including, despite declarations of innocence, a dozen and more who had been arrested in Winnipeg during the labour unrest of June 1919. When legal counsel for several enemy aliens, arrested and interned for having allegedly participated in the violence of the Winnipeg Strike, made application to the justice minister for a hearing of their claims based on new testimony, the response from the deputy minister of justice was that their representations would be carefully considered. Shortly thereafter, to their surprise and astonishment, they discovered that not only was there no effort made to investigate the claims, but that twelve of the alleged co-conspirators had already been deported, despite their petition. The barristers, Noble and Murray of Winnipeg, expressed their dismay and shock with the "summary justice" that had been dealt these men, claiming that the action of the department was "contrary to British traditions."[201] Deportation, however, was not about justice; it was about eliminating a problem and punishing those for their political transgressions.[202]

On 27 October, 438 enemy alien prisoners, under guard, boarded the chartered ship SS *Sicilian* and set sail for continental Europe from Quebec City. Four months later, 27 February 1920, the last group of 112 was expelled from the country on orders of General Otter, who cited the "desirability" of their deportation. At the same time, the director recommended the release of 150 Ukrainians and Croatians who still remained. Hailing from lands that were not part of the new republic of Austria, technically they were now no longer considered enemy alien subjects and therefore entitled to their freedom.[203] The fact that Austria, grappling with questions of post-imperial identity, refused to accept them also settled the matter.

With the final set of deportations, internment operations in Canada had come to an end. The Vernon camp would officially close 20 February 1920, followed by Kapuskasing on 24 February. Unofficially, the former continued to operate as an "immigration station" until early March, when a handful of individuals, deposited at the last moment under special request by immigration authorities, were finally deported.[204] Some of the restrictions imposed on enemy aliens also ended. An order-in-council in December 1919, for instance, had lifted the requirement of enemy aliens to report to police. Meanwhile, the disfranchisement of aliens was eliminated as a result of the introduction of new electoral laws and the expiration of the War Measures Act after the formal signing of the peace treaty on 10 January 1920.

After the signing of the peace, there were scattered expressions of anger that not enough had been done with regard to enemy aliens when the opportunity presented itself. A.E. Moore, former head of the Manitoba Alien Investigation Board, publicly denounced the minister of justice, the Hon. Arthur Meighen, for not having exercised sufficient authority in deporting eight hundred enemy aliens from the province after it had been shown during board proceedings that there was "sufficient reason" for their removal.[205] Nothing, of course, could be done now – the opportunity had slipped away. But as for the country's future, Moore and others argued that it would depend entirely on the quality of immigrants let in and only those who could make good citizens were to be allowed entry.

The public debate about lost opportunity and immigration strategy seemed petty in light of the huge losses that Canadians had suffered during the war. It failed to speak to the unfathomable anguish and pain of those who had sacrificed so much, including Canon Lieutenant Colonel Frederick George Scott, former chaplain to the Canadian Corps, who had lost his son at the battle of the Somme in 1916. Like many others, his grief was so great that, when speaking to a convention of gathered veterans in 1920, he stated that the thought of shaking the hand of his enemy was inconceivable; the anger he felt towards the foe was far from being sinful but "divine virtue."[206] Scott's remarks resonated with the crowd, many of whom had endured and suffered so much. And yet his anger also added to the already complicated situation facing the alien, a former enemy, living in Canada. They were still here and this was their home. Their future was intimately bound to the country they called their own and nothing could detract from the fact that, during the country's trials, the majority did not waiver in their loyalty or commitment to their adopted land.

It was a conundrum to which there were no easy answers. Underscoring the point was the peculiar situation of those persons of former enemy nationality who, under the naturalization law passed by parliament during the war, were denied citizenship until 1929. Speaking of their predicament and in support of changing the law, the *Globe and Mail* contended, "Parliament ought not to regard such men as alien enemies during half a lifetime," adding, "If Canada is not his country, then he has none to which he can turn."[207] Canada was their home. And they deserved better.

## WHO BELONGS?

War often distorts the normal functioning of politics and society. Reason and compassion are often sacrificed to fear and anxiety. In Canada, the alien of enemy nationality was especially susceptible to the vagaries of war and its consequences. Buffeted by forces entirely outside their control, enemy aliens were the last to be hired, the first to be fired, and charged with either "living off the fat of the land" or not doing enough to earn their keep. It was a confusing and arduous time for enemy aliens, as constraints on their movement gave them no place to hide from the constant scrutiny and antipathy of a largely unsympathetic public.

Yet their labour was much needed.[208] As Canadians were siphoned away to fight in Europe and the demand for goods and essentials multiplied, the utility of employing enemy alien labour could not be ignored. They were a resource to be used, and in the rush to obtain their labour, a fierce competition ensued. At a certain level, it highlighted the difficult circumstances industry and agriculture faced. But it also pointed to the incongruity of internment and the irony of prisoner release.[209]

From the perspective of the general public, conditioned to believe that internment was a necessary and prudent measure for dealing with the enemies of the nation, the release of prisoners of war was a shocking proposition. How could these enemies be let loose in the country?[210] The short answer, of course, was that released prisoners enjoyed only conditional freedom. Like enemy aliens in general, they were obliged to comply and conform to regulations governing their person. Authorities were confident that released prisoners would comply, because they undertook to calculate who could be set free without risk. Those who demonstrated obedience and deference to authority during their internment could be let go. As a result, a concerted effort was made to identify precisely this type of individual from among the pool of prisoners. But it was also believed that the employment and liberty granted them should have removed any cause for complaint or trouble.

It was a naive understanding. Employment may very well have addressed part of the challenge that faced the paroled prisoner, but the underlying difficulty of their enemy status remained the same. They were freed from internment, but not from the stigma of who they were said to be. The status of being both an enemy alien and a former prisoner of war exposed them to the contempt of a largely suspicious and hostile public and made of them objects of derision as well as exploitation.[211] Under threat of penalty, once placed with an employer, released enemy alien prisoners were not allowed to move without authorization, making the government complicit in their continuing misfortune.

The circumstances that faced the paroled prisoners were no different from those confronting the general enemy alien population more generally. But the experience of internment was a harsh and constant reminder of what they could expect if they failed to comply. It was for this reason that a large number of former prisoners, desperate in their desire to return home or escape the avariciousness of employers who sought to exploit their predicament, petitioned internment officials to provide them with reprieve by authorizing their movement. When they received none, and despairing of their unbearable lot, many fled. It would add to the public perception of the parolees, and more generally the enemy alien, as a continuing liability.[212]

From the perspective of internment officials who had recent jurisdiction over the internees, the predicament of their former charges was no longer their concern. Once they had been released, it was felt they were now the responsibility of others. In actual fact, however, they were no one's responsibility, except in a perfunctory sense. Under the Farmers Employment Scheme, which saw paroled prisoners placed on farmsteads, farmers became the de facto authorities responsible for the immediate control and care of their enemy wards. This was not to say there were no other checks. Former prisoners of war were still required to register and report to local authorities for purposes of monitoring. Moreover, the police and courts were empowered to deal with those who proved troublesome. Nevertheless, despite these measures, the effort was more of a demonstration than a concerted attempt at control.

The nature of their oversight was not so much a function of lax administration as it was a realistic response to the prevailing conditions. At a certain level, it followed from the observation, frequently made, that released prisoners did not constitute a danger in the conventional sense; their initial internment was a function of unrelated events, notably their poverty and joblessness. In this regard, senior government officials, such as the minister of labour, the Hon. W. Crothers, were clear that these individuals, initially unable to support themselves, might now be given an opportunity to do so through their release, especially given the positive change in the economy. But it also resulted from the fact that enemy alien labour was needed and much in demand. On this point, companies undercut each other in the competition for enemy alien workers, including paroled prisoners.[213] The rivalry made it inevitable that enemy aliens would soon be on the move. Under these conditions, control and surveillance of the population could not be easily affected. Industry protested the mobility of enemy aliens, but in their desperate search for labour, the companies that offered higher wages or better working conditions helped encourage their unauthorized movement. Officials privately grumbled that industries were culprits in undoing the best efforts of government to regulate and provide a reliable source of labour.

During the latter half of 1916 and throughout 1917, the government remained confident that its position regarding the release of enemy alien prisoners was justifiable. Having demonstrated little evidence of hostility toward established authority while interned, those released would not be a cause for concern. By contrast, those whose objectionable attitudes kept them behind barbed wire were precisely the type that could not be released. Their internment was a continuing priority; as long as they remained interned then at least the prospects for trouble were greatly reduced. What to do with them in the future remained an open-ended question, although the exchange of prisoners being negotiated between the belligerents held out the promise that these and other individuals (including the insane, diseased, handicapped, and morally corrupt) might be removed from the country.[214]

Criticism of the release of so-called "non-dangerous" prisoners was mute so long as the situation was stable. This situation, however, would not continue for long with the steady return of servicemen from overseas. The homecoming of the veterans changed the tone and dynamics of the public debate regarding the role and fate of the enemy alien. Jobs became increasingly scarce as the labour market contracted. The place of the enemy alien became a matter that demanded resolution.

Finding themselves on the margins of society, enemy aliens were treated neither fairly nor equitably. In the workplace as well, the situation became difficult for the enemy alien worker. But it did not end there. The competition in the workplace was seen as an extension of the struggle overseas. Veterans demanded that foreigners occupying precious jobs make way for those who fought for king and country; if they did not give way, then they should be removed. When it was discovered that enemy aliens were working on the factory floor at the Russell Motor Company in Toronto, veterans advanced on the building with the view to routing the enemy:

Jumping over benches and shell-making machines as if in a charge on the German trenches, half a hundred returned, disabled soldiers with a few from the Exhibition Camp, last night raided the munitions factory of the Russell Motor Company at King and Dufferin streets with the object of rounding up the enemy aliens employed there. Soldiers went through the great machine shops as they had dashed last summer down the communicating trenches of the Teutons on the Somme, and in less than ten minutes emerged with a score or two prisoners.[215]

It was a scene that played out time and again as veterans effectively organized, using their power, influence, and strength to produce a desired change in policy.

The scarcity of jobs was the catalyst driving the tensions within society, but the context was the war. The conflict had exercised the emotions of individuals on the home front, raising the question of what might be done to help those fighting in the trenches. Very little, of course, could actually be done except in a symbolic way. For those on the home front, therefore, their attention would turn to the enemy alien as the closest object of their anger and frustration. Some of it was motivated by racial antagonism and intolerance – the riots, accusations, and denunciations were symptomatic of the nativist current within Canadian society – but the war also magnified the issues of patriotism, allegiance, and loyalty. Among veterans in particular, at a distance from those still fighting in Europe, fealty to the cause was all they could offer. Consequently, the issues of franchise, military service, and compulsory labour were not simply policy matters but were infused with a meaning and significance that spoke to this heartfelt emotion. The struggle continued at home. And returned soldiers could take some small measure of comfort in the fact that they were doing their small share in ensuring the war would be won.[216]

As veterans applied pressure, politicians' reactions varied. Some, like the parliamentarian Colonel J.A. Currie, seized the opportunity to demand that the government address the enemy alien problem more forcefully. Others were cautious about taking any untoward action that might prove counterproductive in the long run. As a number of officials noted, the dislocation in the economy was situational, not structural, and would naturally adjust with time. Furthermore, displacing enemy aliens from their positions of employment, especially in the mines of western Canada, would add to labour turmoil and unrest. In addition, the question of the long-term role of immigrants in the economy could not be easily ignored or dismissed. Canada's future economic growth would depend on the contribution of immigrant labour to agriculture and heavy industry. Aware of the implications of these issues, Ottawa politicians adopted a careful approach toward the enemy alien question during this critical period.

On some occasions it appeared that caution might be thrown to the wind. On the issue of compulsory labour, for example, the internment of all enemy aliens in Canada was contemplated. Loring Christie, special adviser to the prime minister, was tasked with assessing this option. Christie concluded that, without significant planning and organization, wholesale internment made little economic sense, and he rejected the idea. Nevertheless, the fact that it was even considered showed that the government was treading on thin political and moral ground, a point further underscored by the remarks of the Hon. Charles Doherty. Admitting that enemy aliens were owed consideration since they had been invited to Canada, Doherty also stated that without using a whip there could be no advantage in compelling enemy aliens to work.[217] It was a cold calculation, the mention of which, by any standards, seemed improbable even for the day. Yet it reflected the mood of the country.

In the end, the government was pragmatic in the pursuit of its interests. Still, this approach would lead to a number of questionable actions and formulations. The War Time Elections Act, couched in the language of political necessity, disfranchised a class of citizen on the basis of nationality. The parliamentary opposition and liberal press condemned the measure as "a cheap party trick," observing that it was crudely designed to serve the interests of the governing party. On the other hand, a number of individuals were quick to point out that by gutting the institution of citizenship the government had attacked the foundations of democracy. A matter of philosophical and political debate at the time, disfranchisement constituted a choice, which at its very heart made clear that rights were negotiable.

Other measures were introduced that similarly disadvantaged aliens of enemy birth while limiting their ability to function normally within Canadian society. All of this, of course, touched on the larger subject of rights. This issue would occasionally be taken up in the courts but with little success, if only because the ordinances introduced under the WMA, by definition, were concerned with security and, in the balance of things, security trumped rights.[218] A false dichotomy, it nevertheless helped condone the idea that, in the name of security, not only could rights be ignored but also the questionable logic of government policy and practice could be justified. Such policies included those measures the government adopted that were used to placate an agitated public while averting criticism that it was doing nothing, especially in the face of labour uncertainty.

Some of the measures taken were also borne of suspicion that there was a natural link between enemy alien activity and political radicalism. The extraordinary licence granted Charles Cahan, appointed director of the Public Safety Branch, an agency dedicated to rooting out potential subversives, was a result of this mistrust. Although Cahan had his detractors, the government generally countenanced his aggressive approach. In due course, Cahan would resign from government, but his resignation was not necessarily a consequence of his political views; rather he was pressured to leave because of his public criticism of the country's policing operations and administration. Despite his short tenure in government, Cahan had managed to inflame the already tense situation affecting ethnic communities in the country. This was made possible because senior government officials were not particularly concerned about Cahan's beliefs but more generally persuaded by the director's alarmist suspicions, whose rank cynicism had led to the banning of ethnic organizations and wide-scale censorship.

Although Cahan's views regarding the loyalty of ethnic communities were rooted in deep mistrust if not obsession and fear, this did not mean the various communities were without issues. Radicalism was afoot and there was official concern that the incipient "bolshevism" within these communities might soon become viral. But there was the context to consider. The return of soldiers from overseas and their objections to enemy aliens in the workplace made the situation of the foreign-born more precarious. In the case of enemy aliens, the threat to both livelihoods and families was real. Laws and regulations restricted their everyday routine, reflecting their tenuous position in Canadian society. Although not all enemy aliens turned to a radical form of politics, ideology served as an answer to some.[219]

It was understandable that those most affected were distressed and offended by the ever-mounting restrictions. In September 1918 Reverend C.F. Christiansen wrote to the minister of justice, ostensibly for clarification of order-in-council PC 1908, which required all enemy aliens to register and report whether they had a permanent residence or not. The point of his letter was to bring to the minister's attention the hurtful nature of the order. Was it remotely conceivable, let alone possible, that the parishioners who had sons serving overseas in the cause of country and king were a threat, requiring their registration as enemies? The idea was not simply ridiculous – it was offensive, demeaning, and humiliating.[220]

In a climate of mistrust, unwelcome taunts, and vicious attacks, the enemy alien population looked to the government for protection. They were to be disillusioned, since it appeared that the government was doing little if anything to stem the tide of venomous anti-foreigner sentiment and vigilantism. A variety of groups sent letters to the government, especially after the Winnipeg riot of January 1918, pleading for intervention and relief from persecution.[221] A minority within the Ukrainian community had lost all hope and petitioned that they be allowed to leave the country, ironically invoking the support of the Great War Veterans' Association in persuading the government to let them go. Their pleas would resonate with some, like the member of parliament for Edmonton East, H.A. Mackie, who made a case for the restoration of their rights and a relaxation of government measures.[222] But these efforts were few and largely unsuccessful.[223]

Even with the end of hostilities in Europe, little would change for the enemy alien. The societal attitude that held them in contempt during the war had not improved with the armistice. The idea of the "alien as enemy" had leached into the public's consciousness. Now that the war was over, there remained but one thing to do: purge the country of its enemies. The return of Canadian soldiers from the European battlefields simply reinforced this point. But ridding the country of its enemies was no simple matter. The moniker "enemy alien" had become incongruous with war's end. The cessation of hostilities meant, theoretically, that aliens were no longer enemies. This raised an important question: if they were no longer enemies, on what grounds could they be expelled from the country?

The language used to describe their status soon began to pivot. The label "undesirable" replaced the description of the alien as enemy. In arguing for their removal, it became necessary to portray the alien as a continuing social liability, or in the parlance of the day, a "menace."[224] Still, the initial invitation that was extended to them to come to Canada as settlers and the obligations under international customary law preventing their expulsion had to be considered, especially in the context of postwar diplomacy and prisoner exchange. The meaning of the term "undesirable," therefore, assumed a more rigorous definition. Acceptance by the host society would be conditional. Already settled in the country as a group, the foreign-born did not have to demonstrate that they could stay. But as individuals, they would be judged on the basis of their attitude and demeanour toward Canadian authority and rule. Suspect aliens and especially interned enemy aliens had to demonstrate that there was nothing in their conduct or attitude that would warrant their deportation.[225]

The concept of the alien as acceptable or unacceptable served to inform the investigations being conducted at this time. When veterans' groups insisted the government deport enemy aliens after November 1918, the government responded by introducing order-in-council PC 332 allowing aliens to be vetted before specially appointed courts. The cases would be heard on the basis of a complaint and lead to either deportation or release. As a concession to mob opinion and pressure, however, the process was deeply flawed. The ordinance not only enabled a citizen "sufficiently representative of the feeling of the community" to lay a complaint against any enemy alien that they considered undesirable, it also allowed for the creation of citizens' committees that would assist specially appointed magistrates in their duties. Hastily conducted and with little or no evidence presented, the process favoured the complainant. Order-in-council PC 332 thus represented a quick and convenient measure to deal with individuals deemed objectionable. It also aimed to mollify the many critics demanding the removal of undesirables from the country.[226] Yet the appearance of legal propriety was being observed, and the accused did have access to the courts. This was necessary so that the decisions taken would be seen to be lawful, not only legitimizing the process and strengthening each deportation case but also tempering the unrealistic demand for the wholesale expulsion of the enemy alien population.[227]

Not everyone was satisfied with the process. It was felt to be too cumbersome and inefficient. Veterans' groups, in particular, were incensed that more was not being done to deal with the problem of immigrants and their alleged involvement in radical labour unrest. In Manitoba, where the quasi-judicial Alien Investigation Board had been organized by the provincial government to appease the demands of veterans and others clamouring for government action, veterans insisted that the several hundred who were classified by the board as "objectionable" be immediately deported. With no action forthcoming, veterans' groups met with the Manitoba premier, who informed them that the board had neither the power nor authority to deport; only the federal government could do so. Government foot-dragging on the issue would become a point of contention for the veterans and be used as an argument in their opposition to the government's postwar immigration policies and plans.

The federal government, however, would not be stampeded into taking rash action.[228] Introducing large-scale anti-alien measures would have compounded the mounting labour troubles. Therefore, the designation "undesirable" helped the government to contain the issue. Only those whose actions were deemed disruptive or disagreeable would be interned and deported. But what did this mean in practice? Participation in unlawful gatherings as well as the production, circulation, and possession of literature considered subversive were all cause for the targeted use of administrative and legal measures to rid the country of undesirables. In this way, political agitators were eliminated, much to the dismay and consternation of those who argued justice for their clients.[229] Petty criminals and alleged moral reprobates were also conveniently removed by immigration officials who sought to take advantage of the administrative and legal measures made available, including the use of internment camps as temporary deportation centres.[230] The term

4.6 Demonstration against enemy aliens, Winnipeg, Manitoba, 1919

"undesirable" would prove to be a catchall label for anyone the government wished removed from Canada's shores.[231]

From this perspective, the designation "undesirable" had one final advantage. The fate of interned prisoners of war remained unfinished business. What to do with them was still unclear. Apart from reservists, interned enemy aliens could not be repatriated – repatriation of civilians, according to international convention, required their consent. A majority among the internees were inclined to remain in the country and expressed their desire to do so. It made for a dilemma, but one that could be resolved through deportation. Enemy aliens who were either in violation of the laws or considered hostile were interned under the WMA. By extension, they were considered objectionable and therefore open to deportation. The distinction of being "undesirable" opportunely provided a conceptual framework that would help determine who could be deported. Those who showed themselves unfit and ungrateful would be candidates for deportation, as would those who demonstrated hostile intent toward Canadian authority and rule by way of their political views, opinions, and opposition – a matter of singular importance in the wake of the Winnipeg General Strike.[232]

Counted among those who would be removed from the country were a number who received a "political education" while interned at Amherst.

A sense of injustice fuelled their defiance, as did the views of Leon Trotsky, who helped inform their rebelliousness. An internee at Amherst for a brief time, Trotsky helped galvanize the prison population there, encouraging them to think of their private struggles in wider revolutionary terms. When the facility closed and the remaining group of prisoners was transferred to the last of the remaining camps, Kapuskasing, a majority of the 195 prisoners marched through the compound entrance with red ribbons pinned to their shirts – a symbol of the revolution to come.[233] They did so, already knowing their fate. In short order the government deported them and other "undesirables," including the sick, the infirm, and the insane. As for those who showed no interest in politics or appeared to hold no grudge, they were set free to make their own way in a country still wrestling with the question of the role and place of the enemy alien in the nation's future.

## CHAPTER FIVE

# The Enemy Alien Experience: Towards an Understanding

During the Great War, at the peak of the disfranchisement debate, it was said that naturalized aliens whose origins were in enemy countries at war with Canada could not discharge the highest duty of citizenship. The belief was that origin and especially kinship prevented their impartial judgment. It was further declared that in the choice between blood ties and their adopted country these individuals would invariably resist military conscription. Since they were so disposed, it followed that they needed to be prevented from deciding on war matters.[1] Disfranchisement, therefore, was seen as a necessity. Underlying the argument, however, was a series of suppositions. First, ethnic identity and affiliation were deep and immutable. And, second, the ties that bind – forged in history, nurtured by culture, and rooted in kinship – could not be easily severed. These suppositions supported a world view that maintained the allegiances of such individuals lay elsewhere.

It was a view that informed Canadian government policy from the very start of the conflict. Embedded in the Proclamation of 15 August 1914, for example, was the notion that aliens whose origins could be traced to those countries now warring with the British Empire posed a threat. The Proclamation placed German and Austro-Hungarian immigrants on notice that they would be subject to restrictions and prohibitions, identifying them in the process as "aliens of enemy origin." This designation was rooted in a particular interpretation of ethnicity or, in the parlance of the day, race. Implicit in the label "enemy alien" was the understanding that, once they had quit their place of origin, their homeland ties compelled them to act and think in terms that distinguished them from other members of the host society. Given that these ties were deeply rooted not only in psychology but biology, it was also felt that this enduring connection could not be easily broken. As a result, with ties and interests aligned elsewhere, the alien of enemy birth was considered to exist outside the community. As was stated time and again, the foreigner could not be expected to discard the past for the future, the old for the new, strangers over family.[2]

The strength of ethnic attachment disposed political authority to regard the alien of enemy origin with suspicion.[3] In the context of war, however, this had serious implications for they would be seen as potential adversaries as well. The Proclamation made this point clear: only those who did not act on their foreign loyalties would be left alone to pursue their avocations peaceably. In this instance, a special dispensation was being granted. But also implied was the belief that these individuals were bent on doing harm, and only by curbing their natural impulses would they be allowed to go about their business. The security question, in essence, had become racialized: where you came from would determine whether or not you were an enemy.

The idea of the alien as enemy, however, was also a function of the way in which the political-legal standing of such individuals in the community was conceptualized and understood at the time. By the late nineteenth and early twentieth centuries the idea of nationality had not yet evolved sufficiently to include a wider understanding of the meaning and process of citizenship. At the heart of the modern political community, citizenship is predicated on notions of reciprocal obligations and rights. But in the context of empires and monarchical rule, political allegiance is framed by an idealized understanding of the relationship between subject and sovereign. The sovereign extends protection for which, in exchange, the subject owes their allegiance. Under such circumstances, allegiance is defined in terms of personal union and political hierarchy. It can neither be forsaken nor transferred without the consent of the sovereign. In this regard, the political relationship is considered binding and absolute.

Political loyalty, from this perspective, is informed by the notion of subjectship. And although subjectship competed with liberal notions of political identity in Canada at the time, it was nevertheless an idea that in the public mind generally represented an understanding of what constituted allegiance.[4] It gave credence, for example, to the notion "For King and Country" and underpinned the principle that a subject of a sovereign at war with Britain and the empire "had no rights or privileges whatsoever unless by the King's special favour."[5] But subjecthood was more than a cultural statement about political loyalties. As a practical matter, it made provision for foreign states to intercede on behalf of their subjects who came under threat while living abroad. It also presumed that these same subjects, by way of reciprocity, would naturally return to their former homelands in response to a call to arms.

In the context of early twentieth-century warfare and mass mobilization, this was especially problematic since subjecthood conferred upon virtually every alien of enemy birth the status of a potential combatant. As subjects of a foreign sovereign now at war with Canada, and therefore potential adversaries, they posed a real and immediate threat. It is through this lens that the 15 August Proclamation is interpreted and through which the emergency security legislation, the War Measures Act, is understood. The War Measures Act gave state officials unlimited authority to deal with real and perceived security threats. A legitimate and appropriate response given the circumstances, the act and the Proclamation reinforced the public's perception and growing acceptance of the belief that there were enemies within their midst.

Filtered through the prism of ethnic ties and subjectship, political allegiance was thought to be predetermined. But this conceptual rendering neglected the psychological as well as the social-relational aspects of loyalty and the way it is constructed.[6] Where individuals freely devote themselves to the best interests of the object of their attachment, that devotion is reciprocated. In this regard, the basis for genuine loyalty is free will and mutual acceptance. It is a collaborative process sustained by a deep and abiding appreciation for the role that obligation and responsibility play. The obligation on the part of the immigrant is to respect, uphold, and abide by the rules and laws governing the community. But it is also expected that the government will observe and follow its responsibility to protect in peacetime as well as in war.

This sense of loyalty is often mediated through the process of living and working together, which helps reinforce the values and norms that inform an understanding of what it means to be part of a community. This process of social interaction, however, is neither straightforward nor orderly. War, for example, tests the relationship, and where it is still evolving, tensions naturally occur. Questions invariably surface about ties and ethnicity, bringing attention to differences that, in turn, nominally assist in addressing the issue of who belongs. Ethnicity, with all that it presumes, is a marker of difference and in the context of war is used to identify those whose loyalty could be trusted and who necessarily belonged. Foreshadowing the difficulties associated with this situation, the pressure to change surnames would be intense, while naturalization, if it could be obtained, would provide cover from possible persecution.[7] War, in this regard, strains the fragile bonds of the relationship, highlighting ethnic ties over civic bonds and political responsibility. Who you were would establish whose side you were on, a consideration that, at best, could only be offset by an appeal for understanding and compassion.[8]

In the charged atmosphere of war, however, the Canadian public, suspicious and anxious, abandoned any pretence that an obligation was owed these people. Ethnic origin, subjecthood, and the impact of war became elements that increasingly defined allegiance, loyalty, and trust. Within this context, the official designation "enemy alien" became symbolically important. It reaffirmed the belief that aliens originating from enemy lands had to be watched and, as foreign subjects, treated as adversaries as well. This attitude had consequences. What initially constituted a question – should they be here? – was soon superseded by the belief, held by a majority of native-born Canadians, that they had no business being here at all.[9]

A number of developments followed because of the growing hostility toward the enemy alien. With alleged enemies supposedly everywhere, suspicious and unusual occurrences were attributed to agents and saboteurs, who, it was felt, were bent on doing harm. As a result, a flood of private denunciations inundated the government. These ranged from the banal ("He is well off but had no visible means of support") to the ridiculous ("Must be a spy because he is a clever man who wears glasses and peddles books") to the completely outrageous ("He looks to be German and if not a German he at least owns a German Shepherd").[10] No matter how misguided or shameful the accusations, the cumulative effect was to place pressure on officials to demonstrate that the threat was being taken seriously. In the meantime, security measures were being launched through local initiatives. The purchase of heavy machine guns for militia use against possible rebels in Kingston, for example, was evidence of the prevailing state of alarm and insecurity that gripped the city.[11]

Within this atmosphere, the dominion police and the RNWMP were forced to undertake investigations. They uncovered nothing out of the ordinary, pointing in effect to the uneasy state of the native-born population as the catalyst behind a great many of the allegations.[12] These were anxious moments indeed. That shootings became a regular occurrence was inevitable, an unfortunate but predictable consequence that signalled the public's growing apprehension about living with the enemy.

The notion of an "enemy alien" as described in the 15 August Proclamation elevated the level of the threat, fuelled the public's imagination, and made the unreal possible. The Proclamation also created hostages of individuals of enemy origin by preventing their departure from the country. Although initially conceived by the government as a security measure, the prohibition on travel contained in the 15 August declaration had effectively denied this category of alien access to the United States, where they, along with others, were accustomed to looking for work as seasonal labourers. The decree now not only identified unnaturalized immigrants from Germany and Austria-Hungary as enemies but made virtual prisoners of them as well.[13]

This was a matter of no small importance. The growth that had driven the Canadian economy for fifteen years had come to an end by 1914. As the economy contracted, there was now excess economic capacity and mass unemployment in the country. The tight labour market affected hiring decisions. It was fully expected that every patriot would hire or assist the native-born under these difficult economic conditions. And although preferential hiring was routine, it would now assume a more malign character. Designated an enemy, prevented from leaving the country, and without work, the alien of Austro-Hungarian, Bulgarian, German, or Turkish origin would face unprecedented personal and physical hardship.

The predicament of the enemy alien, whose undoing was the result of government action, was certainly known to officials. There was, of course, the possibility of providing relief and assistance to the enemy alien. At the request of American diplomats, the government did allow the free entry of used clothing from the US for distribution among the Austro-Hungarian poor in Montreal, Sydney, and Fort William.[14] Nevertheless the issue was a thorny one. The restive native-born population insisted that the government act more forcefully in dealing with the perceived threat. Yet how could the government address the problem of widespread enemy unemployment without raising the spectre of betrayal and the charge of capitulating to the enemy? The solution required a deft policy that would simultaneously deal with the problem, appease zealots and patriots alike, yet uphold the principle outlined in the 2 September Public Notice that aliens of enemy nationality would not be interfered with as they went about their normal business – at least not without cause.

Order-in-council PC 2721, issued under the War Measures Act, framed the policy that would eventually take shape. Introduced 28 October

1914, it obligated enemy aliens in designated areas to register and report to officials, creating in the process the foundations of an extensive surveillance system. The order also called for the management and control of the enemy alien by way of internment. Although internment as a security step was already in place at the start of the war, it would now be used more widely to deal with the enemy alien problem as it came to be understood. Clause 7 of the order made this point clear. Specifically, the ordinance obliged enemy aliens to answer the question whether they had "the means to remain in Canada conformably to the laws and customs of the country." Without work, which necessarily meant being without means, the enemy alien became a likely target for internment. But it was the step announcing interned civilian enemy aliens would be put to work as prisoners of war that truly defined the order's extraordinary character. The prisoner-of-war label had effectively turned the issue of the destitute enemy alien into a security problem.

The purpose of PC 2721 was to address more generally the public clamour for the government to do something about the potential danger that enemy aliens posed. It also, however, helped address the specific problem presented by enemy alien unemployment, which underpinned this risk. In this respect, the order-in-council succeeded, effectively granting power to intern enemy aliens as prisoners of war on the basis of whether they could provide for themselves. The government did not wish to convey the impression that the measures taken were punitive, wide-ranging, or discriminatory.[15] After all, as was occasionally stated, resident aliens of enemy nationality were owed a certain amount of "consideration" in view of their immigration to Canada.[16] This point was iterated in the 2 September Public Notice, offering a guarantee of non-interference if there was nothing untoward in terms of their behaviour. Therefore, in achieving the right balance, those authorized to carry out the functions of registration were instructed by government to exercise judgment and personal discretion in ascertaining the facts that established the grounds for internment or parole. A note of caution could be detected: only those who showed evidence of falling within the provisions should be interned.

There were two problems with this policy, however. First, internment, initially understood to be a security measure, had expanded to include the homeless and destitute. The definition of security and what constituted a threat had now been so enlarged as to make it virtually meaningless. Second, as a matter of practice, the latitude over the process granted to registrars and other officials encouraged abuses and violations to occur. Indeed, a number of investigations showed that the decisions taken were based on accusations variously motivated by greed, spite, suspicion, or animosity, highlighting the specious and often arbitrary nature of the process while demonstrating that in the absence of proof, any evidence would do.[17] Nativism, in this regard, was a significant driver behind many of the arrests and internments, giving lie to the assurance contained in the 2 September Public Notice that enemy aliens would not be molested without cause.

A few enemy aliens protested their unlawful arrest and detention, including those naturalized citizens who were caught up in the dragnet and interned. Franz Munsche, for one, pleaded that he committed no criminal offence and as a naturalized Canadian citizen asked to be released so that he might return to his family. Munsche's appeals, however, had limited effect. With Munsche's naturalization paper before him, the director of internment operations questioned the validity of the certificate.[18] In the hands of officials who possessed virtually unlimited power, the fate of Munsche and others was effectively sealed. Many of those in charge were convinced they were simply doing their duty, especially important in the aftermath of the sinking of the *Lusitania*, when the alleged "barbarity of the Hun" was exposed.[19] Aliens of German and Austro-Hungarian origin were enemies whose natural inclination, when given the chance, was to do harm, or so it was presumed. Therefore, what was expected and required of those in authority was to stop the enemy alien before the threat materialized. The nature of that threat was beside the point, for who these people were and what they represented had already been established in principle if not in fact.[20]

The internment of the destitute authorized under PC 2721 had predictable consequences. Although the War Measures Act as a security matter authorized the internment of enemy aliens in the weeks following the declaration of war, administratively the government was unprepared to deal with the large number of aliens being arrested and processed for internment. As a result, many would be released on condition they signed a pledge declaring that they would not engage in hostile acts or activities detrimental to the interests of Canada. But now, with a requirement to intern those who did not have the means to remain in Canada, the embryonic internment system, in place at the start of the war, would have to expand. And expand it did.

Internment operations fell under the authority of the Canadian militia. At the outset of the war only a few existing federal military prisons were in operation. These proved insufficient and were quickly augmented with additional facilities found elsewhere across the country, including provincial buildings and lands, immigration depots, as well as military grounds where units deployed overseas had previously been stationed and trained. The growth in these facilities corresponded to the ballooning numbers being processed. Within four months of the introduction of order-in-council PC 2721, the total number of enemy aliens behind barbed wire swelled to 2,294. Four months later, the number of internees more than doubled, to 5,088.[21]

Internment was a large organizational undertaking. It was also a costly venture, with expenditures being borne entirely by the militia's internment directorate. Rising costs quickly outstripped the initial budget allocation, making any future estimates difficult. The effect was to put into motion the idea of sharing the cost of the operation with potential partners. These included the provincial governments of Quebec, Ontario, and British Columbia as well as the federal Department of Interior. The plan was to use internee labour on assigned public works projects, away from public view in the Canadian hinterland. The militia would continue to provide for the costs associated with security and provisioning the internees while the contracting agencies would be responsible for creating and maintaining the camps, transporting supplies, and paying for any labour performed. Within short order, labour camps on the Canadian frontier appeared in northern Ontario and Quebec, the mountain interior of British Columbia, and the national parks of the Canadian Rockies.[22] The system of internment eventually encompassed some twenty-four facilities, each of varying duration.

The partnership agreement had significant implications. Order-in-council PC 2721 provided for the internment of civilian enemy aliens as prisoners of war. The order also authorized the Canadian militia to oversee the maintenance of enemy aliens as prisoners of war and have them perform work as sanctioned under military law. Under the international Hague Convention outlining the status and rights of prisoners of war, civilian enemy aliens who were apprehended and interned for security reasons – notably reservists – could be treated as prisoners of war. In this regard, Canada was no different from other countries: interned civilian enemy aliens were responsible for their own personal maintenance as prisoners of war. Where Canada would differ was in its prescriptive use of civilians as conscript labour. Because they were unemployed and destitute and relied on the charity and mercy of the state, it was felt that interned civilian enemy aliens should be put to work.[23] Canadian internment policy, initially conceived to deal with security issues, was now being driven by economic concerns.

The economic dimension of internment proved critical in shaping its character. Specifically, the partnership agreements, which set out the division of responsibility between the internment directorate and the contracting parties, were guided by the understanding that costs would be contained and a net benefit derived from the prisoners' labour. The effect of this line of reasoning was threefold. First, the emphasis on cost reduction would lead to austerity practices that bore negatively on the health and welfare of the prisoners. Second, since internees would be paid the daily allotment identified in the regulations governing POWs – a fraction of the cost of the daily wage of a free labourer – an appetite for this type of labour was created. The contracting parties, in fact, looked to secure and use even more prisoners.[24] Finally, and perhaps most importantly from the perspective of the external contracting agencies, it became necessary to take measures to protect their investment. This meant that interned civilian enemy aliens would be forced to work. In effect, the partners in the arrangement insisted there would be a return on the monies spent without regard to military rules or protocol.

Internment in Canada was a nasty and sordid affair because of its crude, calculating nature. In the frontier camps, at sites where internees were put to work – whether clearing forests, constructing roads, cutting through rock cliffs, or simply engaged in quarry work – foremen and overseers representing the interests of the contracting parties insisted that the work not be interrupted, schedules met, and disobedience and laggardness punished. Whether it was at the Revelstoke camp ("a matter [to be] satisfactorily adjusted") or Edgewood ("If left alone we will get the results we want") work quotas took precedence over military protocol and regulations.[25] To the degree that progress on the various projects proved unsatisfactory, the contracting parties threatened to withdraw from their agreements.[26] This placed inordinate pressure on the military to deliver results. Caught in a proverbial vice, commanding officers at the camps sought to impose discipline on the prisoners, which simply served to exacerbate the already complicated relationship between camp authorities and the internees.[27]

The militia's response to situations as they arose varied from command to command. Overall, punishment and abuse against the internees was widespread while the use of coercion was not unknown: beatings, pistol whippings, bayoneting, strappado, solitary confinement, punishment diets, and other forms of physical violence were all used to elicit

5.1 Leaving enclosure, Castle Mountain, Alberta

compliance or submission.[28] The director of internment operations, Major General Wm. Otter, a professional soldier, sought to put a stop to the more egregious violations, but with mixed results. As for the internees, they reacted variously to their situation. Petitions, often ignored, were frequent; strikes or riots less so, as these were brutally suppressed. Escape held the promise of freedom for the most daring. The majority, however, chose to suffer silently in the belief that this was all somehow a mistake and it would end soon.

The underlying principle behind the indifference and the predisposition to take advantage of interned enemy alien was underpinned by the concept of "prize of war."[29] This sentiment informed the thinking of certain municipal officials, commercial enterprises, and even private individuals who sought to get "their fair share" of the opportunity presented by prisoner-of-war labour.[30] It also served as the basis behind the persistent public calls for all internees to be put to work without exception. And yet the notion of prize of war was increasingly untenable, especially as the warring countries attempted to come to a diplomatic agreement on the repatriation and treatment of certain categories of prisoners of war, including civilian prisoners.[31] In dealing with the issue the belligerents were careful to distinguish between combatants and non-combatants. Although interned civilian enemy aliens could be designated prisoners of war, they could not be compelled to work in view of their civilian non-combatant status.[32] In Canada, civilian internees were forced to work. But this was only possible because of the nature of their status. Considered outside the community, they were also at the same time the responsibility of the state. Charged with this duty, government had scant interest in their welfare, except in the most perfunctory of ways.[33]

Subjected to unending diplomatic protests, Canada would reject the political charge of wrongdoing, insisting that the work was not compulsory. According to officials, the internees, in desperate need, were simply being given an opportunity to work. The available evidence, however, was incriminating and irrefutable. From field reports received, British diplomatic officials observed that the internees were compelled to work, although they thought it prudent to keep silent on the matter since the internees did not appear to complain.[34] American diplomats, responsible for the interests of interned enemy aliens of Austro-Hungarian background in Canada, also observed that the work was compulsory, only to countenance what they saw by declaring the work required of the civilian prisoners was similar to what was normally expected of them given their socio-economic standing.[35] It did not matter that this was a violation of international understanding and practice – according to the diplomats this was their lot in life.

The government's claim that the work was not compulsory was plainly a deception – an unfortunate consequence of a policy that attempted to solve the problems of enemy alien unemployment and internment. Invariably, the denials would lead to the disingenuous claim that if it were not for internment, the fate of the enemy alien would have been far worse, an assertion made by none other than the deputy minister of justice, E. Newcombe, in his report to the Committee of the Privy Council.[36] But why the deception? In the end, it was imperative to maintain the pretence in order to deflect discussion away from the strategic role Canadian authorities had assigned to internment. Indeed, the diplomatic controversy around the issue of the compulsory use of civilian internees as prisoner-of-war labour would have been more complicated if it had been acknowledged that internment was used purposefully as a political response to the labour situation in the country.

The strategic use of internment was clearly demonstrated in the government's response to the labour troubles in Fernie, British Columbia. In aiming to solve the problem of labour turmoil in Fernie, order-in-council

PC 1501 was introduced 26 June 1915. Bowing to pressure from the British Columbia government, which illegally detained enemy alien miners at the behest of native-born workers, the federal government retroactively authorized their internment. Remarkably, the government legislated that any enemy aliens competing for work with the native-born would be interned. The order showed that internment was not as benign or charitable as the diplomatic dispatches claimed. It was calculating and political in nature and an illustration of the extent to which the government would use internment to address alleged problems associated with the enemy alien.

But the order also demonstrated that context was a determining factor in shaping government policy. As problems arose, the government reacted accordingly, each situation carrying its own particular challenges. This resulted in contradictions and policy reversals. In mid-year 1916, when labour shortages threatened agricultural and industrial production in Canada, the release of internees into the workforce became as much a priority as their initial internment. In an about-face, the government discharged thousands to farms and industry to address labour shortages. But for this to happen a plan was needed – to simply allow former prisoners of war loose across the country was neither sensible nor practical given the public perception that the internees were genuine enemies undeserving of any indulgence or forbearance.[37]

The approach that the government finally adopted regarding prisoner release developed out of the original policy framework that informed and shaped decisions relating to enemy aliens. Although internment was the logical outcome of a plan that sought to monitor and control the enemy alien population, internment was not the intended goal. Rather, surveillance and control were the objectives. The 15 August Proclamation and order-in-council PC 2721, for instance, made clear that security would best be served by a system of enemy alien registration and reporting. This system, used more generally with respect to the enemy alien population, would now be deployed strategically in relation to the internees. Registration and reporting not only provided the means by which to maintain surveillance and control of the prisoners who might be released but also assured a suspicious public that measures were in place and security concerns were being met. As an additional precautionary step, internment officials conducted their own internal review of the prisoners, determining those assessed to be low risk – the so-called "nondangerous" – on the basis of their behaviour and the attitude they demonstrated toward Canadian authority.[38]

The process of registration and reporting, which had widened in scope and purpose throughout the war, eventually encompassed some 85,000 enemy aliens.[39] All were required to carry a pass card at all times. They had to report regularly to designated officers of the crown – registrars, magistrates, and other officials. From the government's perspective the system was seen as little more than an inconvenience for those targeted and affected. From the perspective of aliens of enemy birth, however, it was an assault on their honour and dignity. In the latter part of the war, when registration was required of domiciled aliens of enemy origin who were in possession of an abode – criteria that had previously exempted them – the response among this group was disbelief and anger. A number had sons who were faithfully serving overseas with the Canadian military. It was simply inconceivable that they would be treated as anything other than loyal subjects. Canada was their home, which, they claimed, they would never betray. From an official perspective, however, what they believed or felt was beside the point. They would follow the law by registering and reporting.

Callous and insensitive, the registration and reporting system was firmly rooted in a racialized understanding of community. It was informed by the assumption that origin was a determining factor in one's loyalty. But it also underlined for the alien of enemy origin the limits of social and political acceptance and the difficulties associated with belonging, especially in the context of war. Rejection occurred because of the fears and the uncertainty that accompanied the conflict. The outcome of the war could not be taken for granted. In many ways, it was felt that only a determined and united effort on the part of the community would enable the country to prevail. If the war was to be brought to a successful conclusion, discord, dissidence, and distractions had to be confronted and eliminated. From this perspective, social cohesion was paramount. But so was rejection. Success depended on weeding out the country's enemies.

The war created an anxious mood on the home front. Accounts of personal heroism and the villainy of the enemy as well as descriptions of battles and casualty lists were featured on the front pages of the leading newspapers. The question of commitment became a gnawing concern. Were the troops being well served? Was enough being done? A sense of pride freely intertwined with feelings of guilt and obligation. On the home front, individuals faced unremitting questions regarding their role and participation. What were they doing to help?

The registration of enemy aliens addressed the desperate need to resolve feelings of guilt associated with what was turning out to be an interminable and unforgiving war. For patriots on the home front, an enemy was needed. Enemy alien registration, in the context of war, was an expression of the deep divisions brought about by war and the estrangement that happens when individuals are separated from each and from the community in which they live.[40] It was an important validation of the notion that the nation was acting as one, and served to identify those who did not belong.

Returned veterans, a large number of whom were wounded in body, mind, and spirit, were a constant reminder of the price of war and the obligations owed to those who had given so much. In gratitude, the general public responded instinctively.[41] As the influx of returning soldiers during early 1917 constricted the job market, solidarity became a pressing matter on the home front. The sacrifice of the veterans and the public's sense of obligation combined to force the issue of patriotic hiring.[42] The overseas struggle, never far from the public mind, shaped attitudes and feelings toward the enemy alien. With disabled soldiers constantly in the public's mind, it became common to confront enemy aliens who were either employed or competing for employment.[43] Transposed to the home front, the overseas struggle had become personal.

From the start of the war it was a difficult time to be an alien of German, Turkish, Austro-Hungarian, or other enemy origin. Suspicion and loathing were accompanied by public calls for the internment of the enemy alien population in Canada.[44] The plan, however, was unrealistic. Officials concluded that without resorting to the use of the whip and gun the scheme would prove unworkable.[45] Nevertheless, the fact that mass internment was even being considered pointed to the degree to which enemy aliens in Canada were living a precarious existence. It is in this context that the various restrictions and prohibitions on enemy aliens regarding their mobility, association, and speech must be understood. Combined with the 1917 Election Act, these were astonishing measures. But the abuse of rights echoed the tenor of the times.

Among enemy aliens, the reaction to these pressures was varied. Some decried the various measures as unlawful and unjust. Others considered their situation as an aberration triggered by war hysteria. They believed that conditions would change, especially if the government were made aware of the loyalty of the affected communities. Still others turned to radical politics to express their sense of injustice. But this only added to the political controversy as to what to do with the enemy alien. Calls for even greater government control of the enemy alien, including the industrial conscription of enemy aliens at the rate of military pay, resulted from the public's identification of radicalism with the alleged political intrigue and duplicity of foreigners.[46] The triangulation of the enemy alien problem – said to be rooted in revolution, conspiracy, and disloyalty – left little room for legitimate protest let alone empathy. Rather, it made possible the emergence of such agencies as the Public Safety Branch and the Manitoba Alien Investigation Board, which had little tolerance for rights or due process.

The government was guided in its approach by the necessity of controlling situations that might prove volatile. This meant continued surveillance of the activity and movement of enemy aliens.[47] It also meant managing public expectations. As anxiety in the country grew over both the growing labour unrest in the country and the perceived disloyalty of the radical foreign-born element, the activity of veterans' organizations and their supporters helped muster opposition and resentment against the enemy alien, thereby complicating the government's efforts to maintain peace, order, and stability.[48] The question for the government, therefore, was how best to manage the situation so as to appease the critics while eliminating the source behind the growing public disquiet. Internment, once again, would provide the solution.

Internment, as it was originally designed, proved effective in dealing with the unemployed and destitute among the enemy alien population. With the improvement in the economy, internment had run its course. Thousands of civilian internees, identified as harmless and compliant, were paroled during 1916–17. As a result, a large number of the frontier labour camps were decommissioned. In 1918, the final year of the war, only those considered bona fide prisoners of war – merchant marines captured on the high seas and interned in Canada – or those who had been judged obstinate and therefore a risk in terms of their possible release were still interned in the few remaining camps. These individuals were to be held and removed once peace terms had been negotiated among the belligerents. But ridding the country of the hostile and incorrigible internees presented an opportunity.[49] Why not use internment, albeit selectively, to remove from the country those who by their behaviour and actions during the ongoing labour crisis demonstrated that they were unsuitable – much like those who remained behind barbed wire?[50]

Internment, in this instance, would be realigned to meet the challenge of labour militancy and radicalism. The effect was twofold: internment helped remove those individuals believed to be contributing to the growing labour unrest and it satisfied the critics. In the realignment of internment, however, new political-legal arrangements that specified the grounds for their eventual expulsion had to be created. Repatriation, the process by which reservists could be returned to their country of origin, applied to those who were still interned. It did not necessarily apply to civilian prisoners whose consent was needed.[51] Nor did it apply to those caught up in the labour disturbances of 1919. The avenue for their removal, therefore, would be deportation, principally under amendments to the Immigration Act as well as other orders-in-council that focused on seditious or other proscribed political activity.[52]

Deportation would be the method used to remove those individuals the government of Canada wished to expel. But for this to occur, a new rationale for deportation was required. The signing of the armistice had made incongruous the idea that aliens (even though of enemy origin) could still be arrested and interned as prisoners of war. Consequently, months after the end of hostilities in Europe, a new classification – "undesirable" – was introduced to describe aliens of enemy origin and others who, once arrested, would likely be deported. The foreigner as an "undesirable" was a more credible alternative to the notion that they were prisoners of war. For the increasingly frustrated public, however, the nuances of their status were of little interest. The country needed to be cleared of individuals who were increasingly described as "a menace that will sooner or later have a demoralizing effect upon the country and militate against the rehabilitation and repatriation of the thousands of men who have suffered and who have bled to make this country possible."[53]

The civilian internees still held in the remaining three camps – Vernon, Kapuskasing, and Amherst – would be assessed on the basis of their "desirability." Some would be released. Others, deemed physically and mentally unfit, or simply found wanting in terms of their attitude, would be gathered together with the recently arrested in preparation for their removal from the country. With labour unrest ubiquitous, it was just a matter of time before most would be transported to Europe.[54]

The state of war between the major belligerents ended shortly after the signing of the Treaty of Versailles. The treaty was variously interpreted. Some saw it simply as an end to the horror that was war. Still others considered it a victory. And then there were those who saw in the treaty an invitation to break with the past – an opportunity to start over, to reject the politics of fear and division in favour of hope and friendship.

But was this even possible? Could the past be so easily ignored? Could the suspicion and distrust, promoted and sustained by the conflict over so many years, simply disappear? Moreover, would those who had endured so much be able to forgive and forget?

With the coming of peace, Canada witnessed the promise of a new beginning. War had helped forge Canada's identity. The country had shown itself worthy of international respect and recognition. Yet, the war forced choices, including the willingness to view and treat the alien of enemy origin as an "outsider."[55] Innocent of wrongdoing, they were pushed aside and subjected to unjust measures and unfair treatment. For those affected, there could be no new beginnings. The cruel lesson of war had been learned: Canada had failed to live up to its initial invitation and obligations.[56] For those officials who spoke frankly yet confidentially about what had happened, they could continue to claim that "these people suffered no hardship worthy of mention ... [and having been] astonishingly well treated ... they ought to be made to realize it."[57] But for those cast in the role of enemy, there could only be silence. The memories of the recent past could not be so easily erased.

# NOTES

## INTRODUCTION

1 National Archives of Canada (hereafter NAC), RG 13 A2, vol. 233, file 422–442, Vernon Internment Camp, Internee Camp Committee to the Duke of Devonshire, Governor General of Canada, 8 February 1919.

2 The brothers Marchuk, for example, interned on the false testimony of an RNWMP constable after an extortion amount of $300 in property was initially paid in order to secure their safety, would not be released, despite the fact that the officer was tried and convicted. The case is described in Bohdan S. Kordan and Peter Melnycky, eds, *In the Shadow of the Rockies: Diary of the Castle Mountain Camp, 1915–1917* (Edmonton: CIUS Press, 1991), 6–7.

Others were sent down for even more mundane reasons. Mike Bundziock was brutally beaten by Constable William Church for allegedly stating that Italians would not be able to stand up to Austro-Hungarian forces in the Alps. He was arrested. With blackened eyes Bundziock was brought before the police magistrate, who had no interest in the fact that Church had a history of preying on Bundziock, beating him on several occasions. He was interned. See NAC, RG 24, vol. 4278, file 34-1-3 (8).

3 The unfolding relationship in the context of the nation-building project is explored in Bohdan S. Kordan, *Enemy Aliens, Prisoners of War: Internment in Canada during the Great War* (Montreal and Kingston: McGill-Queen's University Press, 2002).

4 The issue is examined in Robert Rutherdale, *Hometown Horizons: Local Responses to Canada's Great War* (Vancouver: University of British Columbia Press, 2004).

5  John Herd Thompson, *The Harvests of War: The Prairie West, 1914–1918*
   (Toronto: McClelland and Stewart, 1978); James R. Carruthers, "The
   Great War and Canada's Enemy Alien Policy," *Queen's Law Journal* 4
   (1978); L. Luciuk, *Internment Operations: The Role of Old Fort Henry in
   World War I* (Kingston, ON: Delta, 1980); P. Melnycky, "The Internment
   of Ukrainians in Canada," in F. Swyripa and J.H. Thompson, eds, *Loyalties
   in Conflict: Ukrainians in Canada during the Great War* (Edmonton: CIUS
   Press, 1982); D. Avery, *"Dangerous Foreigners": European Immigrant
   Workers and Labour Radicalism in Canada, 1896–1932* (Toronto:
   McClelland and Stewart, 1983); Howard Palmer, *Patterns of Prejudice: A
   History of Nativism in Alberta* (Toronto: McClelland and Stewart, 1983);
   L. Luciuk, *A Time for Atonement: Canada's First National Internment
   Operations and the Ukrainian Canadians, 1914–1920* (Kingston, ON:
   Limestone Press, 1988); Barbara Roberts, *Whence They Came:
   Deportation from Canada, 1900–1935* (Ottawa: University of Ottawa
   Press, 1988); Art Grenke, "The German Community of Winnipeg and the
   English-Canadian Response to World War I," *Canadian Ethnic Studies* 20,
   no. 1 (1988); Brenda Lee-Whiting, "Enemy Aliens: German Canadians on
   the Home Front," *Beaver* 53 (October–November 1989); O. Martynovych,
   *Ukrainians in Canada: The Formative Period, 1891–1924* (Edmonton:
   CIUS Press, 1991); Kordan and Melnycky, eds, *In the Shadow of the
   Rockies*; P. Melnycky, "'Badly Treated In Every Way': The Internment of
   Ukrainians in Quebec during the First World War," in A. Biega and M.
   Diakowsky, eds, *The Ukrainian Experience in Quebec* (Toronto: Basilian
   Press, 1994); B. Waiser, *Park Prisoners: The Untold Story of Canada's
   National Parks, 1915–1946* (Saskatoon-Calgary: Fifth House, 1995);
   L. Luciuk and B. Sydoryk, *"In My Charge" – The Canadian Internment
   Camp Photographs of Sergeant William Buck* (Kingston, ON: Kashtan
   Press, 1997); D.J. Carter, *POW – Behind Canadian Barbed Wire: Alien,
   Refugee and Prisoner of War Camps in Canada 1914–1946* (Calgary:
   Eagle Butte Press, 1998); L. Luciuk with N. Yurieva and R. Zakaluzny,
   comps, *Roll Call: Lest We Forget* (Kingston, ON: Kashtan Press, 1999);
   L. Luciuk, *In Fear of the Barbed Wire Fence: Canada's First National
   Internment Operations and the Ukrainian Canadians, 1914–1920*
   (Kingston, ON: Kashtan Press, 2001); Kordan, *Enemy Aliens, Prisoners of
   War*; Rutherdale, *Hometown Horizons*; B. Kordan and C. Mahovsky, *A
   Bare and Impolitic Right: Internment and Ukrainian Canadian Redress*
   (Montreal and Kingston: McGill-Queen's University Press, 2004); C.
   Kilford, *On the Way! The Military History of Lethbridge, Alberta, 1914–
   1945* (Victoria: Trafford Publishing, 2004); J. Farney and B. Kordan, "The

Predicament of Belonging: The Status of Enemy Aliens in Canada, 1914," *Journal of Canadian Studies* 39, no. 1 (Winter 2005); George Buri, "'Enemies within Our Gates': Brandon's Alien Detention Centre during the Great War," *Manitoba History* 56 (2007); A. Sendzikas, *Stanley Barracks: Toronto's Military Legacy* (Toronto: Dundurn Press, 2011); Nathan Smith, "Fighting the Alien Problem in a British Country: Returned Soldiers and Anti-Alien Activism in Wartime Canada, 1916–1919," in A. Miller, Laura Rowe, and James Kitchen, eds, *Other Combatants, Other Fronts: Competing Histories of the First World War* (Newcastle: Cambridge Scholars Publishing, 2011); and Peter Moogk, "Uncovering the Enemy Within: British Columbians and the German Menace," *BC Studies: The British Columbian Quarterly* 182 (2014).

6  Ethnicity when aligned with class politics made the enemy alien doubly vulnerable, granting internment a role that availed officials with the necessary powers and authority to deal with the enemy alien threat, which was now increasingly defined as politically radical in nature. This development is the subject of a wider discussion and analysis of radicalism and the ethnic worker in Avery, *"Dangerous Foreigners"*; D. Avery, "Ethnic and Class Tensions in 1918–1920: Anglo-Canadians and the Alien Worker," in Swyripa and Thompson, eds, *Loyalties in Conflict*; and Michael Beaulieu, *Labour at the Lakehead: Ethnicity, Socialism and Politics, 1900–35* (Vancouver: University of British Columbia Press, 2011).

7  The argument is made more fully in Roberts, *Whence They Came: Deportation from Canada, 1900–1935* (Ottawa: University of Ottawa Press, 1988).

8  The nativist phenomenon in the early twentieth century has been the subject of considerable study. See Howard Palmer, *Patterns of Prejudice: A History of Nativism in Alberta* (Toronto: McClelland and Stewart, 1983); Avery, "Ethnic and Class Tensions"; and Art Grenke, "The German Community of Winnipeg and the English-Canadian Response to World War I," *Canadian Ethnic Studies* 20, no. 1 (1988).

The hostile attitude of veterans toward the enemy alien is explored by Smith, "Fighting the Alien Problem"; and Nathan Smith, "Comrades and Citizens: Great War Veterans in Toronto, 1915–1919" (PhD dissertation, University of Toronto).

CHAPTER ONE

1  *Ottawa Evening Journal*, 28 August 1914; and *Saskatoon Daily Star*, 28 August 1914.

2 *Calgary Daily Herald*, 12 September 1914; and *Saskatoon Daily Star*, 8 October 1914.

3 *Lethbridge Daily Herald*, 29 September 1914.

4 *Saskatoon Daily Star*, 30 September 1914.

5 *Globe* (Toronto), 10 August 1914.

6 *Daily British Whig* (Kingston), 31 August 1914.

7 *Winnipeg Tribune*, 19 August 1914; and *Vancouver Sun*, 20 August 1914.

8 *Montreal Gazette*, 16 August 1914; and *Calgary Daily Herald*, 19 August 1914.

9 *Calgary Daily Herald*, 19 August 1914.

10 *Globe* (Toronto), 22 August 1914.

11 "Enemy agents, species and saboteurs were assumed to be everywhere ... The provincial police were forced to investigate alarming reports of flashing lights at night, mysterious vessels offshore, hidden firearms, supposed chase of explosives, suspected radio installations, disloyal talk, and the presence of enemy nationals close to telegraph lines, railway bridges, and train tunnels." Peter Moogk, "Uncovering the Enemy Within: British Columbians and the German Menace," *BC Studies: The British Columbian Quarterly* 182 (2014): 60.

12 *Calgary Daily Herald*, 2 September 1914. See also *Ottawa Evening Journal*, 26 August 1914; and *Globe* (Toronto), 29 August 1914.

13 *Saskatoon Daily Star*, 10 August 1914.

14 *Globe* (Toronto), 17 August 1914.

15 *Ottawa Evening Journal*, 15 October 1914.

16 *Montreal Gazette*, 13 August 1914.

17 *Lethbridge Daily Herald*, 16 September 1914.

18 *Daily British Whig* (Kingston), 15 August 1914. The Ontario Provincial Police also issued "Shoot to kill" orders to watchmen and company employees guarding elevators, telegraph stations, and water supplies. See *Berlin Daily Telegraph* (Berlin, Ontario), 12 August 1914.

19 *Saskatoon Daily Star*, 7 August 1914.

20 *Lethbridge Daily Herald*, 22 August 1914.

21 *Ottawa Evening Journal*, 31 August 1914; and *Saskatoon Daily Star*, 31 August 1914.

22 *Saskatoon Daily Star*, 5 September 1914.

23 *Lethbridge Daily Herald*, 18, 19, 25 August 1914; *Calgary Daily Herald*, 18 August 1914.

24 *Globe* (Toronto), 10 and 11 August 1914.

25 Ibid., 13 August 1914.

26 *Montreal Gazette*, 21, 22, 27, 31 October 1914; *Ottawa Evening Journal*, 21, 22 October 1914; *Calgary Daily Herald*, 21, 23 October 1914.

27 *Saskatoon Daily Star*, 22 October 1914.

28 *Montreal Gazette*, 23 October 1914.

29 *Manitoba Free Press* (Winnipeg), 22 October 1914.

30 Provincial Archives of Ontario (hereafter PAO), Attorney General Records, RG 4–32 (1914) file 1246, E. Bayly, Acting Deputy Attorney General to the Hon. Sam Hughes, Minister of Militia and Defence, 14 August 1914.

31 NAC, Robert Borden Papers, MG 26 H1(c), vol. 46, reel C-4235, page 21039, Prime Minister R. Borden to Sir Wilfrid Laurier, 10 August 1914.

32 The letters tended to be anonymous and often based on hearsay. Typical of the denunciations was the letter addressed "Dear Sir! Keep an eye on Besh the German piano tuner. The writer overheard conversation today. (sgd.) Yours against the Germans." NAC, RG 24, vol. 4412, file 26-3-12 (1), anonymous note to Prime Minister R. Borden, 16 September 1914.

33 Examples of denunciations can be found in NAC, Robert Borden Papers, MG 26 H1(c), vol. 191, reel C-4388, pages 105627-106386. NAC, RG 76, vol. 603, file 884866, also contains denunciations sent to immigration officials for their action.

34 NAC, RG 18, vol. 469, file 1914, no. 436–460, George Bury to Sir Thomas Shaughnessy, 17 August 1914; and NAC, Robert Borden Papers, MG 26 H1(c), vol. 191, reel C-4388, page 105950, Minister of Militia and Defence, Hon. Sam Hughes, to Prime Minister Robert Borden, 28 August 1914. A close confidant of Prime Minister Borden, Sir Thomas forwarded the letter to the prime minister for his attention and action, who in turn asked the minister of militia for his views. Bury also wrote Shaughnessy about information regarding several thousand old Austrian military rifles that were rumoured to have been shipped to Canada and sold for $1.50 to dealers and which could fall in the hands of Austro-Hungarian and German settlers. He urged increasing the number of RNWMP officers by 2,500. NAC, RG 18, vol. 469, file 1914 no. 436–460, Bury to Shaughnessy, 18 August 1914; A.B. Perry, RNWMP Commissioner to L. Fortescue, RNWMP Comptroller, 24 August 1914; and Fortescue to Perry, 26 August 1914.

35 Ibid., M. Donaldson to Colonel A.B. Perry, RNWMP Commissioner, 21 August 1914; Donaldson to Perry, 21 August 1914; "Memorandum re: proposed additional increase of the R.N.W.M. Police," L. Fortescue, RNWMP Comptroller, 27 August 1914; Donaldson to Perry, 28 August 1914; and L. Fortescue, RNWMP Comptroller to Colonel A.B. Perry, RNWMP Commissioner, 9 September 1914.

36  NAC, RG 24, vol. 4276, file 34-1-3 (1), Officer Commanding 51st
    Regiment Soo Rifles to Acting Adjutant General, Military District No. 2
    (Ontario), 28 August 1914.
37  NAC, RG 24, vol. 4695, file 448-14-20, vol. 6, Capt. C.Y. Weaver, Officer
    Commanding "A" Company, 19th Alberta Dragoons to Officer
    Commanding, Military District No. 13 (Alberta), 8 September 1914.
38  The weekly synopses and other police reports are found in NAC, Robert
    Borden Papers, MG 26 H1(c), vol. 191, reel C-4388, pages
    105627–106386.
39  Ibid., page 105989, A.P. Sherwood, Chief Commissioner of Police to L.C.
    Christie, Department of External Affairs, 4 September 1914.
40  NAC, RG 76, vol. 603, file 884866 (3), A.B. Wilmot, Dominion Immigration
    Agent for New Brunswick to W.D. Scott, Superintendent of Immigration,
    21 September 1914.
41  Ibid., D. Morris to W.D. Scott, Superintendent of Immigration, 1 September
    1914. A note of caution, however, punctuated the same report. In the vicin-
    ity of Cobalt, the foreign-born population, largely composed of Austro-
    Hungarians, was considered to be "excitable and not very trustworthy,"
    leading to the recommendation that the powder magazines in the area be
    closely guarded. A number of the immigration reports were repeated in the
    weekly synopses of police reports. See, for example, NAC, Robert Borden
    Papers, MG 26 H1(c), vol. 191, reel C-4388, pages 106069–71,
    "Confidential Report," A. Sherwood, Chief Commissioner of Police to
    Prime Minister Robert Borden, 1–7 September 1914.
42  PAO, Attorney General Records, RG 4-32 (1914), file 1571, letter to J.
    Brebner, Registrar, University of Toronto, 20 October 1914.
43  NAC, RG 25 G1, vol. 1148, file 920, A.P. Sherwood, Chief Commissioner
    of Police to Sir Joseph Pope, Under Secretary of State for External Affairs,
    28 September 1914 and attachment marked "Secret."
44  NAC, RG 76, vol. 603, file 884866 (2), W.D. Scott, Superintendent of
    Immigration to Lt. Col. A.P. Sherwood, Chief Commissioner of Police,
    9 September 1914.
45  NAC, Robert Borden Papers, MG 26 H1(c), vol. 191, reel C-4388, page
    106492, L. Fortescue, RNWMP Comptroller, to Prime Minister Robert
    Borden, 16 October 1914. For undercover police reports on the
    Ukrainian Ruthenian League, see NAC, RG 18, vol. 469, file 1914,
    no. 500-514, A.B. Perry, RNWMP Commissioner to L. Fortescue, RNWMP
    Comptroller with attachment, 13 October 1914; and L. Fortescue,
    RNWMP Comptroller to Prime Minister Robert Borden with two attach-
    ments, 22 October 1914.

46 Ibid., page 106231, A.B. Perry, RNWMP Commissioner to L. Fortescue, RNWMP Comptroller, 16 October 1914.

47 *Daily British Whig* (Kingston), 26, 27 October 1914; *Saskatoon Daily Star*, 26 October 1914; *Edmonton Daily Bulletin*, 26 October 1914; and *Manitoba Free Press* (Winnipeg), 30 October 1914.

48 *Berlin Daily Telegraph* (Berlin, Ontario), 3 September 1914; *Ottawa Evening Journal*, 3 September 1914; and *Edmonton Daily Bulletin*, 10 September 1914.

49 *Calgary Daily Herald*, 13 October 1914.

50 For correspondence relating to this and other British reports on possible raids into Canada by German Americans, see NAC, Robert Borden Papers, MG 26 H1(c), vol. 191, reel C-4388, pages 105928–77; and ibid., vol. 45, reel C-4235, pages 21043–77.

51 *Manitoba Free Press* (Winnipeg), 19 August 1914

52 The "phantom presence of a threat" gave more power to the idea of an invasion than "any facts could hope to muster," the veracity of which, ironically, the government was obliged to investigate. Robert Rutherdale, *Hometown Horizons: Local Responses to Canada's Great War* (Vancouver: University of British Columbia Press, 2004), 132.

53 NAC, Robert Borden Papers, MG 26 H1(c), vol. 191, reel C-4388, page 105932, secret cypher telegram, British Embassy at Washington to the Governor General, 23 August 1914.

54 Ibid., page 106024, Prime Minister Robert Borden to Lt. Col. George T. Denison, 7 September 1914.

55 Ibid., page 106031, A.P. Sherwood, Chief Commissioner of Police to Prime Minister Robert Borden, 8 September 1914. Fear of an invasion of southwestern Ontario and a recommendation to improve defences was also the substance of an anxious letter from the mayor of London, Ontario. See ibid., page 106186, C.M.R. Graham, Mayor, London, to the Minister of Militia and Defence, Hon. Sam Hughes, 14 October 1914.

56 Ibid., pages 106213–14, Member of Parliament, D.C. Ross to Prime Minister Robert Borden, 19 October 1914; and Borden to Ross, 20 October 1914. J. Granatstein and J. Hitsman write: "Chimerical as it was the fear [of invasion] existed, and the government felt obliged to keep enough troops in Canada to guard against invasion or insurrection. At their peak strength, almost 16,000 troops were on guard in Canada, and from October 1915 through to September 1916 there were never less than 50,000 CEF troops in training or serving in the Dominion." J.L. Granatstein and J.M. Hitsman, *Broken Promises: A History of Conscription in Canada* (Toronto: Oxford University Press, 1977), 49.

57 *Daily British Whig* (Kingston), 31 October 1914. When the mayor of
Coleman in Alberta's mining district wrote to local military authorities
about the likelihood of unrest among the local Austro-Hungarian population in the face of certain layoffs, the commanding officer of Military
District No. 13 (Alberta), Col. E. Cruikshank, indicated that the formation
of a unit "would be a difficult matter at the present time owing to pressure
of work in connection with the organization of the contingent for overseas." He advised that the mayor form a rifle association, providing him
with an application to be forwarded to his office. Upon the association's
formation, a rifle for each four members was to be distributed and fifty
rounds of ammunition supplied free. RG 24, vol. 4695, file 448-14-20 (6),
District Officer Commanding Military District No. 13 (Alberta), Col. E.
Cruickshank, to Mr Ouimette, Mayor, Coleman, 4 September 1914.

58 *Globe* (Toronto), 1 August 1914; *Manitoba Free Press* (Winnipeg),
3 August 1914; *Vancouver Sun*, 3 August 1914; and *Montreal Gazette*,
4 August 1914. Prof. Desmond Morton writes: "In Canada, the government had too many other concerns in the early weeks of the war to worry
about internment, and any loyal German or Hapsburg subject eager to do
his patriotic duty had plenty of time to slip over the border to the neutral
United States." Desmond Morton, *Fight or Pay: Soldiers' Families in the
Great War* (Vancouver: University of British Columbia Press, 2004), 87.

59 *Winnipeg Tribune*, 3 August 1914.

60 For a discussion and analysis of the Bishop Budka affair, see Stella
Hryniuk, "The Bishop Budka Controversy: A New Perspective," *Canadian
Slavonic Papers* 23, no. 2 (June 1981): 154–65. On the life and times of
Bishop Budka, see Rev. Athanasius McVay, *God's Martyr, History's
Witness: Blessed Nykyta Budka, the First Ukrainian Greek-Catholic
Bishop of Canada* (Edmonton: Ukrainian Catholic Eparchy of Edmonton,
2014).

61 See, for example, *Manitoba Free Press* (Winnipeg), 12 September 1914.
NAC, M. Petrushevich Papers, MG M-5231, contains correspondence relating to the efforts at exonerating the bishop.

62 NAC, RG 25, series A2, vol. 252, Fr. R. Ambros, Chancellor to Prime
Minister Robert Borden, 11 August 1914; and NAC, Robert Borden
Papers, MG 26 H1(c), vol. 188, reel C-4386, page 104179, Borden to Fr.
Ambros, 15 August 1914.

63 *Manitoba Free Press* (Winnipeg), 7 August 1914; and *Winnipeg Tribune*, 5,
14 August 1914.

64 *Winnipeg Tribune*, 26 August 1914.

65 See, for instance, *Saskatoon Daily Star*, 31 August 1914.

66  *Globe* (Toronto), 10 and 11 August 1914.
67  See, for example, *Winnipeg Tribune*, 7 August 1914.
68  On the Wendt case, see NAC, RG 24, vol. 4695, file 448-14-20 (6), E.A
    Neff, Medical Officer, 9th Battalion to Col. S.M. Rogers, Commanding
    Officer, 9th Battalion, Valcartier, 12 September 1914; Col. J.P. Landry to
    the Secretary, Militia Council, Headquarters, Ottawa, 24 October 1914
    (Secret S/026); Landry to the Secretary, Militia Council, 24 October 1914
    (Secret 5-D S/026); and Col. Denison, Acting Adjutant General to the
    Officer Commanding Military District No. 5 (Quebec), 5 November 1914.
69  Ibid. Col. E.A. Cruickshank, Commanding Officer, Military District No. 13
    (Alberta) to Major R. de L. Harwood, Officer Commanding, 101st
    Regiment, Canadian Expeditionary Force.
70  NAC, Robert Borden Papers, MG 26 H1 (c), vol. 191, reel C-4388, page
    105968, RNWMP Commissioner A. Bowen Perry to RNWMP Comptroller
    L. Fortescue, 31 August 1914. See also *Winnipeg Tribune*, Letter to the
    Editor, P. Lazarowicz, 17 August 1914.
71  See *Saskatoon Daily Star*, 11 September 1914.
72  As quoted in the *Winnipeg Tribune*, 21 August 1914. See also *Berlin Daily
    Telegraph* (Berlin, Ontario), 24 August 1914.
73  Ibid. Moderation and empathy, in this instance, was very much motivated
    by a need to maintain civil order. See Rutherdale, *Hometown Horizons*,
    126.
74  *Saskatoon Daily Star*, 22 August 1914.
75  NAC, Robert Borden Papers, MG 26 H1 (c), vol. 188, reel C-4386, page
    104139, Louis Gurofsky to Military Headquarters, Toronto, 7 August
    1914; and ibid. page 104140, Major General F.L. Lessard, Commanding
    Officer, Military District No. 2 (Ontario) to the Secretary, Militia Council,
    Headquarters, Ottawa, 7 August 1914.
76  Ibid., page 104150, telegram from Russian, Serbian, and Montenegrin
    Committee to the Governor General, 15 August 1914; and NAC, RG 24,
    vol. 4431, file 34-2-18, "Enlistment of Foreigners," Chief of the General
    Staff to the Officer Commanding Military District No. 2 (Ontario),
    25 September 1914.
77  As reported in the *Lethbridge Daily Herald*, 14 September 1914.
78  *Manitoba Free Press* (Winnipeg), 10 August 1914.
79  *Montreal Gazette*, 12 October 1914; and *Ottawa Evening Journal*,
    14 October 1914.
80  For instance, Ukrainian homesteaders in the Henribourg district of
    Saskatchewan drove a wagon laden with vegetables to the nearby munici-
    pality of Prince Albert for distribution among the city's inhabitants facing

the coming winter. It was believed to be "the first occasion in Canada since the war broke out that Galicians [Ukrainians] have taken such action." *Saskatoon Daily Star*, 21 September 1914. Robert Rutherdale argues that the contributions of recent immigrants to the relief effort were viewed as an expression of unity and loyalty, but in accentuating ethnic differences – native-born versus "foreigners" – suspicions were never far removed from the public mind that these individuals were outside the body politic. See Rutherdale, *Hometown Horizons*, 106–7.

81 *Manitoba Free Press* (Winnipeg), 10 August 1914.

82 Ibid., 16 September 1914.

83 Ibid., 26 August 1914.

84 The case for Ukraine's independence was further complicated by the Russophile element in Canada that sought to discredit the independence movement as a German-sponsored project supported in part by Austria-Hungary and an array of opponents historically inimical to Russia. See O. Martynovych, *Ukrainians in Canada: The Formative Period, 1891–1924* (Edmonton: CIUS Press, 1991), 321.

85 *Manitoba Free Press* (Winnipeg), 5 August 1914.

86 Ibid., 11 August 1914.

87 Ibid., 10 August 1914.

88 *Edmonton Daily Bulletin*, 6 October 1914. The editorial was a direct response to the activity and public pronouncements of one Mr P. Crath, a community representative who advocated independence for Ukraine. On the controversy, see F. Swyripa, "The Ukrainian Image: Loyal Citizen or Disloyal Alien," in F. Swyripa and J.H. Thompson, eds, *Loyalties in Conflict*, 47–9. See also Martynovych, *Ukrainians in Canada*, 318–19.

89 See, for example, the open letter of Mr D. Prystash. *Vegreville Observer*, 7 October 1914.

90 *Winnipeg Tribune*, 11 August 1914. See also *Winnipeg Tribune*, 6, 15 August 1914; and *Globe* (Toronto), 7 August 1914.

91 *Globe* (Toronto), 5 August 1914. See also *Winnipeg Tribune*, 10 August 1914.

92 Commenting on the event, the *Globe* urged citizens of Toronto to show restraint. "It is not worth while for the people of other races to attempt any coercion in the use of the British flag by Germans, because throughout Canada and probably also throughout the United States the prevalent feeling among Germans is that their mother country has made a mistake. That is not a good reason for resorting to mob rule against them." *Globe* (Toronto), 7 August 1914.

93 *Vancouver Province*, 6 August 1914.

94 *Montreal Gazette*, 8 August 1914.
95 *Winnipeg Tribune*, 6 August 1914; and *Vancouver Sun*, 7 August 1914.
96 *Calgary Daily Herald*, 19 October 1914.
97 *Globe* (Toronto), 18 August 1914.
98 *Saskatoon Daily Star*, 23 September 1914.
99 NAC, Robert Borden Papers, MG 26 H1 (c), vol. 191, reel C-4388, page 106117, Rev. J. Oberhiemer to Prime Minister Robert Borden (with attached affidavit), 22 September 1914. See also a press report, *Calgary Daily Herald*, 3 October 1914
100 NAC, Robert Borden Papers, MG 26 H1 (c), vol. 191, reel C-4388, page 106117B, Prime Minister Borden to Rev. J. Oberhiemer, 30 September 1914.
101 Ibid., page 106160, RNWMP Comptroller, L. Fortescue, to Prime Minister R. Borden, 7 October 1914. See also ibid., pages 106162–5, "Report Re: Foreign Element in the Irvine District," J.O. Wilson, RNWMP Superintendent "K" Division, 22 September 1914.
102 Ibid., pages 106104–7, "Petition," German-Canadian Provincial Alliance of Saskatchewan to Prime Minister Robert Borden, 21 September 1914. For a discussion of the propaganda campaign conducted by the Anglo-Canadian press against all things German, see Art Grenke, "The German Community of Winnipeg and the English-Canadian Response to World War I," *Canadian Ethnic Studies* 20, no. 1 (1988): 27–8.
103 NAC, Robert Borden Papers, MG 26 H1 (c), vol. 191, reel C-4388, page 106112, Prime Minister Robert Borden to Mr A. Russak, 3 October 1914.
104 *Manitoba Free Press* (Winnipeg), 14 October 1914. See also *Ottawa Evening Journal*, 16 October 1914.
105 Ibid., 15 September 1914.
106 *Globe* (Toronto), 1 August 1914.
107 The issue of naturalization was brought to a head after an application for naturalization failed to proceed under the authority of Justice H. Gervais. The Montreal firm of Campbell, McMaster and Papineau, representing a German client, sought a ruling from the Justice Department after unsuccessfully trying to persuade Justice Gervais. The refusal to naturalize "citizens of enemy nations" occurred in a number of other jurisdictions as well, including Cranbrook. There BC Justice G.H. Thompson ruled: "No enemy alien has a right to apply to the civil courts during war. His civil rights are suspended." More to the point, however, Judge Thompson stated: "I would refuse the application in the exercise of my own discretion [because] I have grave doubt whether a man who is willing and

anxious to divest himself of his own nationality and assume that of an alien enemy would make a good citizen." NAC, RG 6 H3, vol. 793, file 2165-B, letter of Campbell, McMaster and Papineau to the Secretary of State, 15 August 1914; and *Calgary Daily Herald*, 25 September 1914.

108  NAC, Robert Borden Papers, MG 26 H1(c), vol. 46, reel C-4235, page 21156, T. Mulvey, Under Secretary of State to Secretary of State, 17 August 1914; and NAC, RG 6 H3, vol. 793, file 2165-B, W. Stuart Edwards, Acting Deputy Minister of Justice to T. Mulvey, Under Secretary of State, 18 August 1914. The ruling was communicated to justices who made similar inquiries about the legal authority to grant naturalization to subjects of enemy states under the war conditions. See, for example, NAC, RG 6 H3, vol. 793, file 2165-B, Justice E.D. Wood, District Court of Saskatchewan, Weyburn, to T. Mulvey, Under Secretary of State, 18 August 1914, and Mulvey to Wood, 21 August 1914.

109  NAC, Robert Borden Papers, MG 26 H1(c), vol. 287, reel C-4440, page 160388, A. Harcourt, Colonial Secretary to the Governor General, the Duke of Connaught, 29 September 1914. The Canadian position would change slightly in October as a result of the large number of applications for naturalization. Naturalization was not to be permitted "to Germans or Austrians without a certificate from an officer appointed by the government to the effect that after investigation the subject is considered worthy of it." There was also discussion about suspending naturalization where hostility to Britain and the empire could be "disclosed." See *Lethbridge Daily Herald*, 31 October 1914.

110  NAC, RG 6 H3, vol. 793, file 2165-B, "Memorandum," T. Mulvey, Under Secretary of State to Secretary of State, 23 September 1914; and T. Mulvey, Under Secretary of State to Chief Commissioner of Police, 22 October 1914.

111  *Montreal Gazette*, 20 October 1914.

112  *Calgary Daily Herald*, 2 October 1914.

113  "There was no clear consensus in Canada about how or even whether non-British newcomers were to be integrated into Canadian life. Some people believed that there was nothing to impede any newcomer from becoming a citizen and, indeed, people could become legally naturalized after three years in Canada. They were required to swear an oath that put a heavy emphasis on loyalty to the person of the sovereign, a symbolic shift from being the subject of one king to being a subject of the British Crown. They promised to defend King George V 'to the utmost of my powers against all traitorous conspiracies, or attempts whatsoever which shall be made against his person, crown and dignity.' The new Canadian

also promised to inform the King about any 'traitorous conspiracies' of which he was aware. There was also a point of view that held that the foreign-born could never become full citizens with the same relationship to the Crown enjoyed by the British-born." Jim Blanchard, *Winnipeg 1912* (Winnipeg: University of Manitoba Press, 2005), 194.

114  For a discussion of this point, see James Farney and Bohdan S. Kordan, "The Predicament of Belonging: The Status of Enemy Aliens in Canada, 1914," *Journal of Canadian Studies* 39, no. 1 (Winter 2005): 77–82.

115  "That they were imagined by names like 'enemy aliens,' 'the foreigners,' Austrians,' 'Germans,' and that the enemy overseas with which they were associated was so intensively vilified as the 'monstrous Kaiser,' the 'cruel Huns,' or the product of German 'autocracy,' meant there was an array of fluid signs that could blur distinctions between enemy alien ethnic groups, enemy aliens themselves, and the enemy overseas." Rutherdale, *Hometown Horizons,* 121.

116  *Edmonton Daily Bulletin,* 9 October 1914.

117  *Montreal Gazette,* 12, 13 October 1914

118  NAC, RG 24, vol. 4413, file 26-3-12 (2), Officer Commanding 15th Regiment to Officer Commanding 3rd Division, Kingston, 25 August 1914.

119  NAC, RG 76, vol. 603, file 884866 (2), A.P. Sherwood, Chief Commissioner of Police, to W.D. Scott, Superintendent of Immigration, 4 September 1914.

120  NAC, Robert Borden Papers, MG 26 H1(c), vol. 191, reel C-4388, pages 105957–8, T.J. Parkes to Hon. S. Hughes, Minister of Militia and Defence, 28 August 1914.

121  PAO, Attorney General Records, RG 4-32 (1914), file 1354, J.A. Cartwright to E. Bayly, Deputy Minister, Solicitor Attorney General Department, 19 August 1914, and E. Bayly, Solicitor Attorney General Department to M.M. Brown, Crown Attorney, Brockville, 21 August 1914. Sir Joseph Pope also raised the question of suspending habeas corpus. He pointed out that "on the occasion of the Fenian troubles in Canada in 1866, the Habeas Corpus Act was suspended for a year by 29–30 Victoria, Cap. I, which passed both Houses and received the Royal Assent before the Governor General retired after the delivery of his opening Speech from the Throne." NAC, Robert Borden Papers, MG 26 H1(c), vol. 46, reel C-4235, page 21188, "Memorandum for the Prime Minister," J. Pope, Under Secretary of State for External Affairs, 20 August 1914.

122  NAC, RG 18, vol. 469, file 1914 no. 436-460, N.B. Walton, Superintendent to H.H. Brewer, General Superintendent, 20 August 1914.

123  NAC, Robert Borden Papers, MG 26 H1(c), vol. 191, reel C-4388, pages 106108–12, "Petition," German-Canadian Provincial Alliance of Saskatchewan to Prime Minister Robert Borden, 21 September 1914.

124  As reported in the *Saskatoon Daily Star*, 21 September 1914.

125  NAC, RG 25 G1, vol. 1148, file 920, Robert Lansing, US Department of State to Colville Barclay, Chargé d'Affaires of Great Britain, 17 August 1914.

126  NAC, Robert Borden Papers, MG 26 H1(c), vol. 191, reel C-4388, page 105947, W.J. Bryan, US Secretary of State to American Consul, Ottawa, 28 August 1914; and ibid., page 106074, Sir Joseph Pope, "Memorandum for Sir Robert Borden," 11 September 1914.

127  NAC, Robert Borden Papers, MG 26 H1(c), vol. 191, reel C-4388, pages 106108–12, "Petition," German-Canadian Provincial Alliance of Saskatchewan to Prime Minister Robert Borden, 21 September 1914; and ibid, pages 106168–70, "Resolution," German-Canadian Provincial Alliance of Saskatchewan to Prime Minister Robert Borden, 7 October 1914.

128  Ibid., pages 105953–4, T.G. Shaughnessy to Rt. Hon. Sir Robert Borden, 28 August 1914; and Borden to Shaughnessy, 28 August 1914.

129  Peter Moogk documents how personal firearms were also seized from naturalized citizens. See Moogk, "Uncovering the Enemy Within," 62.

130  NAC, RG 6 H3, vol. 793, file 2165-B, Mr Fritz Broo to T. Mulvey, Under Secretary of State (in German), 14 September 1914; T. Mulvey, Under Secretary of State to A.P. Sherwood, Commissioner of Police, 19 September 1914; Mulvey to Broo, 21 September 1914; Sherwood to Mulvey, 22 September 1914; Mulvey to Broo, 23 September 1914; Broo to Mulvey (in German), 23 September 1914; Sherwood to Mulvey, 4 October 1914; and Mulvey to Broo, 5 October 1914.

131  Ibid., J.A. Wall, Barrister, to Secretary of State, 18 August 1914; T. Mulvey, Under Secretary of State to J. Wall, 20 August 1914; T. Mulvey to Deputy Minister of Justice, 20 August 1914; W. Stuart Edwards, Acting Deputy Minister of Justice to T. Mulvey, 21 August 1914; and Acting Under Secretary of State to J. Wall, 24 August 1914.

132  Ibid., G.N. Gordon, City Solicitor, Peterborough, to the Secretary of State, 25 August 1914; Acting Under Secretary of State, P. Pelletier, to E. Newcombe, Deputy Minister of Justice, 26 August 1914; telegram, G.N. Gordon to Secretary of State, 28 August 1914; Newcombe to Pelletier, 29 August 1914; Pelletier to Gordon, 1 September 1914; Gordon to Secretary of State, 2 September 1914; Gordon to Secretary of State, 15 September 1914; A.P. Sherwood to the Under Secretary of State,

18 September 1914; and T. Mulvey, Under Secretary of State to G.N. Gordon, 19 September 1914.

133 Ibid., Baer Bros. Mfg. to Department of State, 6 October 1914; and A.P. Sherwood to Under Secretary of State, 9 October 1914.

134 NAC, RG 24, vol. 4412, file 26-3-12 – vol. 1, Officer Commanding 3rd Division, Kingston, to Chief Commissioner of Police, 15 August; and Sherwood to Officer Commanding 3rd Division, Kingston, 16 September 1914. See also *Daily British Whig* (Kingston), 22 September 1914.

135 NAC, Robert Borden Papers, MG 26 H 1 (c), vol. 191, reel c-4388, page 105980, telegram, E. Busby to Commissioner of Customs, 2 September; and A.B. Perry, RNWMP Commissioner to E. Busby, 4 September 1914.

136 NAC, RG 24, vol. 4542, file 75-1-25, Colonel for General Staff Officer, 6th Division, Halifax, to Major W.H. Gray, Officer Commanding 71st Regiment, Marysville NB, "Petition of Residents of Parish of Canning in vicinity of Minto, Rothwell, and Newcastle Bridge, NB," 12 October 1914.

137 NAC, Robert Borden Papers, MG 26 H 1 (c), vol. 191, reel c-4388, page 106051, Hon. C. Doherty, Minister of Justice to Prime Minister Robert Borden, 10 September 1914.

138 NAC, RG 13 series A 2, vol. 188, file 1392-1411, R. Honeyford, Barrister to E. Newcombe, Deputy Minister of Justice to, 19 September 1914; and Newcombe to Honeyford, 22 September.

139 NAC, Robert Borden Papers, MG 26 H 1 (c), vol. 191, reel c-4388, pages 105983–4, A.B. Perry, RNWMP Commissioner to L. Fortescue, RNWMP Comptroller, 31 August 1914; and ibid., page 105993, L. Fortescue, RNWMP Comptroller, "Memorandum re: seditious articles published in the Regina 'Courier,'" 4 September 1914. The newspapers in question were the *Der Courier* (Regina) and *Der Nordwesten* (Winnipeg) both of which were regularly criticized by the *Manitoba Free Press* (Winnipeg) for their anti-British reporting of events in Europe. See, for example, *Manitoba Free Press* (Winnipeg), 31 August, 1, 8, and 21 September 1914.

140 Ibid., pages 106228–9, L. Fortescue, RNWMP Comptroller, to Prime Minister Robert Borden, 22 October 1914; and ibid, page 106247, Prime Minister Robert Borden to C. Doherty, Minister of Justice, 23 October 1914.

141 *Montreal Gazette*, 14 August 1914.

142 Home-front patriots such as Manley were no doubt motivated by a sense of duty, but also "[a] show of patriotic zeal may have raised their social status as well as their self-esteem." See Moogk, "Uncovering the Enemy Within," 61–2.

143　NAC, RG 6 H3, vol. 793, file 2165-B, "Private and Confidential," R.H. Manley, 7 August 1914; Manley to the Military Secretary, H.R.H. The Governor General (with attached report), 13 August 1914; J. Pope, Under Secretary of State for External Relations to T. Mulvey, Under Secretary of State, 22 August 1914; J.T. Black, Chief Constable, Nelson BC, to Colin Campbell, Superintendent Provincial Police, Victoria BC, 28 August 1914; Mulvey to Pope, 23 September 1914; and NAC, Robert Borden Papers, MG 26 H1(c), vol. 191, reel C-4388, page 105907, Governor General to Prime Minister Robert Borden, 25 September 1914.

144　NAC, Robert Borden Papers, MG 26 H1(c), vol. 287, reel C-4440, page 161216, A. Harcourt, Colonial Secretary to the Governor General, the Duke of Connaught, 3 August 1914.

145　Ibid., page 161213, Governor General to Colonial Secretary, 4 August 1914.

146　NAC, RG 2, vol. 1095, file 843 – 1019E, Prime Minister Robert Borden to the Governor General, 7 August 1914.

147　NAC, Robert Borden Papers, MG 26 H1(c), vol. 46, reel C-4235, pages 21133–4, Prime Minister Robert Borden, to G.H. Perley, Canadian High Commissioner, London, 15 August 1914.

148　Ibid.

149　United Kingdom Public Record Office (hereafter PRO), Colonial Office Records, CO 42/981 "Progress of events in Canada since outbreak of war," 6 September 1914.

150　NAC, Robert Borden Papers, MG 26 H1(c), vol. 191, reel C-4388, page 105925, Prime Minister Robert Borden to the Hon. Sam Hughes, Minister of Militia and Defence, 7 August 1914.

151　NAC, RG 76, vol. 603, file 884866 (1), Malcolm Reid, Dominion Immigration Agent and Inspector, Vancouver, to W.D. Scott, Superintendent of Immigration, 17 August 1914; and Scott to Reid, 25 August 1914. With respect to the uncertainty and confusion in the field, see NAC RG 24, vol. 4413, file 26-3-12 (2), Officer Commanding 15th Regiment, Belleville, to Officer Commanding 3rd Division, Kingston, 10 August 1914; NAC, RG 24, vol. 4694, file 448-14-20 (2), Officer Commanding "G" Division, RNWMP, Edmonton to Col. E. Cruickshank, Officer Commanding Military District No. 13, 27 August 1914; and Cruickshank to Officer Commanding "G" Division, RNWMP, 27 August 1914.

152　There was also the question of manpower. Immigration authorities were "unable to attend to the amount of work necessary" and requested militiamen for assistance in searches conducted on trains. NAC, RG 76,

vol. 603, file 884866 (2), W.D. Scott to Col. W.R. Rutherford, District
Officer Commanding, 12 September 1914.

153 NAC, Robert Borden Papers, MG 26 H1(c), vol. 46, reel C-4235, pages
21015–16, A. Ross Cuthbert, Assistant RNWMP Commissioner, to A.B.
Perry, RNWMP Commissioner, 8 August 1914. See also RG 24, vol. 4695,
file 448-14-20 – vol. 6, P. Primrose, RNWMP Superintendent for the
RNWMP Commissioner to Col. E. Cruickshank, Officer Commanding
Military District No. 13 (Alberta), 20 August 1914.

154 NAC, RG 76, vol. 603, file 884866 (1), E.B. Robertson, Assistant Superintendent of Immigration, to J. Hoolahan, Dominion Immigration Agent
and Inspector, Montreal, 13 August 1914; W.D. Scott, Superintendent of
Immigration to Adjutant General, Department of Militia and Defence,
Ottawa, 19 August 1914; Adjutant General to Superintendent of Immigration, 21 August 1914; and Scott to Hoolahan, 25 August 1914.

155 NAC, Robert Borden Papers, MG 26 H1(c), vol. 46, reel C-4235,
page 21058, A. Ross Cuthbert, Assistant RNWMP Commissioner, to A.B.
Perry, RNWMP Commissioner, 10 August 1914.

156 *Ottawa Evening Journal*, 18 September 1914.

157 See, for example, NAC, RG 76, vol. 603, file 884866 (2), W.S. Homan,
Inspector, Niagara Falls, to W.D. Scott, Superintendent of Immigration,
26 August 1914; and NAC, RG 24, vol. 4413, file 26-3-12 (2), Officer
Commanding 3rd Division, Kingston, to the Secretary, Militia Council,
22 August 1914. Newspapers were full of daily accounts of arrests at the
border and about those hoping to secure passage to Europe. Most were
unaware of the restrictions that made their departure from the country
impossible and whose attempt to leave became grounds for arrest since
most, without evidence to the contrary, were suspect of being enemy
reservists. See, for example, *Montreal Gazette*, 11 August 1914; *Winnipeg
Tribune*, 17 August; *Lethbridge Daily Herald*, 17 August 1914; and
*Saskatoon Daily Star*, 25 August 1914.

158 NAC, Robert Borden Papers, MG 26 H1(c), vol. 191, reel C-4388, page
105953, Sir T. Shaughnessy to Rt. Hon. Sir Robert Borden, 28 August
1914. It was widely reported that "the Government has under consideration the question of appropriating the property held in Canada by
Germans who are aliens or who are engaged in the war against the
Allies." See, for example, *Ottawa Evening Journal*, 26 August 1914.

159 The US consular official in Sarnia, Ontario, observed that twelve Austro-
Hungarians with tickets in hand, who had been arrested, all claimed
"they were going home to see their families." United States National

Archives (hereafter USNA), State Department Records, 736.72115/20, Fred. C. Sloan, US Consulate, Sarnia, to the Secretary of State, Washington, 25 August 1914.

160 *Montreal Gazette*, 11 August 1914.

161 Not everyone, however, was entirely unhappy with the situation. The restrictions on leaving the country provided a veil of protection against the accusation that, as reservists, they deliberately avoided service. Deemed a threat to Canada and prevented from leaving or being arrested, reservists, in this way, were granted immunity against the charge of treason if in the future they decided to return home. In an ironic twist of fate, persons denied the promise of life in a new country would be spared the risk of death in the old. See NAC, RG 6 H3, vol. 793, file 2165B, "Prevent Reservists Leaving Dominion"; and *Manitoba Free Press* (Winnipeg), 1 September 1914.

162 Writing to the Militia Council, the General Officer Commanding 2nd Division noted, "The majority of these prisoners are very illiterate and understand very little of the English language and it is very difficult to secure information regarding them. May I request that the necessary authority be granted for the employment of interpreters?" NAC, RG 24, vol. 4276, file 34-1-3 (2), General Officer Commanding 2nd Division to the Secretary, Militia Council, Ottawa, 15 October 1914. See also NAC, RG 24, vol. 4412, file 26-3-12 (1), Chief Commissioner of Police to the Officer Commanding 3rd Military Division, Kingston, 9 September 1914; NAC, RG 24, vol. 4276, file 34-1-3 (1), Officer Commanding Welland Canal Force to Acting Adjutant General 2nd Division, Toronto, 10 September 1914.

163 NAC RG 76, vol. 603, file 884866 (2), "Undertaking," A.P. Sherwood, Chief Commissioner of Dominion Police, 18 August 1914.

164 See NAC, RG 24, vol. 4695, file 448-14-21 (6), Officer Commanding Military District No. 13 (Alberta), to P.C. Primrose, RNWMP Superintendent, Regina, 22 August 1914; and NAC, RG 76, vol. 603, file 884866 (2), Adjutant General, Department of Militia and Defence, to W.D. Scott, Superintendent of Immigration, 3 September 1914.

165 See NAC, RG 24, vol. 4413, file 26-3-12 (2), Adjutant General, Canadian Militia to Officer Commanding 3rd Division, Kingston, 21 August 1914; and Adjutant General 3rd Division to Major Patterson, 41st Regiment, 24 August 1914.

166 As an example, in Fort Frances, six Austrians were apprehended for attempting to leave Canada. They admitted that they had been called upon for duty "but did not wish to do so." Having expressed a

willingness to sign an Undertaking, "after this was attended to, they were permitted to stay in Canada under parole to report weekly." NAC, RG 76, vol. 603, file 884866 (2), W.D. Scott, Superintendent of Immigration to Col. Sherwood, Chief Commissioner of Police, 1 September 1914.

167 NAC, RG 24, vol. 4694, file 448-14-20 (2), Col. E. Cruickshank, Officer Commanding Military District No. 13 to the Secretary, Militia Council, Headquarters, Ottawa, 28 August 1914.

168 Only part of the Stanley Barracks was used for internment. Aldona Sendzikas writes: "The building designated for internment was the cavalry quarters or the 'West Block' – the privates' barracks on the west side of the fort, originally known as Range No. 2, which had a capacity of ninety men. A plan of Stanley Barracks, drafted by Lieutenant H.J. Burden in 1915 labels Range No. 2 as the 'Prison Block.' The 1915 plan also indicates that a 'Prisoners Yard' had been laid out and enclosed in the southwest corner of the fort, between the officers' quarters and the new hospital." A. Sendzikas, *Stanley Barracks: Toronto's Military Legacy* (Toronto: Dundurn, 2011), 110.

169 See NAC, RG 24, vol. 4412, file 26-3-12 (1), Adjutant General, Canadian Militia to Officer Commanding 3rd Division, Kingston, 14 September 1914; and Officer Commanding 3rd Division to the Secretary, Militia Council, 18 September 1914.

170 NAC, RG 76, vol. 603, file 884866 (2), Adjutant General, Department of Militia and Defence, to W.D. Scott, Superintendent of Immigration, 3 September 1914.

171 See, for example, NAC, RG 24, vol. 4276, file 34-1-3 (1), Officer Commanding 2nd Division, Toronto, to the Secretary, Militia Council, Headquarters, Ottawa, 26 August 1914; and Officer Commanding 2nd Division to Secretary, Militia Council, 8 September 1914.

172 The description "Poultry Building" would stick with the Lethbridge camp and served as a source of amusement to describe the camp and its purpose. "Chicken of a decidedly different type than the winged variety will make Lethbridge their home in the future," wrote the *Lethbridge Daily Herald*. Christopher Kilford noted, "as camp operations began, the authors of numerous military telegrams also took great delight in directing prisoners to the Lethbridge 'poultry buildings' for internment." See C. Kilford. *On the Way! The Military History of Lethbridge, Alberta, 1914–1945* (Victoria: Trafford Publishing, 2004), 21–2.

173 NAC, RG 24, vol. 4412, file 26-3-12 (1), Officer Commanding 3rd Division, Kingston to the Secretary, Military Council, 18 September 1914; Adjutant General, Canadian Militia, to Officer Commanding

3rd Division, Kingston, 22 September 1914; Adjutant General to Officer Commanding 3rd Division, 5 October 1914; Adjutant General to Officer Commanding 3rd Division, 14 October 1914; and Adjutant General to Officer Commanding 3rd Division, 19 October 1914.

174 "Captain Pablo Ferrer said that about 500 miles from Halifax the *Gory* stopped his ship about 9 o'clock Monday morning. The battleship signalled the liner to heave to and be searched and a few minutes afterward a lieutenant from the British ship was on board and examining the *Montserrat*'s passenger list, when he found a suspiciously large number of German names on it. Making inquiries, he ascertained they were German reservists who were bound for Genoa, and as it would be quite easy for them to reach their colors by way of neutral Italy, the captain of the *Glory* ordered the *Montserrat* to go with him to Halifax." *Saskatoon Daily Star*, 19 September 1914.

175 *Vernon News*, 17 September 1914.

176 NAC, RG 24, vol. 4276, file 34-1-3 (1), Adjutant General to Officer Commanding 2nd Division, Toronto, 2 September 1914. See also NAC, RG 13 A2, vol. 190, file 117-136, W. Lawrence, Secretary, Prisoners of War Information Bureau to General Office Commanding in Chief, All Foreign Commands, 24 September 1914; and PRO, Colonial Office Records, CO 323/634, "Prisoners of War Information Bureau," 17 September 1914.

177 The case of one Mr Von Sydow stands out as an exception. Although he was not considered a threat, the inclination was to hold him. Colonel A.P. Sherwood was of the opinion that it was unwise to parole a German officer. But more importantly there was the issue of reciprocity. "In Germany they are not paroling our Officers," declared Sherwood. Referring to the celebrated case of Major Anderson, a Canadian caught at the start of the war in Germany, Sherwood noted: "Major Anderson is now confined as a close prisoner in that country without having been given an opportunity to sign an Undertaking to refrain from hostility. [Von Sydow] should be held." NAC, RG 24, vol. 4412, file 26-3-12 (1), A.P. Sherwood, Chief Commissioner of Police to the Officer Commanding, 3rd Military Division, Kingston, 22 September 1914.

178 NAC, RG 24, vol. 4280, file 34-1-3 (14), "Maintenance of Discipline among Prisoners of War – Abstracts from Royal Warrant of August 3rd, 1914." Also circulated was a typed manuscript copy entitled "Prisoners of War Instructions Re from 'Land Warfare,'" NAC, RG 24, vol. 4695, file 448-14-20 (6). See also PRO, Foreign Office Records, 41/46/14, "Rules enforced upon captives and prisoners," 5 October 1914. The expected

treatment of prisoners of war in Canada was occasionally reported in the Canadian press. See, for example, *Manitoba Free Press* (Winnipeg), 7 September 1914.

179  USNA, State Department Records, 763.72115/65, "Prisoners of War at Fort Henry, Kingston," Felix Johnson, American Consul, Kingston, to Secretary of State, Washington, 17 September 1914, and 20 October 1914.

180  See *Montreal Gazette*, 19 September 1914; *Daily British Whig* (Kingston), 21 September 1914; and *Montreal Gazette*, 12 October 1914.

181  NAC, RG 24, vol. 4412, file 26-3-12 (1), Officer Commanding 2nd Division to Secretary, Militia Council, 22 September 1914.

182  Ibid., Major H.J. Dawson, 14th Regiment, to the Officer Commanding 3rd Division, Kingston, 11 October 1914. They would, however, be supplied with winter clothes: heavy sweater, socks, caps, underwear, and moccasins. See *Daily British Whig* (Kingston), 21 October 1914.

183  Ibid., Officer Commanding 3rd Division, Kingston, to the Commissioner Dominion Police, Ottawa, 8 October 1914. The return of parolees to Fort Henry was reported in the local press. "On Friday, an Austrian, who is about forty years of age, appeared at the gate at Fort Henry and asked the guard who was on duty to take him in again. The request was granted." *Daily British Whig* (Kingston), 13 October 1914.

184  *Montreal Gazette*, 19 August 1914.

185  *Calgary Daily Herald*, 17 October 1914.

186  NAC, RG 18, vol. 470, file 1914 no. 526-544, John Stover to the Department of Interior, 26 October 1914.

187  For this reason, it was often acknowledged that aliens of enemy nationality were in a politically compromised and untenable position. No expressions of allegiance could fully expunge the fact that *their* countries were at war with the empire and as subjects of those countries, they too, technically, were at war with the empire. See, for example, *Winnipeg Tribune*, 7 August 1914.

188  The argument is made more fully in Farney and Kordan, "Predicament of Belonging," 74–89.

189  See *Saskatoon Daily Star*, 14 September 1914.

190  NAC, RG 24, vol. 4412, file 26-3-12 (1), A.P. Sherwood, Chief Commissioner of Police, to Officer Commanding 3rd Division, Kingston, 15 September 1914.

191  The prospect of every enemy alien being a potential combatant also meant that the categories of military and civilian prisoners of war would become blurred, and because of the lack of distinction civilians and actual reservists were freely mixed in the camps.

192  NAC, Robert Borden Papers, MG 26 H1(c), vol. 191, reel C-4388,
page 106083, telegram, B.E. Sunny to Prime Minister Robert Borden,
14 September 1914; ibid., page 106084, "Re: Mr. Van Westrum," A.P.
Sherwood, Chief Commissioner of Police to Prime Minister Robert
Borden, no date; ibid., page 106187, telegram, Sunny to Borden,
15 October 1914; ibid., page 106188, "Memorandum," 16 October
1914; ibid., page 106208, Borden to Sunny, 19 October 1914; ibid.,
page 106209, Sherwood to Borden, 19 October 1914; ibid., page
106215, Chas. Slonin, Chief Constable, to Col. A.P. Sherwood, Chief
Commissioner of Dominion Police, 19 October 1914; and ibid.,
pages 106223–4, Sunny to Borden, 21 October 1914.
193  Copies of both documents are reproduced in Swyripa and Thompson,
eds, *Loyalties in Conflict*, Appendix II, 171–4.
194  *Saskatoon Daily Star*, 22 October 1914.
195  NAC, Robert Borden Papers, MG 26 H1(c), vol. 191, reel C-4388, pages
106228–9, L. Fortescue, RNWMP Comptroller, to Prime Minister Robert
Borden, 22 October 1914; and ibid., page 106247, Prime Minister
Robert Borden to C. Doherty, Minister of Justice, 23 October 1914.

### CHAPTER TWO

1  Byron Lew and Marvin McInnis, "Guns and Butter: World War I and the
Canadian Economy," http://www.trentu.ca/economics/WorkingPapers/
LewMcInnis_Toronto_05.pdf.
2  NAC, RG 76, vol. 603, file 884866 (1), "Notice," Imperial and Royal
Austro-Hungarian Consulate General, Montreal, 12 August 1914.
3  NAC, RG 25 G1, vol.1148, file 920, Sir Joseph Pope, Under Secretary of
State for External Affairs to the Governor General's Secretary, 14 August
1914; and NAC, Robert Borden Papers, MG 26 H1(c), vol. 191, reel
C-4388, page 105947, Jennings Bryan, US Secretary of State to J. Foster,
American Consul General, Ottawa, 28 August 1914.
4  NAC, RG 25 G1, vol. 1148, file 920, A. Harcourt, Secretary of the
Colonies to the Governor General, 20 August 1914; J. Pope, Under
Secretary of State for External Affairs to J. Foster, American Consul
General, Ottawa, 25 August 1914; and Prime Minister Robert Borden to
J. Pope, Under Secretary of State for External Affairs, 12 September 1914.
The Canadian government conveyed to US officials that they were
equally "animated by the same benevolent motive" in providing assis-
tance to the needy. In actual fact, however, according to the undersecre-
tary of state for external affairs, the government was concerned by the

impression that would have been created if it refused the American offer of assistance. NAC, Robert Borden Papers, MG 26 H1(c), vol. 191, reel c-4388, page 106074, J. Pope, Under Secretary of State for External Affairs to Prime Minister R. Borden, 11 September 1914.

5 USNA, State Department Records, 763.72115/274, W.H. Bradley, US Consulate, Montreal to the US Secretary of State, Washington, 17 November 1914.

6 Ibid.

7 The committee was under the impression that the government would not permit the opening of the soup kitchen and made inquiries before there was any objection. After a delegation met with the acting mayor of Montreal and received assurance that the initiative was welcome, the effort to both solicit funds and provide emergency relief went ahead. NAC, RG 13, series A2, vol. 189, file 1608-1638, W.D. Scott, Superintendent of Immigration to the Deputy Minister of Justice, 28 October 1914; and *Montreal Gazette*, 16 and 19 October 1914.

8 NAC, Robert Borden Papers, MG 26 H1(c), vol. 191, reel c-4388, pages 106133-4, Hon. Sir Hugh J. Macdonald to the Rt. Hon. Sir Robert Borden, Prime Minister of Canada, 28 September 1914.

9 NAC, RG 6 H3, vol. 793, file 2165B, Rev. M.C. Kinsale, Presbyterian Mission to the Foreigners, Sydney, to T. Mulvey, Secretary of State, 24 September 1914.

10 Ibid., Thomas Mulvey, Under Secretary of State to Col. A.P. Sherwood, Chief Commissioner of Dominion Police, 29 September 1914; and Sherwood to Mulvey 30 September 1914.

11 NAC, RG 18, vol. 1770, file 1914, no. 170 pt. 92-100, Cpl. G. Binning, RNWMP detachment, North Portal to Officer Commanding RNWMP, Regina District, 18 September 1914.

12 NAC, RG 24, vol. 4413, file 26-3-12 – vol. 2, Officer Commanding 3rd Division to Secretary of Militia Council, Ottawa, 22 August 1914.

13 NAC, RG 76, vol. 603, file 884866 (2), W. Homan, Immigration Inspector-in-Charge, Niagara Falls, to W.D. Scott, Superintendent of Immigration, Ottawa, 26 August 1914.

14 NAC, RG 24, vol. 4412, file 26-3-12 (1), Major H. Dawson, 14th Regiment, Fort Henry, to Officer Commanding 3rd Division, Kingston, 18 September 1914.

15 Ibid., Chief Commissioner of Police to Officer Commanding 3rd Division, 15 September 1914; Officer Commanding 3rd Division to the Chief Commissioner of Police, 19 September 1914; Major H. Dawson, 14th Regiment, Fort Henry, to Officer Commanding 3rd Division, Kingston,

21 September 1914; and Officer Commanding 3rd Division to the Chief
Commissioner of Police, 8 October 1914.

16  *Winnipeg Tribune*, 4 August 1914.

17  Ibid., 7 August 1914.

18  *Edmonton Daily Bulletin*, 3 September 1914.

19  *Manitoba Free Press* (Winnipeg), 21 September 1914. A somewhat similar
view was expressed by the German Alliance of Saskatchewan, which communicated to Ottawa that it had received assurances from a great number
of German farmers who were prepared to care for one or more unemployed by bringing them on to the land, providing work, food, and shelter.
See NAC, Borden Papers, MG 26 H1(c), vol. 191, reel C-4388, pages
106103–7, German-Canadian Alliance of Saskatchewan to the Rt. Hon.
Sir Robert Borden, Prime Minister of Canada, 21 September 1914.

20  See, for example, *Winnipeg Free Press*, 14 September 1914.

21  See Peter Moogk, "Uncovering the Enemy Within: British Columbians and
the German Menace," *BC Studies: British Columbian Quarterly* 182
(2014): 65–6. It had been claimed that the enemy alien could compete with
the native-born, "a touchstone lie, however, that could easily be absorbed
by those ordinarily comforted by the keywords 'British justice.'" Robert
Rutherdale, *Hometown Horizons: Local Responses to Canada's Great War*
(Vancouver: University of British Columbia Press, 2004), 129.

22  *Calgary Daily Herald*, 10 September 1914.

23  Ibid., 26 August 1914.

24  NAC, RG 24, vol. 4278, file 34-1-3 (8), letter signed "BRITISH WAITERS"
to the O.C. Military District No. 2, Toronto, 11 May 1915; and A.A.G.
2nd Division to the Chief of Police, Toronto, 15 May 1915.

25  *Calgary Daily Herald*, 27 August 1914. The effect of unemployment was
to create divisions among labour along ethnic lines, reinforcing British
sensibilities and patriotism while "fragment[ing] the disposition of Calgary
workers to behave as a class." David Bright, *The Limits of Labour: Class
Formation and the Labour Movement in Calgary, 1883–1929* (Vancouver:
University of British Columbia Press, 2011), 139.

26  *Calgary Daily Herald*, 28 August 1914.

27  *Ottawa Evening Journal*, 23 October 1914.

28  The interruption in commerce with Europe caused a large number of the
logging mills across the country to scale back operations. Jobs were shed
not only in the Ottawa Valley but also in New Brunswick. On Vancouver
Island, lumber mills began decreasing production in direct response to falling demand. Also hard hit was the export-driven manufacturing sector in
Ontario and Quebec, which in turn collaterally affected the mining and

steel industries of Nova Scotia as well as transportation across the entire country. In the end, tens of thousands of workers were released from a range of industries with a great many heading to the major cities in search of jobs and relief. In doing so, they added to the stress of municipalities already attempting to cope with the large number of unemployed.

29 *Ottawa Evening Journal*, 7 August 1914.
30 Ibid., 9 September 1914.
31 Ibid.
32 Ibid.
33 NAC, RG 76, vol. 486, file 752149 (1), memorandum, Malcolm Reid, Dominion Immigration Agent and Inspector, Vancouver, n.d.
34 *Montreal Gazette*, 27 October 1914.
35 The secretary of the Charity Organization Society, Rufus D. Smith, wrote to the Montreal Board of Trade: "We probably have somewhere between five and eight thousand of these men, mostly single, and the majority reservists, in the city. Such a body of men, starving and in great distress, may become a serious menace this winter." *Montreal Gazette*, 24 October 1914.
36 *Manitoba Free Press* (Winnipeg), 24 October 1914.
37 *Montreal Gazette*, 27 October 1914. As organizers of the meeting, members of Montreal's Board of Trade solicited support for their position from other municipal boards of trade. They were not disappointed, receiving several endorsements. See, for example, Borden Papers, MG 26 H1(c), vol. 191, reel C-4388, page 106266, F. Morley, Toronto Board of Trade, to the Rt. Hon. Sir R. Borden, Prime Minister of Canada, 31 October 1914.
38 NAC, Borden Papers, MG 26 H1(c), vol. 191, reel C-4235, page 21167, Hon. S. Hughes, Minister of Defence, to the Rt. Hon. Sir Robert Borden, Prime Minister of Canada, 18 August 1914.
39 Borden Papers, MG 26 H1(c), vol. 191, reel C-4388, page 105935, Sir Thomas Shaughnessy to the Hon. Martin Burrell, Minister of Agriculture, 26 August 1914.
40 Ibid., page 105941, Rt. Hon. Sir Robert Borden, Prime Minister of Canada, to the Hon. Martin Burrell, Minister of Agriculture, 27 August 1914.
41 Ibid., page 105951, Hon. Arthur Meighen, Solicitor General of Canada, to the Rt. Hon. Robert Borden, Prime Minister of Canada, 28 August 1914.
42 Meighen was not the only advocate of "a back to the land" movement. The plan was the subject of a public debate carried on the pages of the major dailies. See, for instance, *Vancouver Sun*, 27, 28, 30 October, 2 November 1914. The idea of assisting the unemployed in acquiring plots

of land that would help them while alleviating the unemployment problem was endorsed by the mayor and city administration of Calgary as well as the Regina Board of Trade. See *Calgary Daily Herald*, 29 October 1914, and *Edmonton Daily Bulletin*, 25 November 1914.

43 Borden Papers, MG 26 H1(c), vol. 191, reel C-4388, page 105995, Meighen to Borden, 4 September 1914.

44 Ibid., vol. 192, reel C-4446, page 169306, the Rt. Hon. Robert Borden, Prime Minister of Canada, to the Hon. G.H. Perley, Canadian High Commissioner to the United Kingdom, 20 October 1914.

45 Ibid., vol. 191, reel C-4388, page 106260, Hon. G.H. Perley, Canadian High Commissioner, to Mr Ackland, Parliamentary Under-Secretary to the Foreign Secretary, 22 October 1914.

46 Ibid., page 106262, Hon. L. Harcourt, Secretary, Colonial Office, to the Hon. G. Perley, Canadian High Commissioner, 26 October 1914; and ibid., page 106258, Hon. G.H. Perley, Canadian High Commissioner, to the Rt. Hon. Sir Robert Borden, Prime Minister of Canada, 30 October 1914.

47 NAC, RG 2, vol. 5299, file 1915-2794, copy of letter, A. Chevalier, Director, Philanthropic Societies of Montreal, 17 September 1914. See also *Montreal Gazette*, 19 October 1914.

48 NAC, Borden Papers, MG 26 H1(c), vol. 191, reel C-4388, pages 106153–4, Rt. Hon. Sir Robert Borden, Prime Minister of Canada, to Mr J. Russak, 3 October 1914.

49 See, for example, *Montreal Gazette*, 28 October 1914.

50 NAC, RG 76, vol. 603, file 884866 (3), Memorandum for Mr J.A. Cote from W.D. Scott, Superintendent of Immigration, 23 September 1914.

51 Copies of Order-in-Council 2721 are found in a number of record groups including NAC, RG 2, vol. 3618, file 1157-1164; and RG 6, vol. 819, file "Operations Branch: 1914–1918."

52 For a biographical account, see Desmond Morton, *The Canadian General: Sir William Otter* (Toronto: Hakkert, 1974).

53 As quoted in the *Montreal Gazette*, 28 October 1914.

54 NAC, RG 2, vol. 1104, file 1176 E, "Enemy Alien Relief," 25 November 1914; and NAC, G2, vol. 3620, file 1175-1176, PC 2966, 25 November 1914.

55 *Montreal Gazette*, 30 October 1914.

56 See, for example, NAC, Robert Borden Papers, MG 26 H1(c), vol. 191, reel C-4388, page 106306, Prime Minister of Canada, the Rt. Hon. Sir Robert Borden to the Hon. Sam Hughes, Minister of Militia & Defence, 10 November 1914; ibid., pages 106283–4, "A. Torontonian" to the Rt. Hon. Sir Robert Borden, Prime Minister of Canada, 5 November 1914;

and ibid., pages 106269–71, E. Maud Cory to Premier Borden, 1 November 1914.

On the question of mischief-makers, the case of T.F. Greenhow stands out. Greenhow wrote dozens of letters to federal and provincial authorities as well as to British officials and mayors across the country regarding the threat of an imminent invasion of Canada by German Americans. After several investigations and reaching the limit of his patience, Col. A.P. Sherwood, Dominion Police Chief, concluded, "This man is crazy." NAC, RG 25 G1, vol. 1149, file 1057, Col. A.P. Sherwood, Chief of Dominion Police, to Sir Joseph Pope, Under Secretary of State for External Affairs, 2 December 1914.

57 The line of questioning followed similar questions found in the British memorandum on rules to be observed by police with regard to apprehended enemy aliens. The British document was forwarded to the Canadian government and appears to be the basis for the language contained on identification papers held by registered enemy aliens that were to be presented to police or militia on demand. For a copy of the British document, see NAC, Robert Borden Papers, MG 26 H1(c), vol. 287, reel C-4440, pages 106771–2, "Instructions Relative to the Internment and Treatment of Enemy Subjects," n.d.

58 NAC, RG 13 A2, vol. 191, file 139-159, E. Newcombe, Deputy Minister of Justice to Inspector J.L. Jennings, RNWMP, Edmonton, "Registration of Enemy Aliens," 19 November 1914.

59 It was reported, for instance, that in addition to the official set of queries, the Calgary Registrar, Inspector Pennefather, posed a series of other questions. "These he would not disclose, deeming it inexpedient." *Calgary Daily Herald*, 7 December 1914.

60 NAC, RG 2, vol. 3620, file 1172-1173, PC 2920, 18 November 1914.

61 NAC, RG 13 A2, vol. 191, file 139-159, W.J. Gallon, Provincial Conservative Association (Saskatchewan) to the Hon. C.J. Doherty, Minister of Justice, 1 December 1914; and Doherty to Gallon, 4 December 1914.

62 Armenians and Syrian Christians were exempt from registration and internment. The exemption would be granted only after consultation with the British government. "My Ministers enquire whether this direction [detention of Ottoman subjects] meant to include Syrians, of whom there are about three thousand in Canada. They are all Christians and quiet inoffensive people, which while nominally Ottoman subjects have come to Canada to escape Turkish rule. Officials in touch with these people are of opinion that their detention as a body unnecessary and inexpedient at the

present time." NAC, Robert Borden Papers, MG 26 HI(c), vol. 287, reel
C-4441, page 161406, Governor General to the Colonial Secretary, A.
Harcourt, 13 November 1914. See also Borden Papers, MG 26 HI(c),
vol. 192, reel C-4338, page 106387, V. Alexander Aprahsian to the Rt.
Hon. Sir Robert Borden, Prime Minister of Canada, 2 December 1914.

63 *Manitoba Free Press* (Winnipeg), 29 October 1914. On reports regarding
the establishment of the bureaus and registration, see *Edmonton Daily
Bulletin*, 2 November 1914; *Saskatoon Daily Star*, 2 November 1914;
and *Calgary Daily Herald*, 20 November 1914.

64 NAC, RG 18, vol. 471, file 605-620, cable, RNWMP Commissioner, A.B.
Perry, to Officer Commanding RNWMP, Dawson, Yukon Territory,
12 November 1914; and NAC, RG 24, vol. 4513, file 17-2-40 (1), Chief
Commissioner of Dominion Police, Col. A.P. Sherwood, to Col. J.P. Landry,
Officer Commanding 5th Division, Quebec City, 28 November 1914.

65 In his communication to the prime minister, Aikins underscored the fact
that "the people of the Brandon district have been considerably disturbed
and more so recently because in the dawn of the morning some of the
Brandon people saw an aeroplane flying over the city, and then going
West." NAC, Robert Borden Papers, MG 26 HI(c), vol. 191, reel C-4388,
page 106322, Sir James Aikins to the Rt. Hon. Sir Robert Borden, Prime
Minister of Canada, 12 November 1914; and ibid., page 106322A, Borden
to Aikins, 16 November 1914.

66 Ibid., page 106335, Alex Stewart, Victoria Mayor to the Rt. Hon. Sir
Robert Borden, Prime Minister of Canada, 9 November 1914; NAC, RG
13 A2, vol. 190, file 31-50, Deputy Minister, Department of Naval Service,
to E. Newcombe, Deputy Minister, Department of Justice, 13 November
1914; NAC, RG 2, vol. 3619, file 1171, cablegram, Hon. W.J. Bowser, BC
Attorney General to Hon. C.J. Doherty, Minister of Justice, 12 November
1914; and Ibid., PC 2880, 13 November 1914.

67 See, for example, *Saskatoon Daily Star*, 19 November 1914; and *Calgary
Daily Herald*, 14 December 1914.

68 *Edmonton Daily Bulletin*, 8 December 1914.

69 *Calgary Daily Herald*, 12 November 1914.

70 *Vancouver Sun*, 3 December 1914. In Vancouver alone it was reported that
no less than 1,550 aliens had applied for naturalization since the start of
the conflict, which exceeded the number recorded for the previous eight
months of the year. See ibid., 7 December 1914.

71 NAC, Robert Borden Papers, MG 26 HI(c), vol. 191, reel C-4388, page
106273, British Imperial Association (Toronto) to the Rt. Hon. Sir Robert
Borden, Prime Minister of Canada, 2 November 1914.

72  *Calgary Daily Herald,* 3 November 1914.

73  Ibid., 4 November 1914.

74  *Vancouver Sun,* 3 November 1914.

75  Ibid., 28 November 1914.

76  *Daily British Whig* (Kingston), 5 December 1914; *Edmonton Daily Bulletin,* 17 and 25 December 1914. On the Mueller case, see NAC, Robert Borden Papers, MG 26 H1(c), vol. 192, reel C-4388, pages 106371–4, Sir Edmund Osler, University of Toronto Chancellor, to the Rt. Hon. Sir Robert Borden, Prime Minister of Canada, 27 November 1914; and Borden to Osler, 28 November 1914; and ibid., pages 106409–10, letter, F. Neithdor, n.d.

77  On Canadian naturalization, see NAC, RG 25 G1, vol. 1157, file 105.

78  See *Calgary Daily Herald,* 11 November 1914; and *Saskatoon Daily Star,* 20 November 1914.

79  Ibid., 17 November 1914.

80  In Alberta, among enemy aliens who had been detained but released after having given their parole, it was observed that "most of those so treated have failed to report and their whereabouts cannot be traced." NAC, RG 25 G1, vol. 1150, file 1463, memorandum, Laurence Fortescue, RNWMP Comptroller, 26 November 1914.

81  NAC, RG 18, vol. 473, file 1915 – no. 10, part 1, "Schedule of prisoners of war handed over to the Department of Militia by the RNWMP for internment," 13 January 1915.

82  NAC, RG 24, vol. 4695, file 448-14-20, vol. 5, Major J.S. Stewart, Officer Commanding 25th Battery (Lethbridge), to Col. Cruickshank, Officer Commanding Military District No. 13 (Alberta), 16 January 1915; and Col. Cruickshank, Officer Commanding Military District, to Major General Wm. Otter, Internment Operations, Ottawa, 18 January 1915.

83  Ibid., Horrigan to Perry, 13 January 1915.

84  Ibid., file 1915 – no. 18, part 3, RNWMP Superintendent T.A. Wroughton, "G" Division, Edmonton, to Col. A.B. Perry, RNWMP Commissioner, 18 January 1915.

85  Ibid., file 1915 – no. 10, part 1, RNWMP Sergeant J. Kempston to RNWMP Superintendent J.A. McGibbon, Regina, 2 January 1915; and ibid., Col. A.B. Perry, RNWMP Commissioner, to L. Fortescue, RNWMP Comptroller, 6 January 1915.

86  NAC, RG 24, vol. 4277, file 34-1-3 (5), J. Hoandlen, Assistant Registrar of Enemy Aliens, Toronto, to Lieut. Col. Elliott, 2nd Military Division, 16 February 1915; and Elliot to Hoandlen, 19 February 1915.

87  NAC, RG 13 A2, vol. 191, file 339-357, Maj. General Wm. Otter, Office Commanding Internment Operations, to Co. A.P. Sherwood, Chief

Commissioner of Dominion Police, 19 February 1915. The tag "degener-ate" would stick with Michaelis, who despite some three hundred letters, petitions, pleas, and requests would fail to win his release and was deported in 1919 as a person with "little moral standing." See materials contained in NAC, RG 6 H1, vol. 751, file 1077.

88 NAC, RG 24, vol. 4277, file 34-1-3 (5), Justice E. Coatsworth, Office of Registrar of Enemy Aliens, to Lieut. F. Howland, 2nd Division, Toronto, 20 February 1915.

89 NAC, RG 18, vol. 1770, file 1914, no. 170, part 92-100, Statement Re: Austrian drilling at Alameda, 22 November 1914; RNWMP Crime Report, Weyburn Detachment, Re: F. Kozestkoc – Austrian Prisoner of War, 24 November 1914; and RNWMP Crime Report, Weyburn Detachment, Re: F. Korkoski – Austrian Prisoner of War, 27 November 1914.

90 NAC, RG 24, vol. 4277, file 34-1-3 (4), letter, Mrs J. Doonen to unidentified recipient, 10 November 1914.

91 NAC, RG 24, vol. 4695, file 448-14-20 (6), Acting Adjutant, 101st Regiment, to the Officer Commanding, 101st Regiment, Edmonton, 30 November 1914; and Acting Officer Commanding, 101st Regiment, to the Officer Commanding Military District No. 13 (Alberta), 30 November 1914.

92 NAC, RG 24, vol. 4413, file 26-5-12 (3), O.C.F. Company, 49th Regiment, to Col. G. Hunter Ogilvie, A.A.G. 3rd Division, 24 November 1914.

93 NAC, RG 18, vol. 2174, RNWMP Cpl. T. Wiltshire to the Officer Commanding "C" Division, "Re: Austrians and Germans order in council Sept. 3rd," 9 November 1914.

94 Ibid., RNWMP Const. Fred Allan to the Officer Commanding "C" Division, "Re: War Conditions – Radisson Detachment," 21 November 1914; and Officer Commanding "C" Division to Const. Allan, 24 November 1914.

95 NAC, Robert Borden Papers, MG 26 H1(c), vol. 287, reel C-4440, pages 161278–82, B.B. Cubitt, War Office, London, to General Officer Commanding-in-Chief, Salisbury, 13 November 1914; and ibid., page 161277, B. Cubitt, War Office, to the Under Secretary of State, Colonial Office, 15 November 1914.

96 Ibid., page 161276, L. Harcourt, Colonial Office to the Governor General of Canada, 18 November 1914.

97 *Daily British Whig* (Kingston), 25 November 1914. See also *Saskatoon Phoenix*, 1 December 1914.

98 On the Wagner case, see NAC RG 18, vol. 470, file 524. Regarding the rumoured plot, see *Calgary Daily Herald*, 13 November 1914; and *Lethbridge Daily Herald*, 17 November 1914. The same fate appears to

have befallen Joseph P. Tabinski, who was also tasked with maintaining the quality of the water supply at the Salisbury camp. Discharged because of his Austro-Hungarian nationality, he was arrested on his arrival in Canada and confined at the Halifax Citadel. Tabinski, however, had lived previously in the US for eight years. Friends there hoped to gain his release, convincing US Senator C.E. Townsend to petition for his freedom. On receiving the request, the undersecretary of state for external affairs, Sir Joseph Pope, communicated with Colonel A.P. Sherwood, dominion police commissioner, that "it does seem to me that there would not be much risk in obliging the Senator in this matter, as he, I believe, is a factor of some importance in the United States." On the Tabinski case, see NAC, RG 25 G1, vol. 1151, file 1.

99 "Pilgrims arrive by train loads and boat loads ... Germans planned that they could thus with one stroke capture the big guns which guard the St. Lawrence against the assault of hostile craft. They could seize the rifle and ammunition factories and would be in a position to dominate eastern Canada and open the gates to a general invasion." Ibid., 1 December 1914. See also *Edmonton Daily Bulletin*, 2 December 1914.

100 *Manitoba Free Press* (Winnipeg), 3 November 1914.

101 See *Globe* (Toronto), 6 February 1915; *Edmonton Daily Bulletin*, 9 February 1915; and *Manitoba Tribune*, 9 February 1915.

102 NAC, Robert Borden Papers, MG 26 H1(c), vol. 191, reel C-4388, pages 106348–9, E. Carrington, Vice-President, Thiel Detective Agency, to the Hon. Sam Hughes, Minister of Militia and Defence, 18 November 1914.

103 NAC, RG 76, vol. 603, file 884866 (4), W.D. Scott, Superintendent of Immigration, "Memorandum – Mr. Mitchell," 15 April 1915.

104 Dmytro Apostal, removed from a train at the Windsor–Detroit crossing, was arrested as an enemy alien and sent to Fort Henry as a prisoner of war. Major Dawson, the officer commanding, noted upon Apostal's arrival: "He is sixty three years of age, grey-haired, toothless, a bent old man." Being penniless, he was also supported by his children, who lived in the United States. Apostal was attempting to reach them when arrested. Dawson observed "although he is an Austrian subject, a mistake was made in taking him off the train at Windsor, Ont., and not allowing him to proceed to his destination, in the United States." NAC, RG 24, vol. 4413, file 26-3-12 (2), Major Dawson, 14th Regiment, Kingston, to the Officer Commanding 3rd Division, Kingston, 18 December 1914.

105 See, for example, NAC, RG 24, vol. 4277, file 34-1-3 (3), Fleming, Drake & Foster to Col. A.P. Sherwood, Commissioner of Dominion Police, 30 October 1914. See also *Daily British Whig* (Kingston), 3 February 1915.

106  NAC, RG 76, vol. 603, file 884866 (4), C.E. Wilcox, Immigration
     Inspector-in-Charge, Niagara Falls, to W.D. Scott, Superintendent of
     Immigration, 16 April 1915; and Scott to Wilcox, 28 April 1915.

107  NAC, RG 25 G1, vol. 1151, file 1, Governor General to L. Harcourt,
     Colonial Secretary, 27 November 1914.

108  NAC, Robert Borden Papers, MG 26 H1(c), vol. 191, reel C-4388, pages
     106365–6, S. Schwartz to the Rt. Hon. Sir Robert Borden, Prime Minister
     of Canada, 26 November 1914; and Borden to Schwartz, 30 November
     1914. See also ibid., page 106376, Col. A.P. Sherwood, Chief
     Commissioner of Police, to the Registrar of Alien Enemies, Toronto,
     28 November 1914.

109  *Vancouver Sun*, 26 November 1914. A report to the annual meeting of
     Vancouver's Civic Employment and Relief Association showed that no
     less than $150,000 was spent on city relief efforts during the period
     November 1914 and March 1915. A sum of $72,424.20 was expended
     on food, beds, fuel, transportation, and the like. The additional $75,000
     was appropriated for relief work by the city at $2 a day. See *Vancouver
     Sun*, 10 April 1915.

110  The Associated Charities in Calgary, for example, opened up and oper-
     ated a relief bunkhouse that accommodated a hundred men and eventu-
     ally more, apparently the first shelter of its kind in the country. See
     *Calgary Daily Herald*, 19 November 1914.

111  More than in a political sense was the danger viewed to be real. Increas-
     ingly, it was thought that the growing number of criminal cases was due
     to the high level of unemployment. See *Manitoba Free Press* (Winnipeg),
     4 and 6 November 1914. On the question of liability, see Bohdan Kordan,
     *Enemy Aliens, Prisoners of War: Internment in Canada during the Great
     War* (Montreal and Kingston: McGill-Queen's University Press, 2002),
     16–29.

112  NAC, RG 13 A2, vol. 1929, file 8/1917, D. Atkinson, Police Magistrate,
     to Col. A.P. Sherwood, Chief Commissioner of Police, 13 January 1915.

113  NAC, RG 24, vol. 4277, file 34-1-3 (5), Justice E. Coatsworth, Office of
     Registrar of Enemy Aliens, to Lieut. F. Howland, 2nd Division, Toronto,
     17 December 1915. The precarious position of aliens made them an easy
     target. Allegedly failing to relinquish their ways and incapable of compre-
     hending the nuances of British citizenship, they became objects of deri-
     sion and ostracism, leading to calls for their removal. This objection
     could be attributed in part to racial ideology that framed social accep-
     tance in socio-biological terms. See the discussion in George Buri,
     "'Enemies within Our Gates': Brandon's Alien Detention Centre during
     the Great War," *Manitoba History* 56 (2007): 9–11.

114 The events are described in NAC, RG 18, vol. 470, file 557, Col. A.B. Perry, RNWMP Commissioner, to L. Fortescue, RNWMP Comptroller, 20 November 1914; and *Calgary Daily Herald*, 9 December 1914.

115 NAC, RG 24, vol. 4542, file 75-1-25, Major B.A. Ingraham, 24th Overseas Battery, to A.A.G, 6th Division, Halifax, 12 December 1914; A.A.G, 6th Division, to Officer Commanding, 94th Regiment, Sydney, 15 December 1914; and Officer Commanding, 94th Regiment, to the A.A.G., 6th Division, Halifax, 16 December 1914.

116 PAO, Attorney General Records, RG 4-32 (1915), file 726, letter, Siegfried Atkinson, Police Magistrate, Haileybury, Ont., 26 March 1915; and *Globe* (Toronto), 22 March 1914.

117 Ibid., J.E. Rogers, Superintendent, Ontario Provincial Police to the Ontario Attorney General, 13 April 1915.

118 *Vancouver Sun*, 7 April 1915; NAC, RG 25 G1, vol. 1161, file 696, J.D. McNiven, Fair Wages Officer, to F.A. Ackland, Deputy Minister of Labour, Ottawa, 7 April 1915; and NAC, RG 13 B8, vol. 1368, file 2, UK Ambassador to the United States, Sir Cecil Spring Rice, to the Governor General, 10 April 1915.

119 *Vancouver Sun*, 9 and 12 April 1915.

120 NAC, RG 25 G1, vol. 1161, file 696, J.D. McNiven, Fair Wages Officer, to F.A. Ackland, Deputy Minister of Labour, Ottawa, 20 April 1915.

121 NAC, RG 13 A2, vol. 1929, file 10/1917, part 1, M.B. MacLennan, Chief Constable, to Col. A.P. Sherwood, Chief Commissioner of Dominion Police, 12 April 1915.

122 Ibid., "Certified Copy of a Report of the Committee of the Privy Council, Approved by His Royal Highness the Governor General on the 24th April, 1915."

123 *Vancouver Sun*, 8 April 1915.

124 USNA, Department of State Records, file no. 763.72115/664, Frederick Ryder, US Consul-General, Winnipeg to the Secretary of State, Washington, 27 April 1915. Other reports placed the number at two thousand.

125 In Calgary, for instance, the issue was the civic labour bureau, which provided work on a "first come, first serve" basis. Foreigners regularly camped out in front of the bureau doors and in this way crowded out others. *Calgary Daily Herald*, 4 and 7 May 1915.

126 On the rioting in Victoria after the sinking of the *Lusitania*, see Arthur Richards, "(Re)Imagining Germanness: Victoria's Germans and the 1915 Lusitania Riot" (MA thesis, University of Victoria, 2012), 57–74.

127 See, for example, *Vancouver Sun*, 10 and 11 May 1915; *Calgary Daily Herald*, 14 May 1915; and *Regina Daily Post*, 17 May 1915.

128  See *Globe* (Toronto), 13 May 1915.

129  *Manitoba Frees Press* (Winnipeg), 20 May 1915. See also *Regina Leader Post*, 15 May 1915; *Saskatoon Phoenix*, 15 May 1915; *Saskatoon Daily Star*, 17 May 1915; and *Calgary Daily Herald*, 17 May 1915.

130  *Vancouver Sun*, 19 May 1915.

131  NAC, RG 13 A2, vol. 194, file 1007-1026, RNWMP Inspector H. Townsend to Officer Commanding "G" Division, Edmonton, 30 May 1915.

132  Ibid., Officer Commanding "G" Division to Col. A.B. Perry, RNWMP Commissioner, 1 June 1915. See also *Globe* (Toronto), 14 May 1915.

133  *Vancouver Sun*, 20, 21, 25, 26, 27, and 28 May 1915; and *Calgary Daily Herald*, 20 and 25 May 1915.

134  *British Colonist* (Victoria), 26 May 1915; and *Vancouver Sun*, 29 May 1915.

135  On the strike, see *Fernie Free Press*, 18 June 1915. See also *Calgary Daily Herald*, 8 and 9 June 1915; and *Saskatoon Phoenix*, 9 June 1915.

136  NAC, RG 18, vol. 490, file 433-1915, Confidential Report, J.D. McNiven, Fair Wages Officer, to F.A. Ackland, Deputy Minister of Labour, Ottawa, 23 June 1915.

137  The incident was reported in detail in the *Fernie Free Press*, 11, 18, 25 June. The situation at Fernie was also the subject of commentary in the authoritative industry monthly *Canadian Mining Journal* 36, no. 6 (June 1915).

138  *Vancouver Sun*, 12 June 1915.

139  NAC, RG 13 A2, vol. 1929, file 10/1917, part 1, memorandum, Minister of Justice to Major General Sir Wm. Otter, 26 June 1915.

140  NAC, RG 2, vol. 1118, file 1329 E, PC 1501.

141  *Globe* (Toronto), 28 June 1915.

142  NAC, RG 18, vol. 490, file 433-1915, J.D. McNiven, Fair Wages Officer, to F.A. Ackland, Deputy Minister of Labour, Ottawa, 19 June 1915. On the Hillcrest strike generally, see *Calgary Daily Herald*, 17 and 19 June 1915; and various reports contained in NAC, RG 18, vol. 490, file 433-195.

143  NAC, RG 24, vol. 4542, file 75-1-25, Col. Thompson, A.A.G. 6th Division, Halifax, to Col. Sherwood, Chief Commissioner of Police, 27 June 1915; NAC, RG 13 A2, vol. 1929, file 10/1917, part 1, H. Prudhomme, General Manager, Acadia Coal Company, to Col. Sherwood, Chief Commissioner of Police, 29 June 1915; and ibid., telegram, Hector McInnes to E.L. Newcombe, Deputy Minister of Justice, 30 June 1915.

144  NAC, RG 18, vol. 476, file 1915, no.18, part 5, E. Salmon to the Rt. Hon. Sir Robert Borden, 30 June 1915; Borden to Salmon, 6 July 1915; and

Col. A.B. Perry, RNWMP Commissioner to A. Blount, Private Secretary, Prime Minister's Office, 4 July 1915.

145 NAC, Borden Papers, MG 26 H1, vol. 39, reel C-4231, page 16809, Henry Lyon, Mayor of Blairmore, to the Rt. Hon. Robert Borden, Prime Minister of Canada, 29 October 1914; and Borden Papers, MG 26 H1, vol. 191, reel C-4388, page 106218, John Herron to the Rt. Hon. Robert Borden, Prime Minister of Canada, 31 October 1914.

146 *Calgary Daily Herald*, 10 November 1914.

147 See, for instance, *Edmonton Daily Bulletin*, 6 November 1914; and *Calgary Daily Herald*, 12 November 1914. Contrary to the allegations, American investigators would relay that there was no mistreatment of interned civilians in Germany and that conditions were much the same as in Britain, a conclusion officially conveyed to the US government by its representatives who were responsible for Allied interests in Germany. See *Edmonton Daily Bulletin*, 17 November 1914.

148 NAC, RG 13 A2, vol. 189, file 1639-1659, F.H. Williamson, Deputy Commissioner, Dominion Parks Branch, to W. Cory, Deputy Minister, Department of Interior, "Memorandum: Regarding the Employment of German and Austrian prisoners in the Dominion Parks," 28 October 1914.

149 *Edmonton Daily Bulletin*, 26 November 1914.

150 NAC, RG 13 B8, vol. 1368, file "1 November – 31 December," Sir George Perley, Canadian High Commissioner to the UK, to the Rt. Hon. Sir Robert Borden, Prime Minister of Canada, 2 November 1914.

151 NAC, RG 13 A2, vol. 189, file 1639-1659, C.H. Payne, Private Secretary to the Acting Prime Minister, Sir George Foster, 13 November 1914.

152 NAC, RG 18, vol. 470, file 548, M.L. Jordon, General Superintendent, Department of Public Works, Province of Alberta, to RNWMP Superintendent C. Starnes, 9 November 1914; and Col. A.B. Perry, RNWMP Commissioner, to C. Starnes, RNWMP Superintendent, 13 November 1914.

153 *Globe* (Toronto), 13 November 1914.

154 *Daily British Whig* (Kingston), 13 November 1914; and NAC, RG 24, vol. 4413, file 26-3-12 – vol. 3, Major H.J. Dawson, 14th Regiment, to Officer Commanding 3rd Division, 1 December 1914.

155 NAC, RG 2, vol. 5299, file 2839-3078, PC 2924, 1 December 1914.

156 *Daily British Whig* (Kingston), 10 and 16 December 1914. The creation of the Petawawa internment camp is briefly described in Brenda Lee-Whiting, "Enemy Aliens: German Canadians on the Home Front," *Beaver* 53 (October–November 1989): 55.

157  *Saskatoon Phoenix*, 30 December 1914.

158  USNA, Department of State Records, file no. 763.72115/345, Felix
     Johnson, US Consul, Kingston, to the Secretary of State, Washington,
     17 December 1914.

159  Ibid., 11 December 1914.

160  The idea of putting interned enemy aliens to work on clearing land for
     agricultural purposes in northern Ontario appears to have been the inspi-
     ration of A.D. Davidson, a principal in the land development firm
     Saskatchewan Valley and Manitoba Land Company and land agent for
     the Canadian Northern Railway. W.H. Hearst, who represented the north-
     ern Ontario constituency of Sault Ste Marie and was minister of lands,
     forests and mines (before becoming premier), favourably received the pro-
     posal. PAO, RG 14-157, reel MS 5542, "Kapuskasing Detention Camp
     Re: Clearing Land," A.D. Davidson to the Hon. Sam Hughes, Minister
     of Militia and Defence, "Interned Aliens," 27 November 1914; A.D.
     Davidson to the Hon. W.H. Hearst, Premier of Ontario, 30 November
     1914; and Premier Hearst to J.F. Whitson, Commissioner, Northern
     Development Branch, Ontario Department of Lands, Forests and Mines,
     1 December 1914.

161  For records relating to the possible market sale of wood from the camps
     to mills in Ontario and Quebec, see NAC, RG 17, vol. 2787, file 240779.

162  PAO, RG 14-157, reel MS 5542, "Kapuskasing Detention Camp Re:
     Clearing Land," the Hon. W.H. Hearst to J.F. Whitson, 11 December
     1914; and J.F. Whitson to A.J. Stewart, Government Road Inspector,
     5 January 1914.

163  USNA, Department of State Records, file no. 763.72115/338, the Rt.
     Hon. Sir Robert Borden to W.H. Bradley, United States Consul General,
     Montreal, 9 December 1914.

164  *Saskatoon Phoenix*, 10 March 1915.

165  USNA, Department of State Records, file no. 763.72115/338, Major
     General Wm. Otter, Director of Internment Operations, to US Consul
     General, W.H. Bradley, 12 December 1914. NAC RG 25 G1, vol. 1156,
     file 48-1, Under Secretary of State for External Affairs to the Hon. C.J.
     Doherty, Minister of Justice, 13 April 1915. See also *Saskatoon Phoenix*,
     14 January 1915.

166  NAC, RG 24, vol. 4277, file 34-1-3 (5), Major Clarke, O.C. Kapuskasing
     Internment Camp to the Officer Commanding, 2nd Military Division,
     19 January 1914. The camp, however, was laid out to accommodate one
     thousand prisoners of war. See USNA, Department of State Records, file
     no. 763.72115/581, M.B. Kirk, US Consul, Orillia, to the US Secretary of
     State, Washington, 27 March 1915.

167 NAC, RG 17, vol. 2787, file 240779, J.A. Stuart to the Hon. Martin Burrell, Minister of Agriculture, 24 February 1915.

168 PAO, RG 14 -157, reel MS 5542, "Kapuskasing Detention Camp Re: Saw Mill," Commissioner J.F. Whitson, Northern Development Branch to G.H. Grisdale, Director of Experimental Farms, Ottawa, 25 March 1915.

169 *Saskatoon Phoenix*, 10 March 1915. See also USNA, Department of State Records, file no. 763.72115/644, Felix Johnson, US Consul, Kingston, to the US Secretary of State, 21 April 1915.

170 USNA, Department of State Records, file no. 763.72115/636, W.H. Bradley, US Consul General, to the US Secretary of State, Washington, 20 April 1915; and file no. 763.72115/664, Felix Johnson, US Consul, Kingston, to the Secretary of State, Washington, 21 April 1915. For a detailed description of the Spirit Lake Camp, see P. Melnycky, "Badly Treated in Every Way: The Internment of Ukrainians in Quebec during the First World War," in M. Diakowsky, ed., *The Ukrainian Experience in Quebec* (Toronto: Basilian Press, 1994), 52–78.

171 NAC, RG 25 G1, vol. 1150, file 1463, J.G. Foster, US Consul General, to the Under Secretary of State for External Affairs, Sir Joseph Pope, 16 December 1914; and Pope to Foster, 21 December 1914.

172 See NAC, RG 24, vol. 4513, file 17-2-40, vol. 1, Officer Commanding 5th Division, Quebec City, to the Major General Wm. Otter, Officer Commanding Internment Operations, 19 December 1914; and Otter to Officer Commanding 5th Division, 21 December 1914.

173 Ibid., Officer Commanding 5th Division, to Major General Wm. Otter, 29 March 1915.

174 NAC, RG 13 A2, vol. 1929, file 10/1917, part 1, unidentified letter to the Auditor General, 4 January 1915; ibid., file 591-614/1915, "Memorandum," 25 March 1915; ibid., file 10/1917, part 1, Major General Wm. Otter, Director of Internment Operations to the Minister of Justice, 18 February 1915; ibid., Minister of Justice to the Governor General in Council, 18 February 1915; NAC, RG 25 G1, vol. 1156, file 48–1, "Memorandum of Expenditure on Account of Internment Operations: February 1st to March 31st 1915"; and NAC, RG 13 A2, vol. 1929, file 10/1917, part 1, Minister of Justice to the Governor General in Council, 27 May 1915.

175 See ibid., Lieut. Col. D. Macpherson, Staff Officer, Internment Operations, to the Minister of Justice, 10 April 1915; and Major General Wm. Otter to the Minister of Justice, 19 June 1915.

176 NAC, RG 24, vol. 4513, file 17-2-40 (1), Major General Otter, Officer Commanding Internment Operations, to the Officer Commanding 5th Military Division, Quebec City, 16 December 1914; A.A.G. 5th Division

to S.O.O. 5th Division, 21 January 1915; NAC, RG 24, vol. 4278, file 34-1-3 (7), Major F. Clarke, Officer Commanding Kapuskasing Internment Camp, to A.A.G. 2nd Military Division, Toronto, 5 April 1915; and ibid., file 34-1-3 (8) Major F. Clarke, Officer Commanding Kapuskasing Internment Camp, to Major General Wm. Otter, Internment Operations, 27 April 1915.

177 NAC, RG 24, vol. 4694, file 448-14-20 (1), Major General Wm. Otter, Officer Commanding Internment Operations, to R.B. Chadwick, Superintendent of Neglected Children, 6 February 1915; Chadwick to Otter, 10 February 1915; and Otter to Chadwick, 16 February 1915.

178 NAC, RG 24, vol. 4542, file 75-1-25, A.A.G. 6th Military Division, Halifax, to Major T. Lydiard, 14th Hussars, Kentville, Nova Scotia, 15 December 1914. In the case of Herbert Wirtz and his family, Major General Otter was prepared to make an exception given their penniless condition. Although his case did not meet "the tenor of regulations," Otter indicated that he "would not object to straining a point and providing for the subsistence of the whole family in their own family." The arrangement, however, was that Wirtz would be interned and then a supply of food provided his family, "the cost of which will be paid by the Government on properly certified claims being presented." NAC, RG 24, vol. 4513, file 17-2-40 (2), Major General Wm. Otter, Officer Commanding Internment Operations, to the Officer Commanding 5th Division, Quebec, 27 February 1915.

179 See NAC, RG 6 H1, vol. 819, file 18, "Payment of Prisoners of War," Major General Wm. Otter, Officer Commanding Internment Operations, to the Director General of Engineer Services, Department of Militia and Defence, 14 January 1915.

180 NAC, RG 24, vol. 4541, file 73-1-6, telegram, Major General Wm. Otter, Officer Commanding Internment Operations to Officer Commanding 6th Division, 3 March 1915; Major P. Benoit, C.R.C.E. 6th Division, Halifax, to Major W. Gibson, Q.M.G, 6th Division, 11 March 1915; and Officer Commanding 6th Division, Halifax, 24 March 1915.

181 NAC, RG 24, vol. 4513, file 17-2-40 (1), Major General Wm. Otter, Officer Commanding Internment Operations, to Officer Commanding 5th Division, Quebec, 5 February 1915; and RG 24, vol. 4277, file 34-1-3 (5), Major General Wm. Otter, Officer Commanding Internment Operations to Officer Commanding 2nd Division, Toronto, 5 February 1915

182 NAC, Robert Borden Papers, MG 26 H1, vol. 287, reel C-4440, page 161315, Governor General to Laurence Harcourt, Secretary of the Colonies, 27 November 1914.

183 A request to transfer prisoners of war from Barbados to Canada was also made at a later date by the governor of the Barbados, who was "anxious to find accommodation elsewhere for twelve or possibly more prisoners, since, owing to local conditions, existing accommodation for prisoners of war cannot be enlarged save at a relatively great cost." The Canadian government was also asked to accept prisoners from other West Indian colonies that were faced with similar difficulties. As with the previous arrangements with Jamaica and Bermuda, the Barbados government was prepared to defray the cost of transportation of prisoners of war to Canada and their maintenance while in Canada. A "small number from other West India Colonies" were also sent. See ibid., vol. 289, reel c-4443, pages 164991–2, A. Bonar Law, Secretary of the Colonies, to the Governor General of Canada, 13 June 1916; and page 164917, the Governor General to Bonar Law, 15 July 1916.

184 *Amherst Daily News*, 18 January 1915; NAC, RG 13 A2, vol. 1929, file 10/1917, part 1, Major General William Otter, Officer Commanding Internment Operations, to the Hon. C.J. Doherty, Minister of Justice, 1 April 1915; *Calgary Daily Herald*, 17 April 1915; and *Daily British Whig* (Kingston), 7 May 1915.

185 *Manitoba Free Press* (Winnipeg), 18 May 1915.

186 See BC Ministry of Transportation Records, Okanagan District (1915), file 1752 – section 1, A.D. Ford, Union Club, to Sir Richard McBride, Premier of British Columbia, 5 February; BC Premier Richard McBride to the Hon. Thomas Taylor, Minister of Public Works, 10 February 1915; and the Hon. Thomas Taylor, Minister of Public Works, to R.F. Green, Member of Parliament, 10 February 1915.

187 BC Ministry of Transportation Records , Okanagan District (1915), section 1, Hon. Thomas Taylor, BC Minister of Public Works to R.F. Green, Member of Parliament, 10 February 1915; Major General Wm. Otter, Officer Commanding Internment Operations, to the Hon. Thomas Taylor, 22 March 1915.

188 NAC, RG 13 A2, vol. 1929, file 10/1917, part 1, telegram, Major W. Ridgway-Wilson, Department of Aliens, Vancouver, to Hon. C.J. Doherty, Minister of Justice, 12 April 1915; Chief Constable M.B. MacLennan to Col. A.P. Sherwood, Chief Commissioner of Police, 12 April 1915; and Malcolm Reid, Immigration Inspector for British Columbia, to Col. A.P. Sherwood, Chief Commissioner of Police, 13 April 1915.

189 See NAC, RG 24, vol. 4694, file 448-14-20, vol. 2, Major W. Ridgway-Wilson, Department of Alien Reservists to Capt. J.A. Birney, Officer Commanding Lethbridge Internment Camp, 31 May 1915.

190 BC Ministry of Transportation Records, Okanagan District (1915), file 1752 – section 1, "Memo for the Deputy Minister and Public Works Engineer, J.P. Napier, Assistant Public Works Engineer," 18 May 1915.

191 BC Ministry of Transportation Records, North Okanagan and Salmon Arm Districts (1915), file 211, Ernest Groves with accompanying petition to the Hon. Thomas Taylor, BC Minister of Public Works, 16 June 1915; and Taylor to Groves, 25 June.

192 BC Ministry of Transportation Records, Okanagan District (1915), file 1752 – section 1, the Hon. Thomas Taylor, BC Minister of Public Works, to Major W. Ridgway-Wilson, Department of Alien Reservists, 28 June 1915; and the Hon. Thomas Taylor, BC Minister of Public Works, to L.W. Shatford, M.P.P., 28 July 1915.

193 *Fernie Free Press*, 18 June 1915.

194 Ibid., 11 June 1915.

195 See NAC, RG 24, vol. 4694, file 448-14-20 (2), Capt. J.A. Birney to the Officer Commanding Military District No. 13, Calgary, 3 June 1915; and Col. E.A. Cruickshank, Officer Commanding Military District No. 13, to Major General Wm. Otter, Officer Commanding Internment Operations, 5 June 1915.

196 For details of the discussions that led to the establishment of the first camp in the national parks, see Bill Waiser, *Park Prisoners: The Untold Story of Western Canada's National Parks, 1915–1946* (Calgary and Saskatoon: Fifth House, 1995), 12; and E.J. Hart, *J.B. Harkin, Father of Canada's National Parks* (Edmonton: University of Alberta Press, 2010), 120–2.

197 Canada, House of Commons, *Hansard*, 15 February 1916, 849.

198 *Annual Report of the Department of the Interior*, 1916, 4.

199 NAC, RG 24, vol. 4694, file 448-14-20 (2), telegram, Major General Otter to Col. E.A. Cruickshank, Officer Commanding Military District No. 13, 31 May 1915; NAC, RG 24, vol. 4729, file 3, Col. E.A. Cruickshank to Capt. Birney, Officer Commanding Lethbridge Internment Camp, 10 June 1915; and S.J. Clarke, Superintendent Rocky Mountains Park, Department of the Interior, to Col. E.A. Cruikshank, 17 June 1915.

200 *Calgary Daily Herald*, 15 June 1915; NAC, RG 24, vol. 4729, file 3, Capt. Lorrie, Senior Ordnance Officer, Military District No. 13, to Col. E.A. Cruickshank, 15 June 1915; and Cruikshank to Lorrie, 17 June 1915. Details of the installation of the Castle Mountain camp were recorded in a camp diary. For a record of the setting up and opening of the camp, see B. Kordan and P. Melnycky, eds, *In the Shadow of the Rockies: Diary of the Castle Mountain Internment Camp, 1915–1917* (Edmonton: CIUS Press, 1991), 25–8.

201 The particulars relating to the establishment and opening of the Revelstoke internment camp were reported in detail in the *Mail Herald*
(Revelstoke), 17, 28, and 31 July. See also Waiser, *Park Prisoners*, 17–18
and Kordan, *Enemy Aliens, Prisoners of War*, 105–7.

202 Prof. Waiser notes that Harkin's request for the internees resulted from a
conversation he had with General Otter, who conveyed to him "he could
have as many aliens as he could possibly use." Waiser, *Park Prisoners*, 24.
See also Hart, *J.B. Harkin*, 126-7.

203 On particulars regarding the creation of the Otter Internment Camp, see
Waiser, *Park Prisoners*, 21–2, and Kordan, *Enemy Aliens, Prisoners of
War*, 105–7.

204 *Crag and Canyon* (Banff), 12 June 1915.

205 *Saskatoon Daily Star*, 10 October 1914.

206 *Vancouver Sun*, 29 October 1914.

207 The stampede was a result of advertisements posted late May in a number of ethnic newspapers that three thousand construction jobs on the
Hudson Bay Railway would become available. The men being hungry
and without any work prospects, the situation in The Pas deteriorated,
and violence was narrowly averted after the RNWMP police took it upon
themselves to hand out loaves of bread. The local police officials recommended that the enemy aliens be placed on open flat train cars and sent
back to Winnipeg. This idea was quickly dismissed, only to be followed
by the directive to arrest all those who could no longer support themselves. For reports and correspondence relating to the desperate situation
in The Pas, see NAC, RG 18, vol. 490, file 396-398.

208 NAC, RG 24, vol. 4695, file 448-14-20 (6), Lieut. Col. W.A. Griesbach,
C.O. 49th Battalion, to the Officer Commanding Military District
No. 13, Calgary, 2 January 1915; and RNWMP Superintendent, "G"
Division, to the Officer Commanding Military District No. 13, Calgary,
5 January 1915.

209 NAC, RG 18, vol. 1789, file 170, "Crime Report – Re: Iwan Milan –
Prisoner of War," 15 January 1915. For a discussion of the existential
threat posed by the enemy alien, see Kordan, *Enemy Aliens, Prisoners of
War*, 20–1.

210 On the Therkild Therkildsen/Thomas Ford case, see NAC, RG 25 G1,
vol. 1151, file 1915-1.

211 On social pressure and the changing of foreign-sounding surnames, see
Moogk, "Uncovering the Enemy Within: British Columbians and the
German Menace," 67.

212 For correspondence and an affidavit relating to the detention of imperial
Russian subjects, see NAC, RG 24, vol. 4278, file 34-1-3 (7).

213 NAC, RG 18, vol. 1770, file 170, RNWMP Superintendent, Regina District, re: Thomas Koch, 27 April 1915.

214 For information on the Mike Bundziock predicament, see NAC, RG 24, vol. 4278, file 34-1-3 (8).

215 See NAC, RG 13 A2, vol. 192, file 617-637 (1915), Regio Consolato d'Italia nel Canada, Montreal, to Col. A.P. Sherwood, Chief of Dominion Police, 23 March 1915.

216 The Henion case is documented in NAC, RG 13 A2, vol. 192, file 640–660 (1915).

### CHAPTER THREE

1 NAC, RG 24, vol. 4721, file 1, personal letter, Joseph Leskiw to "General Commander Alberta's Military Forces in Calgary," n.d. See also ibid., file 2, copy of J. Kondro letter to Brigadier General E.A. Cruickshank, 8 February 1916.

2 NAC, RG 24, vol. 4721, file 2, Captain P.M. Spence, Camp Commandant, Banff, to the Officer Commanding Military District No. 13, 17 February 1916.

3 For an account of the escape, see ibid., file 3, "Board of Inquiry," 2 May 1916.

4 NAC, RG 6, vol. 759, file 3656, J. Marchuk to Major P.M. Spence, "Vpovazhnyi Pane Maiora," 22 October 1916.

5 Ibid., Major P.M. Spence, Camp Commandant, Banff, to General Wm. Otter, Director, Internment Operations, 27 October 1916; and Major General Wm. Otter to the RNWMP Commissioner, 10 November 1916.

6 See, for example, ibid., J. Marchuk to Major P.M. Spence, "Proz'ba do Pana Maiora," 22 November 1916.

7 NAC, RG 24, vol. 4721, file 1, letter of J. Leskiw, n.d.

8 NAC, RG 18, vol. 500, file RCMP 1916-31 (3), Major General Otter to the RNWMP Comptroller, 4 March 1916.

9 NAC, RG 13 B8, vol. 1768, file 1 (1 November–31 December 1914), L. Harcourt, Colonial Secretary, to the Duke of Connaught, the Governor of General of Canada, 17 December 1914.

10 NAC, RG 13 B8, vol. 1368, file 7 January – 27 February 1915, L. Harcourt, Colonial Secretary, to the Duke of Connaught, the Governor of General of Canada, 9, 12 January and 1 February 1915.

11 See RG 25, G1, vol. 1156, file 48-1, S. Voska, Bohemian-American Relief Committee, to Sir Cecil Spring Rice, British Embassy, Washington, 28 December 1914; Sir Cecil Spring Rice, British Embassy, Washington,

"Dear Sir," 9 January 1915; Col. A.P. Sherwood, Chief Commissioner of Dominion Police, to Major General Otter, Officer Commanding Internment Operations, 19 January 1915; Major General Otter to Sir Joseph Pope, Under Secretary of State for External Affairs, 23 January 1915; J. Marhonic, National Croatian Society of the United States, to Sir Cecil Spring Rice, British Embassy, Washington, 16 February 1915; ibid., file 7 January–27 February 1915, L. Harcourt, Colonial Secretary, to the Duke of Connaught, the Governor of General of Canada, 22 February 1915; and ibid., file 2 March–30 April 1915, L. Harcourt, Colonial Secretary, to the Governor of General, 2 March 1915. NAC, RG 13 A2, vol. 193, file 813-832 (1915), E. Newcombe, Deputy Minister of Justice, to S. Scott, Member of Parliament, 15 March 1915. NAC, RG 25 G1, vol. 1156, file 48-1, M. Pupin, Royal Consulate General of Serbia, to Sir Cecil Spring Rice, British Embassy, Washington, 8 March 1915; Sir Cecil Spring Rice, British Embassy, Washington, to the Duke of Connaught, the Governor of General of Canada, 17 March 1915; and Major General Otter to Sir Joseph Pope, Under Secretary of State for External Affairs, 31 March 1915. NAC, RG 6 H3, vol. 793, file 2165B, Polish Central Relief Committee, "To the Government of the Dominion of Canada," 14 April 1915; and Sir Joseph Pope, Under Secretary of State for External Affairs, to the Rt. Hon. Robert Borden, Prime Minister of Canada, 19 April 1915.

12 NAC, RG 13 vol. 200, file 262-282, M. Kruszka, *Kuryer Polski*, 12 February 1915; and NAC, RG 6 H3, vol. 793, file 2165B, Polish Central Relief Committee, "To the Government of the Dominion of Canada," 14 and 19 April 1915.

13 Interventions on behalf of interned aliens considered "friendly" were frequent. When political pressure was applied, the director of internment operations would relent, resulting in the slow process of identifying and liberating such individuals. Otter would abide by the distinction and agree to follow the policy as a matter of principle. But as matter of practice, the policy could not be applied generally since the conditions in the country would not allow for it. It was also, according to Otter, "impossible for us to select the 'sheep from the goats' as it were." NAC, RG 13 A2, vol. 195, file 1213-1232, Sir Cecil Spring Rice, British Embassy, Washington, to the Duke of Connaught, the Governor of General of Canada, 26 May 1915; and E. Newcombe, Deputy Minister of Justice, to Major General Otter, Officer Commanding Internment Operations, 3 June 1915. NAC, RG 24, vol. 4414, file 26-3-12, Major General Otter to the Officer Commanding 3rd Division, 8 June 1915. NAC, RG 13, A2, vol. 196, file 1203-1215, J. Smetanka, Bohemian National Alliance of America, to the Hon. C.J.

Doherty, Minister of Justice, 23 July 1915; E. Newcombe, Deputy Minister
of Justice, to J. Smetanka, 13 August 1915; and E. Newcombe to Major
General Wm. Otter, 13 August 1915. NAC, RG 13, vol. 200, file 262-282,
Major General Otter, Officer Commanding Internment Operations, to the
Hon. C.J. Doherty, Minister of Justice, 14 March 1916. NAC RG 24 G1,
vol. 1176, file 15, part II, Major General Otter, Officer Commanding
Internment Operations, to Sir Joseph Pope, Under Secretary of State for
External Affairs, 19 June 1916. NAC, RG 13, vol. 200, file 262-282, E.
Newcombe, Deputy Minister of Justice, to Sir Joseph Pope, Under Secretary
of State for External Affairs, 10 August 1916.

14 See NAC RG 24, vol. 4695, file 448-14-20 (6), "Prisoners of War. Instructions from Land Warfare." For a discussion of the Hague Convention and
articles relating to the treatment of war prisoners, see H.E. Belfield, "Treatment of Prisoners of War," *Transactions of the Grotius Society: Problems
of Peace and War* 9 (1923): 131–47. See also Richard B. Speed, *Prisoners,
Diplomats and the Great War: A Study in the Diplomacy of Captivity*
(New York: Greenwood Press, 1990), 63–79.

15 On the chaotic employment situation in The Pas, see NAC, RG 18, vol. 490,
file 396-398.

16 Examples of restrictions imposed on internees are outlined in various
internment operations orders contained in NAC, RG 24, vol. 4280, file
34-13-4 (4).

17 Instructions regulating military conduct as it pertained to prisoners of war
were first elaborated in the Royal Warrant of August 1914. These were
amended during the course of the war in the form of Army Council
Instructions. For the Royal Warrant, with amendments, in its entirety, see
NAC, RG 25, vol. 1200, file 15, part 2, "Royal Warrant: Maintenance of
Discipline among Prisoners of War. Amended to 16th February, 1917."

The regulations governing internment operations in Canada – administered as "Standing Orders" – derived from the original Royal Warrant
(with amendments) but also from a policy directive issued by Major
General Wm. Otter, Director of Internment Operations, titled "Local Rules
for Internment Camps," issued for the information and guidance of camp
commandants. Commanding officers were "expected to interpret and
administer these regulations in a humane but firm spirit." For a copy of the
abstracts and local rules that applied directly to the operation of internment camps in Canada, see NAC, RG 4, vol. 4280, file 34-13-3 (14), Lt.
Col. Macpherson, Staff Officer, Internment Operations, "Maintenance
of Discipline among Prisoners of War: Abstracts from Royal Warrant
of August 3rd 1914. Subsequent Amendments," 11 January 1915.

18 The regulation pertaining to the work of prisoners of war fell under the section "Local Rules for Internment Camps" within the broader instruction "Maintenance of Discipline among Prisoners of War." There it was stated that prisoners were responsible for the sanitation and health of the camp (Clause D), and compensation at standard rates would be provided for work performed for the state (Clause J). Prisoners of war could be used to perform work for the state but they could not be coerced.

19 The United States had an extensive consular service with numerous consuls located across the country directly reporting to the US Consul General in Ottawa. Swiss and Swedish representation was limited by comparison. The quality of representation varied from person to person; some took their duties seriously, others less so. The US consular service was at times criticized for its pedantry and lacklustre nature. Poultney Bigelow, the celebrated American journalist and author, in an address to the Canadian Club complained that the American consular service comprised "broken down, wheezy political bosses, worn out lawyers and dentists, broken brokers, men who could not earn a living at any honest or respectable business." As quoted in the *Vancouver Sun*, 30 January 1917.

20 Otter was not above conveying his dissatisfaction and frustration with what he observed to be the unconscionable behaviour of local authorities. "Some municipalities," Otter observed, "are attempting to take advantage of the situation to relieve themselves of the taxation necessary for the relief of the unemployed or destitute and I think that Port Arthur and Fort William are in this class." He would repeat this observation in his final report on internment. Desmond Morton, *The Canadian General: Sir William Otter* (Toronto: Hakkert, 1974), 334; and Sir William Otter, *Internment Operations, 1914–1920* (Ottawa: King's Printer, 1921), 6.

21 NAC, RG 24, vol. 4721, file 2, T.J. Stewart, MP, to the Hon. Sam Hughes, Minister of Militia and Defence, 18 December 1915.

22 NAC, RG 24, vol. 4744, file 448-14-298 (2), "Dear General Hodgins," 8 February 1916.

23 Ibid., Brigadier General Cruickshank to Major A.E. Hopkins, Jasper Internment Station, 3 March 1916.

24 NAC, RG 24, vol. 4721, file 2, Brigadier E.A. Cruikshank, Officer Commanding Military District No. 13, to the Hon. Sam Hughes, Minister of Militia of Defence, 5 January 1916; and Brigadier E.A. Cruikshank to the Secretary, Militia Council, Hdqs., 3 February 1916.

25 NAC, RG 24, vol. 4744, file 448-14-298 (2), A.F. Ewing to General Cruickshank, 11 March 1916; and Brigadier General Cruickshank to

Major General Otter, Officer Commanding, Internment Operations,
25 March 1916.

26 See, for example, the case involving Major D. Stuart, the first commandant
of Banff/Castle Mountain Camp. Numerous escapes and problems with
discipline at the camp forced the resignation of Stuart, who subsequently
complained that he had not been treated fairly. Aware of his temperamen-
tal character, Brigadier General Cruickshank "anticipated that he [Stuart]
would endeavour to air his grievance through some other channel." Stuart
would put in for overseas duty after his resignation was demanded and
accepted. NAC, RG 24, vol. 4721, file 1, Major D. Stuart to Brigadier
General E.A. Cruikshank, Officer Commanding Military District No. 13,
27 December 1915; and Brigadier E.A. Cruikshank to Major General
Otter, Officer Commanding, Internment Operations, 28 December 1915.

27 "The foremen and the officers are mutually interested in the advancement
of the work. Of course, they frequently disagree mainly over such usual
points as to who shall keep the prisoners working, etc. There are many
such points which will only cease to be the cause of trouble and loss of
alien time in the different internment camps when the Parks Dept. and the
Internment Dept. agree on a definite ruling for each case." NAC, RG 84,
vol. 124, file Y176, J. Stinson to J.B. Harkin, Commissioner, Dominion
Parks Branch, 7 February 1916.

28 NAC, RG 24, vol. 4360, file 34-6-11 (1), Lieut. Colonel G. Royce, Officer
Commanding Kapuskasing Internment Camp, to A.A.G., 2nd Division,
Exhibition Camp, Toronto, 7 February 1916.

29 Ibid.

30 NAC, RG 24, vol. 4721, file 2, Lieut. Colonel Moffit, Officer Commanding
137th Overseas Battalion, to Brigadier General Cruickshank, Officer
Commanding Military District No. 13, 10 February 1916.

31 Ibid., Brigadier General Cruickshank, Officer Commanding Military
District No. 13, to Captain P.M. Spence, Officer Commanding Banff
Internment Camp, 10 February 1916; Captain P.M. Spence to Brigadier
General Cruickshank, 21 February 1916.

32 NAC, RG 24, vol. 4744, file 448-14-298 (1), Major A.E. Hopkins, Jasper
Internment Station, to Brigadier General Cruickshank, Officer Commanding
Military District No. 13, 19 February 1916.

33 NAC, RG 24, vol. 4360, file 34-6-11 (1), Lieut. Colonel G. Royce, Officer
Commanding Kapuskasing Internment Camp, to the A.A.G., 2nd Division,
Exhibition Camp, Toronto, 10 April 1916.

34 Ibid., Lieut. Colonel Royce to the A.A.G., 2nd Division, Toronto, 16 March
1916. Poaching men for overseas duty was also a problem faced by

Royce's predecessor at Kapuskasing, Lieutenant F. Clarke. See NAC, RG 24, vol. 4279, file 34-1-3 (10), Lieut. Colonel F. Clarke, Officer Commanding Kapuskasing Internment Camp, to the A.A.G., 2nd Division, Exhibition Camp, Toronto, 17 September 1915.

35 Ibid.

36 Detailed copies of all standing orders issued by Major A.E. Hopkins, commandant of the Jasper internment camp, are contained in NAC, RG 24, vol. 4744, file 448-14-298 (1). The file includes copies of the "General Standing Orders," "Orders for the Commander of the Guard," "Orders for All Sentries," "Fire Regulations," "Orders for Barrack Rooms and Other Quarters," "Daily Routine of Duties," "Bugle and Trumpet Calls," and "Prisoners' Routine."

37 The issue of military conduct was a matter of both military and political concern. How well was the Canadian public being served and whether sufficient leadership on security affairs was being exercised would result in periodic questions at the political level regarding measures taken to address possible shortcomings and to enforce discipline. The escape of prisoners of war from the Amherst Internment Camp, for instance, resulted in a political inquiry by the Senate of Canada, which requested "papers, documents and evidence produced at the military court martial held in Halifax, with the court's findings and sentences regarding the officers responsible for the said escape." See NAC, RG 13 A2, vol. 200, file 350-370, Senate of Canada Resolution referred to the Commissioner of Dominion Police and the Assistant Deputy Minister of Justice, 2 March 1916.

38 See NAC, RG 6 H1, vol. 763, file 4911, "Statement of Prisoners of War in Vernon, B.C.," n.d.

39 "Further I do not think it would be advisable to allow any first class prisoner to remain in the present first class compound among the second-class prisoners. It would probably lead to friction as there is not the best of feeling between the two classes." Ibid., vol. 753, file 3196, Major E.A. Nash, Officer Commanding Vernon Internment Camp, to Major General Wm. Otter, Director Internment Operations, 20 June 1916.

40 The privileges and benefits enjoyed by officers and those of officer standing would be extended only on a reciprocal basis. The belligerents would follow each other's actions and respond accordingly. The failure to extend those privileges and benefits resulted in reciprocal treatment. See, for example, NAC, RG 24, vol. 4513, file 17-2-40, vol. 3, Col. Macpherson, Staff Officer, Internment Operations, "Internment Operations Orders," 16 April 1915.

41 A list detailing the movement of prisoners by nationality from December 1914 to August 1918 is contained in NAC, RG 117, vol. 20, file 225. The list is comprehensive and shows that there was a conscious effort to consolidate the camps along national lines. This would change in 1917 when internees were being released and the majority of the camps closed. The remaining prisoners, regardless of national origin, were brought together in several consolidated camps.

42 NAC, RG 24, vol. 4414, file 26-3-12, Internment Operations, "Report for the Week Ending June 5, 1915 – Kingston, Ont. Station" and "Report for the Week Ending May 31, 1915 – Petawawa Station."

43 NAC, RG 25 G1, vol. 1156, file 48-1, Major General Wm. Otter to the Under Secretary of State for External Affairs, 7 July 1915. See also the discussion in Bohdan Kordan, *Enemy Aliens, Prisoners of War: Internment in Canada during the Great War* (Montreal and Kingston: McGill-Queen's University Press, 2002), 75 and 84–5.

44 See NAC, RG 24, vol. 4278, file 34-1-3 (8), A.A.G. 2nd Military Division, to Captain Chisholm, Officer Commanding, Stanley Barracks, 20 May 1915.

45 NAC, RG 24, vol. 4414, file 26-3-12, Major General Wm. Otter to the Secretary, Militia Council, 28 May 1915; Major H.J. Dawson, Officer Commanding Internment Station, Kingston, to the Assistant Adjutant-General, 3rd Division, 10 June 1915; and the C.R.C.E, 3rd Division, to the A.A.G., 3rd Division, Kingston, 11 June 1915. A personal account of internment at Fort Henry is related in Lubomyr Y. Luciuk, *Internment Operations: The Role of Old Fort Henry in World War I* (Kingston: Delta, 1980), 29–33.

46 At the Citadel in Halifax, where a majority of the inmates were German, prisoner of war A. Wyss wrote to the commandant: "Seeing that there is no chance of an early release and find the time rather heavy on my hands through enforced idleness, may I offer you my services in case there is and you know of any odd jobs going. I am willing to do and can turn my hand to anything, so if I finally should get my release I need not go out destitute." NAC, G24, vol. 4541, file 73-1-6, A. Wyss to Captain H. F. Adams, 24 February 1915.

47 On July 20 1915, for instance, the officer commanding the Alberta military district informed Major General Otter that 191 Austro-Hungarians were transferred from the Lethbridge to the working camp at Castle Mountain; among those who remained at the non-working Lethbridge station were forty-five Germans, one Turk, and thirteen Austrians considered "unfit for hard labour." NAC, RG 24, vol. 4694, file 448-14-20, vol. 2, District Officer

Commanding, Military District No. 13, to the Officer Commanding Internment Operations, 20 July 1915.

48 On the issue of internees playing golf, Birney would not countenance the criticism that the prisoners were enjoying themselves, claiming that "any man who knows the game would call it an absolute farce and more of a punishment than a privilege, first because of the exceedingly limited space, and second on account of being under military escort." Ibid., Captain Birney, Officer Commanding Lethbridge Internment Barracks, to the Officer Commanding Military District No. 13, 12 May 195.

49 *Calgary Daily Herald*, 7 May 1915.

50 NAC, RG 24, vol. 4541, file 73-1-6, R. Bell, Automobile Association, to the Assistant Adjutant General, W.E. Thompson, Halifax, 30 June 1915.

51 Ibid., Thompson to Bell, 2 July 1915.

52 BC Ministry of Transportation Records, Slocan District (1915), file 1752, section 5, "Resolution Re: Employment of Interned Aliens to Construct Wagon Road from Nakusp to Hot Springs."

53 BC Ministry of Transportation Records, Okanagan District (1915), file 1752, section 2, J.W. Jones, Mayor, Kelowna, to the Hon. Thomas Taylor, BC Minister of Public Works, 4 September 1915.

54 BC Ministry of Transportation Records, North Okanagan and Salmon Arm Districts (1915), file 211, J. Mizun, Eagle River Farmers' Institute (Malakwa), to the Hon. Thomas Taylor, BC Minister of Public Works, 5 August 1915, and G. Eyre, Eagle River Farmers' Institute (Solsqua), to the Hon. Thomas Taylor, BC Minister of Public Works, 16 August 1915.

55 NAC, RG 24, vol. 4541, file 73-1-6, telegram, Major General Otter to the Officer Commanding 6th Division, Halifax, 13 July 1915, and Major H.F. Adams, Officer Commanding Halifax Internment Camp, to the Assistant Adjutant General, 6th Division, 15 July 1915.

56 See, for example, BC Ministry of Transportation Records, Okanagan District (1915), file 1752, section 3, the Hon. Thomas Taylor, BC Minister of Public Works to J.W. Jones, Mayor of Kelowna, 24 September 1915.

57 BC Ministry of Transportation Records, North Okanagan and Salmon Arm Districts (1915), file 211, the Hon. Thomas Taylor, BC Minister of Public Works, to W. Bowden, Sicamous, BC, 30 July 1915. BC Ministry of Transportation Records, Okanagan District (1915), file 1752, section 2, J.E. Griffith, Deputy Minister and Public Works Engineer, to Hamilton Lang, Road Superintendent, 21 August 1915; and J.E. Griffith, Deputy Minister, to Major W. Ridgway-Wilson, Dept. of Alien Reservists, 27 August 1915.

58 NAC, RG 24, vol. 4661, file 99-221, Fred Binnie, President, Elko Board of Trade, to the Hon. Sam Hughes, Minister of Militia and Defence, 23 October 1915.

59 BC Ministry of Transportation Records, North Okanagan and Salmon Arm Districts (1915), file 211, Major W. Ridgway-Wilson, Dept. of Alien Reservists, to J.E. Griffith, Deputy Minister of Public Works, 3 September 1915.

60 Ibid., R.W. Bruhn, Assistant Road Superintendent to J.E. Griffith, Deputy Minister of Public Works, 7 September 1915; and Griffith to Bruhn, 7 September 1915.

61 Ibid., R.W. Bruhn, "Report showing cost and progress of work on the Sicamous-Mara Road during September, October and November 1915."

62 Biweekly reports, extending to October 1916, are all contained in BC Ministry of Transportation Records, North Okanagan and Salmon Arm Districts (1915), file 211.

63 Ibid, R.W. Bruhn, "Report showing cost and progress of work on the Sicamous-Mara Road, January 1–15."

64 Ibid., R.W. Bruhn, Road Superintendent, to J.E. Griffith, Deputy Minister and Public Works Engineer, 25 December 1915.

65 See, for example, ibid., Bruhn to Griffith, 5 March 1916.

66 Ibid., Bruhn to Griffith, 17 July 1916.

67 "The non-payment to the prisoners of all monies earned by them has created considerable ill feeling among them as it is thought that considering the small amount paid them for their work they should be permitted to use the entire amount while interned. The reason given by the Ottawa authorities for withholding the amount is that they do not wish the prisoners to be turned loose upon the community without funds at the close of the war." NAC, RG 13 A2, vol. 206, file 1753-16, G. Woodward, US Vice-consul, Vancouver, "Inspection of Dominion Detention Camp at Morrissey, B.C.," 19 August 1916.

68 BC Ministry of Transportation Records, North Okanagan and Salmon Arm Districts (1915), file 211, R.W. Bruhn, Road Superintendent, to J.E. Griffith, Deputy Minister and Public Works Engineer, 10 August 1916.

69 PAO, RG 14-157, Kapuskasing Detention Camp, Re: a/c for Board, J.F. Whitson, Commissioner, Northern Development Branch, to J.A. Stewart, Inspector, 14 March 1916.

70 For monthly comparative statements, see ibid., Kapuskasing Detention Camp, Re: a/c for Board.

71 Ibid., J. Stewart, Inspector to the Hon. G. Howard Ferguson, Ontario Minister of Lands, Forests and Mines, 13 December 1915.

72 The figures are derived from monthly statements in ibid., Kapuskasing Detention Camp, Re: a/c for Board.

73 Ibid., J.F. Whitson, Commissioner, Northern Development Branch, to J.A. Stewart, Inspector, 19 April, 1916; and NAC, RG 6 H1, vol. 760, file 4178, Arthur Bruce, Deputy Minister, Northern Development Branch, to Major General W. Otter, Director of Internment Operations, 23 June 1916.

74 For a statement on the work completed in the adjoining townships, see PAO, reel MS 5542 (RG 14-157), Kapuskasing Detention Camp, Re: a/c for Board, "Report done from Kapuskasing Internment Camp in townships of O'Brien – Fauquier – Owens and Williamson," n.d.

75 NAC, RG 24, vol. 4360, file 34-6-11 (1), Lieutenant Colonel G. Royce, Officer Commanding, Kapuskasing Internment Camp, to the A.A.G. 2nd Division, Toronto, 20 March 1916.

76 PAO, reel MS 5542 (RG 14-157), Kapuskasing Detention Camp, Re: a/c for Board, "Alien Labour at Kapuskasing, April 1916"; and "Alien Labour at Kapuskasing, May 1916."

77 *Globe* (Toronto), 16 and 17 May 1916.

78 See NAC, RG 17, vol. 2787, file 240779, J. Grisdale, Director, Experimental Farms, Department of Agriculture, to G. O'Halloran, Deputy Minister, Department of Agriculture, 27 November 1917; and G. O'Halloran, Deputy Minister, Department of Agriculture, to A. Grigg, Deputy Minister, Ontario Department of Lands, Forests and Mines, 29 November 1917.

79 See E.J. Hart, *J.B. Harkin: Father of Canada's National Parks* (Edmonton: University of Alberta Press, 2010).

80 NAC, RG 84, vol. 104, file U60-1, J.M. Wardle to J.B. Harkin, Commissioner of Dominion Parks, 31 August 1915.

81 *Mail Herald* (Revelstoke), 17 July 1915.

82 NAC, RG 84, vol. 104, file U60-1, J.M. Wardle to J.B. Harkin, Commissioner of Dominion Parks, 5 October 1915.

83 NAC, RG 84, vol. 190, file MR176, F. Williamson to Major General W. Otter, 6 October 1915. For a detailed description of the situation at the Revelstoke internment camp, see Bill Waiser, *Park Prisoners: The Untold Story of Western Canada's National Parks, 1915–1946* (Saskatoon-Calgary: Fifth House, 1995), 18–19.

84 NAC, RG 84, vol. 124, file MR 176, W.A. Gordon, Revelstoke City Clerk to J.B. Harkin, Commissioner of Dominion Parks, 5 July 1916, and Municipal Resolution: re: Re-establishment of Revelstoke Internment Camp, n.d.; and RG 84, vol. 190, file MR 176, Harkin to Gordon, 22 July 1916.

85 NAC, RG 84, vol.124, file Y176, E.N. Russell, Superintendent Yoho and Glacier Parks, to J.B. Harkin, Commissioner of Dominion Parks, 12 August 1915.

86  Ibid., E.N. Russell to J.B. Harkin, 10 November 1915.
87  Ibid., Harkin to Russell, 23 November 1915.
88  For a discussion of the working conditions at the Otter camp, see Waiser, *Park Prisoners*, 30–2.
89  NAC, RG 24, vol. 124, file Y176, E.N. Russell, Superintendent Yoho and Glacier Parks, to J.B. Harkin, Commissioner of Dominion Parks, 17 April 1916.
90  Ibid., E.N. Russell to J.B. Harkin, 20 June 1916.
91  Ibid., Russell to Harkin, 9 August 1916.
92  Ibid., Lieutenant G. Brock, Officer Commanding, Yoho Internment Camp, to Major General Wm. Otter, Director, Internment Operations, 23 August 1916.
93  Ibid., J.B. Harkin, Commissioner of Dominion Parks to Major General Wm. Otter, Director, Internment Operations, 30 August 1916.
94  *Golden Star*, 5 October 1916.
95  NAC, RG 84, vol. 124, file Y176, J.B. Harkin, Commissioner of Dominion Parks, to Major General Wm. Otter, Director of Internment Operations, 28 September 1915.
96  After the camp was relocated to Banff, the work undertaken continued to be recorded in the diary maintained by camp officials. For a description of the work, see B. Kordan and P. Melnycky, eds, *In the Shadow of the Rockies: Diary of the Castle Mountain Internment Camp, 1915–1817* (Edmonton: CIUS Press, 1991).
97  NAC, RG 84, vol.124, file Y176, J.B. Harkin, Commissioner of Dominion Parks, to Major General Wm. Otter, Director of Internment Operations, 28 September 1915.
98  NAC, RG 24, vol. 4729, file 3, Major General W. Otter, Director of Internment Operations to the Officer Commanding Military District No. 13, 5 November 1915.
99  *Edmonton Journal*, 19 February 1916.
100  NAC, RG 24, vol. 4744, file 448-14-298, part I, Major A.E. Hopkins "On Work Done by Prisoners of War during the Week Ending February 26th."
101  *Edmonton Journal*, 19 February 1916. See also comments of F.H. Brewster, *Saskatoon Daily Star*, 12 January 1916.
102  NAC, RG 24, vol. 213, file J60, D.W. Johnson, Acting Superintendent of Jasper Park to J.B. Harkin, Commissioner of Dominion Parks, 11 January 1916.
103  For a detailed account of the developments at the Jasper internment camp, see Waiser, *Park Prisoners*, 32–4.
104  *Calgary Daily Herald*, 4 March 1916.

105  Ibid., 6 March 1916.

106  *Saskatoon Phoenix*, 1 May 1916.

107  NAC, Borden Papers, MG 26 H1, vol. 84, reel C-4322, page 4309, President, Dominion Steel Corporation, M. Workman, to the Rt. Hon. Sir Robert Borden, Prime Minister of Canada, 1 February 1917.

108  The case of William Wysk was reported in the *Vegreville Observer*, 16 February 1915.

109  NAC, RG 24, vol. 4279, file 3, Major Peter Spence to the Assistant Adjutant General, 9 December 1916; Assistant Adjutant General to Spence, 11 December 1916; Spence to the Assistant Adjutant General, 20 December 1916 and 5 January 1917.

110  *Manitoba Free Press*, 7 June 1915; *Saskatoon Phoenix*, 7 June 1915; and *Vancouver Sun*, 7 June 1915. On the events at the Brandon camp, see P. Melnycky, "The Internment of Ukrainians in Canada," in F. Swyripa and J.H. Thompson, eds, *Loyalties in Conflict: Ukrainians in Canada during the Great War* (Edmonton: CIUS Press, 1983), 8–9; and George Buri, "'Enemies within Our Gates': Brandon's Alien Detention Centre during the Great War," *Manitoba History* 56 (2007): 8–9.

111  *Saskatoon Phoenix*, 3 May 1915.

112  Ibid., 9 June 1915.

113  *Vancouver Sun*, 23 June 1915.

114  *Calgary Daily Herald*, 1 July 1915.

115  *Globe* (Toronto), 19 January 1916.

116  *Morning Albertan* (Calgary), 1 May 1916. On the escape, see *Lethbridge Daily Herald*, 29 April, 1 and 3 May 1916; *Calgary Daily Herald*, 29 April, 1 and 3 May 1916. See also the account in Christopher R. Kilford, *On the Way! The Military History of Lethbridge, Alberta, 1914–1945* (Victoria: Trafford Publishing, 2004), 32–4; and Robert Rutherdale, *Hometown Horizons: Local Responses to Canada's Great War* (Vancouver: University of British Columbia Press, 2004), 149–51.

117  *Ottawa Citizen*, 5 July 1916. See also NAC, RG 13 A2, vol. 203, file 1066-1085, E. Newcombe to Major General Wm. Otter, Director, Internment Operations, 6 July 1916; "Memo for the Deputy Minister of Justice," 2 August 1916; and Newcombe to Otter, 20 September 1916.

118  *Daily British Whig* (Kingston), 30 April 1915; and NAC RG 24, vol. 4413, file 26-3-12, vol.4, Major H.J. Dawson, Officer Commanding Fort Henry to Major General Wm. Otter, Director, Internment Operations, 29 and 30 April 1915.

119  Ibid., 1 May 1915.

120  Ibid., 3 May 1915.

121 NAC RG 24, vol. 4413, file 26-3-12, vol. 4, Officer Commanding
3rd Division to Major General Wm. Otter, Director, Internment
Operations, 4 May 1915; and ibid., 12 May 1915.

122 *Globe* (Toronto), 25 June 1915, and *Vancouver Sun*, 25 June 1915.

123 *Globe* (Toronto), 16 and 17 May 1916. See also NAC, RG 24, vol. 4360,
file 34-6-11 (1), Major General Wm. Otter, Director, Internment
Operations, to District Officer Commanding 2nd Military Division,
13 May 1916; and Brigadier General W. Logie, Officer Commanding
2nd Military Division, to the Hon. Sam Hughes, Militia Headquarters,
13 May 1916.

124 NAC, RG 24, vol. 4360, file 34-6-11 (1), "Notice to Prisoners Interned
in This Camp," 18 May 1916; and Lieutenant Colonel G. Royce, Officer
Commanding Kapuskasing Internment Camp, to Brigadier General
W. Logie, Officer Commanding 2nd Military Division, 19 May 1916.

125 NAC, RG 24, vol. 4729, file 3, Major Duncan Stuart, Officer Commanding Castle Mountain Internment Camp to the Officer Commanding
Military District No. 13, 4 November 1915; and NAC, RG 13 A2, vol.
201, file 533-551, Officer Commanding Military District No. 13 to
Major General Wm. Otter, Officer Commanding Internment Operations,
5 November 1915.

126 *Rabochyi narod* (Winnipeg), no. 31, 28 October 1915.

127 Ibid., "Copy of letter translated from Prisoner of War No. 98 Nick
Olinyk," n.d.

128 NAC, RG 25, vol. 3413, file 1-1-1918/13, "Comparative Statement Show-
ing Caloric Value of Canadian and German Ration Based on Seven Days
Issue for Non-Working Group," n.d.; NAC, RG 24, vol. 4729, file 3,
Major Duncan Stuart, Officer Commanding Castle Mountain Internment
Camp, to the Officer Commanding Military District No. 13, 13 Septem-
ber 1915; and NAC, RG, 24, vol. 4280, file 34-13 – vol. 4, "Maintenance
of Discipline Among Prisoners of War," n.d. See also Kordan and
Melnycky, eds, *In the Shadow of the Rockies*, 18.

129 See, for example, BC Ministry of Transportation Records, North Okana-
gan and Salmon Arm Districts (1915), file 211, telegram, BC Minister of
Public Works, Hon. Thomas Taylor to Major General Wm. Otter, Director,
Internment Operations, 12 November 1915; J. Griffith, BC Deputy Minis-
ter of Public Works, to Lieutenant Colonel W. Ridgway-Wilson, Officer
Commanding, Department of Alien Reservists, 30 December 1915; J.
Griffith to Major General Wm. Otter, 30 December 1915; and BC Ministry
of Transportation Records, Okanagan District (1916), file 1752, section 4,
J. Griffith to Lieutenant Colonel W. Ridgway-Wilson, 7 January 1916.

130 BC Ministry of Transportation Records, Okanagan District (1916), file
   1752, section 4, J. Black, Edgewood Road Superintendent to J. Griffith,
   BC Deputy Minister of Public Works, 22 November, 3 December 1915
   and 1 January 1916.

131 Ibid., Black to Griffith, 15 December 1915 and 1 January 1916.

132 BC Ministry of Transportation Records, North Okanagan and Salmon
   Arm Districts (1915), file 211, telegram, BC Minister of Public Works, the
   Hon. Thomas Taylor to Major General Wm. Otter, Director, Internment
   Operations, 12 November 1915.

133 See, NAC, RG 13 A2, vol. 1929, file 10/1917 – part 1, Major General
   Wm. Otter, Director, Internment Operations, to the Hon. C.J. Doherty,
   Minister of Justice, 20 December 1915.

134 Ibid., Lieutenant Colonel W. Ridgway-Wilson to J. Griffith, BC Deputy
   Minister of Public Works, 4 February 1916.

135 Ibid., R.W. Bruhn, Mara Lake Road Superintendent, to J. Griffith, BC
   Deputy Minister of Public Works, 21 January 1916.

136 Ibid., J. Griffith, BC Deputy Minister of Public Works, to Lieutenant
   Colonel W. Ridgway-Wilson, Officer Commanding, Department of Alien
   Reservists, 1 February 1916.

137 Ibid., W. Ridgway-Wilson to J. Griffith, 4 February 1916.

138 See ibid., R.W. Bruhn, Mara Lake Road Superintendent to J. Griffith, BC
   Deputy Minister of Public Works, 18 November 1915; and BC Ministry
   of Transportation Records, Okanagan District (1916), file 1752, section
   4, J. Griffith, BC Deputy Minister of Public Works, to Major General
   Wm. Otter, Director, Internment Operations, 7 January 1916.

139 NAC, RG 84, vol. 124, file Y176, J.B. Harkin, Commissioner, Dominion
   Parks Branch, to E.N. Russell, Superintendent Yoho National Park,
   25 February 1916; Superintendent E.N. Russell to Lieutenant G.H.
   Brock, Officer Commanding Otter Internment Camp, 29 February 1916
   and 17 March 1916; J. Stinson, road superintendent, to Harkin, 7
   February; and Harkin to Russell, 28 April 1916. On the situation at
   the Banff internment camp, see NAC, RG 24, vol. 4721, file 2, Brigadier
   General E. Cruickshank, Officer Commanding Military District No. 13,
   to Major General Wm. Otter, Director, Internment Operations,
   28 February 1916. See also Kordan and Melnycky, eds, *In the Shadow
   of the Rockies*, 65n68.

140 "The 48 letters which you forwarded to me last Saturday, I have carefully
   read through, and I have not found anything of importance in them. The
   majority of them are appealing to their friends to help them get away
   from Kapuskasing. A good many are complaining about the cold there."

NAC, RG 24, vol. 4279, file 34-1-3 (11), A. Cash, Official Government Interpreter, 8 Division Station, Toronto, to Lieutenant A.L. Coventry, A.D.I.O. 2nd Military Division, Exhibition Camp, 27 February 1916. See also ibid., 22, 29, and 30 March 1916.

141  NAC, RG 13 A2, vol. 195, file 1192-1212, Mrs F. Munsche to the Hon. C.J. Doherty, 23 June 1915.

142  NAC, RG 6 H1, vol. 759, file 3565, "Translation of Attached Letter," Maria Marchuk, Bienfait Saskatchewan, 22 September 1916

143  "I received twenty-six letters from you yesterday for censor, and I am returning them to you today. I went over them very carefully and found nothing of importance in them. Most of the prisoners wish that they could be home for the coming holidays. They write to their friends that they are very lonely ... Many of them write to their friends to take care of their families; even if it means selling everything ... They say that they have a promise from the Department of the Militia that they will be treated better. A few of them say that they will appeal, to be allowed their liberty." NAC, RG 24, vol. 4297, file 34-1-3 (11), A. Cash to Lieutenant A.F. Coventry, A.D.I.O, Exhibition Camp, Toronto, 17 December 1915.

144  NAC, RG 24, vol. 4729, file 3, "Copy of Letter Translate from Prisoner of War No. 98. N. Olinyk," n.d. Provision was made to support dependents who applied and could demonstrate need. Internment operations would provide a small subsistence amount to 121 dependents of internees at various camps. Not all dependents would apply and not all were aware that they could apply for assistance.

145  NAC, RG 24, vol. 4694, file 448-14-20 – vol. 3, Major General Wm. Otter to Brigadier General E. Cruickshank, Officer Commanding Military District No. 13, 9 March 1916; and Brigadier General E. Cruickshank to Mrs E. Allen, 13 March 1916.

146  Ibid., file 448-14-20 – vol. 2, "Copy of Letter from Mrs. Mudry to her Husband Prisoner of War No. 157, N. Mudry," 18 October 1915.

147  NAC, RG 18, vol. 473, file 10 – part 4, "Crime Report: Mrs. Annie Dandys, wife of interned prisoner of war – destitute," 24 June 1915; RNWMP Comptroller, L. Fortsecue, to Major General Wm. Otter, Officer Commanding Internment Operations, 6 July 1915; and Otter to Fortescue, 8 July 1915. In Calgary a petition was drafted by a group of signatories, Ukrainian and other Austro-Hungarian women, who appealed to the women of Calgary for assistance. "What are we to do if we cannot get work? Are we to starve or are we to be driven to a life of vice. Will not the women of Calgary speak for us?" *Calgary Daily Herald*, 29 February 1916.

148 *Vancouver Sun*, 28 August 1916.

149 On the guard schedule, see NAC, RG 24, vol. 4721, file 1, Major Duncan Stuart, Officer Commanding Castle Camp, to Brigadier General E. Cruickshank, Officer Commanding Military District No. 13, 18 October 1915.

150 See, for example, NAC, RG 24, vol. 4729, file 3, Major Duncan Stuart, Officer Commanding Castle Camp, to Brigadier General E. Cruickshank, Officer Commanding Military District No. 13, 18 October 1915; NAC, RG 24, vol. 4721, file 1, Stuart to Cruickshank, 2 December 1915; and Cruickshank to Stuart, 4 and 7 December. See also Kordan and Melnycky, eds, *In the Shadow of the Rockies*, 100n125, and 105n129.

151 NAC, RG 24, vol. 4721, file 1, Major Peter Spence, Officer Commanding Castle Camp to Brigadier General E. Cruickshank, Officer Commanding Military District No. 13, 12 May 1916. The new commander was reprimanded for having overstepped his authority by freely doling out punishments to his soldiers. The officer commanding the military district, Brigadier General Cruickshank, advised the commander, Major Spence, "that where limited powers of punishment are conferred upon an officer they should be carefully observed by him." See Kordan and Melnycky, eds, *In the Shadow of the Rockies*, 97n121.

152 Ibid., "Liquor Stores and Bars – Out of Bounds – Discipline of Guards," 2 December 1915; and ibid., file 2, Spence to Cruickshank, 21 March 1916.

153 Ibid., Private J. Wiley to Brigadier General E. Cruickshank, Officer Commanding Military District No. 13, 20 March and 4 April 1916. See also the case of Private Albert Morgan, described in Kordan and Melnycky, eds, *In the Shadow of the Rockies*, 100n124.

154 Ibid., Private G. Lomax to Brigadier General E. Cruickshank, Officer Commanding Military District No. 13, 22 April 1916. Others sought different ways to escape their situation. Private J. Elliott asked to be discharged, pleading, "As I have my Mother, who is a widow, to support, I find it impossible to make both ends meet." Elliot's appeal, however, was dismissed as it was noted that when Elliott was taken on strength, he was destitute. Therefore "the claim he makes is not justified." Ibid., file 3, Private J. Elliott to Brigadier General Cruickshank, 3 June 1916; and Major P. Spence to General Officer Commanding Military District No. 13, 8 June 1916. The debilitating effect of camp life on soldier morale at the Banff camp is described in Waiser, *Park Prisoners*, 28.

155 NAC, RG 24, vol. 4694, file 448-14-20 – vol.3, Capt. R.B.C. Thomson, M.O., Lethbridge Internment Camp, to Brigadier General E.

Cruickshank, Officer Commanding Military District No. 13, 25 July 1916.

156  NAC, RG 24, vol. 4744, file 448-14-298 – part 4, Major A.E. Hopkins, Officer Commanding Jasper Internment Camp, to Brigadier General E. Cruickshank, Officer Commanding Military District No. 13, 8 August 1916.

157  *Globe* (Toronto), 3 and 15 March 1916.

158  NAC, RG 24, vol. 4694, file 448-14-20 – vol. 1, Major W.E. Date, Officer Commanding Lethbridge Internment Camp, to Brigadier General E. Cruickshank, Officer Commanding Military District No. 13, 22 September 1916.

159  NAC, RG 24, vol. 4278, file 3-1-3 (7), US Consul Julius Dreben to Lieutenant Colonel, H. Elliot, Assistant Adjutant General, 2nd Division, Toronto, 13 May 1915.

160  See, for example, NAC, RG 117, vol. 14, file 149, L. Lowden to Major General Wm. Otter, Officer Commanding Internment Operations, 22 January 1917.

161  NAC, RG 13 A2, vol. 212, file 962-982, Major General Wm. Otter, Officer Commanding Internment Operations to the Minister of Justice, Hon. C. Doherty, 24 February and 1 March 1917.

162  See, for example, NAC, RH 84, vol. 124, file Y176, E.N. Russell, Yoho Superintendent, to J. B. Harkin, Commissioner, Dominion Parks Branch, 24 January 1916. Prisoners at Yoho were used to supply firewood on an ongoing basis to the Stephen Hotel in Field. At Banff, the internees were used for a host of projects that were spurred on by private and local requests, including cutting hiking trails for the Alpine Club of Canada and creating an ice palace and toboggan glide for the Banff winter carnival as well as extending the golf links at the Banff Springs Hotel. See Kordan and Melnycky, eds, *In the Shadow of the Rockies*, 76n95, 117n148 and 131n155.

163  Documentation on the case of M. Couch, POW No. 198, is contained in NAC, RG 24, vol. 4661, file 99-237 – vol. 1.

164  A total of eighty-one women and 156 children were taken into internment.

165  Documentation on the case of Fanny Priester, POW No. 5003, is contained in NAC, RG 25 G1, vol. 1200, file 15 – part 1; and NAC, RG 6 H1, vol. 752, file 3102.

166  NAC, RG 24, vol. 4721, file 1, Brigadier General E. Cruickshank, Officer Commanding Military District No. 13, to Major General Wm. Otter, Officer Commanding Internment Operations, 16 November 1915.

167  Ibid., Cruickshank to Otter, 16 December 1915.

168  NAC, RG 24, vol. 4695, file 448-14-20 – vol. 4, Major General Wm.
Otter, Officer Commanding Internment Operations, to Brigadier General
E. Cruickshank, Officer Commanding Military District No. 13, 16
December 1915. See also Rutherdale, *Hometown Horizons*, 144–5.

169  Ibid.; and Brigadier General E. Cruickshank, Officer Commanding
Military District No. 13, to the Officer Commanding Lethbridge
Internment Camp, 20 December 1915.

170  NAC, RG 84, vol. 190, file MR 176, telegram, Commissioner, Dominion
Parks Branch, J.B. Harkin, to F.H. Williamson, Deputy Commissioner,
Dominion Parks Branch, 5 October 1915; and J. Wardle to Major
General Wm. Otter, Officer Commanding Internment Operations,
6 October 1915.

171  NAC, RG 24, vol. 4660, file 99-197, Major General Wm. Otter, Officer
Commanding Internment Operations to Officer Commanding Military
District No. 11, 15 December 1915.

172  BC Ministry of Transportation Records, Okanagan District (1916),
file 1752, John Black to J.E. Griffith, Deputy Minister of Public Works,
28 and 29 April 1916.

173  See, for example, ibid., John Black to J.E. Griffith, Deputy Minister of
Public Works, 23 May 1916. See also ibid., R. Bruhn to J.E. Griffith,
29 August, 6 and 9 October 1916.

174  BC Ministry of Transportation Records, North Okanagan and Salmon
Arm Districts (1916), file 211, J.E. Griffith, Deputy Minister of Public
Works to Edmund D. Wood, 10 November 1916.

175  *Revelstoke Mail Herald*, 31 July 1915.

176  Documentation on the strike and efforts to end it is contained in NAC,
RG 84, vol. 124, file Y176. See also Waiser, *Park Prisoners*, 36–8.

177  PAO, RG 14-157, "Kapuskasing Detention Camp Re: Saw Mill," J.F.
Whitson – "Extract from J.A. Stewart's Letter," 9 January 1917.

178  NAC, RG 6 H1, vol. 757, file 3422 (1), Major Peter Spence, Officer
Commanding Castle Camp to Brigadier General E. Cruickshank, Officer
Commanding Military District No. 13, 12 December 1916; and Major
Peter Spence, Officer Commanding Banff Camp to Major General Wm.
Otter, Officer Commanding Internment Operations, 27 April 1916.

179  Provincial Archives of Alberta, 67.172/947, Attorney General, Coroners
and Inquest files. The demise of George Budak was reported in the local
Banff paper *Crag and Canyon*, 30 December 1916.

180  See *Calgary Daily Herald*, 17, 28 April 1915, 10 April 1916, 17 June
1916, and 30 October 1916. See also *Lethbridge Daily Herald*, 17 June
1916; and *Vancouver Sun*, 25 July 1916.

181 *Calgary Daily Herald*, 7 May 1915.

182 *Vernon News*, 27 May 1915.

183 Ibid., 19 October 1916.

184 *Globe* (Toronto), 22 November 1916.

185 See ibid., 15 and 22 November 1916, and 14 April 1916. US Consul, Felix Johnson reported on the provisions at Fort Henry: "I closely examined a prisoner of war, recently released, and questioned him as to food conditions at the fort. He informed me that the food could not be better. There was great sufficiency and that it was better prepared and cooked than that given to the guards at the camp. This statement is corroborated by the Secretary of the Young Men's Christian Association at Fort Henry who frequently takes his meals with the prisoners." NAC, RG 13 A2, vol. 221, file 663-653, US Consul, Felix S. Johnson to the US Secretary of State, Washington, 5 October 1916.

186 NAC, RG 24, vol. 4694, file 448-14-20 – vol. 2, letter of Emily Murphy "Dear Sir," 3 April 1915; Major General Wm. Otter to Col. E. Cruickshank, Officer Commanding Military District No. 13, 22 April 1915; and Cruickshank to Murphy, 27 April 1915.

187 On the effort of the Ukrainian community and the activity of Fred and Florence Livesay, see Melnycky, "The Internment of Ukrainians in Canada," 11–13.

188 *Crag and Canyon* (Banff), 2 September 1916.

189 NAC, RG 25 G1, vol. 1156, file 48-1, George E. Foster, Acting Under-Secretary of State for External Affairs to His Royal Highness the Governor General in Council, 25 August 1915.

190 Ibid., W.H. Walker, Acting Under-Secretary of State for External Affairs, to Major General Wm. Otter, 12 August 1915; Lieut. Col. D. Macpherson, Staff Officer, Internment Operations, to W.H. Walker, 13 August 1915; Lieut. Col. E. Stanton, Secretary, Governor General of Canada, to W.H. Walker, 13 August 1915; and Walker to Stanton, 14 August 1915.

191 Ibid., George E. Foster, Acting Under-Secretary of State for External Affairs, to His Royal Highness the Governor General in Council, 25 August 1915.

192 The Deputy Minister of Justice, E. Newcombe, first articulated the official position. As a report, it was submitted to the Committee of the Privy Council and approved by the Governor General on 28 August 1915 as PC 2039. See NAC, RG 6 H1, vol. 819, file 2616, R. Boudreau, clerk of the Privy Council, 28 August 1915.

193  NAC, RG 13 A2, vol. 1929, file 1633-1916, Major General Wm. Otter, Officer Commanding Internment Operations, to the Minister of Justice, Hon. C.J. Doherty, 3 November 1916.

194  Ibid.

195  Ibid., Deputy Minister of Justice, E. Newcombe, to Major General Wm. Otter, 22 November 1916.

196  NAC, RG 25 G1, vol. 1156, file 48-1, "Note Verbale," to the Embassy of the United States of America, 23 June 1915; and Bonar Law, Colonial Secretary, to the Governor General, 5 and 12 July 1915.

197  Ibid., Bonar Law, Colonial Secretary, to Governor General with copy of Foreign Office telegram, 27 July 1915. On the Canadian position, see NAC, RG 6 H1, vol. 819, file 2616, R. Boudreau, clerk of the Privy Council, 28 August 1915.

198  NAC, RG 25 G1, vol. 1157, file 48-2, "Note Verbale," to the Embassy of the United States of America, 16 August 1915. A report on German allegations of abuses at the Amherst camp appeared in the *Montreal Star*, 23 August 1915, and the *New York Times*, 24 August 1915. Reports of conditions at the Nanaimo detention camp also appeared in the Seattle press, warranting a discussion of bringing in external observers who could counter some of the claims. See ibid., Joseph Pope, Under-Secretary of State for External Affairs, to the Deputy Minister of Justice, E. Newcombe, 23 September 1915.

199  The concern related not only to captured British military personnel but also more particularly to Canadian prisoners. "Reports have recently come to the knowledge of His Majesty's Government to the effect that the German Military Authorities had issued an order that certain classes of prisoners of war were henceforth to be treated with increased severity, this order having application more especially to His Majesty's Canadian troops." NAC, Borden Papers, MG 26 H1, vol. 2884, reel C-4442, page 16377, diplomatic note, Foreign Office to the United States Ambassador, 10 September 1915.

The British Red Cross also raised the issue of reprisals. From its own sources, Red Cross officials were led to believe that as a consequence of alleged maltreatment of German subjects in Canadian camps reprisals against Canadian captives were taking place. See NAC, RG 13 A2, vol. 203, file 1066-1085, Louis Mallet, British Red Cross to the Under-Secretary of State, Colonial Office, 8 November 1915.

Reprisals continued to be a concern into 1916, when, for example, German authorities complained about the abuses and the misdemeanours

of guards as well as the forced labour of civilian prisoners at the
Lethbridge and Banff camps. See NAC, RG 13 A2, vol. 205, file 1450–
1470, Bonar Law, Colonial Secretary, to the Governor General, 8 March
1916. For a report to the British parliament on the issue of reprisals and
the observations of the International Red Cross during 1916, see NAC,
RG 25 G1, vol. 1176, file 15 – part II, "Correspondence with His
Majesty's Minister at Berne respecting the Question of Reprisals against
Prisoners of War," September 1916.

200 NAC, RG 25 G1, vol. 1157, file 48-2, diplomatic note, Foreign Office to
the United States Ambassador, 9 October 1915.

201 NAC, RG 13 B8, vol. 1368, file 14 July–30 October 1915, Foreign Office,
diplomatic note, 9 October 1915.

202 Germany insisted that prisoners interned in the British colonies and
Canada in particular were to be treated in the same manner as those
in the United Kingdom and "are under the same obligations vis-a-vis
Germany, and are equally responsible for seeing that they receive treatment in accordance with international treaties and the laws of humanity
as in the case of the later." Moreover, German authorities were of the
view that there was no need to express complaints or bring attention to
Britain and its Allies unfavourable reports. Rather, it was up to Britain
and its colonies to ensure that reforms and proper treatment were being
accorded the prisoners and abuses stopped. NAC, RG 13 A2, vol. 205,
file 1450–1470, "Note Verbale," Berlin, May 28 1916.

203 Ibid., Bonar Law, Colonial Secretary, to the Governor General, 8 March
1916; and the Under-Secretary of State for External Affairs, Joseph Pope,
to the Minister of Interior, W.J. Roche, 29 March 1916. For the statement
of the Minister of Interior, W.J. Roche, see Canada, House of Commons,
*Hansard*, 15 February 1916.

204 PRO, Foreign Office Papers, FO 383/239, "Prisoners of War Camp at
Banff," 29 June 1916.

205 NAC, RG 24, vol. 4721, file 3, H. Clum, US Consul, "Visit to Internment
Camp at Banff, Alberta," 25 May 1916.

206 See, for example, NAC, RG 24, vol. 4694, file 448-14-20 – vol. 3, Report
of US Consul, "Visit to Internment Camp at Lethbridge, Alberta," H.
Clum, 15 July 1916.

207 The Bulgarian protests originated with the Bulgarian Red Cross.
Allegations of the maltreatment of Bulgarian civilian prisoners at the
Amherst camp resulted in a flood of diplomatic correspondence on the
subject. See NAC, RG 13 A2, vol. 203, file 1066-1085, and RG 25 G1,

vol. 1176, file 15 – part II. On Turkish protests, see NAC, RG 25 G1, vol. 1156, file 48-1; and RG 13 A1, vol. 194, file 1052-1072.

208 The point of complaint was the alleged mistreatment of "Austrian Reserve Officers." A protest was registered with American officials, who conveyed the complaints and in turn to Canadian officials. The prime minister, Robert Borden, citing a report on the subject by the director on internment operations, General Otter, flatly denied the accusation "that any hardships or indignities have been inflicted on Austrian reserve officers or, indeed, upon any alien enemies confined in this country." The matter was urgent because it was reported that two British officers detained at a camp in Salzerbad, Lower Austria, were being harshly handled in retaliation for the treatment meted out to interned Austrian officers in Canada, which was said "to have been the chief cause leading to the alteration in the attitude adopted towards these British officers." NAC, RG 25 G1, vol. 1157, file 48-2, Bonar Law, Colonial Secretary, to the Governor General, 9 September 1915; Major General Wm. Otter to Joseph Pope, Under-Secretary of State for External Affairs, 4 October 1915; and the Rt. Hon. Robert Borden, Secretary of State for External Affairs and Prime Minister, to the Governor General, 6 October 1915.

209 NAC, RG 13, vol. 200, file 262-282, Lieut. Colonel E.A. Stanton, Governor-General's Secretary to Joseph Pope, Under-Secretary of State for External Affairs, 14 February 1916; Major General Otter to the Hon. C.J. Doherty, Minister of Justice, 21 February, 1916; Acting Deputy Minister of Justice to the Under-Secretary of State for External Affairs, 21 February 1916; RG 25 G1, vol. 1176, file 15 – part II, Joseph Pope, Under-Secretary of State for External Affairs, to Lieut. Colonel E.A. Stanton, Governor-General's Secretary, 22 June 1916; and RG 13, vol. 216, file 1912-1932, "Treatment of Serbs, Croats and Yugo-Slavs in this country, races hostile to Austria-Hungary," 15 November 1917.

210 For the charges and allegations, see NAC, RG 25 G1, vol. 1176, file 15 – part II, "Note Verbale," 18 March 1916; Court Inquiry, n.d., RG 6 H1, vol. 819, file 2616, Major General Wm. Otter to Joseph Pope, Under-Secretary of State for External Affairs, "Alleged Forcible Employment German Civilian Prisoners of War," 6 July 1916; RG 25 G1, vol. 1156, file 48-1, Major General Wm. Otter to Joseph Pope, Under-Secretary of State for External Affairs, 8 July 1916; RG 25 G1, vol. 1157, file 48-2, Major General Otter to Joseph Pope, Under-Secretary of State for External Affairs, 20 December 1915; and RG 13 A2, vol. 221, file 633-653, Horace Nugent, British Consulate, Chicago, to Sir Cecil Spring Rice,

British Embassy, Washington, 20 January 1917; and Sir Cecil Spring Rice to the Governor General, 1 February 1917.

211 See, for example, RG 25 G1, vol. 1157, file 48-2, Major General Otter to Joseph Pope, Under-Secretary of State for External Affairs, 20 December 1915.

212 See, for example, the case of Sgt. Mellor, who, charged with brutality, was discharged. The information was conveyed to the German government. NAC, RG 24, vol. 4695, file 448-14-20 – vol. 4, Brig. General E. Cruickshank, General Officer Commanding Military District No. 13, to Major General Wm. Otter, General Officer Commanding Internment Operations, 22 February 1916; Otter to Cruickshank, 29 February 1916; and RG 13 A2, vol. 205, file 1450-1470, Bonar Law, Colonial Secretary to the Governor General with accompanying diplomatic note of the Foreign Office to the US Ambassador, 8 March 1916.

213 NAC, RG 25 G1, vol. 1176, file 15 – part II, F. Johnson, American Consul to the US Secretary of State, 11 May 1916; and Johnson to the US Secretary of State, "Inspection of Fort Henry," 14 August 1916.

214 For a detailed description of the conditions and situation at the Spirit Lake camp, see P. Melnycky, "Badly Treated in Every Way: The Internment of Ukrainians in Quebec during the First World War," in M. Diakowsky, ed., *The Ukrainian Experience in Quebec* (Toronto: Basilian Press, 1994), 51–78.

215 See USNA, 763.7115/2279, G. Willrich, American Consul, to the Secretary of State, Washington, "Report on Conditions of German, Austro-Hungarian, Turkish and Bulgarian Subjects in Quebec Consular District and in the Detention Camp at Spirit Lake, Quebec, 29 December 1916."

216 NAC, RG 25 G1. vol. 1176, file 15 – part III, telegram, Lieut. Colonel J. Rinfret, Spirit Lake, Quebec to Major General Wm. Otter, 21 November 1916.

217 Ibid., Rt. Hon. Robert Borden, Prime Minister and Secretary of State for External Affairs, to the Governor General, 23 November 1916.

218 Ibid., Sir Joseph Pope, Under-Secretary of State for External Affairs, to Sir Cecil Spring Rice, British Embassy, Washington, 24 November 1916; and Sir Joseph Pope to Major General Wm. Otter, 29 November 1916.

219 See, for example, ibid., file 15 – part II, "Note Verbale," Berlin, 19 June 1916; NAC, RG 13 A2, vol. 205, file 1450-1470, "Note Verbale," Berlin, 28 July 1916; Foreign Office diplomatic note, 19 August 1916; NAC, RG B8, vol. 1364, file September 30–October 30, 1916, "Note Verbale," 4 August 1916; ibid., vol. 1369, file 28 June–31 August 1916, "Note

Verbale," 28 May 1916; and file 5 January–21 February, 1917, "Note Verbale," 22 January 1917.

220 This was part of a wider policy whereby 30,000 marks were to be distributed globally for prisoners of war. Funds on the order of 2,000 marks were specifically earmarked for Fort Henry. This was later expanded to cover other internment stations in Canada where prisoners were found, such as Vernon and Amherst and the Citadel in Halifax. NAC, RG 13 B8, vol. 1369, file 5 January–21 February, 1917, "Note Verbale," 22 January 1917; Foreign Office diplomatic note, 25 January 1917; NAC, RG 25 G1, vol. 1200, file 15 – part II, "Note Verbale," 31 January 1917, and German diplomatic note, 28 February 1917; and NAC, RG 25 G1, vol. 1176, file 15 – part II, Swiss Legation diplomatic note, 6 March 1917.

221 NAC, RG 25 G1, vol. 1156, file 48-1, E. Newcombe, Deputy Minister of Justice, "Memorandum: For the Under-Secretary of State for External Affairs," 19 August 1915.

222 Ibid.

223 On the attitude of Germany, Britain, and other belligerents on the question of the treatment of enemy aliens as prisoners of war, see Richard Speed, *Prisoners, Diplomats and the Great War*, 141–53. In addition, see Kordan, *Enemy Aliens, Prisoners of War*, 78–87.

224 The argument is made more fully in Kordan, *Enemy Aliens, Prisoners of War*, 41–51.

225 As a further example, on 18 October 1915, the War Office circulated a regulation that amended the Royal Warrant governing the treatment of prisoners of war. The regulation acknowledged the difference between the civilian and military class of prisoners of war, authorizing that confinement, the most routine of punishments meted out to prisoners of war, "is inflicted only in the case of military or naval prisoners and is inapplicable to civilians." In addition, this form of punishment was not to be commuted to imprisonment in civil jails. See NAC, Borden Papers, MG 26 H1 (9), vol. 288A, reel C-4442, B.B. Cubitt, Assistant Secretary to the War Office, "To All Commands at Home and Abroad and All Government Offices," 18 October 1915.

226 *Lethbridge Telegram*, 4 May 1916.

227 NAC, RG 25, vol. 1200, file 15 – part I, Foreign Office, diplomatic note, 17 January 1917.

228 NAC, RG 24, vol. 4360, file 34-6-11 (1), Brigadier General W.A. Logie, Officer Commanding District No. 2 to Major General Wm. Otter, General Officer Commanding Internment Operations, 19 May 1916.

229 Ibid., Otter to Logie, 25 May 1916.

230 NAC, RG 24, vol. 4661, file 99-237 – vol. 1, Lieutenant Colonel W. Ridgway-Wilson, Department of Alien Reservists to Lieutenant Colonel Jos. Mackay, Officer Commanding 225 Regiment, C.E.F., Fernie, 19 May 1916.

231 For examples of complaints at the Banff camp, see NAC, RG 24, vol. 4721, file 3, "Summary of Complaints made by Prisoners of War at Banff Internment Station," 10 December 1916.

232 See *Calgary Daily Herald*, 25 October 1916.

233 *Crag and Canyon* (Banff), 19 August 1916. For a description of the Konowalczuk escape, see Kordan and Melnycky, eds, *In the Shadow of the Rockies*, 87n108.

234 BC Ministry of Transportation Records, Okanagan District (1915), file 1752, section 4, J. Black, superintendent, Vernon-Edgewood Road to J.E. Griffith, Deputy Minister, BC Department of Public Works, 31 August 1916; and the Hon. Thomas Taylor, BC Minister of Public Works, to J.E. Griffith, Deputy Minister, BC Department of Public Works, 2 September 1916.

235 *Annual Report of the Department of Interior, 1918* (Ottawa: King's Printer, 1919), 6.

236 Sir William Otter, *Internment Operations, 1914–20*, (Ottawa: King's Printer, 1921), 16.

237 *Annual Report of the Department of Interior, 1918*, 6.

238 NAC, RG 25 A2, vol. 264, file P 5/7, Sir George Perley, Canadian High Commissioner, London, to the Rt. Hon Sir Robert Borden, 26 November 1915; and Borden to Perley, 8 December 1915.

239 NAC, RG 13 A2, vol. 196, file 1420, "Translation of letter received from O. Rozdolski, Prisoner of War 948, Bandon, Manitoba," 10 August 1915.

240 NAC, RG 24, vol. 4277, file 34–1–3 (5), Erwin Kohlman to Colonel H. Elliot, A.A.G, Toronto, 11 January 1915.

CHAPTER FOUR

1 *Saskatoon Daily Star*, 31 March 1916.

2 See *Manitoba Free Press*, 5 April 1916; *Calgary Daily Herald*, 5 April 1916; and *Regina Daily Post*, 5 April 1916.

3 *Calgary Daily Herald*, 31 March 1916.

4 *Morning Citizen*, 31 March 1916.

5 *Saskatoon Phoenix*, 10 and 12 April 1916; *Manitoba Free Press* (Winnipeg), 10 April 1916; and *Regina Daily Post*, 10 April 1916.

6 *Regina Daily Post*, 5 April 1916.

7 *Manitoba Free Press*, 11 April 1916.

8 *Vancouver Sun*, 12 April 1916.

9 NAC, RG 13 A2, vol. 196, file 1333, Thomas Tait, President, Minto Coal Company, to the Minister of Justice, Hon. C. Doherty, 28 September 1915.

10 Ibid., D.A. Noble, Dominion Coal Company, to Colonel A.P. Sherwood, Chief Commissioner of Dominion Police, 1 October 1915.

11 NAC, Borden Papers, MG 26 H1, vol. 181, reel C-4382, page 99327, Hon. F. Cochrane, Minister of Railways and Canals, to the Rt. Hon. R. Borden, Prime Minister, 8 November 1915.

12 Ibid., pages 99334–5, Hon. W. Crothers, Minister of Labour, to the Rt. Hon. R. Borden, Prime Minister, 12 November 1915.

13 Ibid., page 99337, Hon. C. Doherty, Minister of Justice, to the Rt. Hon. R. Borden, Prime Minister, 18 November 1915.

14 Various applications and correspondence relating to the release of prisoners of war for private employment can be found in NAC, RG 6 H1, vol. 752, file 3035; and ibid., vol. 753, files: 3203, 3209 – vol. 1 and 3194 – vol. 1.

15 "On account of the enlistment on the one hand and the Internment on the other, we now find the various classes of labour so scarce as to make it impossible to supply the amount of coal now needed by the various consumers of whom we are called upon to supply." NAC, RG 117, vol. 14, file Correspondence – Release of Prisoners, Montgomery B. Morrow, Canmore Coal Company, to Major P. Spence, Officer Commanding Banff Internment Camp, 20 May 1916.

16 NAC, RG 6 H1, vol. 755, file 3326 (1), F. Warrington, Executive Assistant, Canadian Pacific Railway, to Major General Wm. Otter, Officer Commanding Internment Operations, 2 June 1916.

17 Ibid., Major General Wm. Otter, Officer Commanding Internment Operations, to the Officer Commanding Brandon Internment Camp, 12 June 1916.

18 Ibid., Lieutenant Colonel D. Macpherson, Staff Officer, Internment Operations, to the Officer Commanding Brandon Internment Camp, 23 June 1916.

19 NAC, RG 18, vol. 514, file 1916, no. 483-506, S.T. Wood, RNWMP Inspector Commanding Manitoba Boundary Patrol, to Colonel A.P. Perry, RNWMP Commissioner, 22 July 1916. Remarkably, the Brandon camp commandant, Major Coleman, also released prisoners who did not sign an Undertaking, a matter that went against protocol and would be taken up with the Director of Internment Operations. See ibid., letter, "Dear Major Perry," 27 July 1916.

20  For a complete list of companies, see NAC, RG 117, vol. 20, file Sundries re: All Camps, "Companies for whom Prisoners of War were released to work." n.d.

21  Of this number, 255 individuals claimed to be Austro-Hungarian subjects. The rest consisted of ten Bulgarians, eight Germans, and two Turks.

22  NAC, RG 84, vol. 70, file R313, telegram, J H.J. Clarke, Superintendent, Rocky Mountains (Banff) Park, to J.B. Harkin, Commissioner, Dominion Parks Branch, 8 May 1917; and Harkin to Clarke, 8 May 1917.

23  NAC, RG 6 H1, vol. 755, file 3326 (3), Major General Wm. Otter, Officer Commanding Internment Operations to Grant Hall, Vice-President and General Manager, Canadian Pacific Railway, 7 April 1917. In October 1916, when the decision was made to close the Yoho camp after certain difficulties were encountered, all of the prisoners were sent to Spirit Lake in Quebec, despite the policy to discharge, where possible, "non-dangerous" internees.

24  According to British officials, in correspondence with the governor general of Canada, since "it did not appear that there could be any objections on the part of your Ministers, their assent to the stipulated extension has been assumed." See NAC, Borden Papers, MG 26 H1, vol. 288A, reel C-4442, pages 163678–9, Hon. A. Bonar Law, Colonial Secretary, to the Governor General of Canada, 17 August 1916. The promise of repatriation would apply to non-reservists forty-five years of age and older and to invalids.

25  Britain notified Canadian officials that repatriation would occur only on a reciprocal basis and in the totality of the agreement NAC, RG 25 G1, vol. 1176, file 15 – part II, Bonar Law, Colonial Secretary, to the Governor General, 14 August 1916.

26  NAC, RG 13 B8, vol. 1369, file 28 June–31 August 1916, Bonar Law to the Governor General, 4 July 1916.

27  *Calgary Daily Herald*, 28 September 1916.

28  NAC, RG 18, vol. 514, file 1916 – no. 483-506, Colonel A.P. Sherwood, Chief Commissioner of Dominion Police, to L. Du Plessis, RNWMP, 4 August 1916, and unidentified confidential letter "Dear Major Perry," 5 August 1916. Individual prisoners were identified for release by camp commanders and the names were submitted for the consideration of the director of internment operations. These were accompanied by an assessment by the commander and a note detailing the initial reason for internment. See, for example, NAC, RG 6 H1, vol. 753, file 3194 (1), Major D. Coleman, Commandant Brandon Internment Station, to Major General Wm. Otter, Officer Commanding Internment Operations, 5 July 1916.

29  Ibid., vol. 757, file 3466 (1), "For Captain Dillon's Information – From Rates of Pay and Rules governing service of Permanent Maintenance of

Way Employees of the Canadian Government Railways, effective from
March 1st 1916."

30 NAC, RG 18, vol. 514, file 1916 – no. 483-506, Major General Wm. Otter,
Officer Commanding Internment Operations, to the RNWMP Comptroller,
30 August 1916.

31 Ibid., Colonel A.P. Sherwood, Chief Commissioner of Dominion Police,
to L. Du Plessis, RNWMP, 4 August 1916. See also NAC, RG 76, vol. 603,
file 884866 (4), A.P Sherwood, Chief Commissioner of Police, "To Officers
authorized to parole or intern Aliens of Enemy Nationality," 24 July 1916.

32 "These are not hardships. Were no war on, they would be glad to work at
the rate of $1.75, which was current in the city in 1914. Native employ is
now enlisted and is not getting half as much as they receive." NAC, RG 24,
vol. 4540, file 69-1-92, F.I.O. Halifax Fortress to G.S.O., Military District
No. 6, "Alien Labour," 11 July 1916.

33 Ibid., vol. 4577, file 15-1-2, Captain F. Goodspeed, a/D.I.O. Military
District No. 6 to D.I.O. St John, 22 August 1916.

34 Prisoners who were released to employers and subsequently left for higher
wages that were offered by competitor companies became an issue.
Inquiries were made as to whether internment authorities might put a stop
to the practice by restricting the mobility of discharged prisoners. See NAC,
RG 24, vol. 4540, file 69-1-92, F.I.O. Halifax Fortress to G.S.O., Military
District No. 6, "Alien Labour," 11 July 1916; and N.E. Barrett, Halifax
Electric Tramway Company, to General Officer Commanding, Military
District No. 6, 11 August 1916.

35 Citing homesickness, a large number appealed directly to General Otter
for permission to leave their employer. See, for example, NAC, RG 6 H1,
vol. 753, file 3203, letter, Steve Zwarun and Ignacy Klimink to Major
General Wm. Otter, Officer Commanding Internment Operations,
28 February 1917.

36 See, for example, ibid., file 3194 (1), Colonel A. Morris, Commandant
Amherst Internment Station, to Major General Wm. Otter, Officer
Commanding Internment Operations, 23 June 1916, and letter, former
prisoners of war, to Colonel A. Morris, n.d.

37 NAC, RG 13 A2, vol. 208, file 54-73, Major General Wm. Otter, Officer
Commanding Internment Operations, to the Deputy Minister of Justice, E.
Newcombe, 10 January 1917; and Newcombe to Otter, 15 January 1917.

38 NAC, RG 6 H1, vol. 753, file 3203, letter, Cornelius Traczewski to Major
General Wm. Otter, Officer Commanding Internment Operations,
6 December 1916.

39 Ibid., Lieutenant Colonel D. Macpherson, Staff Officer, Internment
Operations, to Cornelius Traczewski, 9 January 1917.

40 NAC, RG 13, vol. 1929, file 10/1917, part 2, Colonel A.P. Sherwood, Chief Commissioner of Dominion Police, to the Deputy Minister of Justice, 24 August 1916; and H. Forder, Chief of Police, Parry Sound, to Colonel A.P. Sherwood, 22 August 1916.

41 NAC, RG 18, vol. 519, file 1917 (no.17), part 2, Lieutenant Colonel D. Macpherson to the RNWMP Comptroller, 5 March 1917.

42 One hundred and thirty-two internees were discharged for employment with the Canadian Pacific Railway on 2 April. A list of seventy Austro-Hungarian prisoners from the Morrissey camp identified for possible release was submitted to General Otter on 11 April for his consideration. At Mara Lake, a list of 184 prisoners was prepared at the same time from which twenty-three were eventually disqualified. The names of 133 were also submitted for consideration from Banff; seventeen from the group were rejected, however. At Vernon fifty-five names were brought forward, and although none were shown to be eliminated from the roster of those to be released, the annotation alongside the name of Jasko Berbes indicated he was blind and unable to work, while William Dumberick was said to be very lame with a broken leg, which had not been properly set. For the lists of released prisoners, see NAC, RG 6 H1, vol. 755, file 3326 (3); and RG 24, vol. 4360, file 34-6-11 (2).

43 NAC, RG H1, vol. 759, file 3473, Maj. General Wm. Otter to Lieut. Colonel MacInnes, A.A.G, Department of Militia, 2 May 1917. As a result of the release of prisoners the internment guard detail, including officers and NCOs, had declined from a high of 1,906 in May 1916 to 846 by June 1917 – a reduction of 1,060 in troop strength.

44 Ibid., memorandum, "Abolished."

45 Reports that released prisoners of war were finding their way back to the mines on Vancouver Island led to a meeting between the BC minister of mines, the Hon. Wm. Sloan, and General Otter, who would assure the minister that no prisoners would be released from the BC camps for mine work. See *Vancouver Sun*, 6 February 1917.

46 NAC, RG 6 H1, vol. 755, file 3326 (3), letter, A. Ostapchuk, et al. to Major General Wm. Otter, Officer Commanding Internment Operations, 9 April 1917.

47 Ibid., letter, J. Alexandruk to Major General Wm. Otter, Officer Commanding Internment Operations, 16 April 1917. NAC, RG 6 H1, vol. 755, file 3326 (3) contains a number of letters requesting the return of funds confiscated or monies earned while interned.

48 "By the terms of the Hague Regulations, POW's personal belongings remained their property; however, they were not permitted to retain money

or items that might facilitate their escape. Consequently, upon their arrival at an internment station, all money and jewellery was at once taken from the internees, and the money deposited in a 'Prisoners of War Trust Fund' saving account at the bank of Nova Scotia; jewellery items were locked in a safety vault. The amounts of money confiscated from each internee were listed for Otter's records. But despite Otter's efforts to keep track of the finances collected from the prisoners, it seems that this was one of the most vexing problems of the administration of the Stanley Barracks internment station. One of the outstanding events of the internment years at Stanley Barracks was the disappearance of several thousand dollars' worth of cash and valuables confiscated from the prisoners during the December 1914 to January 1915 period. No one was charged in the matter, as no records could be found." A. Sendzikas, *Stanley Barracks: Toronto's Military Legacy* (Toronto: Dundurn Press 2011), 112–13.

49 A large number of requests were directed to the internment director ("the Highest Official of the Land") by paroled internees at Sturgeon Falls, where they protested the efforts of the local mayor and police official who would not issue registration cards and threatened them with six months' imprisonment should they leave without the proper documentation. See, for example, the case of Nick Bodnar in NAC, RG 6 H1, vol. 755, file 3326 (3), N. Bodnar to Maj. General Wm. Otter, 16 April 1917.

50 Ibid., Major General Wm. Otter, Officer Commanding Internment Operations, to A.D. MacTier, General Manager, CPR, 8 May 1917.

51 NAC, RG 13 A2, vol. 211, file 551-571, letter, George Werenka to the Hon. C. Doherty, Minister of Justice, 2 April 1917.

52 NAC, RG 6 H1, vol. 755, file 3326 (3), Major General Wm. Otter, Officer Commanding Internment Operations, to A.D. MacTier, General Manager, CPR, 8 May 1917.

53 On the question of industry motives, Crothers believed that many of the applications for the release of enemy alien prisoners "[were] prompted by the thought that their services can be secured at lower than the ordinary rates of wages for such work." NAC, Robert Borden Papers, MG 26 H1, vol. 181, reel C-4382, page 99334.

54 Ibid., vol. 46, reel C-4440, page 120281, M.A. Wood to the Rt. Hon. Sir. Robert Borden, Prime Minister, 16 May 1917.

55 *Globe* (Toronto), 9 June 1917.

56 Ibid., 18 April 1917.

57 A convention of delegates selected from local bodies consisting of an estimated 10,000 men was held in Winnipeg 10–12 April 1917 from which sprang the Great War Veterans' Association. An executive was formed and

a delegation immediately organized to meet immediately with the federal government to discuss matters and concerns affecting the returned soldiers.

58 On 4 June, the day before a scheduled meeting between federal government officials and representatives of the Great War Veterans' Association, a rally was held at Queen's Park in Toronto, where an estimated five thousand supporters appeared. Resolutions were passed favouring selective draft conscription and the immediate suppression of "sedition." Cheers followed the remarks of the Hon. T.W. McGarry, Ontario's provincial treasurer, who declared: "If it was necessary, a gun should be put to the man who would not go." But the loudest roar óf approval was for the veterans' representative Sgt. W.H. Warwick, when, in a blunt phrase, he stated: "Let us have conscription of the foreigner too, not let him stay on here taking the fat jobs and, if necessary, the returned men can fight the French-Canadians." To this was added the declaration of the chairman of the GVWA, Sgt. Major W. Rowe Whitton: "If Canada is good enough to make a living for foreigners and others, it is good enough to fight for." See *Globe* (Toronto), 4 June 1917.

59 On Col. Currie's private member's bill, see *Globe* (Toronto), 1 June 1917. Skepticism of Currie no doubt stemmed from his unpredictability. Currie famously declared, for instance, that he was prepared to use machine guns against a national protest march by farmers to Ottawa in 1917.

60 "In availing themselves of conscientious objections to combatant service, persons thus securing exemption can not be expected to have a voice in a war-time election." NAC, Robert Borden Papers, MG 26 H1, vol. 78, reel C-4319, pages 40300–2, unidentified handwritten memorandum, "War-time election forced on country," n.d.

61 See ibid. vol. 69, reel C-4314, page 35517, London telegram, "For Meighen," Sir Robert Borden, Prime Minister, 20 April 1917.

62 See *Globe* (Toronto), 17 April 1917.

63 There were a number of private letters to the prime minister, especially from Conservative Party members, all of who iterated the importance of eliminating the franchise for naturalized aliens of German and Austro-Hungarian origin if the government was to survive and the conscription issue was to be adopted. See, for example, NAC, Robert Borden Papers, MG 26 H1, vol. 219, reel C-4402, pp. 123088–123092, unidentified letter to Prime Minister Robert Borden, 5 June 1917, and E. Michener to Sir Robert Borden, 11 June 1917. For a discussion of disfranchisment and its impact on the 1917 general election, see John Herd Thompson, *The Harvests of War: The Prairie West, 1914–1918* (Toronto: McClelland and Stewart, 1978), 142–3; and John Herd Thompson, "The Enemy Alien and

the Canadian General Election of 1917," in F. Swyripa and J.H. Thompson, eds, *Loyalties in Conflict: Ukrainians in Canada during the Great War* (Edmonton: CIUS Press, 1983), 25–45.

64 On the connection made by veterans between the overseas conflict and the struggle on the home front, see Nathan Smith, "Fighting the Alien Problem in a British Country: Returned Soldiers and Anti-Alien Activism in Wartime Canada, 1916–1919," in A. Miller, Laura Rowe, and James Kitchen, eds, *Other Combatants, Other Fronts: Competing Histories of the First World War* (Newcastle: Cambridge Scholars Publishing, 2011), 295–6.

65 "Every man who has returned from the front will be of the same opinion. I feel that in speaking as I have done I am only representing their views. I believe that I am also representing the views of the men in the trenches, who know the cowardly enemy that they have to fight at the front. The Germans fight us without any referee to see that fair play is dealt out. Men who have taken up land in the Canadian West are now fighting our men in the trenches. A great many of them have been taken prisoners. Many of the men who are still in the West would be doing the same thing, and if they are not it is simply because they could not get ships or the right to go over. If they could get ships and the right to go they would go tomorrow to fight against our men in the trenches. Under these circumstances what are we going to do? Are we going to have in this House thirty-five or forty members who owe their election to the votes of these Hungarians and Germans, who will foreswear their British citizenship and who will out-vote our soldiers at the front? This House should put a stop to that." *Globe* (Toronto), 27 July 1917. See also *Saskatoon Phoenix*, 27 July 1917; and *Edmonton Bulletin*, 27 July 1917.

66 *Calgary Daily Herald*, 28 July 1917.

67 *Globe* (Toronto), 21 August 1917.

68 See *Montreal Gazette*, 26 November 1917; and *Saskatoon Daily Star*, 26, 27 November 1917.

69 *Globe* (Toronto), 29 December 1917.

70 Ibid., 12 June 1917.

71 Wages, especially in the agricultural sector, increased as a result of growing economic demand and a shortage of labour. In 1912 the wage level was $40 a month, which rose steadily to $100 a month by 1920. The perception of enemy aliens profiting from the war was reinforced by the growing wealth among alien immigrant farmers who capitalized on farm improvements and other factors. See Thompson, *The Harvests of War*, 86; and A. Makuch, "Ukrainian Canadians and the Wartime Economy," in F. Swyripa and J.H. Thompson, eds, *Loyalties in Conflict*, 71–3.

72 The prospect of bringing prisoners of war from Europe to work in Canadian industry had been routinely raised during the course of the war. The last time the proposal was raised, in July 1918, the prime minister asked the Hon. N. Rowell, vice-chair of the cabinet War Committee, to investigate the possibility of bringing over Austro-Hungarian prisoners to address the coal supply shortage in the country. See NAC, Robert Borden Papers, MG 26 H1, vol. 92, reel C-4327, page 48226, the Rt. Hon. Sir Robert Borden, Prime Minister to the Hon. N. Rowell, 6 July 1918.

73 *Lethbridge Telegram*, 6 September 1917.

74 *Saskatoon Daily Star*, 30 November 1917.

75 See *Saskatoon Phoenix*, 20 December 1917, and *Vancouver Sun*, 21 December 1917.

76 See, for example, *Morning Albertan* (Calgary), 19 January 1918. The announcement was offset by relief when news of the rumour that Oriental labour would be brought in to work the farms was declared to be false. *Morning Albertan* (Calgary), 8 February 1918; and *Vancouver Sun*, 15, 21 February 1918.

77 NAC, Robert Borden Papers, MG 26 H1, vol. 241, reel C-4415, pages 134929–31, petition, Great War Veterans' Association to the Rt. Hon. Sir Robert Borden, Prime Minister, 26 March 1918. On the activities of the Great War Veterans' Association, see *Globe* (Toronto), 4, 25, 27 March 1918; and *Vancouver Sun*, 30 March, and 8, 14 April, 1918.

78 NAC, Robert Borden Papers, MG 26 H1, vol. 46, reel C-4440, pages 120421–2, unidentified report on labour situation in Western Canada, 31 December 1917. Although the labour movement, generally speaking, cleaved along national lines, the reintegration of enemy aliens into the workforce and the issues around rights and social justice had the effect of increasing inter-community solidarity. This improvement in relations allowed individuals of enemy alien origin to assume leadership roles within the labour movement. See O. Martynovych, *Ukrainians in Canada: The Formative Period, 1891–1924* (Edmonton: CIUS Press, 1991), 428–9.

79 See *Globe* (Toronto), 10, 11 April 1918.

80 NAC, Loring Christie Papers, MG 30 E15, vol. 2, reel C-3876, pages 1324–5, "Memorandum," n.d.

81 Ibid., pages 1327–33, "Note on the Treatment of Enemy Aliens," 11 February 1918.

82 Canada, House of Commons, *Hansard*, 22 April 1918, 973–1025.

83 "Members of the Force should not be harsh in enforcing the penalties under the Order in Council [2914]. Its provisions are to be sympathetically administered and a man should first be warned to provide himself with a

'certificate of parole' and if after the warning he neglects to do so, action can then be taken against him." NAC, RG 18, vol. 542, file 20 – part 1, "Circular Memorandum No. 771A," Assistant RNWMP Commissioner, J.A. McGibbon, 19 March 1918.

84 *Manitoba Free Press* (Winnipeg), 18 July 1918.

85 NAC, RG 13 A2, vol. 226, file 1874-1899, "Memorandum for the Deputy Minister of Justice," A.P. Sherwood, Chief Commissioner of Police, 20 August 1918. For possessing objectionable material, Leon Mechnavech was found guilty and fined $3,000 or three years in the Kingston Penitentiary. This was a much harsher sentence than internment, which by this time would not have included compulsory labour.

86 Ibid., Sergeant B. James, Dominion Police Headquarters, to Colonel Sir Percy Sherwood, Chief Commissioner of Police, 1 September 1918.

87 From mid-1918 on, the federal government became deluged with petitions demanding the mass deportation of enemy aliens. See D. Avery, *"Dangerous Foreigners": European Immigrant Workers and Labour Radicalism in Canada, 1896–1932* (Toronto: McClelland and Stewart, 1983), 76–7.

88 *Globe* (Toronto), 11 June 1918 and 15 July 1918.

89 For an account of alleged enemy alien sedition in Winnipeg at this time and the response of local authorities, see Jim Blanchard, *Winnipeg's Great War: A City Comes of Age* (Winnipeg: University of Manitoba Press, 2010), 235–7.

90 See *Vancouver Sun*, 3 August 1918.

91 *Vancouver Sun*, 6 August 1918.

92 *Globe* (Toronto), 3 August 1918.

93 *Globe* (Toronto), 3 August 1918; *Manitoba Free Press* (Winnipeg), 7 August 1918; and *Edmonton Bulletin*, 7 August 1918.

94 "There are those who try to palliate the rioting on the grounds that the alien problem is concerned. This is a question of public policy, to be dealt with as such by the constituted authority in a free country. It is no justification for lawlessness and disorder, and cannot be utilized either to incite or extenuate such scenes as have recently disgraced this city. Order must be restored and maintained." *Globe*, 8 August 1918. For a discussion of the grievances of the GVWA in light of the White City Café riot, see Desmond Morton, *Fight or Pay: Soldiers' Families in the Great War* (Vancouver: University of British Columbia Press, 2004), 168–9.

95 NAC, RG 6, vol. 765, file 5294, Report of S. Gintzburger, Consul of Switzerland, Vancouver, to the Consul General of Switzerland, Montreal, 7 September 1917. The director of internment operations, Maj. General

Otter, acknowledged that complaints were made and asked for the Swiss consul's recommendations. In the meantime, the commandant of the Morrissey camp responded to a request to explain the charges contained in the report. See ibid., Major General Wm. Otter to S. Gintzburger, Swiss Consul, 8 February 1918; and Captain J. Mitchell, Officer Commanding Morrissey Internment Camp, to Major General Wm. Otter, 15 March 1918.

96 It would appear that the defensive posture of Canadian officials was the result of a communication that indicated the War Office officials in London were "greatly afraid of German reprisals on Canadians unless the allegations of Gintzburger are disposed of." The cable eventually sent to London in response stated: "In early days few over zealous officers used mild forms of coercion to induce prisoners to work, but this and other complaints in the report, having foundation in fact, have since been remedied." See ibid., vol. 763, file 4738, Dominion Office, London, to Prime Minister of Canada, 11 March 1918; and "Suggested Cable," n.d.

97 "This report is made by Samuel Gintzburger, the Swiss Consul at Vancouver, respecting whom we have most unsatisfactory accounts of his notorious German sympathies. He is a German Jew, and is just as inimical to us as he dare to be." Ibid., vol. 765, file 5294.

98 Babij, however, careful not to appear entirely untruthful, qualified his statement by noting: "There may have been some cases of ill-treatment, but they have never come under my observation, and if so were probably caused by the prisoners' hatred of the Guards." Ibid., 1 September 1917.

99 Ibid., vol. 763, file 4947, David Bergstrom, Royal Swedish General Consul, Montreal, to Major General Wm. Otter, 6 September 1917.

100 Ibid., vol. 765, file 5330, "List of Punishments Awarded to Prisoners of War from Feb. 1 to date," Officer Commanding Kapuskasing Internment Camp, Lieut. Colonel W.E. Date, 17 September 1917.

101 Ibid., Officer Commanding Kapuskasing Internment Camp, Lieut. Colonel W.E. Date, to Major General Wm. Otter, 1 October 1917.

102 Ibid., Date to Otter, 4 November 1917. On Date's orders and warning to prisoners regarding the use of force of arms, see ibid., "Prisoners Orders," 15 October 1917.

103 To ensure that there would be no backsliding, the commandant at Kapuskasing requested the removal of soldiers whose personal loyalties, he felt, were in doubt. For Date, the prospect of disobedience and "collusion" was a concern. Otter approved the request, forwarding it to the officer commanding Military District No. 2 and underscoring the need for "entirely British replacements." NAC, RG 24, vol. 4360, file 34-6-11

(4), Major General Wm. Otter to Officer Commanding Military District No. 2, 11 May 1918.

104  NAC, RG 6, vol. 763, file 4947, Dr K. Schwarze, Chairman of POW Committee, Vernon Internment Camp, to S. Gintzburger, Consul of Switzerland, 14 November 1917; and ibid., file 4738, POW Camp Committee, Vernon Internment Camp, to Swiss Consul, 16 and 19 April 1918.

105  Ibid., file 4738, POW Camp Committee, Vernon Internment Camp, to Beni R. Iseli, Swiss General Consul, Montreal, with request for transmission of letter to the Imperial German Foreign Office, n.d.

106  Ibid., vol. 753, file 3209 – vol. 2, Major General Wm. Otter to Sir Thomas Tait, President Minto Coal Co., 11 September 1917; Charles W. Peterson, Deputy Fuel Controller of Canada to Major General Otter, 20 September 1917; and Otter to Peterson, 22 September 1917.

107  See, for example, ibid. file 3194 (2), S.J. Hungerford, CNR General Manager to Major General Wm. Otter, 31 July 1918. Although the majority of applications were from the railways, other applications were also entertained. Officials were favourably disposed to an application by the Returned Soldiers' Colony at Kapuskasing for the use of eighty prisoners from the nearby camp to help clear land, an application that would only be approved when sufficient guards were procured. Ibid., vol. 757, file 3466 (2), Lieut. Colonel Macpherson, Staff Officer, Internment Operations, to A. Bell, Acting Deputy Minister of Railways, 11 September 1918.

108  See Ibid., vol. 757, file 3466 (3), "Prisoners of War Working Parties in Maritime Provinces for Canadian Government Railways," 16 August 1918.

109  Ibid., vol. 753, file 3194 (2), Major General Wm. Otter to S.J. Hungerford, CNR General Manager, 24 September 1918.

110  Ibid., file 3209 – vol. 2, Major General Otter to Charles W. Peterson, Deputy Fuel Controller of Canada, 22 September 1917.

111  "All Alien Enemies and suspicious persons in Halifax are supposed to be under observation. There is an unwritten 'Black List' of residents, known to this Dept. only, which will be forwarded to you under 'Secret' cover. These comprise what are known as 'Active Surveillance cases,' and are supplemented daily by the transient lists." NAC, RG 24, vol. 4541, file 73-1-1, Major Maclean, Halifax Fortress to the G.S.O., Military District No. 6, 15 January 1918.

112  NAC, RG 13 A2, vol. 222, file 934-955, "Return of Aliens of Enemy Nationality Interned or On Parole within Canada," 27 May 1918; and "Memorandum for the Deputy Minister of Justice," 20 May 1918.

113 Ibid., Freeman Harding, Kamloops, to F.J. Fulton, MP, 18 April 1918.

114 Ibid., Britton Osler to the Hon. J.C. Doherty, Minister of Justice, 24 April 1918.

115 Ibid., "Memorandum for the Chief Commissioner of Police – Registration of Enemy Aliens," 27 May 1918; and Chief Commissioner of Police, A.P. Sherwood, to the Deputy Minister of Justice, 28 May 1918. It was also proposed at the time that a clause be introduced making it an offence for any railway or steamship company to carry enemy aliens without an explicit permit authorizing them to travel. Considered highly desirable, the measure, however, was seen as impractical and dropped.

116 For a copy of the order with appended schedules, see NAC, RG 2, vol. 1203, file 951- 2129E, "P.C. 1908," 5 August 1918.

117 NAC, RG 13 A2, vol. 227, file 2135-2155, Pastor C.F. Christiansen, Denbigh, Ontario, to the Hon. C.J. Doherty, Minister of Justice, 26 September 1918.

118 NAC, Robert Borden Papers, MG 26 H1, vol. 104, reel C-4334, pages 56644–6, memorandum, "Re: IWW," Chief Commissioner of Police to the Hon. C.J. Doherty, Minister of Justice, 23 May 1918.

119 On the USDPC and government attitudes toward the organization, see RG 6 H3, vol. 800, file 1431. On repressive state measures taken against the organization in 1918, see Martynovych, *Ukrainians in Canada*, 436–7.

120 The report was seventeen pages in length. See NAC, RG 13 A2, vol. 222, file 934-955, C.H. Cahan, Montreal, to the Hon. C.J. Doherty, Minister of Justice, 14 September 1918.

121 NAC, Robert Borden Papers, MG 26 H1, vol. 104, reel C-4334, page 56683, Prime Minister R. Borden to C.H. Cahan, 17 September 1918.

122 See NAC, RG 13 A2, vol. 227, file 2009-2028, Deputy Minister of Justice to the Secretary, Canada Registration Board, 16 September 1918.

123 For an interpretation of the order-in-council imposing censorship on the German-language press in Canada, see Werner Bausenhart, "The Ontario German Language Press and Its Suppression by Order-in-Council in 1918," *Canadian Ethnic Studies* 4, nos. 1–2 (1972): 35–48.

124 See, for example, a five-page report to the minister of justice and his report titled "The Social Democratic Party." NAC, RG 13, box 17, file 166-1919, C.H. Cahan, Montreal, to the Hon. C.J. Doherty, Minister of Justice, 26 September 1918; and NAC, Robert Borden Papers, MG 26 H1, vol. 104, reel C-4334, pages 56703–6, Cahan to Doherty, 22 October 1918. See also his correspondence with Prime Minister Robert Borden in NAC, Robert Borden Papers, MG 26 H1, vol. 104, reel C-4334.

125 NAC, Robert Borden Papers, MG 26 H1, vol. 228, file 2246, C.H. Cahan, Director of Public Safety, to the Deputy Minister of Justice, 17 October 1918.

126 Ibid., vol. 229, file 2635-2654, C.H. Cahan, Director of Public Safety, to J.W. Ahlquist, Toronto, 18 December 1918.

127 Speaking in the case of Social Democratic Party of Canada (SDPC) activists Isaac Bainbridge and A.W. Mance, Cahan wrote: "It is inconceivable that the Government should permit Isaac Bainbridge, who is the Chief Executive, and A.W. Mance, who is the acting Dominion Secretary of this organization [SDPC], to proceed with the organization of aliens resident in this country for the purpose of thereby obstructing the work of the Government in carrying on the war." Ibid., vol. 1938, file 2715, C.H. Cahan, Director of Public Safety, to the Deputy Minister of Justice, E. Newcombe, 22 October 1918. Isaac Bainbridge had already been imprisoned on several occasions and Cahan sought his indefinite incarceration. On Bainbridge, see Ian Milligan, "Sedition in Wartime Ontario: The Trials and Imprisonment of Isaac Bainbridge, 1917–1918," *Ontario History* 100, no. 2 (Autumn 2008): 150–77.

128 See NAC, Robert Borden Papers, MG 26 H1, vol. 104, reel C-4334, page 56710, the Hon. N. Rowell, President of the Privy Council, to the Hon. C.J. Doherty, Minister of Justice, 18 October 1918; and ibid. vol. 246, reel C-4417, pages 13871–5, the Hon. T.A. Crerar, Minister of Agriculture, "Memorandum re: position of the Social Democratic Party in Canada under Order-in-Council passed September 24th 1918," 31 October 1918.

129 See, for example, his report outlining the organization, responsibilities, and duties of the Public Safety Branch. NAC, RG 13, box 17, file 166-1919, C.H. Cahan, Montreal, to the Hon. C.J. Doherty, Minister of Justice, 29 September 1918; and NAC, RG 13 A2, vol. 229, file 2463-2483, Cahan to Doherty, "Proposed Organization of Public Safety Branch and Dominion Police," 7 November 1918.

130 See NAC, RG 13, box 17, file 166-1919, C.H. Cahan, Director of Public Safety, to the Acting Prime Minister, Sir Thomas White, 15 November 1918; and ibid., personal letters from the Hon. C.J. Doherty, Minister of Justice, to C.H. Cahan, Director of Public Safety, and to the Deputy Minister of Justice, E. Newcombe, 15 November 1918.

131 "While the conduct of enemy aliens in the Province of Ontario has been fairly good during the war, their presence has caused a certain amount of animosity amongst English people and should there be any provocation on their part there is not the slightest doubt that attempts at retaliation

are likely to be made when the soldiers return." PAO, Attorney General Records, RG 4-32 (1918), file 2785, memorandum, J.E. Rogers, Superintendent, Ontario Provincial Police, to C.H. Cahan, Director of Public Safety, 28 November 1918.

132 On the agreement, see NAC, RG 24, vol. 1206, file H.Q. 240-1-56, "An Agreement between the British and German Governments Concerning Combatant Prisoners of War and Civilians," October 1918.

133 On the correspondence of the director of internment operations with his camp commanders, see NAC, RG 6 H1, vol. 770, file 6712 (1).

134 Ibid. includes replies that detail the character of the internees in accordance with the classification scheme.

135 Trotsky was living in New York City when the February Revolution of 1917 overthrew the reigning Russian tsar. Trotsky, compelled to particpate in the revoutionary events, sailed from New York on 27 March but his ship was intercepted by officials from Halifax harbour. Trotsky was arrested and sent to Amherst, Nova Scotia, for internment. At the request of the Russian Provisional Government, the British government released Trotsky on 29 April 1917. Trotsky would recount his internment at Amherst – "In a Concentration Camp" – in his autobiography (chapter 23). Leon Trosky, *My Life* (New York: Charles Scribners and Sons, 1930).

136 NAC, RG 6 H1, vol. 770, file 6712 (1), Major G. Anderson, Commander, Internment Operations Detail, Munson, Alberta, to Major General Wm. Otter, 22 November 1918.

137 On the Kaminecki case, see NAC, RG 13 A2, vol. 239, file 2497.

138 Ibid., vol. 232, file 3109, Katherine Przycylska to the Minister of Internal Affairs [sic], "Re: Harry Koruna, Prisoner of War No. 2942, Kapuskasing Camp," 3 February 1919.

139 Ibid., vol. 229, file 2484–2502, copy of letter, Mrs Thomas Leubetich, "Translation from French," 18 November 1918.

140 Ibid., E. Newcombe, Deputy Minister of Justice, to Mrs Thomas Leubetich, 23 November 1918.

141 Ibid., vol. 1938, file 12475, E. Newcombe, Deputy Minister of Justice, "Memorandum for Mr. Varcoe," 14 November 1918, and attachment "Memorandum Re: Expulsion of Aliens from Canada," n.d. In theory, enemy aliens as prisoners of war were to be repatriated. Diplomacy, however, made repatriation a problematic proposition in the case of enemy aliens as civilian non-combatants. They were legal immigrants and, therefore, owed consideration. The practical implication of this for internment officials was that they would look to deportation to rid the country of this category of individual, made possible under the WMA. The minister

of justice had the legal authority under the act to remove, expel, or deport enemy alien internees. But this also meant that there had to be sufficient grounds – usually in the form of an arrest report. Barbara Roberts notes: "Enemy aliens did not include prisoners of war, strictly speaking, although the lines between the two groups tended to blur." In actual fact, officials made the distinction and sought to repatriate internees who were known to be reservists and sought to deport the rest. And yet the terms repatriation and deportation were used interchangeably when it came to describing the fate of the internees. For a discussion of deportation of interned enemy aliens and more generally those who might be interned with a view to their deportation, see B. Roberts, *Whence They Came: Deportation from Canada, 1900–1935* (Ottawa: University of Ottawa Press, 1988), 68–9.

142 *Vancouver Sun*, 24 November 1918.

143 See NAC, RG 6 H1, vol. 770, file 6712 (1), Major General Otter to the Deputy Minister of Justice, E. Newcombe, 19 December 1918.

144 For a copy of the order, see ibid. On press reports regarding the order, see the *Globe* (Toronto), 24 January 1919, and *Montreal Gazette*, 25 January 1919.

145 NAC, RG 6 H1, vol. 770, file 6712 (1), "Copy of resolution passed unanimously by the Council of the City of Vancouver on January 27th 1919."

146 NAC, RG 13 A2, vol. 233, file 399-417, Notice of Motion – City of Victoria, 30 January 1919; ibid., vol. 237, file 1384-1403, Petition – City of Toronto, 21 February 1919; Petition – City of Hamilton, 25 February 1919; and NAC, RG 6 H1, vol. 770, file 6712 (1), Alex Morrison, Warden, Victoria County, Ontario, to "The Honourable the Minister of the Crown in charge of the Deportation of Aliens," 1 February 1919.

147 NAC, RG 13 A2, vol. 227, file 2009-2028, "Resolution," Brant Avenue Methodist Church, 5 February 1919. The Methodist Church was an ardent supporter of the war effort, portraying the conflict as a "righteous war." This attitude extended to developments on the home front, easily dovetailing with its radical critique of all that ailed Canadian society. See J. Bliss, "The Methodist Church and World War I," in *Conscription 1917: Essays by A.M. Willms/Ramsay Cook/J.M. Bliss/Martin Robin* (Toronto: University of Toronto Press, n.d.), 39–59.

148 Ibid., vol. 232, file 368, the Hon. Arthur Meighen, Acting Minister of Justice, to the Acting Prime Minister of Canada, Sir Thomas White, 6 February 1919.

149 See *Vancouver Sun*, 21 January 1919. The disposition of the veterans' association toward the enemy alien in Vancouver and divisions of opinion within the organization are described in Elizabeth Anne Lees,

"Problems of Pacification: Veterans' Groups in Vancouver, 1919–1922"
(MA thesis, Simon Fraser University, 1983), 36–9.

150  *Vancouver Sun*, 17 January 1919.

151  As reported in ibid., 27 January 1919; *Edmonton Bulletin*, 27 January
1919; and *Montreal Gazette*, 27, 28 January 1919. For a further description of the riot, see Art Grenke, "The German Community of Winnipeg
and the English-Canadian Response to World War I," *Canadian Ethnic
Studies* 20, no. 1 (1988): 33.

152  As reported in the *Montreal Gazette*, 29 January 1919; and *Vancouver
Sun*, 31 January and 1 February 1919.

153  In Vancouver, various employers agreed to supply lists of enemy aliens
who could be replaced by veterans. Elizabeth Lees, "Problems of
Pacification: Veterans' Groups in Vancouver, 1919–1922" (MA thesis,
Simon Fraser University, 1985), 37.

154  *Vancouver Sun*, 31 January 1919.

155  Ibid., 3 February 1919.

156  *Morning Leader* (Regina), 3 February 1919.

157  *Globe* (Toronto), 23 January 1919.

158  Ibid., 11 February 1919.

159  See *Vancouver Sun*, 5, 11 February 1919.

160  Ibid., 12 February 1919.

161  NAC, RG 13 A2, vol. 237, file 1363-1387, copy of Order-in-Council P.C.
332, and "Statement for the Press," n.d. For press reports, see *Globe*
(Toronto), 4 February 1919; and *Vancouver Sun*, 5 February 1919.

162  NAC, RG 13 A2, vol. 237, file 1384-1403, David Grout, County Court
Chambers, Vancouver, to E. Newcombe, Deputy Minister of Justice,
25 February 1919.

163  The Alien Investigation Board was created under the authority of the
Provincial Act. Manitoba's Premier T.C. Norris had hoped to appease veterans who were pressuring the provincial government to deal with enemy
aliens. According to Norris, the creation of the Board had "a salutary
effect on both the foreigners and returned soldiers," leading to peace and
quiet in the city of Winnipeg. Enemy aliens were being investigated and
sixty to one hundred were registering daily with the Board. Soon, however, the large numbers being processed as well as the growing demand
by veterans that the Norris government act on the Board's findings forced
the premier to turn to the federal government to assume control of the
Board. This came as a surprise to federal officials, who were unsure of the
nature of the Board (except what they read in the press) and its powers
and how these related to federal laws. On the genesis of the Alien

Investigation Board of Manitoba and subsequent controversy, see NAC, RG 13 A2, vol. 234, file 682-701.

164 Immigration meant the arrival of new and radical ideas that constituted a threat to British constitutionalism and the British way of life. See Reinhold Kramer and Tom Mitchell, *When the State Trembled: How AJ Andrews and the Citizens' Committee Broke the Winnipeg General Strike* (Toronto: University of Toronto Press, 2010), 125.

165 As reported in the *Leader* (Regina), 14 April 1919; and *Vancouver Sun*, 22 March and 14 April 1919. The Immigration Act was amended (Section 38), enabling the federal government to prohibit the entry of nationalities that had fought against Canada and Britain during the war, including those from Germany, Austria, Hungary, Bulgaria, and Turkey. The government also used the amended act to prohibit the entry of Hutterites, Mennonites, and Doukhobors due to their religious practices. On public opposition to the Hutterites and other religious denominations, see Howard Palmer, *Patterns of Prejudice: A History of Nativism in Alberta* (Toronto: McClelland and Stewart, 1983), 52–3.

166 *Vancouver Sun*, 17 April 1919.

167 *Leader* (Regina), 21 April 1919.

168 See *Vancouver Sun*, 27 March 1919.

169 *Globe* (Toronto), 14 April 1919.

170 *Globe* (Toronto), 4 February 1919.

171 See NAC, RG 13 A2, vol. 233, file 550-570, minutes of various meetings held in Oshawa (11 February), Toronto (12 February), and Montreal (23 February); and ibid., petition to the Hon. Charles J. Doherty, Minister of Justice, 24 February 1919. For a response to the petition, see NAC, Borden Papers, MG 26 H1, vol. 192, reel C-4389, pp. 106796–801, Parliamentary Under Secretary of State for External Affairs to the Reverends V.T. Rupchynski and P. Crath, 30 July 1919.

172 NAC, Robert Borden Papers, MG 26 H1, vol. 192, reel C-4389, page 106794, "Memorandum," 24 February 1919.

173 The riot had a disconcerting effect on other communities as well. The Ukrainian Canadian Citizens Committee, for instance, petitioned Winnipeg's mayor, Charles Gray, to protect "our very lives against the crusades of youthful looters." See Martynovych, *Ukrainians in Canada*, 439.

174 See NAC, RG 13 A2, vol. 233, file 422-442, Camp Committee, Vernon Internment Camp, to the Governor General of Canada, 8 February 1919.

175 NAC, RG 6, vol. 770, file 6712 – part 1, A. Meyer, POW Committee, Vernon Internment Camp, 21 March 1919.

176  See NAC, RG 13 A2, vol. 236, file 1162, K. Hildebrandt, POW No. 884, Vernon Internment Camp, to the Hon. A. Meighen, Minister of Justice, with accompanying petition, 5 April 1919.

177  Ibid., Prisoners of War, Kapuskasing Internment Camp, to the Hon. C.J. Doherty, Minister of Justice, 17 April 1919.

178  NAC, RG 6, vol. 770, file 6712 – part 2, E. Newcombe, Deputy Minister of Justice to the Major General Otter, 1 May 1919.

179  B. Kordan, "Eaton Internment Camp," *Encyclopedia of Saskatchewan*, http://esask.uregina.ca/entry/eaton_internment_camp.html.

180  NAC, RG 6, vol. 770, file 6712 – part 2, Major General Wm. Otter to E. Newcombe, Deputy Minister of Justice, 2 May 1919.

181  Ibid.

182  Ibid., Lieut. Colonel W.E. Date, Officer Commanding Kapuskasing Internment Camp, to Major General Wm. Otter, 12 May 1919.

183  See *Winnipeg Tribune*, 1 May 1919; and *Saskatoon Daily Star*, 14 May 1919. See also NAC, RG 13 A2, vol. 234, file 746-766, J. Newton, Great War Veterans' Association, to the Hon. T. Johnson, Manitoba Attorney General, Winnipeg, 3 May 1919; the Hon. T. Johnson, Manitoba Attorney General to the Hon. A. Meighen, Minister of Justice, 6 May 1919; and Acting Minister of Justice to the Manitoba Attorney General, 10 May 1919.

184  NAC, RG 18, vol. 581, file 464-477 (RCMP, 1919), "Report. Re: Internment of Enemy Aliens at Winnipeg. Re: Peter Get," 13 May 1919.

185  NAC, MG 26 H1, vol. 5, reel C-4412, pages 002537-41, Sir Hugh Macdonald to the Hon. A. Meighen, Minister of Justice, 3 July 1919.

186  See the *Manitoba Free Press* (Winnipeg), 18, 23 June 1919.

187  "The Immigration Act and regulations provided the government with enough flexibility to prevent admission, to prohibit naturalization, and to effect the removal of those who were perceived as lowering the standards of acceptable citizenry, by their nationality, race, or political opinions." Ninette Kelley and Michael Trebilcock, *The Making of the Mosaic: A History of Canadian Immigration Policy* (Toronto: University of Toronto Press, 1998), 169.

188  Donald Avery notes that the RNWMP, at the height of the troubles, identified one hundred labour activists who were to be deported, of whom thirty-six were from Winnipeg. To this number were added others – "revolutionaries and anarchists" – who were to be deported with the assistance of the Immigration Branch, which had evolved into a quasi-security service. See Avery, *"Dangerous Foreigners,"* 85; and D. Avery, *Reluctant Host: Canada's Response to Immigrant Workers, 1896–1994* (Toronto:

McClelland and Stewart, 1994), 79. The arrests in Alberta are described in Palmer, *Patterns of Prejudice*, 55.

189 NAC, RG 6, vol. 770, file 6712 – part 2, Major General Wm. Otter to E. Newcombe, Deputy Minister of Justice, 21 June 1919; NAC, RG 13 A2, vol. 237, file 1490-1510, Otter to Newcombe, 21 June 1919; and NAC, RG 6, vol. 770, file 6712 – part 3, W.G. Annable, CP Ocean Services, to Major G. Dillon, Supply and Transport Officer, Internment Operations, 18 July 1919. The deportations were covered in the press. See, for example, *Globe* (Toronto), 19, 24, and 29 July 1919.

190 NAC, RG 6, vol. 770, file 6712 – part 3, Major General Wm. Otter to the Hon. A. Meighen, Minister of Justice, 22 July 1919. Otter was inclined, however, to exercise clemency in the case of six British- or Canadian-born women who appeared to be loyal despite being married to enemy aliens, "and seemingly capable of exercising a good influence over the men."

191 Ibid., Meighen to Otter, 13 August 1919.

192 Ibid., Otter to Meighen, 23 August 1919.

193 Regarding the case of J.E. Bieber, POW No. 1012, Amherst Internment Camp, see NAC, RG 13 A2, vol. 240, file 2189-2209.

194 The case of Martin Schweig, POW No. 3214, Kapuskasing Internment Camp, is reported in ibid., vol. 241, file 2384-2404.

195 The circumstances regarding C. Vohwinkel, POW No. 994, Amherst Internment Camp, are described in ibid., vol. 240, file 2189-2209.

196 For information on the Hundt case, see NAC, RG 6 H1, vol. 761, file 4319.

197 "In Canada, the early deportation regime targeted individuals deemed unsuitable on the basis of 'race,' political radicals, the socially undesirable (including the women deemed 'immoral'), and 'foreign' industrial workers." Cynthia Wright, "The Museum of Illegal Immigration: Historical Perspectives on the Production of Non-Citizens and Challenges to Immigration Controls," in Luin Goldring and Patricia Landolt, eds, *Producing and Negotiating Non-Citizenship: Precarious Legal Status in Canada* (Toronto: University of Toronto Press, 2013), 38.

198 On George Hamann, POW No. 2097, Kapuskasing, and the application for his release and the determination, see NAC, RG 13 A2, vol. 240, file 1978-1956.

199 See ibid., vol. 241, file 2210-2230.

200 See ibid., vol. 242, file 2608-2828.

201 For correspondence between the legal firm Murray and Noble and government officials regarding the case of Harry Kizinski and eleven other alleged co-conspirators in the Winnipeg strike and riot, see ibid., vol. 239,

file 1960. The W M A provided not only for the internment of enemy aliens as prisoners of war but also for their deportation if they were shown to be hostile or in violation of the laws. More importantly, declared to be prisoners of war, the internees had "no remedy in law." Internment, in this case, gave administrative legal cover to the deportation of enemy alien agitators.

202 Lieut. Colonel W.E. Date, commandant of the Kapuskasing internment camp, gloated that a hundred "Reds" had been "quietly gathered in" and "without any publicity whatever" deported along with other enemy aliens, adding "more were to go." *Globe* (Toronto), 20 January 1920. For a brief discussion of the issue of deportations of political radicals and labour militants in the wake of the Winnipeg General Strike, see D. Avery, "Ethnic and Class Tensions in 1918–1920: Anglo-Canadians and the Alien Worker," in Swyripa and Thompson, eds, *Loyalties in Conflict*, 86–7. On deportation as a form of punishment, see William Walters, "Deportation, Expulsion, and the International Police of Aliens," *Citizenship Studies* 6, no. 3 (2002): 289.

203 NAC, RG 13 A2, vol. 245, file 41-60, Major General Wm. Otter to E. Newcombe, Deputy Minister of Justice, 29 December 1919, and Otter to Newcombe, 16 January 1920.

204 See Roberts, *Whence They Came*, 70 and 88.

205 *Globe* (Toronto), 27 March 1920.

206 Ibid. See also *Manitoba Free Press* (Winnipeg), 27 March 1920.

207 *Globe* (Toronto), 23 September 1921.

208 The importance of enemy alien labour was an issue throughout the war. Although subject to economic cycles, the value and importance of enemy alien labour to the overall economy was never in doubt. Perhaps this was no more apparent than when, in the context of widespread demands for enemy alien deportation, the chief commissioner of police, Col. A. P. Sherwood, proposed that enemy aliens be prevented from leaving the country – "detained" – after the Declaration of Peace because of the adverse effect their departure would have on the Canadian economy. NAC, RG 13 A2, vol. 228, file 2376-2396, Chief Commissioner of Police, Colonel A.P. Sherwood, to the Deputy Minister of Justice, 6 November 1918.

209 The question of the large-scale use of internment labour for private industry was raised by the minister of railways and canals, the Hon. F. Cochrane, who inquired whether there was "anything in international law which might prevent utilizing the services of prisoners of war to supply this shortage." That this was not the case made the release of the

internees possible. However, the initial inquiry underscored a desire on the part of Cochrane and others to somehow square the conundrum. NAC, Borden Papers, MG 26 H1, vol. 181, reel C-4382, pages 99326–39, the Hon. F. Cochrane, Minister of Railways and Canals, to the Prime Minister, the Rt. Hon. Robert Borden, 8 November 1915.

210 The *Calgary Daily Herald* was particularly incredulous and insisted that those released be re-interned at once. *Calgary Daily Herald*, 28 September 1916.

211 The release of a thousand interned enemy aliens to work in the coal mines of Nova Scotia and Alberta would be regarded as a "foreign invasion" by miners' unions there, according to the *Globe*. See *Globe* (Toronto), 15 June 1916.

212 Fearing being re-interned after public outcry over their release, thirty-five paroled prisoners fled to the United States from their place of employment on Vancouver Island. It was thought that they would make their way across the border. Holding the BC government responsible, critics forced the BC officials to insist that "no further prisoners be released in the province by the Internment Directorate." See *Vancouver Sun*, 13, 26 September 1916 and 6 February 1917.

213 For a list of major companies and corporations (sixty-nine in total), see NAC, RG 117, vol. 20, file "Sundries re: all Camps, Companies for whom Prisoners of War were released to work," n.d.

214 During the course of internment, prisoners took ill and were invalided. Still others were afflicted with a variety of ailments before their internment, having been arrested and interned precisely because they were incapable of maintaining themselves. The question of what to do with them was a matter of ongoing concern, given the fact that they were unable to work, and therefore represented a public charge. Diplomatic negotiations provided for the possibility of the return of wounded prisoners of war. As such, an opportunity was presented for the repatriation of those who would fall broadly within this category. Lists were soon compiled of all the unwanted – the infirm, the invalid, and the insane – for the purpose of deportation. In the end, in excess of one hundred such individuals were identified for deportation. For an example of such a list, see NAC, RG 6 H1, vol. 752, file 3130, Memo: "Incurably Sick P. of W." Lieutenant Charles Harvey, Commandant Edgewood Internment Camp to Major General Wm. Otter, Officer Commanding Internment Operations, 1 June 1916.

On the question of invalids and deportation, Peter Melnycky writes: "Mental and physical health were prominent factors in the selection of internees to be sent out of the country. Some had incurable diseases like tuberculosis; others were slated for deportation as incapacitated invalids for such ailments as chronic inflammation of the bowels and inoperable hernia – all conditions which might well have developed as a result of life in the camps. Anthony Pozlucki, aged fifty-four, was listed as deportation material for suffering from a 'persistent headache.' Many of those interned contracted some form of mental illness during their confinement … A total of 106 internees were confined to mental institutions by Internment Operations, sixty-one of them Austrians; all but three were ultimately deported." Peter Melnycky, "The Internment of Ukrainians in Canada" in Swyripa and Thompson, eds, *Loyalties in Conflict*, 15–16.

215  *Globe* (Toronto), 14 April 1917. For a detailed account of the incident, see N. Smith, "Fighting the Alien Problem in a British Country: Returned Soldiers and Anti-Alien Activism in Wartime Canada, 1916–1919," in Miller, Rowe, and Kitchen, eds, *Other Combatants, Other Fronts*, 293–4.

216  The Great War Veterans' Association met with the prime minister to voice their concerns as soldier-patriots: "As an association of returned soldiers we, to the best our ability and experience, have laid before you the conditions of this alien question as we know it exists throughout the country and in doing so consider our obligation as loyal citizens of Canada to have been faithfully carried out." See *Vancouver Sun*, 30 March 1918. For an account of the veterans' support of the war effort on the home front and its connection to patriotic/anti-alien sentiments, see Nathan Smith, "Comrades and Citizens: Great War Veterans in Toronto, 1915–1919" (PhD dissertation, University of Toronto, 2012), chapters 3 and 4.

217  The comment was made in the context of a wide-ranging debate on the use of interned enemy alien labour. See Canada, House of Commons, *Hansard*, 22 April 1918, 973–1025.

218  See *Globe* (Toronto), 3 April 1918.

219  On radicalism and ethnicity in the Lakehead, see Michael Beaulieu, *Labour at the Lakehead: Ethnicity, Socialism and Politics, 1900–35* (Vancouver: University of British Columbia Press, 2011), 46–62.

220  NAC, RG 13 A2, vol. 227, file 2135-2155, Pastor C.F. Christiansen, Denbigh, Ontario, to the Hon. C.J. Doherty, Minister of Justice, 26 September 1918.

221  NAC, Robert Borden Papers, MG 26 H1, vol. 192, reel C-4389, "Memorandum," G. Maron, Rev. L. Tank, and Rev. W. Kohn, 24 February 1919.

222 See NAC, RG 13 A2, vol. 228, file 2438, H.A. Mackie, Member of Parliament (East Edmonton), to the Rt. Hon. Robert Borden, Prime Minister of Canada, 16 October 1918.

223 H.A. Mackie, member of parliament for Edmonton East, solicited support from his colleagues in the House of Commons on rescinding the War Time Elections Act, which had disfranchised naturalized citizens of "enemy" birth. The response from the parliamentarians was largely negative, including a number of choice comments received by telegraph: "Come off it. Forget it. Run down and urinate in the creek." "Do not concur. No Fightee No Votee." Ibid., "Copies of Telegrams Received."

224 See, for example, ibid., vol. 229, file 2635-2654, F. Warwick, Secretary, Great War Veterans' Association of Canada (Fernie Branch), to the Hon. C.J. Doherty, Minister of Justice, 7 December 1918, and accompanying "Resolution."

225 See ibid., vol. 237, file 2556-223/19, E. Newcombe, Deputy Minister of Justice, to Major General Wm. Otter, 13 December 1918.

226 See *Globe* (Toronto), 4 February 1919. See also NAC, RG 13 A2, vol. 237, file 1363-1383, "Statement for the Press," and accompanying note.

227 Barbara Roberts has observed that considerable effort was exercised to ensure a tight legal case for each deportation so that it might stand up to appeals and objections – "to challenges from the courts, from the transportation companies (who had to pay the costs for taking away 'defective' immigrants they had brought in), from foreign governments, and from interest groups in Canada." Barbara Roberts, "Shoveling Out the 'Mutinous:' Political Deportation from Canada before 1936," *Labour/Le Travail* 18 (Fall 1988): 81–2.

228 The Great War Veterans' Association, at its annual convention, was particularly incensed by what was seen as a cavalier attitude by the government toward its concerns regarding enemy aliens. The government, however, assumed a guarded attitude toward the veterans and their demands. See NAC, Robert Borden Papers, MG 26 H1, vol. 247, reel C-4418, the Hon. F. Calder, Minister of Immigration and Colonization, to the Rt. Hon. Sir Robert Borden, Prime Minister of Canada, "Memorandum: Re GWVA Resolutions," 13 August 1919.

229 At the conclusion of internment operations, Colonel W.E. Date, commandant of the Kapuskasing internment camp, noted that during and after the Winnipeg General Strike, "over 100 prominent Reds" were quietly gathered up, sent to Kapuskasing, and subsequently deported. *Globe* (Toronto), 20 January 1920.

230  NAC, RG 6, vol. 766, file 5484, F.C. Blair, Secretary, Dept. of Immigration and Colonization, to Colonel D. Macpherson, Staff Officer, Internment Directorate, 27 September 1919; and Macpherson to Blair, 2 October 1919.

231  The argument is made in Roberts, *Whence They Came*, chapters 2 and 3.

232  Barbara Roberts notes that the war and its corollary internment gave the Department of Immigration "an unprecedented opportunity to lock up agitators and activists of enemy alien background, and to rid themselves of a raft of people whom they could never otherwise have deported because such deportations were illegal under the terms of the Immigration Act." Ibid., 68.

233  NAC, RG 6, vol. 770, file 6712 (1), Colonel W.E. Date, Commandant, Kapuskasing Internment Camp, to Maj. General Wm. Otter, Director, Internment Operations, 20 December 1918.

## CHAPTER FIVE

1  NAC, Robert Borden Papers, MG 26 H1, vol. 78, reel C-4319, pages 40300–2, unidentified hand-written memorandum, "War-time election forced on country," n.d.

2  Both Sir Wilfrid Laurier and Prime Minister Sir Robert Borden acknowledged the pull of home and familial ties at the outset of the war. See *Winnipeg Tribune*, 21 August 1914; and *Berlin Daily Telegraph* (Berlin, Ontario), 24 August 1914.

3  See NAC, RG 24, vol. 407, file H.Q. 54-21-1-2, letter to Mr C.P. Seyker from the Judge Advocate General and deputy minister, Department of Militia and Defence, 15 August 1914.

4  For a discussion of the idea of subjectship and its relevance in determining allegiance, see James Farney and Bohdan S. Kordan, "The Predicament of Belonging: The Status of Enemy Aliens in Canada, 1914," *Journal of Canadian Studies* 39, no. 1(Winter 2005): 74–89.

5  On the question of enemy aliens and rights and the legal opinion of the Department of Justice, see NAC, RG 13, vol. 189, file 1639-1659, "In the Matter of Josef Chamryk, and Austrian arrested and detained by the military authorities at Winnipeg, and in the matter of his right to discharge on habeas corpus," 5 November 1914.

6  See Montserrat Guibernau, *Belonging: Solidarity and Division in Modern Societies* (Cambridge: Polity Press, 2013), 137–40.

7  For examples of name changes, see *Saskatoon Phoenix*, 5 November 1914; and NAC, RG vol. 192, file 570-589, Lewis Mittenthal to Minister of

Justice, 20 March 1915. As for naturalization, this was no assurance. The BC legislative member for Victoria, H. W. Behnson, was accused of being of German birth, despite testimony that he had taken an oath of allegiance and had been a resident of the province for thirty-four years. *Saskatoon Phoenix*, 3 February 1915. On changing surnames and hiding identities, see John Herd Thompson, *The Harvests of War: The Prairie West, 1914–1918* (Toronto: McClelland and Stewart, 1978), 76–7.

8 Appealing to the governor general, Julius Block, a long-standing resident of Canada, relayed his personal feelings of humiliation and sorrow at being identified an enemy on account of his origin. "In happier times," he concluded, "[Canada] looked upon us as good a body of inhabitants any land could have. Now we get too often the cold shoulder, even abuse and insult, because we just happen to be Germans or bear German names. It is almost looked upon as a crime to be a German." He beseeched the king's representative to communicate publicly "that to be of German nationality or of German origin was not a crime or misdemeanor and that we should be left alone as long as we abstain from any act detrimental to the British Empire, this would I feel sure benefit us greatly." NAC, RG 6 H3, vol. 793, file 2165B, letter from J. Block to the Governor General of Canada, the Duke of Connaught, 30 November 1914.

9 "Though returned soldiers, employers, labour leaders, middle-class spokespeople and politicians did not all agree on how to fix the alien problem there was a broadly-based attitude that the presence of aliens posed problems for society." Nathan Smith, "Fighting the Alien Problem in a British Country: Returned Soldiers and Anti-Alien Activism in Wartime Canada, 1916–1919," in A. Miller, Laura Rowe, and James Kitchen, eds, *Other Combatants, Other Fronts: Competing Histories of the First World War* (Newcastle: Cambridge Scholars Publishing, 2011), 300.

10 See, for example, NAC, RG 24, vol. 4413, file 26-3-12 (3), Wm. A. McCulloch to Colonel Young, Kingston, and the Officer Commanding Division III, 1 December 1914. For a further discussion of disloyalty allegations, see Peter Moogk, "Uncovering the Enemy Within: British Columbians and the German Menace," BC *Studies: The British Columbian Quarterly* 182 (2014): 58.

11 *Daily British Whig* (Kingston), 31 October 1914.

12 See, for example, NAC, Robert Borden Papers, MG 26 H1(c), vol. 191, reel C-4388, page 105989, A.P. Sherwood, Chief Commissioner of Police, to L.C. Christie, Department of External Affairs, 4 September 1914.

13 See ibid., pages 106133–4, Hon. Sir Hugh J. Macdonald to the Rt. Hon. Sir Robert Borden, Prime Minister of Canada, 28 September 1914.

14  NAC, RG 25, vol. 1150, file 1463, Sir Joseph Pope, Under Secretary of State, to J.G. Foster, American Consul General, 21 December 1914.

15  Although the government was able to make the argument that internment was not punitive but rather a relief program, it was accepted by an element of the public and press that the internees were being privileged over "a good many Canadian citizens whose chances of a living would be better if they were enemy aliens." *Edmonton Daily Bulletin*, 1 February 1915.

16  The idea that "special consideration" was owed to those who immigrated to Canada was raised immediately after order-in-council PC 2721 was pro-mulgated and was repeated periodically during the war, including by the minister of justice, the Hon. C.J. Doherty, in a broad debate on the treat-ment of enemy aliens in the Canadian parliament. See *Montreal Gazette*, 28 October 1914; *Revelstoke Mail Herald*, 31 July 1915; and Canada, House of Commons, *Hansard*, 22 April 1918, 973–1025.

17  Investigations were occasionally conducted after complaints were lodged and particulars made known. Some cases were startling in what they revealed. For example, John Kolotelo was arrested by Fort Frances's chief of police and eventually interned, the chief apparently motivated because of his intimacy with the victim's wife. NAC, RG 6 H1, vol. 764, file 5202, J. Kolotelo, Prisoner of War No. 2439, to Swiss Consul General Iseli, 13 September 1917.

18  NAC, RG 13, vol. 195, file 1192-1212, Franz Munsche, Prisoner of War No. 340, to Mr G. Weichel, MPP, 11 July 1915; and Major General Wm. Otter, director, Internment Operations to the minister of justice, 8 July 1915.

19  The link between external events and domestic opinion during the war was compelling. Reports of defeats and setbacks often reverberated throughout the nation, resulting in calls for retribution. The torpedoing of the *Lusitania* had a profound effect on the Canadian public. Riots and vio-lence against individual enemy aliens were widespread throughout the country, underscoring for the government the importance of dealing with the enemy alien "problem." On the loss of the *Lusitania* and its effect on the mood of the country, see *Globe* (Toronto), 11 and 13 May 1915; *Vancouver Sun*, 13, 17, 22 May 1915; and *Calgary Daily Herald*, 14 and 15 May 1915.

20  "I am sending an Austrian Mike Spirak to be dealt with by you. He has been living in the bush at Granite Quarry for some months begging from the farmers in that vicinity and the people there have become afraid of him. He has not reported to me for some weeks, and I should suggest that he be interned." NAC, RG 24, vol. 4279, file 34-1-3 (10), Ralph Vincent,

Chief of Police, Sault Ste. Marie, to Lieut. Colonel S.L. Penhorwood, HQ 51st Regiment Soo Rifles, 18 October 1915.

21 An additional breakdown of the numbers is provided in Bohdan Kordan, *Enemy Aliens, Prisoners of War: Internment in Canada during the Great War* (Montreal and Kingston: McGill-Queen's University Press, 2002), 36.

22 For a description of internment in the national parks, see Bill Waiser, *Park Prisoners: The Untold Story of Western Canada's National Parks, 1915–1946* (Saskatoon and Calgary: Fifth House, 1995), 3–47, and E.J. Hart, *J.B. Harkin: Father of Canada's National Parks* (Edmonton: University of Alberta Press, 2010), 129–32.

23 It was felt that the actions taken "were in accordance with our domestic system to employ at such labour as they are qualified to perform, persons whether native or foreign who are cast upon the charity of the State ... And that neither the state of war nor any rule sanctioned by international convention or practice requires that destitute people of any nationality when seeking relief from the State should be immune from a similar requirement." See NAC, RG 6 H1, vol. 819, file 2616, R. Boudreau, clerk of the Privy Council, 28 August 1915.

24 "I have been endeavouring to lay out a pretty extensive plan of winter work in order that your kind offer with respect to aliens might be accepted in as full a degree as possible. In so far as Banff is concerned, we consider that we have got work to provide for four hundred prisoners, that is, the Castle camp and two hundred more ... A few days ago, Captain Palmer and I inspected the proposed campsite near Field. On this, I think he has also made a report. We figure that can utilize another two hundred at this point. I understand the town of Revelstoke is very anxious to retain the prisoners now in Revelstoke Park, during the winter and that they are submitting a proposition to you in that regard ... I am also anxious to locate a camp in Jasper Park for the winter, where I think work could easily be found for 300." NAC, RG 84, vol. 124, file Y170, J. Harkin, Dominion Parks commissioner, to Maj. General Wm. Otter, director, Internment Operations, 28 September 1915.

25 NAC, RG 84, vol. 190, file MR176, telegram, Commissioner, Dominion Parks Branch, J.B. Harkin to F.H. Williamson, Deputy Commissioner, Dominion Parks Branch, 5 October 1915, and J. Wardle to Major General Wm. Otter, Officer Commanding Internment Operations, 6 October 1915; and BC Ministry of Transportation Records, Okanagan District (1916), file 1752, John Black to J.E. Griffith, Deputy Minister of Public Works, 28 and 29 April 1916.

Notes to pages 276–8

26 See BC Ministry of Transportation Records, North Okanagan and Salmon Arm Districts (1916), file 211, J.E. Griffith, Deputy Minister of Public Works, to R. Bruhn, Assistant Road Superintendent, 17 August 1916.

27 NAC RG 6 H1, vol. 752, file 3130, Lieutenant C. Harvey, Officer Commanding Edgewood Internment Camp, to Major General Wm. Otter, Officer Commanding Internment Operations, 2 May 1916, and Lieut. Colonel, Department of Alien Reservists to Major General Wm. Otter, Officer Commanding Internment Operations, 8 May 1916.

28 In response to a request for information regarding alleged ill treatment of prisoners at the Lethbridge internment camp, the officer commanding noted the circumstances and offered an explanation for each occurrence. The harsh treatment was largely for petty offences and appeared to be motivated by a desire to elicit submission from the prisoner and to provide an example to the others. See NAC, RG 24, vol. 4695, file 448-14-20 (4), copy of letter, Officer Commanding Internment Barracks, Lethbridge, to the Staff Officer Internment Operations, 6 December 1915.

29 The concept "prize of war" is discussed more fully in Kordan, *Enemy Aliens, Prisoners of War*, 113–15.

30 The phrase "fair share" is identified with the request by Kelowna's mayor, J. Jones, who was concerned that the city of Kelowna would be disadvantaged by not making a claim early on, and who insisted that the city was no less deserving than other jurisdictions, which he believed were set to profit from internment labour. BC Ministry of Transportation Records, Okanagan District (1915), file 1752, section 2, J.W. Jones, Mayor, Kelowna, to the Hon. Thomas Taylor, BC Minister of Public Works, 4 September 1915.

31 Diplomatic negotiations regarding the repatriation of civilian internees were long and complicated. It was felt that there was a moral and political duty to work out an agreement that would address plight of these unfortunates. The process of negotiations was shared with the Canadian governments. See NAC, Robert Borden Papers, MG 26 H1(c), vol. 59, reel C-4307, pages 29061–72; and NAC, RG 25, series G1, vol. 1200, file 15 (part 1), "Further Correspondence respecting the Proposed Release of Civilians Interned in the British and German Empires," January 1917.

32 NAC, RG 13 A2, vol. 205, file 1450-1470, Bonar Law, UK Colonial Secretary, to the Governor General, 8 March 1916. The threat of reprisals by Germany against British prisoners was always of concern to UK authorities when they urged Canada to follow the custom of not forcing civilian prisoners to work. See, for example, NAC, RG 13 A2, vol. 195, Bonar Law, UK Colonial Secretary, to the Governor General, 5 July 1915.

33 The point is more widely discussed in Bohdan S. Kordan and Craig Mahovsky, *A Bare and Impolitic Right: Internment and Ukrainian-Canadian Redress* (Montreal and Kingston: McGill-Queen's University Press, 2004), 27–41.

34 In the marginalia of a report on conditions at the Banff internment camp, a Foreign Office official noted that the internees were being forced to work, but since they did not complain he concluded: "I do not think we should say anything about it." PRO, Foreign Office Papers, FO 383/239, "Prisoners of War Camp at Banff," 29 June 1916.

35 NAC, RG 24, vol. 4721, file 3, H. Clum, US Consul, "Visit to Internment Camp at Banff, Alberta," 25 May 1916.

36 The report served as the basis for order-in council PC 2039. See NAC, RG 6 H1, vol. 819, file 2616, R. Boudreau, clerk of the Privy Council, 28 August 1915.

37 The resentment would take on a racial character as protests identified those being released as taking jobs that should be reserved for "white men." See *Vancouver Sun*, 11 September 1916.

38 See *Calgary Daily Herald*, 28 September 1916.

39 It was reported 88,312 enemy aliens were either interned or registered and on parole at the time of the armistice. *Globe* (Toronto), 24 January 1919.

40 The point is discussed more fully in Kordan, *Enemy Aliens, Prisoners of War*, 20–2.

41 See *Vancouver Sun*, 18 October 1916.

42 See, for example, *Vancouver Sun*, 11 June 1917.

43 *Edmonton Bulletin*, 30 June 1917.

44 NAC, RG 13 A2, vol. 227, file 2093-2113, The Great War Veterans' Association, "Aliens: Resolution No. 3," 3 August 1918.

45 NAC, Loring Christie Papers, MG 30 E15, vol. 2, reel C-3876, pages 1324–5.

46 *Globe* (Toronto), 12 April and 7 May 1918; *Vancouver Sun*, 23, 24 April and 7 May 1918.

47 NAC, RG 13 A2, vol. 222, file 934-955, "Memorandum for Chief Commissioner of Police Re: Registration of Alien Enemies," 27 May 1918.

48 *Vancouver Sun*, 23 December 1918 and 17, 18, 31 January 1919; *Globe* (Toronto), 23 January 1919.

49 NAC, RG 6, vol. 770, file 6712 (part 1), "P.C. 158 Certified copy of a Report of the Committee of the Privy Council," 23 January 1919.

50 *Vancouver Sun*, 5 February 1919. The idea of deporting selected individuals who were being interned would devolve into a wider question of interning all 85,000 registered enemy aliens and then determining at a later date those who would be deported. See NAC, RG 13 A2, vol. 237, file

1363-1383, "Memorandum for Acting Chief Commissioner of Police Re: Enemy Aliens," 10 February 1919.

51 There was some question as to what to do in the case of the insane. What was the point, it was asked, of seeking the consent of an individual who was clearly unable to make a competent decision?

52 NAC, Immigration Branch, RG 76, vol. 394, file 663236 (part 7), reel C-10287, page 8542472, Commissioner F. McLure Sclanders to W.D. Scott, Superintendent of Immigration, 5 March 1919.

53 NAC, RG 6 H1, vol. 770, file 6712 (1), "Copy of Resolution passed unanimously by the Council of the City of Vancouver," 27 January 1919. See also *Vancouver Sun*, 25, 28 February 1919; and *Victoria Colonist*, 13 June 1919.

54 On board the transport ship SS *Pretorian* as it was about to depart from Rotterdam, Captain Watson Kirkconnell, the officer commanding the prisoner escort detail, described the prisoners who had just been released as blithe and carefree as they tasted liberty for the first time in many years. Gathered together on the dock, they had one final look at the troops on the ship – their last remaining connection with Canada. "Although there was no malice or vituperation in their parting salutation," there was a Spartan attitude bred from years of captivity, which led some of them to prophesy that "we might expect them back in a few weeks to spread the gospel of 'Bolshevismus' in our sleepy colony." NAC, RG 6 H1, vol. 770, file 6712 (4), Captain T.W. Kirkconnell, Officer Commanding Pretorian Party, to the Staff Officer, Internment Operations, "Prisoners Repatriated per SS Pretorian," 21 September 1919.

55 "The attitude of Anglo-Canadians towards German Canadians had been cordial [initially]. In the war's course people of German ancestry became 'outsiders' – the enemy's kin and the spawn of a murderous and brutal race. It was a dramatic loss of status." Moogk, "Uncovering the Enemy Within: British Columbians and the German Menace," 72.

56 This position was persuasively articulated in a petition to the governor general from the Internment Camp Committee at Vernon. NAC, RG 13 A2, vol. 233, file 422-442, Vernon Camp Committee to the Duke of Devonshire, Governor General of Canada, 8 February 1919.

57 NAC, Robert Borden Papers, MG 26 H1, vol. 192, reel C-4389, page 106802, unidentified author, handwritten note, "Memo," 5 August 1919.

# INDEX

Aikins, James (president, Canadian Bar Association), 82

Alien Investigation Board of Manitoba, 251, 282; number of investigations, 248; provincial government, 265; role of, 246, 366–7n163. *See also* deportation; Moore, A.E.

Allan, Fred (RNWMP constable), 89

Amherst Internment Camp: criticism of administration, 167, 227, 331n37; detention of merchant marines, 129; escape, 158; number of prisoners, 240; prisoner assistance, 349n220; prisoner release, 204, 229; prisoner treatment, 181, 345n198, 346n207; relocating prisoners to, 250; repatriation of prisoners, 253; setup of, 112; shooting of prisoners, 159, 184; Trotsky, 364n135; undesirables, 237, 266–7, 283

Anderson, Major G. (Munson commandant), 237

Apostal, Dmytro, 315n104

Archambault, J.B. (justice), 36

armistice, 3, 235, 236, 264; number of registered enemy aliens, 379n39; prisoner release and, 237, 239, 249; prisoner of war designation, 283

arrest: assurances and, 68; cause, 6, 14, 15, 18, 25, 45, 68, 85–6, 88–91, 123, 125–7, 130–1, 155, 198–9, 212, 220, 224, 237–8, 254, 285n2, 315n104; destitution, 93, 122, 128, 132, 136, 165, 325n207; Fernie, 100–1, 114–15, 121; German-Canadian Alliance, 40; labour unrest, 255; militia, 48; nativism, 274; police authority, 49, 81; Proclamation (15 August), 36, 37, 60, 61; radicalism, 225, 252, 253; reservists, 107, 314–15n98; suspicion, 62, 86–7; threat of, 214; UK instructions, 47; Undertakings, 50–1, 77; US border 96, 112, 301n157; USDPC, 233

Arsenych, W., 27–8

Austria-Hungary, 29, 183; national minorities, 58–9, 133, 183

Austrian Philanthropic Committee, 65, 66

Bruhn, R. (road superintendent), 145, 146, 164

Bryan, William Jennings, 39

Buchs, Reinhold, 88

Buck, Private William, 11

Budak, George Luka, 174

Budka, Nykyta (bishop), 23, 57–8

Bulgarians, 181, 240, 272, 346n207, 352n21

Bundziock, Mike, 126

Burrell, Martin (minister of agriculture), 73

Bury, George, 17, 200, 289n34

Bury, Lieutenant A.C., 167

Cahan, Charles (director, Public Safety Branch), 233, 234, 235, 262–3

Calder, J.A. (minister of immigration), 240

Calgary, Alberta: nativism in, 30, 70, 86, 98–9, 201; registration, 78, 311n59; relief effort, 316n110, 317n125, 340n147; request for POW labour, 155; unemployment, 308n25, 309–10n42

*Calgary Daily Herald*, 12, 13, 14, 20, 35, 57, 70, 155, 175, 209, 219, 371n210

Campeau, Oliver (Montreal chief of police), 72

Canadian National Railway, 14, 204, 243

Canada Registration Board, 234

Canadian Pacific Railway, 205, 207

Canmore Coal Company, 204

Castle Mountain Internment Camp: conditions at, 152, 160, 161, 166–7, 170; escape from, 195; public attitudes toward, 177–8;

relocation to Banff, 206; segregation of prisoners, 332n47; setup, 117; work regime at, 149, 153. *See also* Cruickshank, Col. E.A.; Spence, Capt. Peter; Stuart, Major Duncan

Catrin, A.H., 44–5

charities, 70, 92, 119, 166, 309n35, 316n110

Cherumachzynsky, A., 211

Chevalier, Albert, 76

*Chicago Tribune*, 184

Chiskolook (prisoner), 170

Christiansen, Rev. C.F., 232, 263

Christie, Loring (legal adviser), 223, 261

Church, Const. William, 126

Church, Thomas (Toronto mayor), 216, 218

Citadel Internment Camp (Halifax): closure, 206; holding station, 213; POW labour proposals, 111, 142; re-internment, 210; role, 52; setup, 53

citizenship, 33, 40, 296–7n113

Clarke, S.J. (Banff park superintendent), 117

Cloran, Henry (senator), 168

Coatsworth, Emerson (Toronto registrar), 88, 93, 122

Cobalt, Ontario, 16, 94, 290n41

Coblenz, Manitoba, 38

Cochrane, F. (minister of railways), 203, 370–1n209

Cohen, Issac, 42

Coleman, Major. D. (Brandon commandant), 202, 205, 351n19

conscription, 216, 217, 218, 220, 268, 356n58, 356n63

Copsh, Stanley, 85

for families during, 120, 132, 165, 166, 322n178, 340n144, 340n147; system of, 129, 274; work projects, 143–4, 147–8, 153, 154, 164, 196–7, 207, 229, 275–6, 320n160, 342n162, 361n107, 377n24. *See also* prisoners of war; registration

Jamaica, 111–12, 240, 323n183
Jasper Internment Camp, 118, 137, 153; and Maligne Canyon, 154, 167
Johnson, Felix (US consul), 54, 63, 185, 344n185
Jones, J. (Kelowna mayor). *See* Kelowna, British Columbia

Kaminecki, John, 237
Kaminecki, Rev. Peter, 237
Kapuskasing Internment Camp: closure, 256, 267, 283; conditions at, 110, 137, 236–7, 250, 339–40n140; diplomatic protest, 178, 181; guards, 139–40, 360n103; numbers at, 213, 240, 253; prisoner resistance, 160, 173, 193, 227; provincial arrangements, 111, 196, 320n160; rationale for, 106, 108; relocation of prisoners, 201, 204, 207; setup, 105, 129; work projects, 147–9, 229, 361n107. *See also* Date, Major W.E.; Royce, Lieut. Col. G.
Kelowna, British Columbia, 143, 378n30
Kingsford, Rupert (justice), 30
Kingston, Ontario, 22
Kinsale, Rev. M.C., 67
Kirkconnell, Capt. Watson, 227, 380n54

Kitchener, Ontario, 220. *See also* Berlin, Ontario
Kitt, Mike, 68
Klenzing, Fred, 88
Koch, Thomas, 126
Kohlman, Erwin, 199
Kondro, Jacob, 130–1, 198
Kondro, John, 130–1, 132
Konekovitch, Martus, 68
Konowalczuk, Peter, 195
Konrat, Simon, 157
Krasij, Harry, 85
Kulik, Mike, 93, 122

labour shortage, 201, 202, 214–15, 221, 279
Lakehead, 136
Lake Minnewanka, 153
Lansing, Robert (secretary of state), 21
Larivitch, Tom, 68
Laurier, Wilfrid (opposition leader), 25, 26, 57
Law, Bonar (colonial secretary), 182
Lebeuf, M. (justice), 35
Leskiw, Joseph, 132
Lethbridge Internment Camp, 115, 116–17, 303n172; closure, 206; conditions at, 137, 165–6, 167, 170, 176, 184, 345–6n199, 378n28; escapes, 158, 168, 191; German prisoners at, 142, 175, 332n47; setup, 51–2, 129
*Lethbridge Telegram*, 191, 221
Leubetich, Mrs Thomas, 238–9
Licki, Mike, 55
Likahatcheff, S. de (Russian consul), 125–6
Livesay, Florence and Fred, 177
Logie, Brig. General W.A., 193–4